Learning from Clients

LEARNING FROM CLIENTS

Interpersonal Helping as Viewed
by Clients and Social Workers

Anthony N. Maluccio

THE FREE PRESS
A Division of Macmillan Publishing Co., Inc.
NEW YORK

Collier Macmillan Publishers
LONDON

The Free Press
A Division of Macmillan Publishing Co., Inc.
866 Third Avenue, New York, N.Y. 10022

Collier Macmillan Canada, Ltd.

Library of Congress Catalog Card Number: 78-67753

Printed in the United States of America

printing number

1 2 3 4 5 6 7 8 9 10

Library of Congress Cataloging in Publication Data

Maluccio, Anthony N
    Learning from clients.

    Bibliography: p.
    Includes index.
    1. Family social work--United States. 2. Social
service--Research--United States. 3. Social service--
United States--Evaluation. 4. Helping behavior.
I. Title.
HV699.M33   361'.06   78-67753
ISBN 0-02-919820-8

TO JANICE

I think they do a marvelous job
and I think their prices are right!
If you ever get into trouble with
your marriage, I invite you to go
to a marriage counselor. . . . If they
can't help, they can't hurt you!

A client

Contents

Preface

The 1970s have witnessed a marked increase in the numbers of people seeking help with personal or interpersonal problems from practitioners using diverse methods and associated with various professions such as the clergy, psychology, psychiatry, and social work. At the same time the effectiveness of these methods — which may generally be described as *interpersonal helping* — has increasingly been questioned. In response, there has been growing interest among practitioners and researchers in improving practice theory and service delivery. One emerging approach is to obtain the views of consumers.

This book reflects this interest and represents my commitment to the notion that we can learn a great deal directly from clients. We can learn how they view our services, what they find effective or ineffective, and what suggestions they have for improvement. Ultimately, through the input of clients, we may be able to improve our skills and our methods of training future practitioners.

The book is based on findings from an intensive qualitative study of the helping process in a family service agency, as perceived by clients and their social workers following termination of the service.

Part I presents the objectives of the study and its conceptual as well as methodological framework. Critical questions about interpersonal helping are raised in the context of prior research and current imperatives in the field of social work. The agency, workers, and clients in the study sample are described. Part II focuses on how clients and social workers perceive the helping process, from the beginning phase to the outcome. Part III covers the clients' and workers' views on the factors that significantly influence the helping process and its outcome, particularly the client-worker relationship, life experiences, social networks, and the agency environment. Part IV discusses what we have learned from this study — and might learn in future replications — by listening to clients.

Finally, the appendixes include additional material that may be useful, especially to readers interested in pursuing formal or informal research in the area of client perception of services, such as guides for research interviews with clients and practitioners and complete transcripts of several interviews.

While my basic frame of reference is that of social work, I believe that the findings of the study are relevant to a variety of other professions that focus on interpersonal helping. As I hope that the book will show, as practitioners we can enhance our skills by learning from clients through regular feedback concerning our helping efforts. Obtaining the views and insights of those whom we help is an essential means of critically examining our practice and refining our knowledge and skills. If we allow ourselves to learn from clients, we may well be able to enhance our own competence as well as theirs.

Acknowledgments

One of the joys of completing a book is the opportunity to thank those who contributed to it. Many persons have been most helpful to me since this book first emerged as a dissertation.

First of all, I wish to thank professors David Fanshel, Irving Miller, and Hervé Varenne at Columbia University; professors Albert Alissi, Morton Coleman, Carel Germain, and Martha Williams at the University of Connecticut; and Dr. John E. Mayer, of the Albert Einstein College of Medicine. Each of them provided not only needed encouragement but substantial help with the study's methodology and/or my writing efforts. John Mayer originally inspired the study through his own research with Noel Timms on client perception of casework. In addition, he gave generously of himself by consulting with me in the early stages of the study and later reviewing and thoughtfully commenting on the entire manuscript.

Many thanks also to Gladys Topkis, my editor at The Free Press, who contributed more than she can imagine through her unusual combination of consistent support and incisive critique.

Above all, I owe a special debt of gratitude to those who made the book possible and worthwhile: the clients, social workers, and administrators at the agencies where the research was carried out. It was a unique pleasure to learn with and from them, and I hope that I have faithfully portrayed their views and insights.

Finally, I am grateful to Georgia Bialy, Diane Denton, Grace Derrick, and Margaret Partridge, not only for their secretarial skills, but also for their patience and promptness in responding to my sometimes frantic requests.

ANTHONY N. MALUCCIO

Part I

THE STUDY AND ITS CONTEXT

There is no question about the value of client observations of social work methods. . . . Our clients can tell us more about how they are influenced. . . . They can if we develop better methods of asking.

Alice Overton (1960)

Chapter 1

Interpersonal Helping and Client Perception

We went there for marriage counseling and we saw Mrs. Albert. . . . I can't honestly say that she did a lot of *counseling* other than listening. She did mostly listening, and maybe in her own mind that was the thing to do with us . . . like getting the two of us to talk with each other. . . . Well, I wasn't sure at first—but it worked out and I would recommend that anybody who needs marriage counseling go there!

This is what Mrs. Fort, a young secretary, had to say when I asked what she thought about the help she had just received from a social worker at a family service agency. She had gone to the agency reluctantly. But, as the "counseling" went on, she found, rather unexpectedly, that she was quite satisfied with it.

What happened? What was there about the helping process that made it worthwhile to Mrs. Fort? In general, what makes for effective interpersonal helping in social work or related disciplines? These are questions with which practitioners continually struggle. In order to pursue these questions, I carried out an intensive, qualitative study of the helping process as perceived by clients and social workers in a family service agency, with a particular focus on the processes of engagement.

The study is exploratory in nature and relies on in-depth, focused interviews as the chief medium of data collection. The emphasis is on similarities and differences in client and worker views concerning the process and outcome of their interaction. As Mrs. Fort and other clients and their workers speak in the research interviews, they stimulate numerous insights and implications that are useful in reexamining social work and its underlying assumptions. Their remarks and observations suggest ways of making practice more effective with diverse client populations.

The idea for this study emerged over a decade ago, when as a practitioner I often found myself wondering what clients thought regarding my effort to help them—and whether my services made any difference in their lives. My colleagues had similar questions, and we tried to obtain the answers in countless supervisory conferences, staff meetings, and consultations with experts from pyschiatry and psychology. At the time it did not occur to us that one potentially meaningful method of learning what clients thought about our services was to ask *them.*

In those days it seemed a bit farfetched to think that clients might have expertise in examining our services: weren't they too involved to be objective and too fragile to participate in formal or informal research projects? And so we went on — talking among ourselves as professionals and struggling to infer through indirect evidence the clients' views and opinions of our services and of us. On the basis of these inferences, we effected changes in our practice and hoped that we were responding more appropriately to the needs and expectations of clients.

The issue of how consumers perceive our services is still with us today. If anything, it is more compelling and pervasive than ever, as social work again finds itself under intense scrutiny from internal as well as external sources. Questions are being raised about its values, the efficacy of its methods, the validity of its theoretical perspectives, and the relevance of its functions in contemporary society. Evaluative studies of the outcome of social work intervention — particularly casework — abound with negative or inconclusive findings (Fischer, 1973; Fischer, 1976; Mullen, Dumpson et al., 1972; Siegel, 1972). Agency administrators are increasingly frustrated, as public and private funding sources are drying up. And some writers declare, with a sense of gloom and impending disaster, that the social work profession is undergoing a grave identity crisis (Richan and Mendelsohn, 1973).

In the midst of such seeming despair, it is noteworthy that social workers are increasingly showing interest in how their clients perceive them and their services. It is no longer incompatible with professional wisdom to see consumers as potentially useful informants. Practitioners as well as researchers are asking their clients about their views, their ideas, their suggestions, and their expectations. There is something refreshing in all of this; perhaps it is a mark of the growth of a profession to have its members interested in seeking consumer views about their efforts.

This book exemplifies this growing interest and the expanding role of client feedback in service delivery. Through it, I hope to contribute to the continuing efforts to improve theory and practice by examining the findings of my study and their implications within the context of related research on client perception of interpersonal helping. Before proceeding with the study and its findings, however, I will present in this chapter the key conceptions and theoretical perspectives on interpersonal helping that guided me in developing the research design and analyzing and interpreting the data.

Since my purpose is not to test any specific hypothesis or to illustrate any given orientation, I am hesitant to present a particular theoretical framework as the one underlying the study. However, I do have various notions about relevant considerations and these should be made explicit, inasmuch as a researcher's conceptual system is one of the factors shaping his or her observation of social phenomena (Sjoberg and Nett, 1968: 169–173). Furthermore, theoretical considerations are useful in organizing, illuminating, and explaining empirical observations.

The underlying conceptual system in the study as well as the book consists of selected ideas from general systems theory, psychology (especially ego psychology), socialization theory, role theory, and recent research on patterns of human interaction. Within this context, the interpersonal helping process is viewed as an interactional phenomenon in which client and social worker come together to form a social system that is temporary and initially fragile. It is assumed that their participation in the helping process and their perception of it was influenced by numerous external as well as internal factors, including their expectations, personal qualities, life spaces, roles and statuses, social networks, and the agency environment.

THE HELPING PROCESS AS AN INTERACTIONAL PHENOMENON

Interpersonal helping comes in various shapes and colors (Fischer, 1972). Within the field of social work, it refers to such forms as casework, group work, and clinical social work. On a broader scale, it may be described through a variety of terms, including psychotherapy, counseling, and social treatment. It may be based on one of many theoretical frameworks, ranging from the highly specialized to the eclectic.

Definitions of interpersonal helping consequently vary among different disciplines and, indeed, even within a given discipline. However, there is at least one widely accepted common element, namely, emphasis on helping people through some form of personal contact between the practitioner and the client or "significant others" in the client's environment. For instance, Whittaker (1974: 49) defines "social treatment" as "an approach to interpersonal helping which utilizes direct and indirect strategies of intervention to aid individuals, families, and small groups in improving social functioning and coping with social problems."

My approach to interpersonal helping is consistent with Whittaker's formulation. In addition, I view interpersonal helping in general — and the process of client-worker engagement in particular — as an interactional phenomenon incorporating these phases:

1. *Getting engaged.* As the client gets to the agency, he or she and the worker go through a process of interaction through which they determine whether they should go on together for one or more sessions.

2. *Staying engaged.* The client and worker then go through a phase in which they attempt to work on the client's problems or needs.

3. *Ending the engagement.* As the client's needs are met or the client and/or worker decide that they cannot be met, they go through a process of becoming disengaged.

These phases are interrelated and overlapping and follow an uneven rather than a linear course of development. There are different levels and kinds of involvement in each. Moreover, during each phase client and worker are confronted with specific tasks or challenges that must be successfully resolved in order to lead them to an effective therapeutic relationship and a successful outcome. In the beginning, for example, there must be exploration of the person's presenting request and engagement of his or her motivation to work on it (Hollis, 1972: 247-259). Client or worker may perceive each phase differently, as a result of a variety of factors that will be considered later in this chapter. For this reason, the present study emphasizes the client's and worker's respective views at different stages of their interaction.

The major phases in interpersonal helping as outlined above reflect the traditional view of the helping process in social work and other disciplines as consisting of a beginning, a middle, and an ending. But in my view there is special emphasis on the ongoing and dynamic process of *engagement* between client and worker and the importance of understanding the internal and external factors that in each phase may be affecting the course, quality, and outcome of the client-worker interaction.

The interactional nature of the client-worker relationship and of the process of their engagement is highlighted by Lennard and Bernstein (1969: 18-25). On the basis of extensive research, these authors stress the role of the "interactional environment" in human behavior. By interactional environment, they mean the context and patterns of interactions that characterize social action involving two or more human beings. Lennard and Bernstein (p. 22) theorize that, in addition to analyzing the *content* of human interaction, it is essential to appreciate "the formal and contextual properties of the interaction process itself":

> These patterns of interaction within social systems, such as the family or therapy, are often as significant as knowledge of the content is for understanding the behavior of individuals in those systems. Both the content and the context convey meaning.

Scheduling of appointments, for example, is an important contextual property of an interaction system, since it influences the development and continuity of a client's involvement in therapy (Lennard and Bernstein, 1969: 23).

According to these authors (pp. 168-170), the major contextual properties in therapeutic interaction include:[1]

1. *Duration:* The interaction can be expected to continue for a certain period of time.

---

[1] Several of the contextual properties proposed by Lennard and Bernstein (1969), such as *duration* of the therapeutic encounter, are identical to group properties defined by Robert K. Merton (1968: 364-380) in his classic formulation of reference groups and social structure.

2. *Noninterruption:* There is assurance that the interaction will be scheduled without unnecessary interruptions.

3. *Total attention:* Both the client and the worker concentrate on the client's behaviors, feelings, and needs.

4. *Continuity:* There is emphasis on congruence and relevance in pursuing themes, topics, and activities.

5. *Process analysis:* There is exploration of procedural difficulties that interfere with the helping process.

6. *Boundaries:* In contrast to many other social contexts, there is clear definition of temporal, spatial, physical, and social boundaries (e.g., frequency and length of interviews).

Role learning in relation to these and other characteristics of the therapeutic encounter is a prerequisite for effective psychotherapeutic interaction:

> A patient learns that in that particular social setting there are certain behaviors, attitudes, expectations, sequences, and programs that are appropriate and certain others that are not. His induction into the therapy system occurs through his receipt of explicit instructions and through inferences drawn from various therapist behaviors (Lennard and Bernstein, 1969: 167).

In this book, we will therefore explore clients' and workers' views on role learning in respect to the context of their interaction. To what extent does this type of role learning occur? How does it occur? How does the worker contribute to the client's role learning and role induction? How do clients and workers view the configuration and patterns characterizing their interaction? For instance, how do they see the scheduling of appointments? Do they see the *experience* of participating in their encounter as significant as the *content* of the communication itself?

CLIENT-WORKER INTERACTION AS AN OPEN SYSTEM

In addition to appreciating the immediate context of client-worker interaction, it is useful to consider the broader ecological framework within which it occurs. In this regard, general systems theory is helpful in conceptualizing client-worker interaction in dynamic terms as an open system in ongoing transaction with other systems in the environment.[2] Through concepts such as boundary, energy, reciprocity, input, and output, this perspective suggests ways of analyzing and understanding client-worker interaction as a social system. Above all, it is useful in shifting our lens from a linear to a transactional purview. Thus, it sensitizes us to the importance of considering various forces and processes operating outside as well as within the context of

---

[2] For application of general systems theory to social work, see Hartman (1970); Janchill (1969); Leighninger (1977); and Stein (1974).

client-worker interaction that may be influencing the client's—as well as the worker's—behavior and perception of what is happening to them and between them.

Various ideas from environmental psychology and social psychology enrich and render a bit more concrete some of the abstract notions from systems theory. Especially useful are concepts of the environment and of "social situations." Barker (1968), a leading environmental psychologist, has formulated the concept of "behavior setting," through which he calls attention to the environmental features that in any given situation influence a person's behavior. A similar notion is that of the "operational situation," advanced by Meier (1965) as part of her work on diagnostic treatment classifications in casework. *Operational situations* are sites within which a person is expected to function; they comprise "those factors and influences that are *external* to the person but that are relevant to his functioning in that they provide the stimuli affecting his ways of thinking, feeling, and behaving" (Meier, 1965: 544).

These concepts are pertinent in that they help to illuminate the multiple social and environmental forces impinging on the client's and worker's behavior and perception of their situation. For example, a client's satisfaction with and continuance in treatment may be influenced by such variables as the nature of the informal network (Mayer and Timms, 1970: 37–61) and the availability of alternative resources (Mayer and Rosenblatt, 1964).

The concept of the social environment is analyzed by Stein (1960), who clarifies several key ideas: (1) a person's environment is much broader than what is readily and concretely accessible to perception; (2) the environment is not "external" to the person but is internalized through significant influences on such aspects as his or her values, self-image, and coping patterns; and (3) the environment is not static but is constantly changing.

In examining client and worker perceptions of services, it will be important to go beyond the immediate situation to explore the broad environmental context in which clients find themselves and the specific social situations impinging upon them at any particular time. For this reason, our research deals with those factors within and without client-worker interaction that influence the outcome and their satisfaction with it.

The notion of the person's internalization of the environment highlights the importance of moving beyond simple description of the client's environmental situation and into his or her perception, understanding, and interpretation. Useful in this connection are various ideas from sociology and social psychology that point to the role of a person's subjective and unique perception of the situation in influencing his or her behavior. For example, in his analysis of situational fields, Cottrell (1942: 377) postulates that "the person responds in a social situation according to his own definition of the situation." Cottrell draws in part from Lewin's "field theory," whose fundamental principle is that human behavior is a function of the person's life space (Lewin, 1935). In Lewin's formulation, the "life space" refers to the configuration of the person and the psychological environment; it represents the totality of all possible facts or events capable of influencing the behavior of a human being at any given time. The person is surrounded by the psychological environment, which in turn represents the objective or non-psychological environment as it is interpreted by him or her or filtered through more or less permeable boundaries.

Lewin's dynamic formulation of behavior as a function of the individual's life space supports the validity of viewing a client's perception of services as the consequence of the interplay of multiple factors in the client's ecological context. The concept of life space guides the researcher's efforts to probe each respondent's views in depth as well as in breadth: for instance, by exploring clients' inner thoughts and feelings in relation to their total life situation, one is more likely to gather information concerning the significant determinants of their satisfaction or dissatisfaction with social work services.

Symbolic interactionism provides further theoretical support for a study of client and worker perception of social work services, particularly through its emphasis on viewing social phenomena from the perspective of the actor. A key idea flowing from symbolic interactionism is that human beings perceive and understand what is happening in their lives through *a process of interpretation,* through which they handle and modify the meanings of people, things, and events (Blumer, 1969).

CLIENT AND WORKER ROLES AND EXPECTATIONS

Spiegel (1968: 393) defines "social role" as "a goal-directed pattern or sequence of acts tailored by the cultural process for the transactions a person may carry out in a social group or situation." A role does not exist in isolation but is patterned to fit in with the reciprocal functions of a partner in a relationship. Building on the work of sociologists such as Parsons, Bales, and Shils (1953), Spiegel (1968: 393-402) discusses the concept of "role complementarity," that is, the interlocking set of expectations and behaviors in interpersonal systems. In his analysis of family conflict, Spiegel also formulates a variety of possible causes of failure of complementarity that are useful in examining the functioning of role systems in general, including the interaction between clients and social workers:

1. *Cognitive discrepancy*—Resulting from lack of knowledge of required roles on the part of one or more members of the role system.
2. *Discrepancy of goals*—The goals of different persons involved in the role system may become discrepant due to such reasons as shifts in motivation, illness, lack of maturation, or sociocultural differences between the partners.

3. *Allocative discrepancy*—This refers to disagreement between role partners regarding a person's rights to the role he or she wishes to occupy.
4. *Instrumental discrepancy*—Deprivation or insufficiency of required instrumental resources (such as technical equipment) interferes with role transactions.

When there is no complementarity, role transactions are characterized by disequilibrium and the role partners experience disappointment in each other, resulting in tension, hostility, frustration, or other negative consequences. The lack of complementarity between client and worker may help to explain the high attrition rate of clients in many social work agencies and the frustrations and dissatisfactions that clients and practitioners frequently experience in their efforts to interact with each other (Mayer and Timms, 1970; Silverman, 1969; Stark, 1959). Consequently, we will examine the findings on client and worker perceptions in terms of complementarity and the possible causes of its failure as formulated by Spiegel. For instance, is there evidence of cognitive discrepancy in situations in which clients express dissatisfaction with services? Do clients and workers feel that there is sufficient discussion of mutual expectations and preparation for assuming the role of client in their initial contacts with workers? What happens when clashes in perspective occur between client and worker and the equilibrium in their role system is upset? How do they cope with discrepancies in their expectations at different points in their interaction?

Spiegel's ideas on role complementarity and the various types of discrepancy arising in role systems can also be helpful in analyzing data on use of the client-worker contract. The explicit contract between client and worker has been proposed as a means of clarifying their mutual expectations, resolving any discrepancies, delineating their respective roles and tasks, and facilitating their joint activities (Maluccio and Marlow, 1974). In what ways and to what extent do workers use the explicit contract or one of its variations? Does negotiation or renegotiation of the contract in social work practice contribute to role complementarity in client-worker interaction by reducing the various types of discrepancy conceptualized by Spiegel?

The issue of role complementarity is especially crucial in interpersonal helping, inasmuch as client and practitioner occupy different statuses and therefore bring different expectations into their interaction. This is particularly true in social work practice, since frequently there are substantial differences in the sociocultural backgrounds of client and worker. As a prospective client approaches an agency, he or she enters a process of socialization into the client role, which Lennard and Bernstein (1960: 25) call "one of the crucial and necessary tasks in the construction and maintenance of therapeutic systems." They suggest (1969: 29) that, as in all major role relationships, there are four basic dimensions involved in socialization into psychotherapy:

1. *Activeness*—allocation of responsibility for activity and participation in the relationship.
2. *Differentiation*—variations of behavior or the basis of the direction of the relationship.
3. *Selectivity*—decisions about proper subject matters and types of interaction.
4. *Timing*—estimating the time needed to accomplish treatment goals.

Writers on role induction or socialization have stressed the changes that the prospective client needs to make (Hollis, 1972; Lennard and Bernstein, 1969; Siporin, 1975). There has been less attention to the complementary need for the worker to become socialized to a particular client by modifying his or her expectations, beliefs, or attitudes toward that person. That this is another crucial function of the socialization process is suggested by research on interpersonal helping in social work as well as in other fields. Chance (1959: 97) has found that therapists tend to exaggerate the client's pathology. Goldstein (1962) and Heine and Trosman (1960) have reviewed research showing that patients and therapists often hold expectations that are not complementary and that are consequently disruptive. Smale (1977: 1-2) has argued that "the expectations of the professional helping person will tend to act as a self-fulfilling prophecy and thus affect the outcome of his efforts."

Various researchers have also highlighted the significance of compatible role expectations in therapeutic relationships. Goldstein (1962: 64-69) has written extensively about the importance of mutuality in expectations between patient and therapist. Similarly, Lennard and Bernstein (1960: 153) have pointed to the role of expectations in psychotherapy:

> When both members of a dyad are in agreement regarding their reciprocal obligations and returns, there is consensus or similarity of expectations, and harmony or stability occurs in their interpersonal relations. But when there is any degree of discrepancy or lack of consensus between the participants and their expectations are dissimilar, the role system is disequilibriated and manifestations of strain appear in their interpersonal relations. If expectations are too dissimilar, the social system disintegrates unless the differences can be reconciled.

Thus, complementarity in role behaviors and expectations is in many ways essential in interpersonal helping, since much emphasis is placed on the therapeutic relationship as the major vehicle of intervention. In order for treatment to be effective, it is assumed that the client-worker relationship should be characterized by mutual regard or positive interpersonal attitudes. Thus, Hollis (1972: 228-244) has stressed that a positive client-worker relationship is an essential component of casework treatment. Truax and Carkhuff (1967) have emphasized that the helper's personal qualities—such as empathy, warmth, and genuineness—are critical in the outcome of the therapeutic relationship. Wilson et al. (1968) have suggested that the client-therapist relationship influences the outcome of the various behavior therapies.

As one means of dealing with the problems of clashes in expectations and the resulting lack of complementarity, there has been extensive consideration of influences on "interpersonal attraction" between clients and practitioners in the initial phase of the helping process. In particular, Goldstein (1971) has carried out research on "psychotherapeutic attraction" and has written about maximizing the initial relationship by increasing the attraction between clients and helping persons (Goldstein, 1969). He has noted that therapists in general prefer the YAVIS type of patient—"Young, Attractive, Verbal, Intelligent, and Successful"—and dislike or find it difficult to become engaged with the non-YAVIS or HOUND type of patient—"Homely, Old, Unsuccessful, Non-verbal, and Dumb" (Goldstein, 1969; Goldstein, 1971).[3] Problems arise when—as so often happens in practice—a HOUND-displaying client meets a YAVIS-preferring therapist. There has therefore been much concern over the issue of optimal matching of clients and workers (Moore, 1977). But in reviewing research in this area, Goldstein (1969: 446) has concluded that most of it has involved "simplistic or uni-dimensional matching studies on patients and therapists" which have "failed to yield meaningful results on a variety of outcome criteria." This is not surprising in view of the complexity of interpersonal behavior. And it suggests a major focus for the present book—namely, analysis of the clients' and workers' views regarding their respective qualities and the specific components of their relationship that make for effective helping.

THE CLIENT AS AN ACTIVE PARTICIPANT IN THE HELPING PROCESS

Thus far we have considered how client-worker interaction may be affected by such variables as the environment, the helping context, and client and worker roles, expectations, and qualities. In addition, we should focus on the client as an active participant in the interpersonal helping process. In this regard, ego psychology offers a number of pertinent insights, especially through its more recent emphasis on independent ego energies and ego autonomy, activity, and competence.

In the classic Freudian view, the ego was seen as arising out of conflict between the id, superego, and reality and as having the function of "mediator" or "synthesizer." Departing from this view, Hartmann (1958) postulates the existence of a "conflict-free sphere" of the ego, from which emerge "executive" functions, such as thought, perception, and motility. Hartmann conceptualizes the individual's biologically endowed potentialities

[3] Schoefield (1964) first called attention to the YAVIS syndrome in his provocative analysis of the sociology of psychotherapy.

as emerging and developing in response to the reality situation encountered in the environment. In his view, the organism not only adapts to the environment but is also capable of changing it in a creative process of mutual adaptation.

Erikson (1959), in his psychosocial, epigenetic formulation of ego development, places further stress on the role of the environment in personality growth. Erikson views personality growth and the achievement of ego identity as occurring through the successive resolution of developmental crises characterizing each stage of the life cycle. Elaborating on Hartmann's earlier formulation concerning the person's adaptation to "an average expectable environment," Erikson defines the individual's constant and active interaction with the environment as particularly crucial for his or her development.

White (1963) postulates that an autonomous drive toward competence motivates the person to keep trying out the effectiveness of his or her capacities for action. He defines "competence" as the individual's achieved capacity to interact with the environment — or the cumulative result of the history of transactions with the environment. The individual is compelled to seek competence in dealing with instinctual as well as environmental demands through the force of his or her independent ego energies. The ego is strengthened through the individual's "action upon the environment, feelings of efficacy, and cumulative growth of a sense of competence" (White, 1963: 150).[4]

The perspectives of Hartmann, Erikson, and White are quite useful for social work, especially through their emphasis on the autonomous development and functioning of the ego, the dynamic transaction between the person and the environment, and the crucial role played by a person's activities in adaptive coping efforts and in the ongoing struggle to achieve personal autonomy, competence, and identity. Above all, these views help to solidify the notion of the human organism as an *active* rather than simply a *reactive* participant in interaction with the environment.

These formulations of ego psychologists are akin to the views of René Dubos, a renowned microbiologist who has written extensively on human adaptation. Dubos (1965; 1968) sees adaptation as a creative process based on a continuous, dynamic interplay between the person and his or her environment. The person plays an active role in this process through the force of his or her unique qualities. While agreeing that an individual's behavior is in part conditioned by the past (i.e., evolutionary and experiential factors), Dubos adds:

Experience has shown that human beings are not passive components in adaptive

---

[4] White's (1963) biopsychological perspective on competence is complemented by the views of others, especially social psychologists, who add the importance of sociocultural referents (e.g., social feedback) to his notion of the person's intrinsic motivation (Foote and Cottrell, 1955; Gladwin, 1967; Inkeles, 1966; Smith, 1968).

systems. Their responses commonly manifest themselves as acts of personal creation. Each individual person tries to achieve some self-selected end even while he is
responding to stimuli and adapting to them (1965: xviii).

Numerous questions are stimulated by these formulations. For instance,
is there any relationship between a client's satisfaction with services and the
quality and quantity of his or her participation in the helping process? How
does each person's self-concept as a client influence his or her participation,
and vice versa? How do clients perceive the differential efforts of workers to
involve them in the treatment process? What particular features of the
worker's efforts lead to a greater sense of satisfaction and competence in the
client? How do workers try to mobilize a client's personal resources and latent
potentialities? Are there certain activities of the worker or features of the service delivery system that interfere with the client's motivation to achieve
competence? Are there factors in the client-worker engagement that influence the worker's own sense of competence? Are different kinds of worker
competence needed for clients with diverse types of problems, personalities,
and socioeconomic backgrounds?

As these questions suggest, the concept of competence is of particular interest, because of its potential value in developing practice theory that emphasizes the client's maximum participation in the helping process (Maluccio, in press, a). As the reader will undoubtedly notice, I will devote special
attention to this variable in the analysis of data.

The emphasis on competence reflects my preference for a humanistic
orientation toward interpersonal helping—an orientation that stresses the
client's as well as the worker's strengths, potentialities, and creative strivings.
In concert with the view of the helping process as an interactional phenomenon, the humanistic orientation offers a powerful framework for examining and learning from clients' and workers' perceptions of interpersonal
helping.

Chapter 2

The Background, Objectives, and Methods of the Study

Client participation in the processes of social work intervention has traditionally been accepted as a basic professional tenet and a prerequisite for effective practice. In casework, for example, most theorists explicitly recognize the importance of client participation (Roberts and Nee, 1970). In their formulation of task-centered casework, Reid and Epstein (1972) emphasize the client's definition of target problems and interventive tasks. In the emerging life model of social work practice, the client — or, better, the consumer — occupies a central role in the helping process as a striving, competent, and active agent (Germain, 1973; Gitterman and Germain, 1976). In her imaginative reformulation of social work practice, Studt (1969) assigns central importance to the client as the chief actor in social work intervention. In her view, while both the client and the worker have important tasks to perform, the worker has a secondary responsibility, that is, "to provide the conditions necessary for the client's work on his task" (p. 24). Others have stressed ways of strengthening the client's role through use of the client-worker contract (Maluccio and Marlow, 1974) and client activities and life experiences (Maluccio, 1974).

THE BACKGROUND

Despite the long-standing emphasis on client participation, until recently there has been very little research on client *perception* of services. In the past decade, however, researchers have generated fresh insights when, as in the seminal work of Mayer and Timms (1970), they have dared to ask the client to speak. Practitioners have reported that it is helpful to ask clients what there is about the helping process that produces or does not produce positive changes in their lives (Papp, Silverstein, and Carter, 1973). And theorists have argued that practice theory and services delivery should increasingly be geared to the client's definition of crucial problems and choice of interventive methods. Stressing that practice models should evolve from empirical research, Meyer (1973: 97) observes that through research "we should find

15

out what it is that people in different statuses want and need from social workers, and carefully define, classify and explicate those findings." Similarly, Germain (1973: 330) highlights the need for a shift in research activity "away from the present concern with the effectiveness of treatment to the exploration of consumer needs, interests and expectations."

The growing interest in client perception of services is also related to an emphasis on consumerism throughout our society, persistent criticism of social work effectiveness, and increasing demands for accountability emanating from consumer groups, funding bodies, and social workers themselves. The pressure of accountability is reflected in numerous recent writings on the subject (Glisson, 1975; Hoshino, 1973; Newman and Turem, 1974; Tropp, 1974). As one writer has observed, "The social work literature is replete with messages exhorting the profession to further efforts to account for social services intervention" (Cruthirds, 1976: 179). Stressing the need to measure objectively the outcome of social work intervention, Newman and Turem (1974: 15) note:

> The current crisis in social services is a crisis of credibility based on an inadequate system of accountability. Social programs are in trouble because they focus on processes and not results.

Although there is agreement that social workers should be accountable to their clients, in reality there has been reluctance to obtain client feedback as a part of program evaluation:

> In only a few instances have the independent perceptions of clients themselves been incorporated in the evaluation data. While it could be argued that client perceptions . . . are not real criteria of effectiveness, nevertheless such data constitute an element of program evaluation and are essential to the concept of accountability (Hoshino, 1973: 378).

While there is still a gap between expressed goals and actual performance in this area, there has long been clear indication of interest among social workers in using client feedback to develop social work theory and improve practice and services delivery.

Nearly two decades ago, Alice Overton (1960) urged social workers to "take help from our clients" by finding out how they view social work services. Her plea resulted from her experience in a series of meetings with a group of clients in the well known "Family-Centered Project of St. Paul." Overton was surprised to find in these meetings that supposedly inarticulate, inadequately motivated, and poorly educated clients from multiproblem families had much to say about social work services that was instructive as well as provocative. Impressed by the "clarity of perception and vigor of conviction of the multi-problem family," she concluded:

> There is no question about the value to us of client observations of social work methods. Our hypotheses about behavior and how it can be influenced need all the correction or verification we can find. Our clients can tell us more about how

they are influenced, or pushed away. They can suggest more effective stimuli for change. They *can—if* we develop better methods of asking (Overton, 1960: 50).

Even before Overton's plea, researchers and practitioners had been expressing their conviction about the value of client perception studies. Graham and Blumenthal (1955) conducted an informal study in which clients who had dropped out of marriage counseling were seen in unstructured, in-depth, follow-up interviews. They discovered wide discrepancies between what caseworkers provided and what clients expected. For example, many clients were surprised to find workers who tended to be cold and impersonal, were hesitant to give advice, and did not seem to understand their needs. Graham and Blumenthal concluded:

> We have learned, above all, that a vast field for productive research lies in cooperation with our clients and in finding, with their assistance, ways in which we can improve our services (1955: 94).

Writing in the late 1950s, Beck (1959: 390) examined various approaches to research in the family service field and pointed to the "critical importance of tapping client perception directly." At the same time, in analyzing the findings of a study of caseworkers' perceptions of clients at a family service agency, Fanshel (1958: 550) observed that clients themselves represented an important source of data and advocated research into clients' perceptions of what they experience at an agency.

REVIEW OF PREVIOUS STUDIES

A brief review of the limited research carried out thus far in the area of client perception of services helps us to identify key themes and issues for further exploration.

A number of studies focus on a comparison of client and worker views. These studies reveal marked disparities between clients and workers in their respective judgments on the process and outcome of services. Kogan (1957) explored the views of clients and caseworkers with a large sample of short-term cases at a family service agency, most of which had been terminated by the client's "premature" withdrawal from services. In most cases, the workers attributed client discontinuance to resistance or lack of interest. Most of the clients, however, indicated that they had ended treatment because of improvement in their lives or because practical problems such as transportation prevented them from keeping office appointments.

In another study, Silverman (1969) explored the perceptions of a small number of clients who had dropped out of treatment in family service and mental health agencies. These were black persons from lower socioeconomic backgrounds who had been offered casework or psychiatric treatment but had not followed through. Silverman found substantial differences between these clients and their workers in the way they viewed the clients' problems and the helping process; these discrepancies led to marked conflict between them and early withdrawal of the clients from treatment. The conflict appeared to be largely due to the fact that clients and practitioners entered into the helping process with different conceptions of help: to the workers, "help" generally meant enhancing the clients' understanding of their reality, while to the clients it meant finding an immediate solution to their problems.

In an extensive survey, Perlman (1975) investigated the views of over four thousand predominantly black clients involved during a two-and-a-half-year period with a multiservice neighborhood center in an inner-city area. Finding that people approached the center with different expectations and behaviors, he delineated three types of consumers (p. 33):

1. The "buffeted people" — who bring multiple problems to the center and who keep coming over and over in search of help.
2. The "problem-solvers" — who present a few difficulties and who are willing to contact the center more than once or twice to get help, but not as often as people in the first group.
3. The "resource seekers" — who emphasize one or two problems and get involved in a limited way with the center.

Perlman found that the "problem-solvers" and the "buffeted" clients had the most favorable outcomes in terms of having their expectations met and their problems acted upon by the staff. The "resource seekers," who went to the center expecting solutions to problems in such areas as housing and employment, were frustrated more often than those in the other groups.

Perlman's findings suggest that there is an association between the ways in which consumers approach social service agencies and the outcomes that they experience. He notes that a feedback process seems to be operating:

> The process is a complicated one in which clear-cut "causes" and "effects" are hard to come by. Even before it is clear what the outcome will be, people are forming judgments and in some instances deciding not to continue their contacts (1975: 54).

Consumers appear to adjust their behavior toward the agency and to use its services "in accordance with at least two criteria: (1) how close will the organization come to meeting their needs as they define them and (2) how high a price will they be required to pay" (Perlman, 1975: 63).

Perlman's study provides empirical evidence of the impact of clients' expectations and problem definition on their use of agency service and points to the need to explore in greater depth how individuals approach an agency and how their impressions and perceptions help to shape the process and outcome of the client-worker engagement.

In a pioneering study carried out at a family service agency in Great Britain, Mayer and Timms (1970) employed unstructured, in-depth and probing interviews to examine clients' perceptions of, and reactions to, casework services. A distinctive feature of this study was that it relied on data supplied by consumers on the basis of their own perspectives and in their own language, in contrast to the more traditional method of obtaining client perceptions through structured interviews or questionnaires.

Mayer and Timms analyzed their findings by dividing the respondents into (1) satisfied versus dissatisfied clients and (2) those who sought help with material problems (e.g., financial assistance) versus those who wanted help with interpersonal difficulties (e.g., conflict with a spouse). The central findings of their investigation were as follows:

1. Inadequacies in the client's informal social network (such as absence of helpful friends or relatives) generated a tendency to seek external, formal help through an agency.

2. Formal and informal referral agents played a significant role in fostering contact with the agency (e.g., by pushing some persons to seek help).

3. There was a substantial group of dissatisfied clients, particularly those seeking material help. Within this group, there was considerable evidence of clash in perspective between client and worker in respect to mutual expectations and conceptions of the helping process.

4. There was a large group of clients who sought help with interpersonal problems and who were satisfied with casework. These clients felt that they were helped through the worker's provision of emotional support, suggestions, advice, and opportunities to unburden themselves.

5. Clients seeking material help who were satisfied received not only material aid but also supportive help.

6. Some clients who were seeking material help did not get it and were unhappy not only about not having received help but also about having been treated through "insight-oriented" procedures.

7. Satisfied clients seemed to view the worker as active and involved and ready to give suggestions; dissatisfied clients, on the other hand, apparently regarded the worker as aloof and disinterested.

In their nationwide study of clients' and counselors' views on family service agencies, Beck and Jones (1973) found further evidence of differences in perspective between clients and workers. Where heavy reality stresses were present, clients were less likely than counselors to give positive reports on outcome. Workers were less aware than clients of environmental problems, more aware of problems related to personality adjustment or mental illness, and less aware of changes in family relationships. These discrepancies suggested "that continued study of the opinions of both parties on the same situations and mutual in-person exploration of the sources of these differences would be a productive area for further research" (Beck and Jones, 1973: 10).

Many agencies in recent years have investigated client satisfaction with their services. Family Counseling of Greater New Haven (1974) carried out a survey in which a questionnaire was mailed to the 200 clients who had completed treatment during a six-month period. The questionnaire was returned by nearly half of the clients. The results showed a strikingly predominant pattern of satisfaction with agency services: more than two-thirds of the respondents indicated that they were helped by the agency and that there was no other kind of service or help that they had expected. The few clients who expressed dissatisfaction had expected more guidance and more concrete aid such as financial assistance. At a large, metropolitan family service agency, Riley (1975) found that 86 percent of the clients were satisfied with both the counselor and the services. At a smaller urban agency, Park (1975) concluded that "nine out of ten clients considered the method of service— counseling—to be useful to them in their efforts to handle their own problems."

The results of these family service agency investigations are consistent with the findings of similar studies of client satisfaction in a variety of other settings. In the area of mental health, most consumers have been found to be satisfied in study after study. For instance, in a survey of nearly one hundred clients of an outreach program at a large community mental health center, an overwhelming majority expressed positive attitudes toward staff and services and indicated that the service had been helpful in solving their problems (McCoy et al., 1975). Similarly, in a small outpatient clinic, four-fifths of former clients returning a mail questionnaire indicated that they were satisfied with clinic services (Goyne and Ladoux, 1973). In another study which compiled the findings of client satisfaction surveys conducted in forty-eight community mental health centers throughout the country, McPhee, Zusman, and Joss (1975: 401) concluded as follows:

> Despite the variety of measurement methods employed, patient satisfaction with service was found to be routinely high. Seventy-two percent to 100% of patients from centers surveyed indicated that they were satisfied with services received.

In the field of foster care, Jenkins and Norman (1975) found that about half the mothers in their investigation "expressed positive, satisfied feelings about the placement experience" five years after their children had entered foster care; about one-fourth were negative and another one-fourth were ambivalent or neutral. In another study conducted at a public social service department in Great Britain, two-thirds of the clients said that they were satisfied and less than one-fifth noted being dissatisfied; 90 percent said they had received some help (McKay, Goldberg, and Fruin, 1973).

In short, the findings of consumer surveys in a range of settings indicate that there is overwhelming satisfaction with services among clients. There is evidence of client satisfaction even in studies that have strongly questioned the effectiveness of social work intervention. A case in point is *Girls at Vocational High*, a controversial report that shook the social work profession over a decade ago, with its conclusion that professional services were largely ineffective. In this investigation, nearly two-thirds of the adolescent girls who had been exposed to social work services in the experimental group reported that their workers had been helpful to them (Meyer, Borgatta, and Jones, 1965: 197–198).

While the results of these studies seem to be encouraging, there is a question about how meaningful they are, in view of various methodological limitations. First, the research design usually involves a fixed-alternative questionnaire or structured interview as the chief data collection instrument, thus precluding the client from freely evaluating the service and expressing his or her own ideas and concerns. Professional workers are usually responsible for originating and formulating the questionnaire items, and it is possible that they do not include dimensions that may be important to the consumer (Gottesfeld, 1965).

Second, the studies tend to be simplistic in their methodology and superficial in their scope, typically focusing on an overall measure of satisfaction or dissatisfaction rather than exploring in depth *why* clients are satisfied or dissatisfied with agency services. As McPhee, Zusman, and Joss (1975: 401) observe, the concept of "client satisfaction" is too simplistic:

> Assessments of satisfaction sometimes consist merely of asking, are you satisfied, would you return, would you recommend the agency or service? Essentially, these questions are equivalent to asking, "Is everybody happy?"

Third, most previous investigations stress client perception of variables related to client-worker interaction and devote little attention to other factors in the client's life situations that may significantly influence their use and perception of services. Finally, in many of these studies there is the issue of biased sampling, since most of them rely on mail questionnaires, which are typically returned by less than half of the clients receiving them. It may well be that satisfied consumers are more likely to respond than those who are dissatisfied. Researchers should develop

> mechanisms . . . for dealing with patients who are illiterate, who drop out of service, or who otherwise refuse to participate. Sample attrition of this type can significantly lower or destroy the reliability of any study (McPhee, Zusman, and Joss, 1975: 403).

This selective review of the literature suggests a number of themes and issues for further study. In particular, there is indication of high client satisfaction with services, along with extensive evidence of substantial discrepancies between clients and practitioners in their view of the helping process, as well as in their expectations and in their approaches to problem solving. These findings lead to various questions:

1. What are the sources of discrepancies between clients and practitioners? What is the impact of these discrepancies on the helping process and its outcome?

2. Why are clients satisfied with services? What are the particular aspects

with which they are satisfied, and why? It is especially important to explore the reasons for satisfaction, since in previous studies satisfied consumers have been found to be less able to explain their views than dissatisfied ones (Gurin, Veroff, and Feld, 1960: 321-323; Mayer and Timms, 1970: 94-95).

3. What are some of the processes that produce satisfaction in clients and that are not expressly initiated by the worker? Mayer and Timms (1970: 94-95) note that various influences independent of the therapist seem to have an important bearing on the outcome of treatment. Herzog (1959: 32) observes that "the secret of the practitioner's success—or his failures—may lie in features of his practice that are not part of his explicit theory and of which he himself is not aware."

4. Why are some clients dissatisfied with the service as a whole or with some of its aspects?

5. What are workers satisfied or dissatisfied with, and why? Why is it that, as suggested in some studies, workers are less satisfied with services than are clients? (Sacks, Bradley, and Beck, 1970: 85.)

In addition, there is evidence in various studies that clients prefer an active, "advice-giving" worker. However, most of these studies have involved subjects from the lower socioeconomic classes, and the usual explanation of researchers has been that client preference for active qualities in their workers is class linked. There should also be exploration of the views of clients from other socioeconomic groups. It may be that under certain conditions clients from middle and upper socioeconomic classes also prefer a worker who is active and involved. This hunch is supported by the findings of laboratory experiments in which middle-class subjects were asked to indicate what they viewed as the desirable characteristics of a potentially helpful person; active, forceful, and interested workers were preferred by a group of college students (Thomas, Polansky, and Kounin, 1955), as well as by a group of white, female high school students in a suburban area (Worby, 1955).

Some studies suggest that clients from lower socioeconomic backgrounds find it hard to use social work services, at least partly because of fundamental differences between their cognitive styles and approaches to problem solving and those of their social workers. Thus, Mayer and Timms (1970: 143-148) observe that these clients seem to be characterized by a unicausal, moralistic, suppressive approach to problem solving, in contrast to the practitioner's probing, multicausal, insight-oriented approach. Especially in light of research findings questioning the effectiveness of social work intervention, various questions should be raised: What is there in the workers' approach that may be irrelevant to these clients' needs, qualities, and life styles? What is there about the processes of social work that needs to be changed? What is there that should be done in order to adapt social work services to the needs of people rather than vice versa?

Finally, there is a need to explore, more intensively than has been done in previous studies, other variables that in subtle ways may be influencing client-worker satisfaction with services as well as the outcome of client-worker interaction. In other words, it is important to go beyond the immediate phenomenon of client-worker interaction and into the client's overall life space or ecological context, so as to see whether external forces may be playing a role in client perception and use of the interpersonal helping process.

THE OBJECTIVES

The study on which this book is based seeks to build on prior research, particularly that of Mayer and Timms (1970), by examining some of the issues and questions listed above with clients from varied socioeconomic backgrounds and their social workers in a typical family service agency. Its overall purpose is to contribute to the effectiveness of practice and service delivery by obtaining clients' views on the interpersonal helping process and comparing these with the views of their social workers.

The major questions to be explored are:

1. How do clients view the helping process?
2. How do clients perceive the *outcome* of the helping process?
3. How do clients' views compare with those of their social workers?

Within the framework of these broad questions, the study examines a variety of specific issues, including:

1. What expectations of social work services do clients have which are met or not met? How do these expectations influence the course and outcome of the helping process?
2. In the opinion of clients and workers, what are the significant factors, either within or outside their engagement, that influence the outcome of interpersonal helping, and their satisfaction with it?
3. In addition to those perceived by clients and workers, are there other factors that may be influencing clients' perception and use of services?
4. Are there differences in client perception of social work services on the basis of characteristics such as age, race, and socioeconomic status?

The theoretical rationale for these and other related questions was discussed in the preceding chapter. At this juncture, it should be reiterated that much research in social work (and in the social sciences) is formulated in simplistic terms; consequently, it does not capture the essence of the phenomenon being investigated. In previous studies, client or worker perception of services has usually been conceptualized in linear terms, that is, as being determined by separate or discrete factors. In contrast, in this study it is viewed in a multilinear or transactional context, that is, as a function of various interrelated factors in areas such as the following:

1. The client—for example, presenting problem, personal qualities, and life experiences.
2. The social worker—for example, training, style, and personal qualities.
3. The agency—for example, philosophy and social and physical environment.
4. The service—for example, referral process and client and worker activities.

The thrust of the study and the book, consequently, will be to identify not only the clients' and workers' views, but also the particular set of factors which lead to their respective perceptions. There will be an effort to go beyond clients' and workers' initial statements and into their world, so as to explore the reasons for their perception and the pertinent processes operating within as well as outside client-worker interaction. For instance, I am interested not simply in ascertaining *levels* of client satisfaction with service but in examining *in depth* what it is the clients and workers are satisfied with and what lies behind their satisfaction or dissatisfaction.

THE METHODS OF THE STUDY

To help the reader in evaluating the data and my interpretations, I would like to explain at this point the central features of the research design and methods that I employed. Further details on methodology may be found in Appendix A.

BASIC PLAN AND RATIONALE OF THE RESEARCH

The basic plan of the research consisted of a combined exploratory-descriptive design.[1] Individual, in-depth, focused interviews were conducted with a small, random sample of clients as well as with their social workers soon after termination of service. Data were collected primarily in qualitative form.

Several underlying assumptions should be made explicit at the outset. First, I believed that what clients and workers report retrospectively as their perceptions of service generally represents their thoughts and feelings, although there may be difficulties in recall or other areas. Second, I assumed that client reports are of value in any effort to examine and improve social work theory and practice.[2] Third, I thought that clients' and workers'

---

[1] For a detailed explanation of the purposes and procedures of exploratory-descriptive research, see Tripodi, Fellin, and Meyer (1969: 49–54).

[2] Several studies provide empirical evidence of the reliability and validity of client evaluations. In a study at a university-based mental health clinic, it was found that clients' evaluations of their progress agreed more closely than those of their therapists with the evaluations of independent judges (Horenstein, Houston, and Holmes,

perceptions of services are influenced not only by factors inherent in the client-worker interaction (e.g., worker's qualities) but also by other variables in the agency environment and in the client's life situation. Consequently, the study also examines the respondents' views concerning factors outside the immediate context of their interaction.

The rationale for the study design was derived from emerging conceptions of "qualitative methodology" in social science research.[3] Filstead (1970: 6) defines qualitative methodology as

> those research strategies, such as participant-observation, in-depth interviewing, total participation in the activity being investigated, field work, etc. which allow the researcher to "get close to the data," thereby developing the analytical, conceptual, and categorical components of explanation from the data itself—rather than from the preconceived, rigidly structured, and highly quantified techniques that pigeonhole the empirical social world into the operational definitions that the researcher has constructed.

In a similar vein, Blumer (1969), a leading exponent of qualitative methodology, stresses the importance of research approaches that clearly take into account the subtleties of the empirical world under study. He criticizes traditional research practices that allow the theory, techniques, or scientific protocol to coerce the research and the analysis of findings. Blumer states that

> what is needed is to gain empirical validation of the premises, the problems, the data, their lines of connection, the concepts, and the interpretations involved in the act of scientific inquiry. The road to such empirical validation does not lie in the manipulation of the method of inquiry; it lies in the examination of the empirical world (p. 34).

Exploratory inquiry is thus conceived as being open, flexible, and responsive to the empirical nature of the phenomenon being investigated. In contrast, quantitative research methods adapted from the natural sciences are frequently insufficient or inappropriate in efforts to capture the complexity and richness of human phenomena of interest to researchers in the social sciences, particularly in the social work area.

In the present study, I regard the exploratory design as the best means of

---

1973). In another study in a medical setting, it was concluded that client evaluation of physician performance corresponded closely with a variety of criteria of quality in medical care generally accepted by health professionals; contrary to expectations, patients were found to be reliable judges of the quality of medical care that they were receiving (Kish and Reeder, 1969). In a survey of family service agencies, Beck and Jones (1973: 11) concluded that clients represent an indispensable resource in assessment of the outcome of social work intervention: clients are more aware of the changes that may take place in their life situations and can evaluate these changes for their own perspective.

[3] For excellent practical texts on qualitative research, see Bodgan and Taylor (1975); Filstead (1970); and Lofland (1971).

getting as close as possible to the respondents' views of interpersonal helping. While there are real limitations, such as the small size and questionable representativeness of the sample,[4] in terms of our purposes, these are offset by the strengths of qualitative research—strengths such as the freedom of respondents to speak their own minds; closeness to the subtleties and intricacies of the subjects' own world; and the resulting richness of data.

In particular, the in-depth interview provides the opportunity for clients and workers to express their perceptions and ideas as freely and spontaneously as possible. Thus, the chief value of qualitative research is that it allows us to get close to the respondents' empirical world, with as little contamination as possible from the research itself. Through in-depth analysis and appreciation of the clients' and workers' views and insights into interpersonal helping, we may be better able to derive practice implications. At the same time, we may contribute to knowledge building by clarifying concepts, identifying pertinent variables and their interrelationships, and formulating potentially significant questions and hypotheses for further study.

COLLECTING THE DATA

The study took place at a sectarian family service agency located in an inner-city area. In the next chapter I will present details on the characteristics of the agency, the social workers, and the clients, along with a description of the criteria used in selecting the sample and the process followed in obtaining the subjects' cooperation. At this point, I should note that the sample consisted of eleven social workers and thirty-three clients who had recently terminated their contact with the agency.

Confidentiality was safeguarded in various ways: by assigning code numbers to clients and workers in the study sample; disguising identifying data about them in the study report; and maintaining anonymity by insuring that the views of individual clients and workers would not be shared by me with anyone within or outside the agency.

Data were collected between June and August 1975 by means of the following techniques:

1. In-depth, Open-ended Interview with Each Client

I conducted all interviews with clients as well as with workers. The interview with each client took place in a location selected by him or her. All clients chose to have the interview in their home except for five who preferred the agency office, my office, or, in one case, the public library. At least half of the interviews lasted somewhat over one hour; about one-fourth lasted between three-quarters of an hour and one hour, and the other fourth between one-half and three-quarters of an hour. In cases of couples, I interviewed each partner separately.

[4] See Appendix A for further discussion of the study's limitations.

All of the clients agreed to have the interview tape recorded, with the exception of the one who was seen in a library in her town. In the latter case, with her permission I took brief notes during the interview and, soon after it was over, recorded the interview in long hand as faithfully as I could reconstruct it.

2. In-depth, Open-ended Interview with the Worker in Each Case

The interviews with social workers took place in their offices. Nearly all of these lasted between three-quarters of an hour and one hour. A few went over one hour.

In all cases, I interviewed the worker within a few days *after* having seen the client. By plan, I did not share with the worker anything that the client had told me, because of the need to maintain confidentiality as well as to avoid influencing the workers' own responses. Workers were often understandably curious about their clients' views, although they appreciated that I could not reveal any information.

Prior to the individual interviews with them, I had met with the workers as a group on two occasions during the early phase of the research process. In these sessions, I explained the purposes of the study, elicited staff members' questions or suggestions in such areas as procedures for involving clients and safeguarding confidentiality, and solicited their participation in the study. The workers' response was enthusiastic from the beginning.

3. Schedule of Identifying Data on Each Client

Demographic and other socioeconomic data in each case were obtained directly from the client, by means of a schedule that I completed at the beginning of each interview (see Appendix B).

4. Schedule of Identifying Data on Each Worker

Following completion of the last research interview with each worker, I obtained from him or her data concerning age, education, and employment (see Appendix C).

5. Informal, Concluding Interview with Each Worker

After completing the interviews with workers pertaining to their specific cases, I held a brief, informal interview with each of them. The purpose was to obtain some idea of the workers' orientation to practice, clients, and agency (see Appendix C).

THE INTERVIEWING PROCESS

The research interview, a popular method of data collection in the sociobehavioral sciences, constitutes a complex interpersonal transaction bringing into play not only the specific objectives of a given research project, but also the varied personal and sociocultural characteristics of interviewer as well as respondent. This reality creates numerous difficulties in planning and in use of the interview. There has been extensive consideration of methodological issues that arise in the construction of interview schedules, in conducting the interview, and in measuring and analyzing the data (Cannell and Kahn, 1968; Hyman, 1954; Richardson, Dohrenwend, and Klein, 1965). Chief among the potential problems are the dangers of interviewer and/or interviewee bias.

In view of the many complexities, a great deal of thought went into the interview in this study, since it was the major method of data collection. To help the reader in judging the quality of data that were gathered, I will describe the interviewing process in some detail.

The interview with the client in most cases was held within one month of his or her last contact with the worker, and in a few cases within two or three months of the last worker contact. As already noted, I conducted all interviews. I had no prior information on the client other than his or her name and address. I hoped that this would help to control for interviewer bias while facilitating the desired freeflowing and spontaneous researcher-subject interaction.

Each interview began with a brief preliminary discussion intended to explain the purpose of the study, to establish some rapport with the respondent, and to help him or her feel at ease. I indicated that the purpose was to learn how people view the services that they receive from a family service agency. I emphasized that: (1) the agency had agreed to cooperate because of its interest in improving services; (2) their responses would be held in strictest confidence; (3) I had not been told anything about the client except the name and the fact that he or she had had some contact with the agency; (4) obtaining the client's frank views was extremely important; and (5) I would follow an outline. After this explanation, I asked the respondent if it would be all right to tape the interview.

The type of research interview used with both clients and workers can best be described as the *focused interview* delineated by Merton, Fiske, and Kendall (1956:3–5). It is characterized by emphasis on the subjective experiences of persons exposed to a particular situation and by use of an interview guide setting forth the major areas of inquiry. It allows for coverage of the respondent's views in breadth as well as in depth.

As explained later in this chapter, the interview guide was developed following considerable pretesting in a pilot study conducted at a different family service agency in a nearby city. The guide was very useful in providing me with a list of areas to ask about, while also facilitating the respondent's efforts to speak freely in his or her own terms. It included an outline of specific content areas and sample questions in each. It covered the client's or worker's views, impressions, feelings, and perceptions in regard to each of the following:

presenting problem and prior coping efforts

referral to the agency

initial session with the worker

subsequent contacts with agency and worker

agency characteristics

worker or client qualities

reasons and process of termination

outcome of contact

client or worker satisfaction

changes in client functioning

client's life situation

influences on outcome and satisfaction

summary assessment of the service and its impact

The guides for interviews with client and social worker are reproduced in Appendix B and Appendix C, respectively.

I began each section of the interview with a general, open-ended question, in essentially the same form with all respondents. Then I followed up with more specific, probing inquiries as seemed appropriate. While the sequence, content, and format of the questions were adapted to each situation and flowed naturally from it, I was guided by the variety of content areas germane to the study. There was an effort to cover each area in depth.

The interview with each worker basically followed the same procedure, plan, and content as the one with the client. In addition, there were questions about how the worker thought the *client* had perceived various aspects of the service. The workers were asked to review the case prior to the interview, if they were not familiar with it. In the interview itself, they were encouraged to speak from memory and to avoid referring to the case record.

I found that respondents became quickly involved in the interview and were quite interested in the study as a whole. Both clients and workers shared their views openly and in depth. Frequently, clients brought out personal details about which I had not specifically asked. In many cases, they were ready to continue talking beyond the formal end of the interview. A number of them expressed their pleasure in having been asked what they thought about the service and their sense of satisfaction in contributing to a worthwhile cause.

Pilot Study

A critical part of the entire research process was a pilot study that helped to refine the methods and procedures of data collection and analysis. The pilot study, which is described in further detail in Appendix A, was carried out at a smaller family service agency in a nearby city. Its purposes were to test and refine the research approach, particularly the interview, and to help in delineating the critical dimensions in client and worker perceptions of service.

The pilot study proved to be extremely useful in various ways. First, the procedure for obtaining client participation was streamlined and made more effective. Second, the interview guide was substantially modifed by including a number of key questions asked of all respondents in essentially the same terms and by clarifying the wording of certain questions. Third, various rating scales on such aspects as "satisfaction with outcome" were eliminated from the study when both clients and workers repeatedly pointed out that their use interfered with the free flow of the research interview itself.

Finally, in consultation with an experienced social worker who reviewed all of the taped interviews, the strengths and weaknesses in my approach as the interviewer were highlighted, leading to a number of important changes. For example, it was evident that I tended to influence the results by engaging in discussion of interesting points, showing more enthusiasm in response to some comments of clients or workers than to others, or eliciting primarily positive responses. In preparation for the main study, I was thus helped to modify my personal style so as to be more objective and to establish a climate in which respondents would be more likely to express their views freely.

ANALYZING THE FINDINGS

It has been stated that "qualitative analysis is addressed to the task of delineating forms, kinds and types of social phenomena; of documenting in loving detail the things that exist" (Lofland, 1971: 13). In practice, this is difficult to accomplish, and I realized this when, at the conclusion of the data collection stage, I found myself faced with the need to make sense out of over sixty hours of taped interviews with clients and workers. As a matter of fact, data analysis typically presents serious problems in exploratory, qualitative research. A crucial issue is: How can the data be organized and analyzed in a way that is accurate as well as interesting?

My main response to this issue was to employ primarily the procedure of "inspection" described by Blumer (1969: 42–47). The essence of this procedure is the intensive, focused examination of the empirical material relating to the "analytical elements" or concepts and variables being studied. Thus, I gathered and examined the various instances of client and worker satisfaction or dissatisfaction and then viewed this material from different angles, asking different questions, comparing client and worker perceptions, and identifying emerging differences, patterns, and relationships.[5]

---

[5] Additional guidelines in the process of data analysis were suggested by the works of Glaser and Strauss (1967) and Lévi-Strauss (1970). Through their discussion of the "constant comparative method of qualitative analysis," Glaser and Strauss (1967: 101–115) reminded me of the need to inspect empirical data over and over in the search for potentially meaningful categories. Also helpful was Lévi-Strauss' formulation of structural analysis, with its emphasis on the multiplicity and interrelatedness of different themes, the idea that organizational principles governing a subject matter emerge as the analysis progresses, and the need to reduce arbitrary data to some order by developing an inventory of pertinent patterns (Lévi-Strauss, 1970: 1–14).

After listening over and over to several randomly selected sets of interviews with clients and their workers, I found that certain variables, themes, and patterns emerged, and that it was possible to extract the data onto a two-page schedule. The schedule closely followed the framework used in developing the interview guide. (See sample of completed schedule in Appendix D.) It covered broad categories such as the various phases of the helping process, with subgroups of data in each category. For instance, under the category of the "beginning phase," I included the respective views of clients and workers in such areas as presenting problem, referral process, expectations, and initial session.

After extracting pertinent data from each interview onto a schedule, I followed the procedure of inspection: by repeatedly examining and reviewing the data in each category and its subgroups, I was able to discover key patterns, themes, and variables as well as atypical occurrences. Then I analyzed variations by different groupings of respondents, such as satisfied versus dissatisfied clients or cases with "planned termination" versus those with "unplanned termination."

While data analysis was for the most part of a qualitative nature, there was some quantification of findings through simple reporting of frequencies. However, statistical analysis was not appropriate, because of the small size of the sample and inexactitude of measuring instruments. In addition, as a result of the small sample, it was not possible to analyze differences on the basis of such variables as duration of contact or sex, age, and race of client and worker.

REPORTING THE FINDINGS

In his discussion of guidelines for the qualitative analysis of social settings, Lofland (1971: 7), an urban ethnographer, observes:

> The sociological researcher of a qualitative humanistic bent . . . seeks neither purely novelistic reportage nor purely abstract conceptualizing. His aim is judiciously to combine them, providing the vividness of "what it is like" and an appropriate degree of economy and clarity.

Lofland's statement is very pertinent to the reporting of findings in this study. It highlights the need to strike a balance between description and quotes, on the one hand, and discussion of concepts and implications, on the other hand.

Accordingly, I try to report the findings from the perspective of clients and workers, using their own words and displaying the raw data as much as possible. There is extensive use of excerpts from research interviews, to illustrate data collection methods, to highlight the central findings, and to convey the substance and complexity of interpersonal helping as perceived by clients and workers. With these purposes in mind, the full transcripts of interviews with two clients and their workers are reproduced in appendices E and F. It should be noted that I did very little editing of these transcripts or the excerpts in the text. As a group, these clients proved to be surprisingly articulate and literate.

Going beyond description of the findings, I discuss emerging insights, themes, patterns, and issues that seem pertinent for service delivery and practice theory in relation to interpersonal helping, particularly within social work. I make no attempt to place the findings within any single theoretical framework, which would be inappropriate for this type of research. Instead, I relate them to a variety of theoretical perspectives, as it seems germane and productive.

THE SIGNIFICANCE OF THE STUDY

Studies of client perception have several functions: (1) sensitizing researchers to new considerations; (2) refining what is currently known about treatment; and (3) identifying significant variables affecting the helping process (Mayer and Timms, 1970: 9-11). In addition, by providing us with their views, clients can help to "curb the excesses of ideology by letting practitioners know what works and what does not work" (Mayer and Rosenblatt, 1974: 440).

The potential significance of the present study lies in its yield of empirically derived data on clients' and workers' perception of services that may suggest hypotheses for further investigation, implications for refinement of social work theory and practice, and changes in the service delivery system. Theory and practice and service arrangements in the field of social work rarely take into account the client's direct observations and views. If clients' views are considered at all, they are generally inferred from the observations of others.[6]

While the client is not the *only* source of information concerning ways of advancing social work theory and practice, he or she *is* a significant source and can no longer be neglected. Further knowledge of how clients view services and how their perceptions compare with those of their workers may help us to reverse the traditional trend of adapting our theories, practices, and service arrangements to the unique and dynamic needs, qualities, and coping patterns of human beings. In short, the consumer of social work services has something to say that should be heard and that can enrich theory and practice. Ultimately, consumer studies can also contribute significantly to decision making and policy formation by providing agency administrators and staff with the opinions and suggestions of users of their services.[7]

[6] This criticism is not limited to social work. Linn (1968) points out that, while there has been a voluminous discourse on the psychiatric patient and the mental hospital, the patient's views of their hospital experience have not been systematically tapped as a source of information.

[7] For further discussion of this and other functions of consumer feedback studies, see Neigher, Hammer, and Landsberg (1977: 365-390).

Chapter 3

The Agency, Social Workers, and Clients

Several of the more significant recent investigations of client perception of interpersonal helping have been carried out in family service agencies (Beck and Jones, 1973; Mayer and Timms, 1970; Sainsbury, 1975). Partly for this reason, I chose another family service agency as the setting for the research on which the present book is based. The agency's services, staffing patterns, and clientele are comparable to those of agencies in earlier studies, allowing for some replication, comparative analysis, and cumulative building of knowledge.

There were additional reasons for selecting this particular agency. First, as a field education consultant from a nearby school of social work, I had an ongoing relationship with various members of the staff and administration. Second, the administration and staff were receptive to research, particularly in areas such as client perception of their services, and had expressed their readiness to become engaged in a practice-related project. My entry into the organization as a researcher was therefore considerably facilitated. Furthermore, the diversity of the agency's clientele in relation to such variables as age, race, and socioeconomic background made it possible to obtain the heterogeneous sample of subjects desired for the study.

THE AGENCY

The study was conducted at a sectarian, multifunction family and children's agency located in an urban area in the northeastern United States. The agency, which I shall refer to as the Family Service Bureau, was established in 1920.

Structurally, the Family Service Bureau is affiliated with the Roman Catholic Church and is part of the diocesan network of social agencies. As such, in relation to major policy issues it is accountable to the diocesan network's Board of Trustees and Director of Charities. In practice, it operates independently of the Church. It is autonomous, particularly in respect to

33

funding and programming. Its staff members are not in any way restricted by the connection with the Church in carrying out their professional roles.

The Bureau has a lay board of directors that sets policy and an executive director who has overall responsibility for administration and service delivery. Nearly two-thirds of its operating funds annually come from the United Way, and the rest from client fees and contracts with public agencies such as the local welfare department. Its main office is located in a building owned by the Catholic Church and provided rent-free. The agency serves a metropolitan population of over one quarter million in twenty-five towns, through a central office located in a downtown area awaiting urban renewal as well as a small branch office in a suburban town. Like the area surrounding it, the main building has been deteriorating rapidly in recent years, in anticipation of relocation.

As stated in one of its recent annual reports, the primary purposes of the Family Service Bureau are as follows:

> 1. To promote and strengthen family life by providing professional counseling, consultation and guidance through individual, couple, families, and group treatment methods and through family life education.
> 2. To initiate and support social action and become advocates to improve social conditions affecting families, individuals, and children.

The Bureau is a fully accredited member of the National Conference of Catholic Charities, the Child Welfare League of America, and the Family Service Association of America. It is typical of most member agencies of the latter organization in respect to size, staff, and programs. In addition to its counseling service, it operates a variety of specialized programs, including outreach services to black families and Spanish-speaking people, an adoption program, outreach to ex-offenders, services for the elderly, family life education, and premarital counseling. The latter service is provided specifically at the request of the Catholic Church, which requires premarital counseling for couples under nineteen years of age. In recent years, the agency has increasingly been moving toward involvement in social action and advocacy programs. At the same time, it has been expanding its programs for black and Hispanic persons, in response to the marked growth of the minority population in the area which it serves. Over half of the agency's services are delivered to minority individuals or families.

Counseling and adoption fees are charged, based on a sliding scale relative to the family's income. However, all services are available to any individual or family in the community, without regard to race, creed, sex, age, or economic circumstances. Nearly two-thirds of the clients are Catholic, and most of the others are Protestant.

At the time of this investigation, the professional staff of the Family Service Bureau consisted of thirty-five members, as follows:

Administrators	3
Supervisors	5
Social Workers	13
Social Work Associates	14
	35

All of these were lay persons, although occasionally a priest or nun is appointed to the staff.

Approximately half the staff members were Catholic, while most of the others were Protestant. Nearly half of the staff was of minority background. All of the administrators and supervisors and all but one of the social workers held a Master of Social Work degree. The one worker without it had an M.A. in psychology. Of the fourteen social work associates, all but four held a B.A. or B.S. degree in social work or in one of the sociobehavioral sciences. In addition to the full-time staff, the agency employs a psychiatrist, a psychologist, and a public relations expert on a part-time or consultative basis. During the academic year, there is also a substantial group of trainees from graduate and undergraduate social work programs as well as from related fields.

The agency follows a traditional approach to staff supervision. Each staff member is assigned to a supervisor, with whom he or she meets on a regular weekly basis. There is also an active staff development program that often includes guest lecturers or discussion leaders from outside.

The research focused on the agency's counseling program, which includes services such as individual or joint counseling, family treatment, and crisis intervention on behalf of an individual, couple, or family unit or subunit. Although there is some group treatment, the major method employed is casework. Very few of the clients in the sample had been involved in group approaches other than family treatment. Therefore, the study did not explore client and worker perception of the totality of social work services, but primarily casework services as provided in a family service agency.

THE SOCIAL WORKERS

Each of the eleven social workers who were active in the agency's counseling program agreed to participate in the study after I explained its purposes at a staff meeting early in the research process. All were employed by the agency on a full-time basis. All but one held M.S.W. degrees. The only exception was a B.A.-level social worker with training in counseling and extensive practice experience in the same agency. Of the ten practitioners with formal social work education, all had majored in casework, except for one person whose training had been in "generic social work." Six graduate schools of social work were represented.

TABLE 3-1. Characteristics of Social Workers Participating in Study (N = 11)

AGE	No.
30 or under	4
31–40	3
41–50	3
51–60	0
Over 60	1
	11

RELIGION	No.
Catholic	6
Protestant	5
	11

SEX	No.
Female	9
Male	2
	11

MARITAL STATUS	No.
Married	6
Divorced	1
Single	4
	11

RACE	No.
Black	2
White	9
	11

YEARS OF POST-M.S.W. EXPERIENCE	No.
2 to 3	2
Over 3 & up to 5	2
Over 5 & up to 10	3
Over 10 & up to 20	2
Over 20	1
	10*

*One worker had no M.S.W. but over five years of experience in this agency.

CHARACTERISTICS OF THE WORKERS

Characteristics of the workers are presented in Table 3-1 in aggregate form. Although it would be interesting for the reader to have personal details about each specific worker, I am not free to provide these data on an individual basis because of confidentiality. Since the sample of workers is rather small, most of them could be easily identified by other staff members or administrators at the agency.

Most of the workers where white, female, married, and between thirty and forty years of age. As a group, they were highly experienced, with years of post-M.S.W. employment ranging from two to over twenty. Most had at least five years of experience and had been with the agency a minimum of five years. Five held supervisory positions while also being engaged in direct practice.

WORKERS' ORIENTATION TOWARD SOCIAL WORK

Soon after the final research interview, I met with each worker for an informal discussion of his or her orientation toward practice, clients, and agency. In this informal discussion I followed an interview guide (see Appendix C) that included a variety of open-ended questions in these areas:

agency characteristics
relevance of social work training
preferred theories and practice approaches
expectations from clients

A brief summary of the workers' responses at this point may be of interest to the reader, since it provides some picture of their views concerning social work education and practice in general.

When asked to describe briefly the agency's goals, workers referred to broad purposes such as "to be available to families," "to reach out to the community and meet human needs," "to help people with emotional or situational problems," or "to provide counseling." Some workers supported the agency's multifunction orientation; others questioned it, noting that the agency might be trying to achieve too much with limited resources.

In response to questions regarding the impact of the agency's characteristics on their professional functioning, workers pointed to various factors that in their opinion contributed positively to their performance, especially the commitment of staff and administration, the in-service training program, and the freedom to develop their own interests and potentialities. The main factors that were viewed as interfering with professional functioning were the agency's inadequate physical facilities, the multiplicity and expansion of agency services in the midst of increasingly limited financial resources, and the shifting emphasis in agency functions in response to changing community pressures and needs, such as increased investment in advocacy.

Workers expressed mixed feelings regarding the relevance of their social work education. Some noted that it had provided a basic knowledge framework or general orientation useful in understanding and working with people. Others brought out that the knowledge and skills that had been emphasized in schools of social work had little relationship to the realities of practice, and that on-the-job training had been more helpful to them than their professional education. Nearly all concurred in singling out field work as the most relevant component of the M.S.W. program, since it had afforded them the opportunity to develop and practice their skills.

Most of the workers indicated that, while they may have been exposed to one or another theoretical orientation in the course of their social work education, they had developed an eclectic approach in which they were guided by what "felt right" or comfortable for them and the client, and by what they perceived as the needs in each case situation. They stressed in particular the following components of "good" social work practice: the worker's human concern and understanding; the worker's sensitivity to the client's underlying feelings and needs; and the client-worker relationship.

The workers in this group apparently preferred clients who had the potential to become involved with them and with the helping process. This was reflected in their responses to the question: "What do you expect from clients in order to be able to help them?" Nearly every worker indicated having one or more of the following expectations of clients:

1. Sufficient motivation to change so that the client can get involved in working on the problem.

2. Capacity to share something of themselves, to express their feelings honestly.

3. Feedback from the clients about the client-worker relationship—that is, what is happening in it and how they feel about it, whether positively or negatively.

THE CLIENTS

My original plan was to select a random sample of 25 to 30 clients for participation in the study. This number was considered sufficiently small to permit in-depth interviewing and large enough to include a variety of clients representing different personality characteristics, socioeconomic backgrounds, presenting problems, duration of contact, and social workers. As explained before, I eventually arrived at a sample of 33 clients who were involved in 25 cases.

SELECTING THE CLIENTS

In selecting clients for the study, I collaborated with the agency's Director of Professional Services. The social workers themselves were not at all involved in this process. To arrive at the study sample, the Director and I first formed a pool of all clients in the agency's counseling program whose cases had been closed during April and May 1975 by the workers participating in the study.[1] This procedure yielded a pool of 76 cases, from which an initial study sample of 37 cases was derived by selecting the last three or four cases closed by each worker that met the following criteria:[2]

1. Primary client was at least eighteen years old and English-speaking.

2. Client(s) had sought help voluntarily or had been referred in connection with difficulties in such problem areas as interpersonal relationships, personal functioning and growth, or material needs.

3. Client(s) had been assigned for treatment following intake screening.

4. During the initial interview, client and worker had agreed to continue with further sessions. (Thus excluded from the study sample were persons

---

[1] There was an exception to this for three workers who had had no termination during this period and for whom we therefore included the last three cases that they had closed between January and March 1975.

[2] We selected three cases each from the caseloads of seven workers and four cases each from the caseloads of four workers.

who did not keep the initial appointment or in whose cases service was completed in the first interview.)

Obtaining Client Participation

The procedure for obtaining client participation in the study was as follows: the agency's receptionist telephoned clients in the sample to invite their cooperation and obtain their consent to give their names to me as the researcher. Once the person agreed, the receptionist notified me, and I followed up with the client by making arrangements for the interview as soon as possible. A letter was sent to the few clients who could not be reached by telephone, asking them to return an enclosed postcard to indicate whether or not they were willing to participate. (See Appendix A for copy of letter as well as further details on these procedures).

As a result of the above process, 25 individual clients or client couples (68%) agreed to participate, while 3 (8%) refused. The other 9 (24%) could not be reached either because they had moved out of state (in 4 cases), had no address (2 cases), or did not respond to our letter (2 cases).[3]

The three clients who declined to participate gave these reasons:

I'm not interested in talking about it at all.

We're in the process of building a house and will be much too busy for the next few months.

I don't have any opinion about your service. Besides, I'm seeing someone else now.

Except for these three, all clients who were reached not only gave their consent but frequently expressed their recognition of the receptionist and their pleasure in hearing from her. It appears that the receptionist was a key factor in the high rate of positive responses. Their relationship with her influenced at least some clients to respond affirmatively.

Of the 25 cases in the group of clients who were interviewed, there were 8 in which both husband and wife were seen separately, yielding a total of 33 interviews with former clients. The worker was interviewed in all 25 of these cases, as well as in 10 of the 12 cases in which the client was unavailable or refused to be interviewed. Each of the workers had two or three cases in the sample.

Characteristics of Clients

Most of the interviewed clients were white women under forty years of age who came from diverse socioeconomic backgrounds and who had sought help with marital or parent-child relationship problems.

[3] These rates compare as follows with those obtained in another study, in which clients were paid for participating in research interviews: 71 percent agreed to participate; 5 percent refused; and 24 percent could not be reached or were ineligible (Mayer and Timms, 1970: 22).

TABLE 3-2. Characteristics of *Interviewed* and *Noninterviewed* Clients in Study Sample

	Interviewed	Noninterviewed
	(N = 33 persons)	(N = 10 persons)*
Age	%	%
30 or under	43	40
31–40	24	30
41–50	18	10
51–60	9	20
Over 60	6	0
Sex		
Female	73	80
Male	27	20
Race		
Black	6	40
White	94	60
Religion		
Catholic	70	50
Protestant	30	40
Unknown	0	10
Marital status		
Married	48	30
Divorced	16	10
Separated	8	30
Single	28	20
Widowed	0	10
Social class		
I	0	0
II	20	10
III	32	0
IV	24	30
V	24	60
Duration of agency Contact		
3 mos. or less	40	20
3–6 mos.	28	50
6–12 mos.	28	20
Over 12 mos.	4	10
Number of interviews with worker		
1	4	0
2–5	24	30

TABLE 3-2. *(Cont.)*

	Interviewed	Noninterviewed
	(N = 33 persons)	(N = 10 persons)*
Age	%	%
6–12	28	30
13–20	36	30
21 & up	8	10
Primary focus of service		
Marital relationships	34	30
Parent-child relationship	26	30
Other family relationships	23	20
Environmental problems	6	10
Out-of-wedlock pregnancy	11	10

*Data not available in two cases.

The characteristics of *interviewed* as well as *noninterviewed* clients in the study sample are summarized in Table 3-2.

The social class of each client was determined on the basis of Hollingshead's two-factor index of social position (1957), which proved to be the simplest method in relation to the data available. Following this scheme, the two major indicators of social position—that is, occupation and education—were scaled according to an established system of scores to ascertain each client's social class (Hollingshead, 1957: 2-11). Most of the interviewed clients fell into classes II and III, while nearly all of the noninterviewed clients were in classes IV and V. For purposes of analysis, clients in classes II and III were combined into the "middle socioeconomic group" and those in classes IV and V into the "lower socioeconomic group."

The subgroup of interviewed clients is skewed in that it includes a higher proportion of white, Catholic, married, middle-class clients than the subgroup of noninterviewed clients. An important question therefore is whether their responses provide a biased picture of the total sample. For this reason, partial data in the cases of noninterviewed clients were obtained by interviewing their workers. These findings will be compared, where appropriate, with data on interviewed clients.

There is no major difference between the groups of interviewed and noninterviewed clients in respect to characteristics of agency contact such as number of interviews, duration of contact, or primary focus of service. The number of treatment interviews ranged from one to forty-five. Most clients had fewer than twelve interviews. Duration of contact was six months or less in two-thirds of the cases. The "primary focus of service" (as determined at intake by the agency worker) involved a personal or interpersonal problem in all but a few cases.

COMPARISON OF INTERVIEWED CLIENTS WITH AGENCY'S TOTAL CLIENTELE

In examining the findings, the reader may be interested in knowing how the clients interviewed in the study compare to the agency's overall client population in relation to key demographic variables and characteristics of agency contact. For this reason, in Table A-1 (Appendix A), I compared interviewed clients with the total number of cases closed by all workers at the Family Service Bureau during 1975.

The sample of interviewed clients is comparable to the agency caseload in relation to age and sex. In both groups, over two-thirds of the clients are under forty years of age and approximately three-fourths are women. The two groups are different in respect to ethnicity: the study sample has a smaller number of blacks. In addition, by plan Hispanic clients were not included in the study, because of the language factor, although they constituted over one-tenth of the agency's caseload. The two groups could not be compared on the basis of religion, marital status, or socioeconomic class, since only fragmentary data were available on these variables for the total client population. However, the two groups are comparable in relation to family income, except for a substantially larger proportion of persons with annual income of under $3,000 and over $12,000 in the agency's overall population.

The two groups are also comparable in relation to *primary focus of service*, except that the study sample includes a higher proportion of marital relationship and parent-child relationship cases. This difference is probably accounted for by the category of "other" focus of service, which includes mostly engaged teenage couples seen for one interview for the premarital evaluation required by the Catholic Church. These persons were excluded from the study sample since no treatment was involved. The two groups are also comparable in respect to duration of contact but differ somewhat in number of interviews, with the study group including fewer one-interview cases and more cases with thirteen or more interviews. Again, this difference may be explained at least in part by the exclusion of teenage premarital evaluations from the study sample. With these exceptions, the group of interviewed clients is representative of the general client population at the agency.

COMPARISON WITH RELATED STUDIES

Going beyond the Family Service Bureau itself, it may be useful to compare the clients in the present study with the ones in similar investigations. My sample shows similarities as well as differences when contrasted with the one in the research carried out by Mayer and Timms (1970: 23-26) in a British family service agency. Both groups were composed largely of women under age forty. The British sample, however, consisted largely of working-class clients, while mine was more heterogeneous in that it included almost equal proportions of persons from the lower and middle socioeconomic groups. In addition, clients in my sample were primarily seeking help with personal or interpersonal problems, while many in the Mayer and Timms study wanted aid with environmental or economic difficulties.

The respondents in the present study are in various respects similar to those in the nationwide investigation by Beck and Jones, who surveyed a sample of nearly four thousand clients active with 266 agencies during a one-week period in 1970. These researchers followed most of these clients until closing or for two years, yielding the largest pool of client responses ever accumulated on family agency service and providing an informative national perspective (Beck and Jones, 1973: 16–36).

As with the group of clients in the present study, the Beck and Jones sample was composed primarily of women under forty-five who were about evenly divided between the lower and middle socioeconomic groups.[4] Most of the clients in both samples were seeking help with personal or interpersonal problems. However, the two samples are quite different in respect to race and religion of clients: as a result of the Family Service Bureau's sectarian affiliation, most clients in the present study were Catholic and less than one-tenth black, whereas in the nationwide Beck and Jones sample most clients were Protestant and over one-fifth were black. Since respondents in the present study were not in every respect representative of family agency clients as a whole, the applicability of the findings to other settings with different populations remains to be examined through further research.

CHARACTERISTICS OF INDIVIDUAL RESPONDENTS

As noted in the preceding chapter, in presenting the findings I will make extensive use of excerpts from research interviews with the respondents. Therefore, it may be useful for the reader to have a basic understanding of each client as an individual, helping him or her to appraise more insightfully the quoted passages and related discussion. Accordingly, there follows at this point a listing of the clients and their individual demographic characteristics.[5]

All names are, of course, fictitious. In addition, in some instances other identifying details such as age and occupation have been disguised, so as to maintain confidentiality.

---

[4] Precise comparison in respect to socioeconomic background is not possible, since different methods of determining social class status were used in the two studies.

[5] A listing of demographic characteristics for each of the noninterviewed clients may be found in Appendix A.

Demographic Characteristics of Interviewed Clients in Study Sample

No.	NAME	RACE*	AGE	MARITAL STATUS	RELIGION†	HIGHEST GRADE COMPLETED	OCCUPATION	SOCIO-ECONOMIC CLASS ‡	INDEX OF SOCIAL POSITION ‡
1	Appel, Joan	W	19	Single	RC	1 yr. college	Typist	III	40
2	Bates, Louis	W	43	Married	RC	1 yr. college	Management Consultant	II	26
3	Bates, Sylvia	W	42		RC	12	Housewife		
4	Becker, Diane	W	20	Single	RC	12	Secretary	IV	44
5	Bogdansky, Eleanor	W	38	Married	RC	12	Office manager	III	37
6	Brown, Esther	B	20	Single	P	12	None (Welfare Recipient)	V	65
7	Cain, Roberta	W	31	Married	RC	3 yrs. college	Registered Nurse	II	26
8	Crompton, Albert	W	30	Married	RC	2 yrs. college	Draftsman	III	40
9	Crompton, Laura	W	29		RC	12	Housewife		
10	Donnelly, Judy	W	33	Divorced	P	1 yr. college	Beautician	III	33
11	Foley, Mary	W	41	Divorced	P	8	Waitress	V	69

No.	Name	Race	Age	Marital Status	Religion	Education	Occupation	Class	
12	Fort, Michael	W	35	Married	P	10	Truck Driver	V	62
13	Fort, Anne	W	29		P	12	Secretary		
14	Gates, John	W	28	Separated	P	B.A. degree	Accountant	II	22
15	Gates, Carol	W	29		P	B.S. degree	Teacher		
16	Grover, Thomas	W	50	Married	RC	12	Car Repair Shop Owner	III	37
17	Grover, Dawn	W	50		RC	11	Housewife		
18	Kraft, Elizabeth	W	22	Single	P	12	Office Clerk	IV	44
19	Lodano, Vincent	W	25	Married	RC	2 yrs. college	Laboratory Assistant	III	39
20	Lodano, Maria	W	24		RC	1 yr. college	Executive Secretary		
21	Molina, John	W	51	Married	RC	12	Factory Worker	IV	58
22	Molina, Mary	W	51		P	12	Secretary		
23	Moore, Joyce	W	20	Single	RC	2 yrs. college	Physio-therapist	III	39
24	Mosca, John	W	39	Married	RC	B.A. degree	Personnel Manager	II	22
25	Mosca, Lydia	W	39		RC	B.A. degree	Teacher		
26	Norton, Ann	B	35	Separated	P	10	Hospital Aide	V	62
27	Porter, Barbara	W	29	Divorced	RC	1 yr. college	Computer Programmer	III	39

Demographic Characteristics of Interviewed Clients in Study Sample

No.	Name	Race*	Age	Marital Status	Religion†	Highest Grade Completed	Occupation	Socio-Economic Class‡	Index of Social Position‡
28	Spaulding, Ethel	W	69	Married	RC	10	Retired Factory Worker	V	62
29	Stewart, Carol	W	37	Divorced	RC	B.A. degree	Unemployed Teacher	II	22
30	Talcott, Ruth	W	55	Married	RC	8	Unemployed Sales Clerk	IV	48
31	Vinter, Louise	W	74	Single	RC	12	Retired Sales Clerk	IV	44
32	Voltaire, Albert	W	50	Married	RC	4	Unemployed Laborer	V	67
33	Xavier, Joan	W	18	Single	RC	12	Office Clerk	IV	44

*B = Black; W = White.
† P = Protestant; RC = Catholic.
‡ Based on Hollingshead (1957).

Part II

The Helping Process and Its Outcome

I had been so unhappy for so long that when my mother suggested I go to the agency I thought, Wow! I'll be all fine and cured! . . . *So . . . When I first went in there, I went with this kind of illusion that there was this Good Fairy who was going to wave the magic wand and I'd be just so happy and peaceful. . . . Well, it took me a couple of months to realize that the counselor wasn't a Good Fairy. Oh, she was just a nice lady to talk with. . . . She . . . she gave me time to talk about myself and after a while I felt better . . . . but it didn't happen overnight.*

From research interview with a client in this study

Chapter 4

The Beginning Phase: Getting Engaged

What forces propel someone to get to a family service agency? Once an initial connection is made, what is there that influences the person's and the social worker's efforts to *get engaged* with each other and decide to continue? What role do client expectations play in the helping process?

To explore these issues, the research interviews with clients and workers included a variety of questions concerning the presenting problem, prior coping efforts, the referral process, expectations, and the initial client-worker encounter.

PRESENTING PROBLEM

Clients and workers were asked to describe the difficulties that initially led each person to the agency. As seen in Table 4-1, most persons went to the agency because of difficulties in their marriage or in their relationships with other family members. Other problems included out-of-wedlock pregnancy, depression or personal dissatisfaction, teenagers' school difficulties, and difficulties in dealing with other agencies such as public welfare.

Aside from two exceptions, workers agreed with the client in their recollection of the difficulties initially bringing the latter to the agency. In the two cases where this was not so, the clients saw the presenting problem as their teenager's school difficulties, while the workers defined it as a conflict in family relationships. In seven of the eight cases in which both spouses were interviewed by the researcher, there was also agreement between the spouses; in the remaining case, one partner viewed the problem in terms of marital conflict while the other defined it as the spouse's depression. The latter case was categorized as a "marital conflict" case, since that is how the worker and at least one spouse defined it.

As clients talked about their presenting problems, their descriptions reflected a common theme of desperation and confusion. Over half of the respondents used words or phrases such as "confused," "didn't know where to

49

TABLE 4-1.   Difficulties Bringing Client to Agency, as Seen by Clients and Workers (N = 25 cases)

DIFFICULTY	CLIENT	WORKER
Marital conflict	10	10
Parent-child conflict	2	2
Family relationship problems	3	5
Depression or personal dissatisfaction	2	2
Out-of-wedlock pregnancy	4	4
Teenagers' school problems	2	0
Dealing with other agencies (public welfare, housing bureau)	2	2
TOTAL	25	25

turn," "was discouraged," "couldn't think straight anymore," "chaotic situation," "I felt like I was in a stormy sea." Some typical statements were:

Mrs. Stewart: My husband and I had been having so many problems. . . . Things were so chaotic that I felt maybe I should find out where I was going wrong. . . . I felt like I was losing my mind.

Miss Appel: I had been feeling bad about myself. . . . I didn't like myself at all. . . . I had some friends but didn't think they liked me either and . . . oh . . . I closed myself off from them. The more I did that, the more unhappy I became.

Mr. Mosca: The marriage had been going downhill slowly . . . then things began to fall apart suddenly. . . . I didn't know what to do. . . . I knew my wife was depressed and we were both confused and unhappy.

Mrs. Spaulding: I was so discouraged that I didn't care about nothing . . . . I didn't want to live. . . . Ever since my son died, all I did was brood over him day and night.

While in a few instances clients reported that there had been a precipitating event such as the death of a family member, in most cases they pointed to the chronic nature of the presenting problem. There were indications that the search for outside help was typically triggered not so much by a specific event as by the feeling that the situation had become intolerable and that the client had no one else to turn to. Social workers also pointed frequently to the progressively deteriorating nature of a client's problems rather than to any one precipitating cause. As found in studies of applicants for mental health services, most respondents had been experiencing high levels of stress in the period immediately preceding their application to the agency (Overbeck, 1972; Smolar, 1976).

PRIOR COPING EFFORTS

Most clients had engaged in a variety of efforts to cope with their difficulties prior to going to the agency, including seeking help from close family members and other informal or formal helping agents.

Particularly striking was the high proportion of clients who sought help from professionals in the period immediately preceding their contact with the Bureau. Over two-thirds indicated that they had discussed their difficulties with one or more professionals—for example, physicians, clergymen, and school personnel. Similarly, over two-thirds said that they had talked with friends and/or relatives about their problems. Most people had sought help from both types of resources. This suggests that, for the population represented in the study, there is some acceptance of the need for outside help in connection with personal or interpersonal problems.

Thus, nearly all of the clients had access to potential formal and informal sources of help in their social networks. However, their contacts with these people usually proved to be insufficient or unsatisfactory. The professionals, in general, were persons who did not specialize in counseling (e.g., family physicians or teachers) and who apparently recognized their limitations and encouraged clients to seek help from a more appropriate resource. With a couple of exceptions, clients who had previously been involved with a psychiatrist, social worker, or psychologist expressed dissatisfaction with the service:

> He seemed interested only in getting his forty dollars an hour.

> She seemed too busy to pay attention to us.

> It was a waste of time.

Most clients also indicated that they had not been satisfied with the help they had received from informal sources such as friends or neighbors. While in general they had access to other persons, they felt that discussing their problems with them was not sufficient or appropriate. In some cases, they were reluctant to expose their difficulties to others:

> Our friends saw us as a model couple. How could we tell them we were having trouble in our marriage?

> I wouldn't go to my mother. She always puts me down.

Other clients questioned the capacity of their friends or relatives to be of help:

> I could talk with my sister, but she couldn't possibly help. . . . She has too many problems of her own right now.

> All a friend can do is listen to you.

> I was too sick. . . . I needed psychiatric treatment.

Another common theme was that it was difficult for friends or relatives to be objective, since they are too close to the problem and the people involved in it:

> You can't talk with your family or neighbors about your marriage. It's hard to confide in them. . . . They're too close. . . . You want someone outside who can see both sides better.

As seen in other investigations,[1] respondents in this study initially tried to cope with their personal or interpersonal difficulties by turning to friends, relatives, colleagues, and others in their social networks whom they trusted or whose opinion they respected (Smolar, 1976: 156). Eventually, however, they became motivated to seek professional help, as they experienced loss of social support (Overbeck, 1972) or as they perceived their informal helping agents as unsuitable or inadequate (Mayer and Timms, 1970: 37-51). In a number of cases, despite their discouraging experiences with their earlier efforts to seek help, these respondents were sufficiently motivated or desperate to reach out to the agency.

REFERRAL PROCESS

A review of research on pathways to treatment in mental health settings (Smolar, 1976: 26-39) shows that a person's reference group strongly influences the referral process:

> Pathways to treatment are in good part dependent upon available resources, social customs, and group support for help seeking behavior. The beliefs and attitudes toward mental illness are important determinants of the perception of a problem in mental health terms. Also, the decision to seek help and the source selected will depend greatly on how well informed the seeker is regarding the possible resource and whether he has a favorable orientation toward the effect professional help may have (Smolar, 1976: 148).

TABLE 4-2.   Sources of Referral (N = 25 cases)

Source of Referral	No. of Cases
Self	7
Relative or friend	4
Clergyman	3
Family physician	1
Employer	1
School	2
Other social agencies	7
TOTAL	25

[1] For a concise summary of many of these investigations, see Smolar (1976: 26-39).

Some pertinent questions therefore are: How does a person eventually get to a particular agency, in this instance the Family Service Bureau? What goes on in the referral process? How informed is he or she in regard to the agency? What choices, if any, does the prospective client have in respect to agencies?

As seen in Table 4-2, over one-fourth of the clients in the study were self-referred; over half were referred by formal agents (e.g., clergymen, school, or other community agencies); less than one-fourth were referred by informal agents (e.g., relative or friend).

Nearly all of the self-referred clients were in the middle socioeconomic group, whereas almost all of those referred by other social agencies were in the lower group. There were no differences by social class in referrals by professionals such as physicians or clergymen.

Most of the clients, regardless of socioeconomic status, suggested that they had gone to this particular agency because they did not have or were not aware of other options. For example, several of the self-referred clients knew about private practitioners or mental health clinics; however, they were not able to afford their cost and were attracted to the Family Service Bureau at least partly because of the lower fee. A clear example of this is provided by Mrs. Donnelly, who had been in treatment with a private practitioner for a few months and then transferred to the Bureau for financial reasons. In the research interview, in discussing her feelings about transferring from one worker to another, Mrs. Donnelly observed:

> I didn't want to change . . . really from Mr. Smith to another worker . . . but financially I couldn't afford it. . . . Okay, that was one of the reasons.

As for the clients who had been referred by other social agencies or professionals, in general they noted that they had been sent specifically to the Bureau. They had not been told about other resources, although there are three other family service agencies in the community, two of which are nonsectarian while the third is Jewish. It would appear that, although each of these agencies is open to all persons regardless of religion, the Bureau is viewed by referral agents as the most appropriate one for Catholics.

Most clients said that they knew very little about the agency at the point of referral and were uncertain about what they would find. This was particularly true of the clients referred by formal agents. Informal referral agents were more likely to give specific information about the agency and the helping process. One man talked extensively during the research interview about his sister, a guidance counselor who had received marriage counseling in another state and who not only urged him to seek help but also carefully explained what would be involved. In another case, a woman indicated that her older sister, who had been a client of the same agency, had described the counseling service to her in detail.

Most of the clients referred by professional persons or other agencies said that they had been told very little about the Family Service Bureau. Several of those referred by professional persons noted that they had been given vague information about several agencies and that they were urged to seek counseling. The main function of the referral agent seemed to be to offer encouragement to the client in his or her movement toward professional help. From what the clients brought out, it did not seem that referral agents exploited one potential use of the referral — that is, the opportunity to clarify the person's expectations, to discuss the services provided by diverse agencies, and to help the person to make an informed choice.

The agency's religious affiliation played an important role in the referral process in one out of four cases. This is illustrated by the case of a young woman who indicated that her father had been totally opposed to her "going to a shrink," until he learned that the agency was associated with the Catholic Church. Several of the self-referred clients also explained that they had chosen this particular agency on the basis of its religious connection. One woman said that she looked through the telephone book and called the first agency with "Catholic" in its title.[2]

In summary, in most cases the person's distress, usually coupled with some encouragement from a formal or informal referral agent, propelled him or her to seek help at the Family Service Bureau. In a few cases, the client went to the agency even though there was opposition from significant figures such as friends or relatives. In these cases, it seems that the clients were sufficiently desperate or overwhelmed by the problems to be able to overcome the resistance to counseling that they encountered in their social network. Mrs. Stewart was one of these people. She had numerous relatives who gave her much comfort as she struggled with an abusive husband; but none of them could accept her need for outside help:

> My parents and aunts in their own way were trying to help . . . but they just couldn't see that it wasn't enough. Oh. . . . Oh. . . . They figured that you should hang in there like everybody else and solve your own problems. And they made me feel like I was nuts. . . . They were negative toward psychiatrists and counselors. . . . My parents had old-fashioned ideas. Oh. . . . They thought your problems would eventually be solved if you tried hard enough . . . if you had common sense and a lot of hobbies to distract yourself. I finally had to go somewhere for help . . . couldn't take it anymore!

In contrast to the clients, workers usually recalled very little about the referral process. This may be due to the fact that, as explained later in this chapter, in this agency the initial intake call is often handled by a different worker. However, Sainsbury, in another study (1975: 18), also noted that "the clarity and focus of clients' memories of referral are in contrast to the increasingly generalized recollections expressed by their social workers." Perhaps workers do not actually attribute much significance to the referral

---

[2] See Chapter 10, "The Agency Environment," for a discussion of the influence of the Bureau's religious affiliation on the helping process and its outcome.

process, despite considerable emphasis in social work on the role of referral agents and the quality of the referral. It may also be that the large number of cases to which workers are exposed makes it difficult for them to recall details of the beginning phase of the service in each individual case.

At any rate, since the nature and process of the referral do exert an influence on the prospective client, it seems important for workers to be cognizant of its meaning for each person. By clarifying the prospective client's response to the referral, the worker may gain a greater understanding of his or her motivation and exploit this motivation in the engagement process. Furthermore, discussion of the person's referral early in the contact may serve to clarify his or her expectations and to deal with any discrepancies between the client and the worker.

EXPECTATIONS

As someone takes the step of getting to an agency, what does he or she expect to get out of it? This is a critical issue in practice, in view of findings that expectations significantly influence the counseling process. Goldstein (1962; 1971; 1973) has carried out extensive research on patient and therapist expectancies in psychotherapy. On the basis of this research, he has concluded that mutuality of expectations is necessary to enhance the therapeutic relationship (Goldstein, 1962: 64–75). Goldstein's early findings have been confirmed by later studies in social work and other fields. Various researchers have found that clashes in expectations between client and worker can seriously interfere with the helping process (Lennard and Bernstein, 1969; Lerner, 1972; Mayer and Timms, 1970; Mayer and Rosenblatt, 1974). Others have argued that a person's expectations from the "helper" can be a positive force in the outcome of treatment (Frank, 1974; Friedman, 1963).

In the present study, most clients indicated that, in going to the agency, they had hoped to find a quick solution to their problems. Some commonly used phrases were:

Find a cure.

Straighten things out.

Looking for a miracle.

Get quick answers.

Find a snappy solution.

Miss Appel responded in a particularly interesting way to the question about her initial expectations from the agency and the worker:

I had been so unhappy for so long that when my mother suggested I go to the agency I thought, *Wow! I'll be all fine and cured!* . . . So . . . when I first went in there, I went with this kind of illusion that there was this Good Fairy who was going to wave the magic wand and I'd just be so happy and peaceful! . . . Well, it took me a couple of months to realize that the counselor wasn't a Good Fairy. Oh, she was just a nice lady to talk with. . . . She . . . She gave me time to talk about myself and after a while I began to feel better . . . but it didn't happen overnight.

In addition to global or vague hopes, most respondents brought out a variety of specific expectations that fell in these categories, in descending frequency:

1. Achieving change in *one's self* or in *one's interaction* with significant others, usually the spouse (e.g., learning to communicate better with a spouse; being better able to make decisions; "feeling better about myself").
2. Achieving change in *another person,* such as spouse or child (e.g., changing spouse's abusive behavior; getting teenage son to return to school; convincing spouse to accept reconciliation).
3. Achieving some *concrete* change in *one's situation* (e.g., obtaining a rent reduction; making adoption plans for a baby; finding better housing).

Three clients indicated that they did not know what they had expected, while another one emphasized that she had not expected anything from the agency. In all four of these cases, the client had been pressured to come to the agency by some outside institution such as the school. Each of these clients eventually dropped out and was dissatisfied or ambivalent about the outcome. As will be noted later, these were among the cases in which the worker might have been more active in helping the client to clarify the focus of service.

With the exception of the above four cases, there was no difference in the pattern of expectations between clients who were self-referred and those who were other-referred. There were differences, however, on the basis of socioeconomic class. Clients were more likely to expect either *change in someone else* or *concrete help* if they were from the lower socioeconomic group. In contrast, they were more likely to expect *change in themselves* if they were from the middle socioeconomic group.

These findings substantiate the conclusions of previous investigators that lower-class clients, more than those from middle and upper classes, seem to be less concerned with psychological problems and more interested in obtaining concrete assistance or help in changing the behavior of another family member (Aronson and Overall, 1966; Jones, 1974; Mayer and Timms, 1970; Overall and Aronson, 1963). The different expectations apparently result from different belief systems concerning the causes and treatment of personal or interpersonal problems. For example, as noted in an earlier chapter, working-class clients seem to approach problem solving from a unicausal, moralistic perspective, in contrast to the probing, multicausal, insight-oriented approach of persons from middle or upper socioeconomic groups (Mayer and Timms, 1970: 143-148).

Along with high expectations of the service, at the point of referral most clients expected the worker to take an active role in solving their problems or meeting their needs. There were no differences in regard to this expectation on the basis of socioeconomic background, nature of presenting problem, or duration of contact. In short, many clients clearly viewed the referral as potentially providing a quick solution to their problems. Therefore, they moved into the counseling process with high expectations of the worker and of the service. This was illustrated in particular by Mr. Bates, a middle-aged professional man who had been involved with several agencies and mental health clinics in different parts of the country, in connection with his teenage son's severe psychiatric problems:

> Naturally, every time you go to a counselor you hope that a cure will follow. . . . You expect to move immediately toward solution of the problem as they do in medical treatment. But with psychiatric problems it's not the same. Even though you know this, you still expect a quick cure. . . . The average person wants immediate help, immediate relief. . . . That's why counselors have never really met our expectations. . . . Every time my wife and I go to a new clinic, we have high hopes . . . but we're always disappointed. . . . We usually feel that we're getting the runaround and that the counselors aren't really helping. . . . We feel like this even though we understand counseling a little bit after having been to so many places in the past ten years.

Despite their understanding of the complexities inherent in the process of problem solving, some clients tended to have high or unrealistic expectations. Several examples illustrate the ambivalence felt by clients as they recognized that they were expecting too much:

Mrs. Bogdansky: Sure, I was hoping that my daughter's problems would be taken care of right away. But you can't expect to have 17 years changed in a couple of months.

Mrs. Mosca: I was hoping to get snappy solutions and answers from the counselor without having to put my mind to work. . . . I knew this wasn't the sensible way of doing it, but I wanted the counselor to do the work for me, to tell me what to do.

Mrs. Lodano: I wished that we would come up quickly with a cut-and-dried solution for the troubles in our marriage. . . . But I knew it wouldn't be done that way, since I had some training in psychology and sociology in college.

On the basis of the research mentioned earlier by Goldstein (1962; 1971; 1973) as well as others, it could be predicted that the client's initial expectations represented a significant element in the helping process in the beginning phase. We will therefore consider the workers' handling of these expectations, as we examine the respondents' views on the initial client-worker encounter.

INITIAL CLIENT-WORKER ENCOUNTER

THE INTAKE PROCESS

Before moving into the findings on the client-worker encounter, the reader may be interested in a description of the typical intake process at the Family Service Bureau. Social workers are assigned to intake duty on a rotating basis. The intake worker initially screens each inquiry or referral over the telephone or, in a few instances, in person in case of those who walk in. If the intake worker judges the referral to be appropriate, the applicant is assigned to a social worker and given an appointment for intake evaluation. In about half of the applications, the worker is the same as the one who initially screened the referral. In the other cases, the applicant is assigned to another worker, usually on the basis of availability and in consultation with the Director of Professional Services. Worker and applicant then meet for an initial session, in which they decide whether or not further service is indicated. If so, the case is assigned for treatment, usually to the same worker.

The agency receptionist comes in contact with nearly all applicants, since she is the one who first greets people as they enter the agency's offices. Moreover, her work area is located directly across from the waiting room. This affords her the opportunity to observe and talk with clients while she is seated at her desk and carrying out other functions. She is the only receptionist, expect for volunteers or other staff members who occasionally substitute for her. During the period covered by the study, the receptionist was a warm, friendly, and open middle-aged woman who related easily and spontaneously to clients. She had had no special training. She seemed to be ideally suited to her role, very effective in meeting people and making them feel comfortable and accepted. Her behavior with clients seemed to reflect primarily her personality but also, to some extent, agency policy. Although her role was not necessarily viewed as a therapeutic one, the agency's philosophy encouraged her as well as other staff members to be positive in their interaction with clients. As the findings of this study will reveal, clients in general viewed the receptionist as an integral member of the staff who played a most important role in the process and outcome of interpersonal helping.

TASKS IN THE BEGINNING PHASE

In social work, as in other "helping" professions, there is wide agreement about the crucial importance of the initial encounter between client and worker. Consequently, the initial interview has been extensively examined by practitioners (Argelander, 1976; Perlman, 1960; Rosenblatt, 1962) as well as researchers (Blenkner, Hunt, and Kogan, 1952; Goldstein, 1969 and 1971; Pfouts and Rader, 1962; Polansky and Kounin, 1956). However, it is not clear precisely *how* the initial encounter affects the process and outcome of interpersonal helping. In particular, there is a need to identify the essential tasks that client and social worker must perform in their efforts to cope constructively with the initial phase of the helping process.

With these issues in mind, research interviews included questions that elicited the clients' and workers' spontaneous views on their initial meeting. In response to these questions, many clients vividly recalled the first session with the worker and freely shared their impressions. Excerpts from research interviews with several clients are reproduced below, to illustrate the substance of clients' views as well as the interviewer's methodological approach.

CASE OF MRS. CAIN

Interviewer: What do you remember about that first meeting?
Respondent: They were very nice; very pleasant. They tried to make us feel at ease. The woman we had—the counselor—tried to make us as relaxed as possible and just, you know, relaxed enough where we wouldn't feel on edge or tense and would be able to talk to her. It's difficult to go to a stranger and talk to somebody, but she did everything in her power to relax us and she was very good at that.
I: What were some of the things that she did that made you feel relaxed?
R: Oh, she used very good communication techniques and she stressed the positive, talking about things other than our problems, asking us about the children and talking about everyday common things that would just kind of make you at ease with somebody you don't know . . . a stranger.
I: What do you think about that way of doing it?
R: It's good, because it relaxes you. I think I realized what she was doing . . . that in a way she was using communication techniques. I use some of these myself in my work. I know people who use these techniques routinely. . . . It's their job and they do it but they don't really feel for you. That's why at the beginning I was a little . . . hesitant, you know, and I was going to feel her out a little bit more, just a little, so see if she was superficial or deeper in her interest in us or just as another case.
I: How did that work out as it went on? How did you feel about that?
R: I found that she was quite interested in us. It seemed to her more than just a job. I think you can usually pick it up if it's just a job.
I: What gave you that impression? What was it about her or her approach that made you feel that she was interested?
R: She just seemed like a very natural person. . . . She just seemed very natural and not . . . I don't know . . . you can tell in somebody's voice whether they're interested or whether it's just a talk for conversation or talk just for talk.

CASE OF MRS. MOSCA

Interviewer: Could you tell me about your first meeting with the social worker?

Respondent: It was a good meeting. . . . I liked it.

I: Could you tell me a little more about your impressions?

R: I was very nervous in going there . . . even though I really wanted to go and I pushed my husband to go into counseling. I was very nervous because we're not the types who tell their problems to anyone. . . . Even our close friends and relatives didn't know. . . . But, after we got there and the counselor asked us questions we started talking . . . and we told him everything.

I: What else do you remember?

R: Actually, I did more crying than talking. . . . Once I got going I went through many feelings and emotions in that first meeting. . . . I guess I had to get it off my chest . . . and then I felt good . . . as if I had taken a giant load off my shoulders . . . emotionally drained but good.

CASE OF MR. FORT

Interviewer: Now, if we could talk a little about that first session, how did you feel going there?

Respondent: Stupid! Absolutely stupid!

I: How do you mean . . . "stupid"?

R: Uh, oh, I felt like . . . what am I doin' here, baring my troubles to the world? I don't need to be here, I haven't done anything wrong. . . . You sit there and—I don't know—I just couldn't bring myself to admit that we had gone that far that we had to be someplace like that.

I: What else went on in that first session?

R: Mostly she just listened to us. . . . I realized that she was interested in us . . . that she was trying to see what was going on with us . . . how she could help. . . . And I felt better after we began to talk. . . . She seemed like she knew what we were going through.

As reflected in the preceding excerpts, in recalling their initial impressions, most clients brought out effective themes dealing with how they felt in approaching the worker, with what went on in their interaction with the worker, and with their obtaining emotional relief through the initial interview. There were fewer references to the worker's skills, knowledge, or competence. For most of the clients, the initial session apparently was quite effective in relieving their anxiety.

The clients' views reflected a number of themes that are basic in social work practice, particularly the therapeutic value of appropriate support and reassurance, ventilation of one's feelings and anxieties, and the experience of being accepted in a relationship with another human being. From the perspective of the client, the emotional aspects of the client-worker relationship begin to emerge as a central factor in counseling as early as the initial session. This finding supports Lennard and Bernstein's emphasis (1969) on the therapeutic value of the interactional environment in which client and worker operate.

The workers' recollections of the initial phase of the encounter were not as vivid as those of the client. Furthermore, while clients tended to recall their feelings and reactions, workers tended to talk more about their initial impressions of the clients' problems and their activities in engaging the prospective client in a treatment relationship. Some representative impressions of the initial interview by workers follow:

> I wondered whether I could help them. . . . They seemed to be so troubled and depressed. . . . We talked about what their concerns were, what they wanted to do about them . . . and how I could help them.

> We went over a general overview on their situation . . . and what services we provided. Both of them brought out their dissatisfaction with each other . . . how they were both busy and had been going their separate ways.

> It was so long ago that I don't remember much about it. I imagine I did what I usually try to do . . . try to help the client to define the problem . . . understand what I can do, . . . decide if she wants to go in treatment and on what basis.

There may be various reasons for the differences between clients and workers in recollections of the initial sessions. For one thing, although both were usually asked the same questions in identical terms, their frames of reference are quite different. Workers are involved with many clients and may find it difficult to recall details about early sessions in a specific case. The initial meeting is not as intense an experience for them as it is for the client. Also, the worker is guided by the requirements of the professional role, such as the need to arrive at some assessment and treatment planning in each situation. For these reasons, for the worker, the content of the interaction may be more salient than the process. For the client, the reverse seems to happen. It is as if the initial session is an intensely meaningful life experience for the client, while for the worker it is an ordinary part of the job — another moment in time or a ritualistic activity.

A comparative analysis of clients' and workers' views regarding their initial encounter suggests that they are confronted with a sequence of mutual tasks, from (1) opening up the client's "life space" to (2) assessing the client's needs and determining the appropriateness of the service; (3) establishing an emotional connection; (4) mobilizing client motivation; and (5) reaching a beginning working agreement. Each of these tasks involves complementary functions and responsibilities for both parties. For example, "opening up life space" is dependent on the client's willingness to share himself or herself as well as on the worker's readiness to provide encouragement and support.

The data on the first two tasks are not extensive. The suggestion is that clients and workers actively struggle with the need to have the client open up the life space—that is, tell his or her story—and with the task of assessing the problem and determining whether the service is appropriate. In somewhat different terms, these tasks have been viewed as two of the major functions of the psycho-social study in the initial phase of casework (Hollis, 1972: 247–259).

There were more extensive data on the other three tasks—*establishing an emotional connection, mobilizing the client's motivation,* and *reaching a beginning working agreement.* Therefore, these will be considered in some detail at this point. It should be noted at the outset that these tasks appeared to have been adequately handled in about two-thirds of the cases and inadequately in the remaining third.

ESTABLISHMENT OF EMOTIONAL CONNECTION

In two-thirds of the cases, clients typically indicated that in the initial session they expressed their concerns, feelings, and fears about seeking help and that the worker listened to them and helped them to relax or feel more comfortable. In most of these cases, the workers' responses in the research interviews showed that they were tuned into the clients' feelings and concerns and that they had deliberately focused on these at some point during the initial session. Thus, these clients and workers were able to establish an initial emotional connection or a beginning positive relationship. For example, this is in part how Mr. Lodano talked about his initial meeting with the worker:

> I wasn't sure that anyone could help us . . . or if there was a solution to our problem. . . . But, soon after we met John [the worker], I decided that there was hope. I can't tell you what it was. . . . It's just that we got along very well from the beginning. . . . It was like we had always known each other. . . . Some kind of bond grew between us. . . . John seemed like someone I had known for a long time, even though I had never met him before.

Mr. Lodano, who was described by the worker as a hypersensitive young man unable to relax, was assigned to an easygoing worker whose steadying influence turned out to be a major factor in the favorable outcome of the service.

In the other third of the cases, the clients did not recall having expressed their feelings or having been helped with their feelings by the workers. At the same time, the workers recalled very little expression or discussion of feelings in these cases; furthermore, several of them during the research interview brought out their dissatisfaction with the client's inability to relate at an emotional level. In contrast to the experiences of respondents in the first group, these clients and workers apparently were not able to establish some kind of emotional connection during the initial phase of their interaction.

In some cases, it seemed that the clients had ended up with workers whose styles or qualities were unsuited to their needs. As an example, Mrs. Bates, a middle-aged woman with extensive prior experience in psychotherapy, spoke this way about the importance of client-worker matching:

> When you finally decide to go to a counselor, you go with a great deal of anticipation that you're going to get help. . . . When you first meet the counselor . . . you wonder if she can help you . . . how you will get along. . . . A meeting of personalities is necessary. . . . I can't explain it . . . but if you clash . . . you're not going to open up. . . . You won't feel like getting involved.

Mrs. Bates equated professional competence with formality and structure; she was assigned to a worker with an informal and spontaneous style. She was critical of the worker's "overly casual approach" and did not feel sufficient confidence in the worker's ability to help her. After a few sessions, Mrs. Bates withdrew.

In at least some instances, then, it appears that idiosyncratic qualities, such as the style or personality of a particular worker, play a major role in the process of the client and worker becoming engaged with each other, influencing the quality of their interaction.

In social work practice it is assumed that, although professional education "signifies a minimum of competence with respect to all clients, workers nevertheless possess additional ability in relation to certain types of clients" (Moore, 1976). Practitioners generally appreciate the importance of modifying their style and approach so as to accommodate them to the client's needs. But there may be a limit as to how far or how well this can be done by the worker in the reality of practice. In addition, it is not at all clear just what constitutes optimal client-worker matching. There has been considerable research in this area in psychotherapy; numerous studies have investigated the relationship between the outcome of therapy and the matching of patient and therapist on the basis of expectations, attitudes, and personality dimensions, such as authoritarianism, tolerance, flexibility, self-acceptance, and social presence. After reviewing many of the studies published prior to 1970, Goldstein (1971: 116-139) determined that the findings were inconclusive. Pointing to the complexity of interpersonal behavior, Goldstein (1969: 446) noted that these "simplistic or unidimensional matching studies on patients and therapists have failed to yield meaningful results on a variety of outcome criteria."

More recently, there has been research pointing to the eventual development of a conceptual framework for matching of clients and practitioners on the basis of their human qualities (Moore, 1976). At the present time, however, there are no specific guidelines in relation to matching of clients and workers. Perhaps the most important implication is that practitioners should be sensitive to any evidence of grossly poor matching between themselves and prospective clients in initial sessions. As this evidence becomes apparent in some situations, they should be responsive to it and, at the least, raise it as an issue with the client, so as to consider whether an immediate transfer to another worker might be indicated.

MOBILIZING CLIENT MOTIVATION

Most of the clients in the satisfied group also reported that they had left the initial session with confidence in the worker's ability to help them, a sense of relief, and renewed hope that by continuing in counseling they would achieve the improvement that they had been seeking:

I knew that things would finally get better.

She was obviously very good at her work. . . . Made me feel that she knew what I needed and that she would give it to me.

Somehow, after a lot of crying in that first meeting, my problems didn't seem to be so bad.

I finally could see that there was something I could do.

My prayers were beginning to be answered.

In different ways, these respondents brought out that their worker by the end of the session had managed to convey to them a sense of hope about their situation, some conviction that things *could* change for the better, some recognition that their problems were not beyond solution.

The importance of hope in the casework relationship has been stressed by practitioners (Oxley, 1966) and also documented through empirical investigations (Boatman, 1975; Bounous, 1965; Van Dyke, 1962). In addition, there has been extensive consideration of the role of hope in psychotherapy. Stotland (1969) has defined hope as the perceived possibility of attaining a goal. Writing about the significance of hope as an antecedent variable in the outcome of therapy, Frank (1974: 137) has noted: "Unless the patient hopes that the therapist can help him, he will not come to therapy in the first place, or if he does, he will not stay long."

The findings of the present study show the role of hope in the helping process and also the significance of the "interactional environment" described by Lennard and Bernstein (1969): by experiencing relief and hope through their interaction with the worker, clients became ready to begin dealing more effectively with life tasks or challenges. Above all, it appeared that, by heightening the client's sense of hope, the worker began to mobilize his motivation and capacity to get engaged in the problem-solving process.[3]

[3] The role of motivation in the problem-solving process in casework has been carefully analyzed by Ripple, Alexander, and Polemis (1964).

Thus, another cardinal task in the initial phase of interpersonal helping is that of *mobilizing the person's motivation*. This task seems to be a prerequisite for the prospective client's decision to continue with the service. Apparently, increasing the client's hope is a major component of this task.[4]

Other hypotheses are suggested by the above data. As emphasized by Frank (1974), the client's faith in the worker may in itself be healing or therapeutic. It also seems that the worker's favorable expectation of client improvement is useful in maintaining and strengthening the client-worker relationship (Heller and Goldstein, 1961).

REACHING A BEGINNING WORKING AGREEMENT

Workers in general seemed to be well aware of their clients' expectations. However, they did not uniformly talk about these with the clients.

In most of the cases of satisfied clients, both parties recalled some discussion of their mutual expectations and roles and of their definition of the problem, along with consideration of what would be involved in the helping process. It was evident, in other words, that they had begun to engage in the contracting process by raising questions, sounding each other out, expressing their concerns, and confronting some of the differences in their views and expectations.

In the cases of dissatisfied clients, very little attention was given to the issue of the contract. The majority of these clients were from the lower socioeconomic group. In these cases, the person usually expected help with one kind of problem while the worker focused on something else. Mr. and Mrs. Molina, for example, wanted the worker to induce their teenage son to return to school, while the worker tried to help them with their tendency to control his life. These were typically cases in which the client either had come to the agency through pressure from someone else or expected the worker to effect changes in another family member. The workers recognized the inappropriate or unrealistic nature of the client's request but indicated that they did not explicitly discuss it with the client.

In the two-thirds of the cases in which there was ample discussion of their expectations, clients and workers reported that the initial session had ended with a definite conclusion, such as a plan for future meetings, delineation of actions to be taken by client and/or worker, and definition of the focus of service. Several clients mentioned that they were especially helped by the worker's careful review of their discussion and conclusions toward the end of the initial session:

Mrs. Gates: Before we got through with our first meeting she went over what we were talking about . . . what we had more or less agreed to do. . . . We had to decide if there was any more purpose to our

---

[4] It is interesting in this regard that *motivation* is defined by French (1952: 50-53) as the "push" of discomfort and the "pull" of hope.

marriage. . . . Well, it was good the way she put things so clearly. . . . Oh . . . she made you think.

Mr. Voltaire: She was okay. . . . The first time we talked she made things clear. . . . I don't understand English too much . . . but . . . oh . . . I know what we do. . . . She told me many things. . . . Not to be too strict with my daughter.

Mrs. Mosca: It was amazing how he could remember and summarize everything that we had been saying with me and my husband. . . . It made you think and realize what you should do. . . . I began to see that my husband and I should do more things together.

In social work practice, workers often conclude initial interviews with generalities concerning the problem and the planned intervention. The clients in this study evidently responded most positively to workers who took an active role in reviewing the client's concern and proposed ways of dealing with it in specific and concrete terms.

In the group of cases in which there had been limited or uneven discussion of expectations, clients brought out the vagueness and uncertainty that they felt at the conclusion of the initial interview. Several of them noted that the worker suggested his or her availabilty for continuing contacts but did not offer a specific appointment. Mrs. Molina, for example, said:

> I wasn't so sure that she wanted to see me again. . . . She said we could get together anytime . . . but she didn't give me an appointment. She made me feel like my problem wasn't that important. . . . Maybe she had other people with more serious troubles. . . . The next week I called her back . . . hoping to get an appointment. . . . She said she wasn't sure what she could do for me . . . oh, she told me to think about it and call her back. . . . I never did. What was the use?

The worker in this case indicated in the research interview that Mrs. Molina's request for counseling in the initial session was very vague, and that she had tried to encourage her to clarify what she was looking for and what she wanted. However, it seemed that the client interpreted her efforts to clarify the request for help as rejection or lack of interest on the part of the worker.[5]

There were other examples of misunderstanding between client and worker, of uncertainty on the part of the worker about the nature of the client's request for help or its appropriateness for this agency, and of consequent vagueness in the conclusion of the initial session. In effect, in these cases clients and workers had not been able to resolve satisfactorily the task of

[5] This case supports the hypothesis by Thomas and his associates that a client's commitment to continue in a therapeutic relationship beyond the initial interview is in part a function of his conception of the intensity of the counselor's motivation to help (Thomas, Polansky, and Kounin, 1955: 173).

reaching a beginning working agreement. There was insufficient clarity or mutuality as to the target problem or solution desired by the client.

Similar difficulties were evident in the ten cases in the study sample in which clients were not available or declined to be interviewed. Most of these involved people from the lower socioeconomic group. In eight of these cases, workers brought out their uncertainty or dissatisfaction concerning the conclusion of the initial session in terms like these:

> The client was very confused . . . didn't know what she wanted. . . . And I couldn't help her to clarify things.

> I couldn't figure out why she was here. . . . She wouldn't tell me. I felt so frustrated.

> They agreed to come back but they were not enthusiastic about counseling. I doubted that they would last long.

> Even though we went over this, at the end of the session they still didn't understand what was involved in treatment. . . . They continued to think that I would be tutoring their daughter in science and arithmetic.

While at the end of the initial session these clients had agreed to continue their contacts, most of them either did not return for their next appointment or soon dropped out. These were evidently cases in which there was insufficient role complementarity between clients and workers (Spiegel, 1968). Since the lack of complementarity was not overcome, these cases eventually resulted in discontinuance or premature withdrawal. These findings are consistent with those of Silverman (1969), who concluded in her study of "spoiled helping relationships" that, at the end of intake interviews, there was no common or clear definition by clients and workers about the nature of the problem to focus on, their mutual expectations, or the purposes and methods of their future contacts.

GETTING ENGAGED

In the initial phase of the helping process, clients and workers were confronted with a variety of essential tasks. In large measure, the resolution of these tasks determined whether they got engaged, that is, whether they decided to continue their contacts.

In the majority of cases, clients and workers were able to resolve most of the tasks satisfactorily and therefore went on with subsequent meetings. This does not mean that they agreed on everything or that they achieved total congruence in their role expectations and behaviors. On the contrary, many disparities continued to pervade their interaction. Findings on how clients and workers coped with these ongoing disparities will be discussed in the next chapter.

Clashes in expectations and other differences between clients and workers emerged more intensely in a smaller number of cases (about one-third of the sample) in which the participants had decided to go on with each other, even though the necessary tasks had not been adequately resolved. In these instances, the person's distress or pressure from external sources continued to be sufficiently strong to force him or her to go one despite dissatisfaction with the worker and/or the initial encounter. In addition, Erving Goffman's concept of "face-work" may help to explain why some prospective clients and their workers agreed to continue despite mutual doubts and dissatisfactions. In his provocative analysis of ritual elements in interpersonal behavior, Goffman (1967: 5–46) argues that a person's activity in any social encounter can be viewed as face-work through which he or she tries to develop, maintain, or improve his or her self-image (that is, "face"):

> Much of the activity occurring during an encounter can be understood as an effort on everyone's part to get through the occasion and all the unanticipated and unintentional events that can cast participants in an undesirable light, without disrupting the relationships of the participants (p. 41).

In Goffman's view, much social interaction is organized along accommodative lines:

> Each of the members guarantees to support a given face for the other members in given situations. To prevent disruption of these relationships, it is therefore necessary for each member to avoid destroying the other's face (1967: 42).

In other words, human beings tend to "save face" in social situations through a variety of strategies designed to neutralize or minimize unpleasant or unacceptable aspects of interpersonal behavior. Thus, in social work practice it may be that the worker and prospective client at times agree to "get engaged" despite their lack of conviction, in order to save face.[6]

When viewed in the light of Goffman's formulation of face-work, the findings of the present study highlight the importance of focusing on the client's expectations as early as the beginning session, by bringing them out, discussing them, and clarifying them. Such an emphasis can help to accomplish several purposes. It enables the worker to heighten his or her sensitivity to the client's feelings and needs, thus conveying his or her understanding and caring (Lieberman, 1968). It provides the opportunity to clarify the solution sought by the client and to define as specifically as possible the purpose of the service (Schmidt, 1969).[7] It helps to establish the optimal level of expectations in any given situation. The practitioner needs to work with the

[6] For a more elaborate presentation of his views on the organization of social experiences, see Goffman (1974).

[7] In her analysis of purpose in casework practice, Schmidt (1969) stresses that clarifying the solution sought by the client is a specific task of the beginning phase of casework.)

client on modifying those expectations "that are either too high or too low. This will be a necessary first step in many situations" (Smale, 1977: 88).

Above all, an explicit focus on expectations early in the beginning phase could enable social workers to provide more effective services to clients from lower socioeconomic backgrounds, who constitute a large proportion of the people coming to the attention of social agencies. Because of their particular perspectives and frame of reference, discrepancies between these clients and their mostly middle-class social workers are inevitable. Therefore, there is an even more urgent need for workers to be attuned to their expectations, their definition of problems or needs, and their proposed solutions. In this study, with many of these clients, the person's predisposition toward premature withdrawal or dissatisfaction with the service could have been predicted on the basis of evidence that the initially crucial tasks had not been dealt with successfully.

In some of these cases, it would be possible to overcome the early predisposition toward withdrawal through greater understanding of and more deliberate attention to the client's special needs, qualities, and views. When this is not done, as we will see in a later chapter on the termination phase, there is a persistent lack of mutuality or complementarity between client and worker that eventually leads to discontinuance and, in Silverman's terms (1969), to "spoiled helping relationships."

Chapter 5

The Middle Phase: Staying Engaged

Most persons enter into the treatment encounter with high or unrealistic expectations. Once client and worker establish some connection with each other and agree to continue, what happens as their interaction proceeds? How do they define the problem? How do they approach problem solving? Are there disparities in their views and expectations and, if so, how do they deal with them? In short, how do they manage to *stay engaged?*

These issues were pursued in the research interviews through a series of questions eliciting the clients' and workers' views on their interaction during the period following their initial session. The questions centered on problem focus and problem-solving activities. The data show that, while clients and workers generally agreed on definition of the problem, they held disparate views concerning formulation of goals and approaches to problem solving. This chapter presents these findings and also discusses how clients and workers attempted to cope with disparities in their views.

PROBLEM FOCUS

As we have seen, clients came to the agency with a specific presenting problem or complaint. What did clients and workers focus on, as they became further involved with each other? The findings reveal that the problem focus was increasingly expanded as they proceeded with their interaction. Twenty of the twenty-five clients in the study sample indicated that they had covered a variety of topics extending beyond the initial definition of the problem. Workers generally concurred with the clients' description of these topics, although they tended to use more sophisticated terminology.

Both clients and workers referred to a wide range of difficulties in areas such as the clients' feelings about themselves, their interaction with others, and their functioning in key life roles. It appears that clients were able to share more of their "life space" as they became more comfortable with the workers and more aware of their own feelings and concerns. At the same time, workers became more comfortable with clients and more forceful in their efforts to probe into the clients' lives.

Although the degree of congruence between clients' and workers' views about problem definition was generally high, there were exceptions in six cases. In one of these, for example, the worker described the husband's drinking as a major problem focus, whereas the client did not mention this at all but talked instead about the marital relationship. In each of these six cases, according to the worker, there was an indication that the client needed to deny the reality of a specific problem in his or her life (e.g., drinking) and therefore disagreed with the worker's problem definition. In addition, these were cases in which the workers indicated that the clients had resisted their efforts at confrontation: This is how one worker talked about Miss Xavier, a young woman who had come to the agency requesting help in planning for her unborn baby:

> Joan was having all kinds of problems with her parents. . . . She was locked into a hostile, mutually destructive relationship with them. I tried to help her with this, but she wouldn't let me. . . . Our relationship was great as long as we focused on the baby; but things got worse as I began to explore her feelings toward her parents. She then started to cancel appointments. It seemed like she wasn't ready to handle this whole area.

Miss Xavier, on the other hand, related in the research interview that she was aware of other problems; however, she stressed that she had not gone to the agency for help with these difficulties, but simply for aid in planning for her baby. She seemed quite clear about what she wanted from the agency in relation to the baby, but not ready to go into other areas of her life at that time. In her case, as with several others, her reaction on one level could have been interpreted as "resistance." But there was also evidence that it represented her careful assessment of what she wanted and was ready for at that point in her development.

Perhaps, in some cases of seeming resistance on the part of the client, the worker needs to accept more readily the client's decision as sound and appropriate, even though it may conflict with his or her own interpretation. In practice, it seems that workers themselves at times show resistance, that is, rejection of the client's views and choices.

PROBLEM-SOLVING ACTIVITIES

Workers and clients agreed that the main problem-solving activity in which they had engaged was talking; however, they disagreed about its value or utility. Workers offered such comments as the following:

> Mr. and Mrs. Gates were finally able to start talking with each other, after years of poor communicating. . . . That's when they began to see not only what their problems were, but also how to solve them.

Joyce [Moore] and I talked a lot . . . about her life, her relationship with men, her feelings about herself and her future. . . . She gradually gained some insight into herself . . . how she was keeping people at a distance.

Perhaps reflecting the emphasis on verbal communication that is characteristic of their education and of most therapeutic modalities, workers evidently perceived talking as an important problem-solving activity and as a fundamental component of client-worker interaction. This bias was seen even more dramatically in several cases in which workers mentioned somewhat reluctantly that they had been heavily involved in such concrete activities as advocacy on behalf of the client or accompanying the client on an apartment hunting trip or to an interview at the welfare department. They described these activities apologetically and expressed uncertainty about their value as well as concern about how to reconcile them with their image of professional social work. The cases in question involved people from a lower socioeconomic background who had tangible needs rather than personal or interpersonal problems. It may be that professionally trained social workers in general do not find involvement in these concrete activities as rewarding or prestigious as clinical activities in such areas as development of insight.

In contrast to the workers, most clients openly wondered what talking had to do with their needs or difficulties. This was true of clients from both the lower and middle socioeconomic groups. Their doubts and questions were reflected in the following representative statements:

Mrs. Spaulding: We talked for a long time. She asked me how I felt . . . well, I told her. But then we agreed that just talking wasn't going to help . . . I needed more than talk. Oh, I needed psychiatric treatment and, well, some kind of medicine.

Mrs. Cain: The social worker never did anything except listen and let me try to come to my own conclusions. This wasn't too helpful because . . . what good is it, if you have a problem and the person you're seeing can't do anything for you other than talk? That's why I stopped going. . . . What can they do really?

Mr. Molina: We had a serious problem with Tom [teenage son] and we told her that we didn't know what to do with it. . . . But she didn't give us any suggestions. . . . We simply talked. . . . We didn't know any more after we had been there.

Clients seemed to distinguish between *talking* and *helping* and thus to question the value of talking. This was typical of clients from the lower *and* middle socioeconomic groups. There was an occasional exception, primarily in cases of clients who were college educated and/or knowledgeable about psychotherapy. For example, a high school teacher who had been in marital counseling jointly with her husband said:

Mrs. Mosca: It was very helpful to talk about our relationship with an objective and perceptive third party. The counselor would give us a leading question and then encourage us to talk . . . to pull out what was bothering us. . . . We would answer and soon we found out a lot about each other. . . . We could see things more clearly. . . . I know what he was doing. . . . He was encouraging us to talk as a way of straightening things out.

In contrast to Mrs. Mosca, most clients doubted the value of talking, even though they may have liked it. Furthermore, it is evident from the responses of workers as well as clients that there was usually little explanation concerning the use of talking or other techniques. In her study of "dropouts" from treatment, Silverman (1970: 634) also noted that workers did not seem to explain the role of talking in the treatment process and that clients made a distinction between talking and helping:

> Although the clients could acknowledge the value of talking, they did not see how talking would solve their current problems. They consulted the workers because the workers had special expertise not otherwise available to them. At the end of the interview they did not understand what this expertise was, and they were unable as clients to question the workers.

A related theme was frequent questioning by clients about the role of listening on the part of the worker. While they were pleased to have the worker listen to them, clients were puzzled as to how this was supposed to help them. Mrs. Fort replied as follows when asked in the research interview what she thought about the service as a whole:

Interviewer: Could you tell me what you think now about the agency's service in general?
Respondent: Well, we went there for marriage counseling and the lady that we had, Mrs. Albert, was a marriage counselor, as far as I was concerned. I can't honestly say that she did a lot of *counseling* other than listening. . . . She did mostly listening, and maybe in her own mind that was the thing to do with us . . . like getting the two of us talking with each other. . . .Well, I wasn't sure at first—but it worked out and I would recommend that anybody who needs marriage counseling go there!
I: You mentioned that she did mostly listening but not counseling. What do you mean by counseling?
R: Well, when I first went I thought she would tell me . . . "You do this" and "He'll do that" or something like this. But it didn't happen. . . . It really shocked me that it didn't happen.
I: It shocked you? . . . What do you think about it, now that you've gone through it?

R: Oh, well, I didn't understand what was happening or what we were doing there. . . . And it made me wonder whether we should even be there. . . . But looking back on it, I think that was a good way. . . . It worked for us. . . . It got us straightened out.

Mrs. Fort and her husband went on to be very satisfied with the service and its outcome. However, for a long time they had serious doubts about its usefulness and at various points early in the contact they considered dropping out. It seems that it would have been helpful if the worker had told them a little about her methods, about the role of talking and listening in the help-ing process.

In social work, as in other helping disciplines, the art of "listening with the third ear" is stressed (Reik, 1948). Furthermore, it is believed that "the paradigm of the therapeutic process is the dynamic flow of the patient talk-ing and the clinician listening" (Barish, 1977: 220). While talking and listen-ing are thus taken for granted by practitioners, they may make little sense to clients. It seems therefore that workers have a responsibility to explain help-ing methods and techniques to clients, particularly those that clash with the client's expectations or conceptions. These explanations are an essential part of the role learning clients must do in order to facilitate their participation in the helping process. Apparently they are necessary not only in the beginning phase but throughout the contact. Role induction, in other words, extends beyond the early sessions.

As the preceding excerpt suggests, another major difference in role ex-pectations between clients and workers concerned advice-giving. Clients from diverse socioeconomic groups indicated that they expected the worker to play a more active role by expressing opinions, giving advice, and offering sugges-tions. While they seemed to accept their ultimate responsibility in resolving their problems, they clearly looked to the social worker, as the expert, to sug-gest options and guidelines. Over half of the clients expressed dissatisfaction with what they perceived as the worker's failure to offer advice and guidance. This is reflected in the following comments:

Mrs. Cain: I asked her [the worker] pointblank about our situation as she saw it. Her answer was that she wasn't there to come to conclusions, she wasn't there to say "yes" or "no"; she was there to help us to come to our own conclusions and then from that point to help us to find solutions to our dilemma. . . . She felt very strongly about giving her own opinion—about *not* giving her own opinion—but, rather, having us think for ourselves. . . . That's good if you can come to your own conclusions, but what do you do if you can't? . . . I would like her to offer an opinion as to how *objectively* she saw everything.

Mrs. Bogdansky: My husband and I did most of the talking. . . . They [social workers] don't say too much. . . . They want *you* to talk. They just try to bring up topics. . . . They don't give you their opinion about the problem.

. . . I wish they would say more. . . . I wish they could be more opinionated . . . and give you advice. . . . I'm an open person. . . . I may not do what you say but I'd like to hear your opinion. . . . I wish they would give me more advice about my daughter . . . how to handle her, things like that.

Social workers, in contrast, rarely referred to their giving advice or offering opinions. When questioned directly about this in the research interview, they indicated that they were aware that many clients liked to get advice or suggestions. They explained that they usually refrained from doing so, in order to promote the client's decision making and avoid increasing his or her dependency. As Ewalt and Kutz (1976: 3) point out, it appears that "advice-giving as a therapeutic intervention has generally been held in low esteem" in the field. A leading casework theorist in fact has questioned the use of advice:

> Only the beginner or the clumsy worker makes major use of advice. The skillful practitioner finds ways of stirring his clients to thoughtfulness, for the most part simply by making a suggestion, or better still, by merely reinforcing the client's own ideas (Hollis, 1972: 101).

In the same vein, a psychologist has strongly questioned the use of advice, asserting that "the inefficacy of advice is widely recognized by psychotherapists and caseworkers—but it is still frequently given by mental health counselors" (Mosher, 1965: 86).

Reflecting these strong convictions, social workers in the present study, as in others, seemed to be reluctant to give advice. For example, in a study of parent counseling in an outpatient clinic for children, Davis (1975) found that less than 8 percent of all worker statements involved advice or other forms of direct influence. On the other hand, various studies have demonstrated that a substantial number of clients from diverse socioeconomic backgrounds go to an agency expecting to receive advice (Ewalt and Kutz, 1976; Goin, Yamamoto, and Silverman, 1965; Reid and Shapiro, 1969). Furthermore, there is empirical evidence that advice is found to be helpful by clients and that it is positively correlated with client satisfaction (Ewalt and Kutz, 1976; Davis, 1975) and with outcome (Davis, 1975; Reid and Shapiro, 1969).

Some researchers have suggested that advice is expected primarily by clients from the lower socioeconomic groups (Aronson and Overall, 1966; Overall and Aronson, 1963). However, the evidence from this study, as well as from others cited above, shows that this is a simplistic view. Advice seems to be significant for clients from diverse socioeconomic backgrounds. Furthermore, advice-giving is not a simple technique. There is need to clarify the variety of forms it can take; to delineate the "circumstances in which advice may be acceptable, used, and found helpful by clients" (Ewalt and Kutz, 1976: 17); and to redefine its functions in social work practice. Further research can help in clarifying which kinds of advice "may be effective with various types of patients, in various settings, at various points in treatment, and with various types of presenting problems" (Ewalt and Kutz, 1976: 6).[1]

Several clients in the present study explained that, by offering a suggestion or an opinion, the worker encouraged them to think about alternative courses of action.

Mrs. Gates: My trouble was that I was trying to do too much at the same time — with my family, my friends, and my career. She [the worker] advised me to choose one or two goals to concentrate on at any one time. . . . When I did that, things got easier . . . I was able to accomplish more . . . I didn't feel so confused.

Mr. Mosca: He was very skillful in asking questions or making suggestions that made us think. . . . Like, "You seem to be expecting too much of each other." In thinking about this, we could see that we were complicating our lives by feeling that we should meet almost all of each other's emotional needs by ourselves. . . . We began to see that we had other relatives and friends with whom we could get closer and . . . oh, get more satisfaction.

Thus, in some cases, the worker's opinion or suggestion seemed to be a source of cognitive stimulation, "a prod to constructive thought and action" (Reid and Shapiro, 1972: 172). Similarly, in their study of clients at a child guidance clinic, Ewalt and Kutz (1976: 15) found that advice in the form of a leading question or a professional opinion was helpful in stimulating parents to consider more constructive ways of dealing with their children's problems.

Other clients interpreted advice-giving as a manifestation of the worker's sensitivity to their feelings or acceptance of them as human beings who were struggling with difficult issues:

Miss Appel: Many times she told me that I should get on the phone and call some of my friends . . . even though I hadn't seen them for a long time. . . . She really knew how I felt, . . . how scared I was that they might not like me any more. . . . She kept suggesting that I risk a little . . . and in this way she encouraged me a lot. Eventually, I called up my friends and I was surprised. . . . They were actually pleased to hear from me!

Miss Moore: For a long time I didn't really know what I should do about the baby. . . . I was torn between keeping him and giving him up for adoption. . . . The social worker told me to talk it over with my parents and my boyfriend. . . . She really knew how I felt . . . that I wanted to talk about it with my family and friends, but that it was hard to do. . . . She gave me the courage to go ahead and face them.

Conversely, when their workers did not give advice, some clients felt that they were not accepted and questioned whether the workers truly cared for them or appreciated their plight.

Mrs. Talcott: He just sat there while I was trying to save my marriage. . . . I didn't know if he really cared.

[1] See Ewalt and Kutz (1976) for an extensive discussion of advice-giving.

Mrs. Cain: She could at least say what she thought. . . . Sometimes I felt like I was just another case as far as she was concerned.

Mrs. Bogdansky: I asked her what she would do if she was in my shoes. . . . She avoided the question. . . . I don't think she realized what I was going through, . . . how desperate I was.

The absence of suggestions or opinions on the part of the worker created considerable resentment and frustration in these clients and was apparently interpreted by them as rejection or lack of interest. As speculated by Lennard and Bernstein (1960: 188), it may be that "therapist passivity and lack of participation is equated with rejection and reacted to with frustration," whereas "verbal output on the part of the therapist is . . . interpreted as a 'gift' from the therapist."

These findings call for reexamination of social work perspectives on problem-solving methods. It appears, first of all, that clients from diverse socioeconomic backgrounds prefer an active worker who uses techniques such as advice-giving. Second, these techniques are quite complex, involving varied forms and meanings for clients in different contexts. Third, such basic features of interpersonal helping as talking and listening appear to be puzzling to most clients, suggesting that their effective use in practice requires continuing explanation by the worker in each case. Finally, the worker needs to be attuned to the special meaning that each technique has for a particular client. The worker's advice, for example, may be interpreted as control by one person and as caring by another. In this context, Robert K. Merton's classic distinction between conscious motivation and objective consequences is most relevant. Merton (1968: 114–136) differentiates between the *manifest* or intended functions of social behavior and the *latent* functions or objective consequences that are neither intended nor recognized by participants in a given social system. Thus, in interpersonal helping, the worker needs to be cognizant of the latent functions of various problem-solving or interventive techniques as they are perceived and mediated by each client in a particular case situation.

DEALING WITH DISPARITIES

Thus, as clients and workers went on with each other in the middle phase of their interaction, there were numerous indications of disparities in their role expectations, orientations to problem solving, and formulation of treatment goals. These disparities were evident in cases of satisfied as well as dissatisfied clients; they constituted a major, recurring theme in the middle phase of the helping process, as the different worlds of client and worker encountered each other and sometimes clashed with even greater intensity.

While the disparities were most prominent in cases of persons from the lower socioeconomic group, they also became apparent with clients from a middle-class background, as I probed more intensely into their views. The discrepancies between clients and practitioners should not be surprising, in view of their different frames of reference and perhaps even different belief systems concerning the causes and solutions of personal or interpersonal problems (Edgerton, 1967; Mayer and Timms, 1970; Wiseman, 1970).

Despite the many disparities and the unrealistic expectations with which clients generally entered treatment, it is noteworthy that most of them not only continued but also felt, as we shall see later, that they had been helped and that they were satisfied with the service. Although they found that counseling does not provide miracles, in a substantial proportion of cases these clients reported that they had gotten some benefit from treatment. We should therefore consider various important issues: How do clients and workers deal with disparities in their perceptions and expectations? How do they, in most cases, manage to overcome the potentially negative impact of these differences? What happens in cases in which the differences are not overcome and the client-worker system disintegrates?

Goffman's concept of face-work (1967) provides one possible explanation. In at least some cases, there is evidence that clients and workers went on with each other in order to *save face*. Several of the dissatisfied clients, for example, noted that they did not want to displease the worker and therefore did not initiate discussion of termination, even as they became convinced that they were not getting the help they wanted. Beyond the notion of face-work, several prominent variables emerged as clients and practitioners offered their views on their interaction in the middle phase of the helping process. These were the client-worker relationship; the interactional environment; and the contracting process.

The *client-worker relationship*, which came up over and over in the responses of both clients and workers, seems to be a critical variable that served to counteract or overshadow the possible negative impact of other factors, such as differences in expectations or orientations toward problem solving. As we will discuss in further detail in Chapter 8, disparities between clients and workers were minimized as their relationship grew.

A second significant variable is the *interactional environment* of client and social worker, that is, the context and patterns of interaction that characterize their functioning as a social system (Lennard and Bernstein, 1969: 18–25). This concept helps to explain why clients derived benefit from the service despite ongoing disparities between them and their workers. As suggested by research on patterns of human interaction, both *context* and *content* of the therapeutic enterprise convey meaning to the participants. Contextual properties such as *continuity* in the relationship and the worker's *total attention* to the client's needs and feelings were instrumental in reducing the impact of cognitive differences or disparities in expectations between them. These and other properties that characterize patterns of human interaction between client and worker may have been more significant for outcome and satisfaction than the verbal content of their communication, such as their different definitions of the problem or goals of intervention.

Third, there is considerable evidence that the *contracting process* plays a noticeable role in workers' and clients' efforts to cope with their initial and ongoing disparities. These findings will be discussed in some detail at this point, since they serve to refine the concept of the contract as a tool in interpersonal helping.

In social work, the contract has been defined as the "explicit agreement between the worker and the client concerning the target problems, the goals and strategies of social work intervention, and the roles and tasks of the participants" (Maluccio and Marlow, 1974: 30). The concept of the contract is much talked about in the field (Estes and Henry, 1976; Maluccio and Marlow, 1974; Schwartz, 1961; Seabury, 1976); but there is a question as to how frequently or systematically it is employed in practice.

With the exception of one or two of the eleven workers in the sample, there was no evidence of deliberate and explicit use of the contract. From what the respondents indicated, it was apparent that early in the process — usually in the initial session — most workers engaged with the client in efforts to arrive at a "working agreement" concerning goals and methods. In some cases, the agreement appeared to have been reached prematurely: the client did not really comprehend what he or she was agreeing to or politely complied with the worker's suggestion. In another study that focused on contract negotiation in early interviews, it was also found that most explicit contract activity occurred in the first session (Rhodes, 1975: 108-133).

Beyond the initial phase, it was evident that little conscious attention was devoted to the contract or that contract negotiation between client and worker evolved in a casual or fragmentary fashion. This is illustrated by the following excerpts from research interviews with workers:

> In the first session I usually go over why they're here now, what they hope to achieve, what they expect from me, what will be happening in counseling, etc. After that, I don't usually stop to consider things but try to respond to what the clients bring and what they need.

> I rarely discuss goals or my role with the clients in advance or in a formal way. Generally, I tend to handle these questions as they come up.

> How did the client view the objectives of our work together? I don't really know. . . . You *keep asking me* this question and it makes me think about my approach. The client usually comes in here with certain hopes and expectations. Some, like Miss Kraft, almost feel that the problems will magically disappear. She and I initially discussed what she was looking for, what her goals were. With this client, as with others, we agreed early on what we should be working toward. But, once we got going, many other things came up and we went into different directions. . . . I usually don't stop in the middle of things and ask, "What do you

think is happening?" or, "What do you think we should be doing?" Maybe I should. Most of the time I go on assuming that the client is right beside me.

Although workers and clients reported that they were not consciously and systematically involved in contract negotiation and renegotiation, their recollections suggested that much of their activity and energy goes into this area. In listening to their respective views on the helping process, I was struck by the frequency with which they were involved in efforts to define their tasks and roles, to deal with their divergent expectations, and to explain or clarify their ideas in such areas as problem definition, desired goals, and treatment methods. These efforts consumed a great deal of energy on the part of clients and workers, not only in initial sessions but throughout the middle phase of their interaction. As suggested earlier, this should not be surprising, in view of their different orientations to problem solving in general, their different roles and frames of reference, and their divergent perceptions of their life situations.

In about two-thirds of the cases, there was evidence of ongoing negotiation and renegotiation between clients and workers that facilitated their interaction. For instance, the positive and influential role of the contract in the helping process is exemplified by the comparative views of client and worker in the following case:[2]

CASE OF MR. AND MRS. PORTER

Mrs. Porter: The social worker explained from the beginning what would happen . . . that it would get rough . . . but that this was necessary in order to work things out between me and my husband. She was right! It did happen, it got worse later on . . . so much so that both of us felt: "Why bother?" . . .

But we continued. . . . She had prepared us well, since in the first few sessions we discussed together why we were there, what she could do for us. . . . When it looked like we were unsure about going on, she reminded us of our earlier agree-

Worker: In the early sessions, the Porters and I reached an agreement as to what we would try to accomplish, why we would be meeting, and for how long. I asked them to stay in counseling long enough to find out what it was like and whether it could be beneficial to them.

Very early I had sensed, particularly with him, that he might drop out even though he wanted to be here and work on their problems. I asked for a minimum commitment to counseling from each of them. . . . And when the going got rough and they were thinking about stop-

---

[2] In this, as in subsequent chapters, comparative comments of clients and workers in response to similar questions will occasionally be offered, so as to convey the flavor of the respondents' views. However, precise comparison may be misleading, since some of the comparative comments may be out of time sequence or context.

ment . . . and we went on even though it was hard.

ping, I reminded them of our agreement . . . and why they were here . . . why they should not be panicky. . . . It worked. . . . They responded positively.

In this example, the clients and workers negotiated a contract early in their encounter and then used it to guide their activities at difficult points. In other cases, it seemed that a "treatment" crisis arose, necessitating reexamination and renegotiation of the contract. In the case of Miss Appel, both the client and the worker indicated in the research interviews that after a while they were not getting anywhere and had reached such an impasse that the client was considering withdrawing. Instead, she called the worker's supervisor to ask for a transfer to someone else. The supervisor urged her to take this up with the worker. Miss Appel eventually did so and both she and the worker were then able to bring out their mutual frustrations and dissatisfactions. This led to clarification of the client's expectations from treatment, recognition of the worker's concern and caring for her, and negotiation of an explicit contract for the first time in their engagement. As related by the worker during the research interview, negotiation of the contract proved to be a turning point in client-worker interaction:

> At first I was pretty angry that she had called my supervisor. . . . But then, well, we talked about what it all meant, what she wanted to accomplish, what she expected from me, what I could and could not do for her. From that point on, things improved between us. We got down to work. We hit the real issues and I was extremely pleased. . . . She began to respond much more positively.

In other cases, incongruent perceptions or expectations and other issues around contracting also emerged over and over. However, they were not handled as openly and directly as in the preceding illustrations. Instead, in these instances there was evidence of inability or reluctance on the part of client and/or worker to share their questions or differences openly with each other, resulting in considerable mutual frustration. Similarly, in the ten cases in which clients could not be reached or declined to be interviewed, most workers also pointed to various contracting problems, particularly their failure to arrive at a "working agreement" with the clients.

Thus, there was a substantial number of cases (approximately one-third) in which the contracting process was not adequately handled. While some of these clients and workers decided to continue with their interaction, they did so with little or no agreement regarding target problems, goals, or strategies. As various manifestations of strain between them emerged, clients and workers were not able to cope with them successfully. Differences between clients and practitioners were not reconciled. Consequently, there was insufficient complementarity between them, and eventually the majority of these cases resulted in the client's "premature" withdrawal. Without sufficient complementarity or equilibrium, the client-worker system disintegrated (Lennard and Bernstein, 1960: 153). In some cases, it was clear that termination was not premature but long overdue and could have taken place in a more constructive fashion if it had been possible for client and worker to be more open and direct in confronting their divergent views. In other cases, the client's dissatisfaction and withdrawal could be traced to the worker's failure to deal explicitly with the client's unrealistic or inappropriate expectations.

As I explored further what had happened in these unsuccessful client-worker transactions, two typical patterns emerged. In one, client and worker were aware of their differences in respect to choice of target problems or treatment objectives and methods but did not explicity discuss them. There was little consideration of the purpose or focus of client-worker interaction. As Schmidt (1969) concluded in an earlier study of casework practice, the absence of discussion about purpose led to misperceptions between clients and workers. Mr. Grover, for example, felt that his main problem was limited finances, while the worker thought that it was his personality, and therefore she directed treatment efforts toward changing him.

In the second pattern, the client and worker discussed their different views of the problem but did not confront the issue of whether they should continue or not. They simply went on with their contact despite obvious mutual frustration and dissatisfaction. As one worker observed:

> Mrs. Talcott desperately wanted me to save her marriage. . . . We discussed how I couldn't do this, especially since her husband didn't want to get involved. . . . But she simply couldn't consider any other alternatives. . . . We went on for a while, even though it was clear that both of us were frustrated with each other and could see that we weren't getting anywhere. . . . I guess it was easier to go on rather than face the issue of our different views of the problem and how to approach it.

The findings in cases of satisfied as well as dissatisfied clients point to the need for more systematic attention to the concept of the contract in social work practice. The contract emerges as a much more complex concept than is reflected in social work literature; it is not only an *event* or a *product* but also a dynamic, ongoing *process* that influences the quality and outcome of the client-worker engagement in ways that need to be explored and understood more precisely. As the concept of the contract is refined through further analysis and application in different practice contexts, its effectiveness in interpersonal helping can be increased:

> The therapeutic contract is a central dynamic in the therapeutic process which, when used purposefully, furthers individual and group conflict resolution and contributes to increased client participation in both the means and ends of professional social work intervention (Estes and Henry, 1976: 621–622).

Through involvement in the contracting process, many clients and workers in fact were able to reduce discrepancies between them, achieve greater mutuality and role complementarity, and thus accomplish more through their interaction. Where there was limited or inadequate use of contracting, clients and workers were not able to overcome disparities between them, and their social system broke down.

Finally, to exploit the advantages of the contract, workers need to use it much more explicitly and systematically than they seemed to do in this study. Even in cases that were eventually successful, it appeared that clients and workers wasted a certain amount of time and energy in their efforts to understand each other and to clarify their expectations and goals. At times, they struggled at great length in order to decipher the meaning in their verbal communication. Time and energy could have been saved through more deliberate use of a tool such as the contract. In this connection, it is noteworthy that, in the research interviews, workers frequently brought out the need to engage in more explicit contract formulation in many of their cases. A representative comment by one worker follows:

> In this case I should have clarified the focus earlier. In general, I tend to go with the flow of things and sometimes, as with this couple, that's not good. We were all confused or working in different directions for too long. I can see now how important it is to be as specific and concrete as possible as we try to define the client's goals and ways to achieve them.

Chapter 6

The Ending: Becoming Disengaged

Much has been written about the importance of the termination phase in social work with individuals, families, and groups. Theorists from the "functional" school of thought have emphasized that the ending is a psychological experience that can be used to promote growth in the client (Smalley, 1967). In group work, Schwartz (1971: 3-24) has highlighted the final period of "transitions and endings" and the resulting problems of leaving and separation faced by group members. Many practitioners have written about the intense feelings triggered by the inevitable separation and the varied coping behaviors shown by clients and workers in response to their anxiety (Bolman, Fox, and Nelson, 1969; Moss and Moss, 1967; Levinson, 1977).

Despite the significance widely ascribed to it, there has been limited research on termination, except for numerous continuance-discontinuance studies, most of which were carried out more than a decade ago.[1] In a recent review of the literature, Pearlman (1976) concluded that more follow-up studies are needed to assist practitioners in understanding the complexity and richness of the termination process. In particular, there should be more research on the nature of the client-worker relationship during termination and on the worker's own reactions:

> Although much attention is given to the necessity for, and the methods of, structuring the opening phase of treatment, relatively little is devoted either to the process of the ending period or to the problems arising at this time. More surprising, minimal consideration is given in the literature to the nature of the patient-therapist relationship during termination; to the therapist's emotional reaction in ending treatment; and to the therapist's experience of loss in separating from the patient with whom he had a prolonged and intimate experience (Levinson, 1977: 480).

Therefore, some pertinent questions in the present study include: What happens as clients and workers move toward ending their engagement? Why do they terminate it? How do they become disengaged from each other? How do they feel about ending? How do they cope with their reactions? These and related questions were pursued through exploration of clients' and workers' views regarding the reasons, process, and significance of their termination.

[1] For excellent reviews of many of these studies, see Levinger (1960) and Briar (1966).

TYPE OF TERMINATION

Data were analyzed by dividing cases in the study sample into two groups:

1. *Planned termination.* Cases in which clients and workers had discussed ending their engagement and reached a mutual agreement to terminate.

2. *Unplanned termination.* Cases in which clients and workers either did not discuss ending their engagement or clients withdrew prior to an agreed-upon point.

TABLE 6–1. Type of Termination, by Socioeconomic Group (in percent)

| | INTERVIEWED CLIENTS (N = 25 cases) | | NONINTERVIEWED CLIENTS (N = 10 cases) | |
	Lower Socio- economic Group	Middle Socio- economic Group	Lower Socio- economic Group	Middle Socio- economic Group
Planned	28	36	10	10
Unplanned	20	16	80	0

As shown in Table 6-1, of the twenty-five cases in which at least one client participated in a research interview, two-thirds were in the "planned termination" group and one-third in the "unplanned termination" group. There was no significant difference between the interviewed clients from the lower socioeconomic group and those from the middle socioeconomic group in relation to type of termination. On the other hand, nearly all of the clients who could not be reached or declined to be interviewed were from the lower socioeconomic background *and* in the unplanned termination group. Clients from a lower socioeconomic status evidently were more likely to drop out. This is consistent with the findings of a number of previous studies (Beck, 1962; Rosenberg and Raynes, 1976).[2] Social workers should give much more attention to ways of adapting services to the needs and qualities of clients from lower socioeconomic backgrounds, since many of them apparently do not view social work intervention as relevant to their needs.

PLANNED TERMINATION

In most cases in the "planned termination" group, clients indicated that they were the ones who took the initiative to end, whereas workers indicated

[2] In an extensive review of research on attrition in mental health settings, Rosenberg and Raynes (1976) concluded that the typical "dropout" is from a lower socioeconomic background.

that the decision to terminate was arrived at mutually. This compares with Beck and Jones' finding in their national survey of family service agencies that 76 percent of the clients indicated that termination was the client's decision, whereas 56 percent of the workers saw the decision as mutual (Beck and Jones, 1973: 83). Perhaps workers feel the need to stress the theme of mutuality in the decision-making process around termination, in view of the philosophical commitment to client participation that is characteristic of social work practice.

In the sixteen cases in the planned termination group, there was nearly unanimous agreement between clients and workers concerning the reasons for ending. The prevalent reason, given in fourteen cases, was the client's readiness to terminate. In the other two cases, the reason was that the client needed a referral elsewhere. As clients and workers expanded on these reasons in further discussion of the termination process, both used phrases dealing with three interrelated themes: (1) goal achievement; (2) readiness to function independently; and (3) limited productivity of further sessions:

GOAL ACHIEVEMENT

We accomplished what we came here for.

We could cope with our problems much better.

Their marital relationship had improved considerably.

My husband and I were finally getting along pretty well.

READINESS TO FUNCTION INDEPENDENTLY

I reached the state where I needed to try things out on my own.

She was ready to go out there by herself.

He was doing well on his own.

LIMITED PRODUCTIVITY OF FURTHER SESSIONS

Our final sessions were not too productive.

It got so that it was nice going there — but we weren't really discussing anything serious.

There was nothing more that the counselor could do.

Especially revealing are the comments of client and worker in the following two cases, in response to questions about how they happened to terminate treatment and how they felt about it:

CASE OF MISS APPEL

Client: We ended because it seemed like I had gone as far as I really

Worker: We terminated gradually. We talked about it for a long, long,

needed to go with her. . . . I started feeling strong . . . like I had grown a lot. . . . And I got involved in other things . . . . volunteer work with young children . . . a job that I liked . . . and an awareness group. . . .

I began talking about ending. It was funny, in the beginning. . . . I remember her saying, "We should talk about terminating," and my first reaction was "*No! No! No!*" I felt like she was kind of leaving me, you know? So I grabbed on and said, "No, no. Not yet, not yet," and then in the end, it was me who did it. . . . I just said, "What do you think about ending it soon?" and I felt like she was almost holding on. . . . That was flattering in a way . . . to feel that I was someone with whom she wanted to go on.

long time. . . . Then we started seeing each other perhaps once a month for a few months, again constantly talking about what it was going to be like to terminate, to separate . . . the whole thing.

We left it at a point that we both felt good about where Joan was. . . . Things had changed for her, she had tried herself out in some new ways and they were working for her. By that time, she was feeling much better about herself. . . . My guess is that she had a lot of ambivalence about the termination—but, then, anybody does . . . . She was definitely ready to try things out by herself, to go at it alone. . . . I didn't like to see her leave. . . I had grown fond of her . . . but I knew it was time.

CASE OF MRS. DONNELLY

Client: We both agreed. Um, we decided as soon as I felt I could make my own decisions, that I could handle everything myself without getting too emotionally upset . . . um, you know, that I could leave. And that was funny. After all that time, . . . I really felt bad in leaving. I was glad and then I felt bad at the same time. You know, I was going to miss her in my life because I had grown fond of her but then . . . I had to leave some time—I couldn't go there forever. . . . She gave me the confidence that I could do it. . . .

I told her I felt bad leaving because I had grown to like her—you see, then we were getting closer after the early sessions, after we broke that

Worker: [We ended because] she was ready, and I'll tell you why I felt that. She was ready, I thought, quite a while before she actually terminated. She was willing to take a few risks in relationships and other situations to see how she functions. She knew that you can talk, talk, talk for twenty-nine sessions but if you're not really going to plunge in and see how you function . . . You can talk about how you'd handle future relationships but unless you're willing to engage yourself in a present relationship, you're not going to see. And that's the point that I feel we reached.

We gradually began declining sessions back last fall. She was am-spell. . . . I felt much closer, much better.

She also felt that it was time for me to leave and she felt that somebody else might need her much more . . . that I was doing well . . . that it was time for me to make the decision to go.

bivalent about becoming too dependent on me. There was a part of her that really wanted to be dependent and there was the other part . . . that competitive, striving, achieving part; dependence was very scary to her, you know.

She was a lady that canceled quite a few appointments but not from disinterest or whatever. What I figured out and what I checked out with her later was some of the times that she canceled, that was sort of her signal that, "Hey, I'm all right this week, I'm doing pretty good, I don't need you," you know? So, finally when I realized that that was in the wind, we moved to an every other week and then I think we went a couple of times once a month. She was reluctant to let go but she wanted to try some of these things on her own and I think we reached the point where allowing her to come in every week and talk about it was encouraging her to postpone. She was getting out there and seeing what she could do.

As these excerpts illustrate, in most of the cases in the planned termination group the client and worker reviewed their work together, concurred in their decision to terminate, actively discussed their ending, and made plans to do so in a gradual way. Frequently, as in Mrs. Donnelly's case, it was evident that client and worker had been thinking about termination and even hinting at it long before they explicitly considered it. In these instances, both client and worker were ambivalent about ending, as seen in the pattern of canceling appointments or arranging less frequent sessions. Eventually, as Mrs. Donnelly's worker put it, the practitioner would realize what "was in the wind," namely, that the client was communicating her readiness to terminate.

In several of these cases, it was impressive to see how thoughtfully and deliberately the workers had used the termination experience for therapeutic purposes. In so doing, they demonstrated a variety of significant practice principles, including being attuned to evidence of the client's growing ability to cope more effectively in key areas of his or her functioning; being sensitive to the client's sometimes subtly or tentatively conveying his or her readiness to end even before cancellation of appointments makes it obvious; reviewing changes in the client's functioning and overall situation not only to decide about termination but also to help in reinforcing the client's gains and coping capacity; and implementing the termination not merely as an event but as a gradual process—a process of disengagement tailored to the unique needs and qualities of each client.

UNPLANNED TERMINATION

Respondents in the "unplanned termination" group expressed different views from those who had ended by plan (Table 6-2).

TABLE 6-2. Reasons for Termination Given by Client and Worker in "Unplanned Termination" Cases

Case No	Client	Worker
1.	Not getting anywhere.	She never called back.
2.	Nothing happening. We had been going on ad infinitum.	We had gone as far as we could.
3.	I felt we weren't doing anything. I canceled our last appointment and never called back.	She just stopped coming.
4.	Obvious that she couldn't help me with my problems.	He pulled out when the pressure was off.
5.	He wasn't doing me any good.	We weren't getting anywhere.
6.	She wasn't helping us.	We weren't making any progress.
7.	Our marriage was better. There was no reason to keep going.	They couldn't tolerate any more probing.
8.	My daughter had improved a lot.	I'm not sure why they dropped out.
9.	I would have kept going but the counselor didn't give me another appointment.	She didn't seem to want to continue in treatment.

In the first six cases, the client's stated reason reflects dissatisfaction with the help received and frustration over lack of progress. The worker seems to be similarly dissatisfied and frustrated and, in three of the cases, he or she stressed the client's *failure* to continue. In cases number 7 and 8, the clients indicate that they dropped out because they received the help they wanted, while the worker either is not sure about the reasons or points to the client's resistance. In case number 9, there is the suggestion that the client responded by withdrawal to what she perceived as the worker's insufficient encouragement to continue, while the worker pointed to the client's ambivalence about treatment.

More detailed comments of clients and workers in several cases from the unplanned termination group shed light on the process that leads to their becoming disengaged:

CASE OF MRS. FOLEY

Client: The kids started to act different . . . there wasn't as much fighting and arguing . . . there was no more reason to go. . . . And so we just stopped going there.

Worker: There were many cancellations and then she stopped altogether. I had been pushing her to get into family issues and she was saying in a way: "That's all I can take."

CASE OF MRS. BOGDANSKY

Client: I kept thinking, *Why go back? I have better things to do with my money . . . and my time.* I stopped going when I could see there was no use in talking anymore.

Worker: There was no real termination . . . no discussion about it. . . . After a while, she just phased out. . . . I was pretty busy at the time. . . . I guess I just let her slide out the door.

CASE OF MR. AND MRS. GROVER

Mr. Grover: I felt I wasn't getting anywhere. . . . I was concerned about my financial problems and the counselor kept talking about my personality. . . . I don't know how it stands now . . . whether I'm supposed to go back or what. . . . I think we left it that she would call me about another appointment, but she never did.

Worker: We terminated when I went on vacation. . . . He had been recognizing what his problems were, but wasn't sure he wanted to change . . . so we left it that after my return from vacation he would call me to set up our next appointment . . . but he never did.

While it is not possible to generalize from such a small number of cases, these findings suggest a number of themes that are consistent with the conclusions of earlier studies and clinical reports on attrition in social work. In a few cases, the client evidently got what he or she was looking for and therefore terminated. In others, the client was dissatisfied with the lack of progress or the service as a whole. In some cases, the client forcefully took the initiative and withdrew. In others, he or she apparently sensed the worker's growing frustration and/or diminished interest, which reinforced his or her own ambivalence and led to withdrawal. Similarly, in a study at a child guidance clinic, it was found that the most common reasons for client withdrawal from treatment were: (1) the parents' expectations of therapy were not fulfilled; (2) the parents were generally dissatisfied with the service; and (3) there was no improvement in the children (Farley, Peterson, and Spanos, 1975).

In all of the cases in the unplanned termination group, there was evidence of lack of openness between client and worker and lack of clarity or agreement in respect to their roles, goals, and expectations. As noted in an earlier chapter, these were cases in which problems in client-worker interaction were evident as early as the initial session. The views of these clients and workers about the initial sessions showed that, in contrast to cases in the planned termination group, these clients and workers had a vague sense of what would be happening in treatment, were unable to establish an emotional connection between them, did not actively engage in contract negotiation, and ended the first session with vagueness and uncertainty about future plans. Furthermore, in most of these cases there was a lack of congruence in client and worker expectations. This lack is associated with discontinuance from the service, as shown by various investigators (Heine and Trosman, 1960; Lazare, Eisenthal, and Wasserman, 1975; Overall and Aronson, 1963). On the basis of those findings, it could have been predicted early that the client would be dropping out, even though he or she may have agreed to continue. Thus, there are various predictors or "early warning signals" that should have alerted the worker to the need in these cases to be more active in confronting the client's ambivalence and/or clarifying the focus of the service.

It appears that workers and clients go on in these cases with little conviction about the usefulness of the contacts and with much uncertainty about their roles. These are also cases in which workers apparently have much difficulty in dealing with termination and in using it as a growth-producing experience. In considering these cases during the research interviews, workers critically examined their functioning. In particular, they questioned their failure to terminate earlier despite various clues given by the client about not wanting to continue or despite their awareness that the service was inappropriate or unproductive.

As one worker observed:

> This couple just stopped coming. I called them several times and they would agree to come in but never actually followed through. . . . Thinking about the case at this point, I probably should have terminated soon after the initial session, when it became clear that they weren't motivated to look at the problems in their relationship and instead kept focusing on their daughter's problems. Maybe I should have faced them with these things and referred them to a child guidance clinic.

Workers expressed similar frustrations in eight of the ten cases in which the client was not available for the research interview. According to the worker, in each of these cases the client and/or the worker felt that they were not getting anywhere. There was no formal ending; the client simply dropped out. Several of these cases involved persons who were pressured to seek counseling by someone such as a spouse or a representative of an institution like the public school. As the workers reviewed these cases during the research interviews, it seemed that these prospective clients viewed the problem as being located not in themselves but in some other person or institution. Apparently, they required a different approach from "voluntary clients" who were more likely to perceive the problem as their own inability to cope.

SIGNIFICANCE OF TERMINATION

It has been noted frequently in the social work literature that the task of termination can be difficult and at times painful for workers as well as clients (Levinson, 1977). But it is assumed that the "pleasures of completing a task, resolving a problem, and fulfilling a helping contract are counterbalanced by the pains of separation and loss that accompany many termination experiences, for client and social worker (Siporin, 1975:337). The data in this study show that termination is an intense phase provoking a variety of reactions in clients and workers. Becoming disengaged is in some ways more complicated than becoming engaged.

Clients expressed their feelings openly and directly, using phrases such as the following:

It was a traumatic experience.

I felt like losing a lifelong friend.

I felt bad even though I didn't need to go on any longer.

It took me a while before I could accept the idea of not seeing her anymore.

It was like losing an arm you no longer needed.

I was unhappy about it for a long time.

I wanted to be on my own, but didn't want to lose her.

I felt bad because I had become so fond of her.

Several excerpts from research interviews with clients follow:

Miss Appel: I didn't want to stop going because it was like a security blanket. I knew in my mind that I was okay . . . but her support was gone all of a sudden. It was kind of scary. . . . Well, nothing could be done about it. . . . If I kept going indefinitely, she wouldn't be doing her job.

Mrs. Stewart: It was very hard when he let me go . . . like losing a good friend . . . someone who had brought me a long way and then let me walk the rest of the way by myself. . . . He had warned me . . . had told me in advance that we would have so many meetings and then stop, but . . . well, it still hit me like a ton of bricks.

Miss Moore: I was unhappy about stopping. . . . I would have liked to be able to continue seeing her . . . oh, to have a personal relationship outside the office . . . but after a while I got over it.

These and other similar comments from clients reflect themes such as dependence on the worker, investment in the relationship, ambivalence about ending, and loss of support. It should be noted that all of these comments came from clients in the planned termination group. Clients in the unplanned termination group, because of their lesser investment in—or dissatisfaction with—the worker, were more likely to deny having any feelings about termination.

How about the workers? What did termination mean to them? How did they feel about ending the engagement with their clients, in whom they often had invested a great deal of themselves? It would be expected that workers also experience feelings and reactions as they go through the process of ending with clients. Writing in a social work journal, a clinician recently asserted:

> Simply and essentially viewed within an interpersonal model of psychotherapy, it is not surprising to find that at termination the therapist also has feelings of anxiety, anger, and depression as well as relief, satisfaction, and joy and longing for other experiences and new beginnings (Levinson, 1977: 489).

Contrary to what might have been predicted, workers in this study, with occasional exceptions, did not express their own feelings directly, although they were typically open and articulate about their clients' reactions to termination. However, in most of the cases the workers' feelings emerged indirectly in a variety of ways: through frequent references to their disappointment in not having helped the client further; dissatisfaction with the degree of change that had taken place in the client or his or her situation; concern over the client's continuing problems; and doubts about his or her capacity to cope with future life crises.

Typical comments of workers were:

I wonder how she'll be able to manage by herself.

There was a lot of unfinished business.

We didn't even touch the underlying issues.

I didn't give them enough help in relation to their sexual difficulties, which is what had brought them here in the first place.

The big question is what he will do when he is confronted with the next crisis.

I felt shaky about their readiness to terminate but went along with their decision.

She will always have problems.

For some workers, these comments seemed to represent a less intense or less painful way of coping with their real and human responses to termination. In other words, it may have been easier for them to bring out their concerns about the effectiveness of treatment or about the client's capacity to cope rather than to face their own feelings about separation. Practitioners at times may find it necessary to cope with termination through distancing, that is, by trying to "keep themselves from being affected by the emotional reactions of either the patient or themselves" (Levinson, 1977: 480).

Further details of workers' reactions to the ending are seen in the following excerpts:

CASE OF MR. AND MRS. LODANO

I felt comfortable with their decision to terminate. . . . I didn't have any qualms other than the usual ones. . . . [Jokingly] I thought, *How could they possibly make it without me?* I do remember having some doubt about whether I had given them enough help, especially with their sexual relationship. . . . They were saying that it was okay . . . but it still left me with a question, not so much about whether they could make it on their own but, more, *Have I given them enough? Did I really help them?*

CASE OF MRS. TALCOTT

I hope she comes back here or goes somewhere else to get some counseling. . . . I wish I could have helped her more. . . . I feel badly that I didn't. . . . Somehow what I did wasn't enough. . . . At the end she said she was doing better but I'm not so sure.

CASE OF MR. AND MRS. GATES

I felt rather shaky about the termination. . . . They had come a long way but there were still many issues to get into, many treatment issues we didn't touch. However, at the time they couldn't have gone any further. . . . I felt that it was time to terminate but was uncertain about how things would work out, particularly for Mr. Gates.

It is noteworthy that the preceding excerpts were drawn from cases in the planned termination group, in which clients and workers had agreed that it was time to end. While clients were in general satisfied with this decision, doubts were expressed by workers even in cases in which they indicated that treatment objectives had been achieved. Moreover, it is interesting that, while clients in general entered into treatment with high expectations,[3] they

---

[3] For further details on the initial expectations of clients, see Chapter 4, "The Beginning Phase: Getting Engaged."

left it with more realistic views of what could be accomplished. In contrast, as workers became more involved with their clients, their expectations appear to have been heightened. The discrepancies between clients and practitioners in this regard may reflect such factors as the worker's broader view of the problems versus the client's need to deny, the worker's traditional emphasis on pathology and cure, differences in the client's and the worker's orientations toward problem-solving, and the worker's gratification from client dependence.

The study's findings suggest that workers are influenced by their own rather high expectations of themselves as well as of their clients. Practitioners may be motivated "to produce a perfect case" (Levinson, 1977: 484). As another writer has observed, it may be that, "in spite of his special training, the worker is subject to three narcissistic snares—the aspiration to heal all, to know all, and to love all" (Reid, 1977: 601). One wonders what messages the client gets through this emphasis on perfection or cure. The worker's doubts may be conveyed to the client in such a way that they interfere with a major therapeutic task of termination—that is, helping the person to consolidate and internalize treatment gains.

In view of these complexities, considerable effort is required on the part of workers to make the termination phase as growth producing an experience as possible for the clients—and perhaps even for themselves. In particular, workers need to accept more readily the idea that the client needs not so much to be "cured" as to get help in mastering various developmental tasks at the individual and/or family level and in preparing himself or herself for more effective coping with future life challenges.

PLANS FOR FOLLOW-UP

In social work practice, a case is generally considered either "open" or "closed." In other words, termination is *final*. Serious questions are usually raised about a worker or a client who may wish to maintain some kind of relationship beyond termination.

In view of the intensity and meaning of the client-worker relationship for both parties, I explored how they felt about the possibility of continuing their contact, or whether they made arrangements for any kind of follow-up contact. In more than half of the cases in the present study, clients and workers left the door open for less formal contact through such means as plans to meet for lunch, to be in touch with each other by telephone or letter, or to have a follow-up session several weeks later. Many clients stated that they liked these opportunities to maintain some contact with the workers. Similarly, most workers indicated that they liked the idea.

While there was a high level of interest in continuing their relationship in some form beyond official termination, in most situations clients and workers had not followed through. As exemplified by the Donnelly case, they were often vague or ambivalent in their planning for future contacts.

INTERVIEW WITH MRS. DONNELLY

Respondent: She always said, "Once you leave, if you ever have any real emotional problems, you always can come back, just call." So it wasn't that you went forever, and I think with that in your mind, the chances of going back are probably one in a million.

Interviewer: How do you mean?

R: Well, because, um, she, in her way, gave you the confidence that you can do it, right? And, then just knowing you can go back, you just try to be self-sufficient, see?

I: Oh! Do you think that if anything came up you might go back to this agency or a similar person?

R: Oh, yeah, I would go back to the same agency . . . if it was still there.

INTERVIEW WITH MRS. DONNELLY'S WORKER

Respondent: I wouldn't be a bit surprised if, after she has dated a few people, depending on how the relationship went, that I would hear from her again. . . .

Interviewer: Why do you think you might hear from her?

R: Because the relationship thing was really the big unresolved issue. She was . . . ready to start dating, but said: 'I don't need anybody." You know that when you hear that, it means that a person really isn't making an effort to meet others.

I: Did you make any arrangements for any kind of follow-up?

R: Well, yeah. . . . Within the context of this being a closed case she had had the follow-up; but she might, at some time in the future, check back with me, depending on how things are going.

As with other clients, Mrs. Donnelly apparently perceived a mixed message in the worker's invitation to call. On the one hand, Mrs. Donnelly heard the worker say that she could call and come back at any time; on the other hand, she also heard the worker's emphasis on calling *if* there was a need or problem. As in other cases, the worker's message implied that returning to the agency would be a negative step, perhaps a sign of deterioration, or at least further difficulties in the client's functioning. As a result, it is no wonder that Mrs. Donnelly was hesitant about the possibility of returning, particularly to this worker.

The worker's response in this case is not unusual. Particularly prior to the recent emphasis on brief treatment and task-oriented casework, there has been a general reluctance in social work practice to encourage clients to come back for further help. As a result of the preoccupation with "cure" that was noted earlier in this chapter, a client's return to the same agency has often been viewed as indicative of the worker's or agency's failure to provide competent service.

There is no question that at present the issue of planning for further contacts or continuing the client-worker relationship beyond termination is highly controversial in the field. For instance, a practitioner recently advocated exchanging photographs between clients and student workers, as a means of helping them to deal with their reactions to termination and to appreciate the continuity in their relationship even after they end (Wikler, 1977). Another social worker, however, quickly condemned this practice, stressing that it infantilizes both the client and the student by playing into their fantasies, encouraging avoidance of the reality of their separation (Rubin, 1977).

In light of the intensity of the client-worker relationship in many cases and its significance for all involved, it may be asked whether practitioners should not consider moving toward a more natural and individualized approach to "ending the engagement" — an approach that recognizes the worker's and client's respective qualities and needs and makes use of the human, positive features of their relationship beyond the point of official termination.

Chapter 7

The Outcome

> I can't think of anything we haven't covered. . . . I think they do a
> marvelous job and I think their prices are right! If you ever get into trou-
> ble with your marriage, I invite you to go to a marriage counselor. . . . If
> they can't help, they can't hurt you!

As reflected in his concluding comment above, Mr. Fort, who had gone
into treatment with many doubts, came out feeling that it had "saved my
marriage." Like most of the clients interviewed in this study, Mr. Fort felt
that he had been helped and attributed much of this to the service itself.
Similarly, in the nationwide study of family service agencies, nearly half of
the clients viewed the service as the major factor in improvement, while
another fifth reported that it was one of several contributing factors (Beck
and Jones, 1973: 93).

These findings should be gratifying to practitioners. However, beyond the
matter of client satisfaction, there is a continuing need to search for elusive
answers to recurring questions related to the effectiveness of interpersonal
helping. What do clients get out of their interaction with the worker? Why
are they satisfied or dissatisfied with the service? In the opinion of clients and
workers, what accounts for the outcome?

Data related to these issues were gathered by exploring the clients' and
workers' evaluation of the outcome, their satisfaction or dissatisfaction, and
their views on sources of influence on the service. There was a special focus
on the responses of clients who were satisfied, in the light of evidence from
prior studies that satisfied clients, unlike those who are dissatisfied, find it
difficult to explicate their feelings and tend to talk in vague or general terms
(Gurin, Veroff, and Feld, 1960: 323; Mayer and Timms, 1970: 94-95).

EVALUATION OF OUTCOME

In eighteen, or over two-thirds, of the cases, clients and workers agreed
that the former had gotten some benefit from the service. In the other seven
cases, clients felt that they had not gotten anything out of it; all but one of
the workers agreed with this evaluation. In these seven cases, there was

evidence of clashes in expectations between clients and workers, inappropriate demands on the part of clients, lack of negotiation of a contract, or inability on the part of clients and/or workers to communicate openly and honestly with each other.

Most clients felt that they had been helped by their interaction with the worker. What was it, more specifically, that they got out of it? What were the areas of improvement in their functioning and life situations? The respondents' comments were categorized by use of the following scheme developed by Beck and Jones (1973: 95-100).

1. Improvement in areas of family relationships — e.g., communication.
2. Improvement in specific problem areas — e.g., child-rearing.
3. Improvement in problem-coping — e.g., understanding of problem.
4. Improvement in individual family members — e.g., self or other.

Most respondents indicated improvement of varying degrees in different areas; however, only the areas in which they noted major improvement were categorized. As seen in Table 7-1, the largest category of improvement was in "individual family member," followed by "family relationships," "specific problems," and "problem-coping." A high level of agreement is seen between spouses and between clients and workers regarding areas of improvement.

TABLE 7-1. Areas of Improvement, as Seen by Clients and Workers (N = 18 cases)*

AREA OF IMPROVEMENT	CLIENTS	WORKERS
Individual family member	14	12
Family relationships	7	6
Specific problems	6	6
Problem-coping	2	2
TOTAL	29†	26†

*In the other seven cases, clients reported no improvement.

†Total number of responses is greater than 18, since some clients and workers thought that there was more than one major area of improvement.

The high congruence in clients' and workers' evaluation of the outcome is noted in the following randomly selected examples of client-worker pairs:

CLIENT	**WORKER**
My husband and I were able to communicate much better with each other.	Better communication with spouse.
We got along better, and this saved our marriage.	More satisfying marital relationship.

Learned to accept myself.

My husband and I realized what we wanted.

I became more confident.

Learned to communicate with my daughter.

More comfortable with himself.

Clearer about their respective needs and wants.

Greater self-confidence.

Better parent-child communication.

In contrast to the present study, Beck and Jones (1973: 95) found that clients tended to report more improvement in each problem area than workers, particularly in respect to changes in family relationships and individual family members. Beck and Jones suggested that a key reason for this discrepancy is that practitioners face "a major information handicap," since they have access only to information reported or observed in weekly interviews. There seems to be some validity to this suggestion, since in this study too it was evident that in many cases information about the client's life situation outside the office was not readily accessible to the worker.

There were no differences in evaluation of the outcome on the basis of referral source (self or other), socioeconomic background of client, duration of contact, or type of termination. Due to the small size of the sample, it was not possible to classify views on the outcome by other variables such as the presenting problem or the worker.

Further details about clients' and workers' views on the outcome of their interaction are provided in comparative excerpts, to highlight recurring themes. First, a case in which client and worker concurred in their positive evaluation of the outcome:

CASE OF MISS APPEL

Client: I began to feel better about myself . . . was able to get on the phone and call friends I hadn't seen in a long time and they were glad to see me. It felt great! I got feeling more comfortable and confident about myself.

Before I left, I told the worker I thought I might want to start volunteering at a counseling agency because I liked relating to people and I thought it would be good to get out myself and just talk with other people about their kind of problems. I have been doing that and it feels real good.

Worker: I think things worked out very well. . . . I'm pleased with the results. I feel good about where Joan is at. I think she feels freer to try herself out and to experience herself differently. . . . She is more aware of getting her own needs met, that she doesn't always have to come second. . . .

When I first met her, she had absolutely no social life . . . her whole world revolved around her room and her dog. . . . Now, she gets out and is involved with people.

She has made some good friends . . . she is working as a volunteer

> with young people. . . . Her whole
> appearance has changed. . . . She
> lost a lot of weight.

As illustrated by this case, clients and workers who evaluated the outcome positively in general pointed to evidence that the client was functioning more effectively in key areas.

Next is a case in which client and worker disagreed in their evaluation of the outcome.

CASE OF MR. AND MRS. BATES

Mr. Bates: Looking at the experience as a whole, I think I was helped. . . . I went from a rotten relationship with my son to one in which we were at least talking. . . . Also, I found out things about myself and it changed me . . . in my attitudes toward life . . . being too strict with my children . . . too concerned about my business.

Mrs. Bates: We eventually dropped out . . . but I feel that we were helped because, well, we started talking again with each other . . . that had been one of our problems. . . . No, there was no other way we were helped.

Worker: I don't feel that there was any change, that they got any help from me. . . . Somehow, we didn't hit it off. I didn't feel I cracked the door or made any impact. . . . To my way of looking, it was a disastrous case. . . . This family came in here with serious problems and I didn't give them any real help.

I think it was just one of those things that happens once in a great while. I think they got the wrong person.

This case is especially interesting, since it was one of those in which the clients dropped out of the service after a few sessions because of dissatisfaction with the worker and with the pace of change in their situation. Mr. Bates not only evaluated the outcome positively but also offered evidence about his functioning and that of his family that supported his assessment. Mrs. Bates, who had gone into treatment with higher expectations than her husband, was particularly dissatisfied with the worker and her lack of competence. However, even she acknowledged that there had been some improvement in relation to the communication problem with their teenage son. The worker, on the other hand, viewed the outcome in totally negative terms. There was similar disagreement between clients and workers in several other cases. A major reason for this discrepancy was that the worker typically had much higher expectations than the client. In addition, the worker did not seem to know enough about the client's functioning outside the clinical setting.

With a few exceptions, such as the one illustrated in the above excerpt, clients and workers concurred in their positive evaluation of the outcome and expressed their views in similar terms. However, there were substantial differences in their assessment of the client's strengths and coping patterns. These differences became evident as respondents were asked about the clients' functioning since beginning at the agency. The questions in this area centered around the following aspects:

1. How the client and other family members were getting along with each other.

2. How the client was getting along with others outside the family.

3. How the client felt about the problem or need and how he or she was handling it.

4. Whether the client had made any decision or taken specific action in connection with the problem.

5. How the client was coping with any new crisis or with life in general.

As usual, both clients and workers were asked these questions. The content and quality of their responses were strikingly different in nearly two-thirds of the cases. In general, clients presented themselves as *proactive,* autonomous human beings who were able to enhance their functioning and their competence through the use of the service and of resources in themselves and their social networks. Workers, on the other hand, tended to view clients as *reactive* organisms with continuing problems, underlying weaknesses, and limited potentialities. These differences are reflected in comparative excerpts from a number of client-worker pairs:

CASE OF MR. AND MRS. MOSCA

Mrs. Mosca: I still have some of the same problems that took me there, but I realized I had more strength than I thought. . . . I'm learning I don't have to be so dependent on my husband. . . . I can do some things on my own. . . . It's making me feel better and the two of us are happier together.

Worker: I was surprised that she felt as good as she did about our work and the changes in her life. . . . She told me she was doing better . . . but I'm not so sure. . . . We didn't touch the underlying issues . . . her low self-image, her rigid defenses, her ambivalence toward men. . . . She was cooperative in the counseling process but extremely dependent and resistive. . . . I worry about her.

CASE OF MISS XAVIER

Client: After I decided to give up the baby, I wasn't as confused as I

Worker: She was like a little girl trying hard to be an adult. . . . But she

had been for over a year. Mrs. Moriarty [the worker] kind of straightened me out. . . . She helped me to see what I wanted to do. . . . And I realized that I had always wanted to get something out of life. . . . Since then, I've been working harder and enjoying my job. . . . I'll be getting a promotion soon.

had been severely traumatized as a child and there was only so much she could do. . . . The out-of-wedlock baby was just one piece of the problem. . . . She has many, many conflicts that we didn't even touch. . . . I don't think she got much out of coming here.

CASE OF MR. AND MRS. GATES

Mr. Gates: I got rid of a lot of guilt over separation from my wife and began to consider my own needs and interests much more. . . . The counselor enabled me to think more clearly. I could see there was a lot I could do to determine my fate. . . . There have been many changes in me. . . . I'm more honest with myself . . . more self-confident . . . more open with others.
Mrs. Gates: The counseling was very helpful. . . . I realized I wasn't doing myself or anyone else any favors the way I had been acting . . . feeling sorry for myself and guilty about the divorce. . . . There has been tremendous change in me in the past six months. . . . My whole outlook has changed. . . . About a year ago, I spent almost a month in this house . . . not wanting to see anyone, . . . feeling so depressed . . . yelling at the children. . . . I'm finding it doesn't have to be that way. . . . I can handle the children. . . . I'm able to cope with my job even though the pressures have increased. . . . We had a big crisis not too long ago when someone fouled up our records and the boss asked me to straighten things out. . . . I did it and it felt good to be in charge. . . .

Worker: This case worked out much better than I had expected. Mr. and Mrs. Gates eventually became good friends, once they were reconciled to the idea of their separation. . . . Nevertheless, both of them have a long way to go. . . .

Mr. Gates has some serious characterological problems. . . . Didn't make any radical changes. . . . He learned to understand himself better. . . . Developed some new friendships. . . . Was able to stand up to his father a little more. . . . On the whole, I feel he'll continue to view life as he has been. . . . He'll still be very fearful of taking risks. . . . For example, he'll never make it with an assertive woman.

As for Mrs. Gates, I think she got what she was looking for . . . some insight into her problems, better understanding of her relationship with her husband, . . . increased self-esteem. She was then able to function much better. . . . She got involved in social activities, she got a job. . . . She felt good as she found out that there were many things she could accomplish independently of her husband. . . . I imagine she is functioning well . . . but she could do much better with further therapy

Even my co-workers have noticed the difference in me.

. . . maybe involvement in a therapeutic women's group. . . . She needs to deal with women's issues . . . how she feels as a woman. . . . Otherwise, she'll suffer the next time she gets involved with a man.

The different perspectives of clients and workers are revealed over and over in these excerpts. Clients were satisfied and felt that they received help. They gave evidence to support their conviction that they were functioning adequately and that they were strong enough to cope with life challenges. While showing some recognition of their limitations, they underlined significant resources in themselves and in their environments. Workers, on the other hand, stressed the clients' problems and weaknesses, highlighted their underlying conflicts, and raised doubts about their capacity to cope in future life situations.

The workers' more pessimistic outlook was evident even in cases such as the next three, in which they acknowledged that there were positive changes in the clients' functioning. In a sense, the practitioners in these cases played down the progress made by the clients as well as their own accomplishments.

CASE OF MISS MOORE

Client: She helped me to realize things about myself, about my parents . . . that my father wasn't as bad as I thought. . . . I learned how to assert myself more with my parents. . . .

All of it helped a lot. . . . I've been getting along very well. . . . It's amazing! I know what I want out of life. . . . I've grown up a lot. . . . I'm closer to my father and have a better relationship with my mother.

Worker: Many good things happened with Joyce. . . . She was satisfied with her decision to have the baby adopted. . . . She became more comfortable with herself. . . . Was more in touch with her feelings. . . . But I was still frustrated that I couldn't keep the case open . . . that we didn't have a chance to get deeper into family conflicts. . . . Once the baby was born and placed for adoption, her main issue was resolved and she didn't want to get into things further. . . . There was still a lot she needed to work on.

CASE OF MRS. CAIN

Client: Going there for counseling didn't help us very much. . . . My husband really needed psychiatric treatment. . . . Maybe a few more sessions would have helped. . . .

Worker: Both Mr. and Mrs. Cain made some strides. . . . He learned to cope a little better with her demands. . . . She was more difficult to work with . . . although she

Anyway, I have to say I came out of it being a little stronger. . . . or rather I found out I was pretty strong all along. . . . Eventually I was able to stand up to my husband . . . and I told him to leave the house when he continued to be so uncooperative. . . . This must have done the trick. . . . He came back after a week and we've been getting along better ever since.

gradually loosened up a bit. . . . I touched bases with them and helped them some . . . but we hardly scratched the surface. . . . I wasn't satisfied with how far we went. . . . When we terminated, they had the same problems they came with— problems in their identity as adults, in their communication as a married couple.

CASE OF MR. AND MRS. LODANO

Mrs. Lodano: Going there was one of the smartest things I ever did. . . . I found out it was okay to be different . . . that I wasn't really an oddball . . . that I had something to give other people, including my husband.

Mr. Lodano: For me it worked out very well. . . . Helped me to relax with my wife. . . . I realized that I had good friends . . . people that I liked and who liked me. . . . There were things that still bothered me . . . but I felt better able to face them.

Worker: This case worked out well. I felt okay about what we achieved. . . . In hindsight, I think that we were still in phase 1—just touching on the issues. . . . But they still have many problems and reality pressures. . . . I suspect that at some point in the future their problems will demand that they get into phase 2: eventually they will feel the pressure and get help with some of their basic issues, like in the sexual area. . . . I felt pretty satisfied that we worked on what they were ready for . . . but we didn't even explore some of these other issues.

As these excerpts illustrate, workers in most cases agreed that clients had received some benefit from the service. In other words, they concurred with clients in their positive evaluation of the outcome. However, this did not mean that they were satisfied. On the contrary, as seen in the above examples, the practitioners in general tended to be dissatisfied with the extent of the benefit or change in the client's situation. Moreover, some workers expressed, with much feeling, their concern that they had not gone as far as they would have wanted with a particular client. They wished that the client had been ready for deeper involvement and further work on the problems. At the same time, however, they clearly respected the client's right to choose what to work on and how far to go. The worker in one of the excerpts above, for example, related her dissatisfaction and sense of pain in seeing Mr. and Mrs. Gates leave treatment with a number of problems that she considered unresolved. In reviewing this case in the research interview, the worker thoughtfully indicated:

I sensed that Mr. Gates in particular was not at all comfortable with my efforts to probe deeper into his problems in relating with women. After testing it out and seeing how reluctant he was, I respected the fact that he did not want to deal with it. . . . In my view, the *client* decides. . . . I'm not going in after a problem that he doesn't want to deal with. . . . I would not impose it on a client.

There are alternative explanations for these marked differences in perspective. Perhaps workers do not know enough about their clients' functioning outside the office. Clients may need to exaggerate their positive qualities and their capacity to cope. Perhaps they overemphasize their progress so as to be protective of the worker or to justify their investment of time, energy, and money in the service. Perhaps the workers' training in uncovering pathology makes them overly preoccupied with it. At any rate, clients and workers come to their encounter with different frames of reference that influence their involvement in it — and their evaluation of the outcome — in significant and persistent ways. The discrepancies between clients and workers will become even more pronounced as we examine in further depth their satisfaction or dissatisfaction with the outcome of the service.

SATISFACTION WITH OUTCOME

Before presenting the findings in this area, we should briefly consider the concept of *satisfaction*, since it refers to one of the major variables explored in the study.

Client satisfaction may be viewed along a continuum from total satisfaction to total dissatisfaction. *Total satisfaction* includes such dimensions as overall satisfaction with one's situation, with the worker and with the outcome of services. *Total dissatisfaction*, on the other hand, is marked by the absence of all of these. Client satisfaction may also be conceptualized along the *instrumental* dimension (e.g., satisfaction with what the worker does about the problem) and the *expressive* dimension (e.g., satisfaction with qualities of the worker or with the relationship).

Client satisfaction or dissatisfaction was operationalized through questions such as the following in the research interview: Did the client feel satisfied or dissatisfied? Did he or she feel helped or not by various aspects of the service, such as talking about the problem or need? What did he or she like or dislike about the worker's approach and about the agency as a whole?

In respect to the worker, this concept referred to the practitioner's sense of satisfaction or dissatisfaction with such aspects as accomplishments, personal gratification, client qualities and response, and client participation in the helping process. It was operationalized through questions such as: On the whole, how do you feel about the way things worked out in this case? What

TABLE 7-2. Clients' and Workers' Satisfaction with Outcome (N = 25 cases)

	CLIENT	WORKER
Satisfied	64%	36%
Dissatisfied	16	36
Ambivalent	20	28

particular satisfaction and/or frustrations did you experience in working with this client?

In response to these questions, most clients and workers readily expressed their feelings about the outcome of their interaction. In cases where this was not so, they were asked directly about their satisfaction. The responses are summarized in Table 7-2. The "ambivalent" category includes respondents who were evasive, vague, or ambivalent in expressing their satisfaction with the outcome. Also included in this category was the only case in which a husband and wife clearly disagreed with each other.

Although most clients and workers, as noted earlier in this chapter, had concurred that the former had derived at least some benefit from the service, there were striking differences in their *satisfaction* with the outcome. Positive evaluation of the outcome, therefore, was not equivalent to satisfaction with it. As seen in Table 7-2, most clients were satisfied with the outcome, whereas most workers were either dissatisfied or ambivalent. Clients and workers in cases with "unplanned termination" were less likely to be satisfied than those in cases in which termination was planned. In two-thirds of the cases, client-worker pairs were in agreement in relation to their satisfaction or dissatisfaction. In the other cases, in general, the client was positive while the practitioner was either dissatisfied or ambivalent.

In addition, workers expressed strong dissatisfaction with the outcome in nearly all of the cases originally in the study sample in which clients could not be reached or declined to be interviewed. Since most of these clients dropped out prematurely, it is likely that they were also dissatisfied with the service and its outcome. The rate of client satisfaction in the study as a whole, therefore, would probably have been much lower if these clients could have been interviewed.

The following excerpts further illustrate the discrepancies between clients and practitioners in relation to their satisfaction.

CASE OF MISS BECKER

Client: The counseling was worthwhile. It felt good . . . . because it was the first time in years I could talk with someone about what's on

Worker: We were still in the beginning phase of treatment when she pulled out. . . . Some important things got out on the table, but we

my mind. . . . She helped me to gain confidence. I began to get out more with people, to get along easier. . . . I still have a long way to go . . . but I speak out more for my rights.

didn't really deal with them. . . .I wasn't happy, because we couldn't get in and deal with these issues. . . . I couldn't penetrate her defenses. . . . I didn't feel that we were making progress.

CASE OF MRS. BOGDANSKY

Client: There is no doubt that it helped. Counseling made me see what my daughter is like and what she is going through as a teenager. . . . Naturally, I expected more. . . . You always do . . . but I was satisfied with what I got.

Worker: It was a frustrating case in its fluidness. . . . My relationship with the mother in particular was tenuous. . . . It was hard to see what she wanted and how she felt. . . . My satisfaction was minuscule.

CASE OF MISS BROWN

Client: I'm glad I went to the agency. The counselor did me a lot of good. Before I went there, I didn't know where I was headed, I felt like committing suicide. . . . It really helped to talk with her. . . . I realized I ain't so bad. . . . People liked me. . . . I had something to live for.

Worker: I think that Esther got what she wanted . . . some help to get over her immediate crisis. . . . But I wasn't satisfied. . . . I guess I didn't get what I wanted . . . to have her stick it out in treatment so that we could deal with the underlying issues . . . especially why she kept running away from people as soon as she got close to them.

The substantial proportion of satisfied clients is consistent with the findings of previous studies in diverse practice settings.[1] Questions may appropriately be raised, however, about the validity of the findings in the present study as well as earlier ones. The high rate of client satisfaction may in part be due to a variety of methodological limitations inherent in research of this type. For instance, client samples are typically biased toward those who are satisfied. Also, the particular methodology that is usually employed to gather data, such as structured interviews or questionnaires with global questions, tends to elicit positive responses. In addition, the rate of satisfaction may be influenced by the respondent's need to "save face" in interpersonal transactions and his or her inclination to view the service in favorable terms when his or her image of the worker is positive.

For these reasons, as explained earlier, I chose a qualitative method-

[1] See Beck and Jones (1973: 74); Goyne and Ladoux (1973: 627-628); McKay, Goldberg, and Fruin (1973: 488); McPhee, Zusman, and Joss (1975: 401); and Sainsbury (1975: 116).

ological approach for this study and also the in-depth interview as the instrument of data collection. I wanted to obtain more than simplistic measures of client satisfaction. I found that clients could offer critical comments regarding certain aspects of the service, even though in general they were satisfied with it. As seen in the previous chapter on "the middle phase," they were able to express their dissatisfaction with certain problem-solving techniques. Also, as will be discussed in subsequent chapters on "the client-worker relationship" and "the agency environment," clients were frequently critical of certain qualities in the workers as well as some of the regulations and physical features of the agency. A good case in point is provided by Mrs. Donnelly, whose research interview is reproduced in full in Appendix E. Although she definitely felt that she had been helped by the service and was satisfied with its outcome, Mrs. Donnelly was critical of the worker's style (e.g., her quietness), the physical location of the agency, and the size and appearance of the worker's office.

Although the high rate of overall client satisfaction was not surprising in view of earlier studies, the high level of dissatisfaction among the workers was not anticipated. This finding is particularly striking, since worker dissatisfaction was evident even among cases in which clients and workers had concurred that clients derived some benefit from the service and that mutually agreed-upon goals were achieved. In other words, while agreeing with clients in their positive evaluation of the outcome, workers were nevertheless dissatisfied to one extent or another.

The data suggest that workers frequently were not aware of the positive impact that they made on clients. During the course of treatment, workers rarely solicited feedback from the clients about the outcome of their intervention. Furthermore, once a case was closed, the workers in most cases did not engage in any kind of follow-up and therefore had no way of knowing how their clients were functioning. Yet workers continued to be interested in their clients beyond the point of termination. In the research interviews, they would ask me how the client was doing. Even though they realized that I could not reveal information obtained in the interview with the client, they kept asking, expressing their intense — and understandable — curiosity. On occasion, I would suggest to the worker that he or she call the clients to learn about their functioning. Some workers did so and later reported how pleased they were to learn that the client was functioning quite well months after termination.

Even more striking than the workers' lack of awareness of their impact on clients was their tendency to have high expectations of the service, of themselves, and perhaps even of clients. Further evidence for this was presented in the chapter on termination: unlike the clients, workers expressed considerable dissatisfaction and doubt about their helpfulness to clients and concern with the clients' continuing or underlying problems. It seemed that, whereas clients were satisfied with having obtained help in relation to specific "problems in living," workers were concerned with overall "cures" or broad changes in an individual's situation or personality structure. Social work theorists have emphasized the positive role of worker expectations as a dynamic in the client's motivation for change. Oxley (1966: 437)[2] has observed that "clients must be motivated to grow and change":

> The social worker's responsibility is to help the client develop this motivation. The reality of the client-worker relationship as well as the weight of professional responsibility places the worker in the role of motivator.

The results of the present study suggest that, in addition to the positive impact of the worker's expectations, there should be careful consideration of their possible negative influence on the service, when they are unrealistic, inappropriate, or not relevant to the client's needs and goals.

The study's findings are congruent with those of previous investigations revealing marked discrepancies between clients and workers in respect to their expectations from "treatment" and their orientations toward problem solving. In their research with mostly middle-class clients in a family service agency in a small urban location in the United States, Sacks, Bradley, and Beck (1970: 64) found that "clients seem naturally oriented toward a crisis coping perspective on treatment. They want immediate relief, even temporary, from the acute pressures of their problems." Workers, on the other hand, "are clearly more attuned to the cognitive and perceptual precursors that facilitate decision and action and help guide the individual in productive directions" (Sacks, Bradley, and Beck, 1970: 64). In their study of working-class clients at a British family service agency, Mayer and Timms (1970: 136-148) concluded that clients were characterized by a unicasual, moralistic, suppressive approach to problem solving, in contrast to the workers' probing, multicausal, insight-oriented approach. In her investigation with clients who dropped out of treatment at family service and mental health agencies, Silverman (1969: 212-213) observed that there were major differences in the clients' and workers' definition of *help*: while for clients "help" meant concrete intervention geared to their specific needs, for the workers it consisted of developing a relationship with the clients.

In response to the overwhelming evidence concerning discrepancies in perspectives between clients and workers, there has been a great deal of emphasis on the process through which applicants are socialized into the role of clients (Hollis, 1972; Lennard and Bernstein, 1969; Siporin, 1975). Hollis (1972) has discussed how the applicant gradually becomes acculturated to the role of client and adapts himself or herself to the treatment process. Mayer and Timms (1970: 144-148) have suggested, as one possibility, the resocialization or reeducation of working-class clients, since their attitudes

---

[2] The impact of caseworkers' expectations on the motivation of clients is carefully considered by Oxley (1966).

and views on "helping" are drastically different from those of the workers. Others have written extensively about "anticipatory socialization" of applicants for service (Orne and Wender, 1968).

In these writings, an underlying assumption is that clients should become adapted to social work methods and delivery systems. Especially in light of research findings questioning the effectiveness of social work intervention (Fischer, 1976), this assumption needs to be challenged. There is a need to consider more intensely how practice methods and service arrangements should be changed so as to adapt them to the styles and qualities of clients. Furthermore, it is urgent to take another look at the socialization of social workers themselves. What is there in the educational process, for example, that leads to excessive worker preoccupation with pathology and cure, despite long-standing emphasis in social work on human strengths and potentialities?

INFLUENCES ON THE OUTCOME

What influences how satisfied clients and workers are with the helping process and its outcome? In the opinion of clients and workers, what accounts for the outcome of their interaction? Are there other factors of which they are not aware? There is a great deal of material relating to these questions from the research interviews, since both clients and workers considered, thoughtfully and extensively, the service as a whole and what there was about it that was helpful or not helpful. In contrast to the findings of previous studies (Gurin, Veroff, and Feld, 1960: 323; Mayer and Timms, 1970: 94-95), clients as well as workers specified the reasons for their satisfaction as well as dissatisfaction, in response to probing questions. Clients in particular were able to go beyond their global ratings of satisfaction and to share significant insights into the reasons for their satisfaction with the process and outcome of interpersonal helping.

These data will be presented in detail in the next three chapters. By way of anticipation, I should indicate that, while most clients and workers concurred in their view of the service as productive, they differed in regard to the perceived sources of influence on the outcome. Workers ascribed more importance to the client-worker relationship, whereas clients emphasized the role of external factors such as life experiences and resources in their social networks. In addition, clients more than workers reported that the agency environment influenced the course and outcome of the service in positive as well as negative ways.

Part III

INFLUENCES ON THE HELPING PROCESS AND ITS OUTCOME

Client: The counselor was of great help. . . . I can't say exactly what it was. . . . I don't think I could have done all these things without her. . . . She gave me the courage to do it.

Worker: The case worked out so well because she was ready to work . . . . She was well motivated. . . . She would have worked whether it was me or anyone else.

Client: When I was promoted, my life began to change. . . . I felt better about myself, more positive toward my wife, more optimistic about our relationship and our future together.

Worker: We didn't talk much about the promotion. . . . This wasn't directly related to treatment goals, which had to do more with looking at himself and his relationship with his wife.

From interviews in this study

Chapter 8

The Client-Worker Relationship

In the social work literature, the client-worker relationship is regarded as a major vehicle of help. In casework, for example, it is portrayed as *the* medium through which change takes place in the client's situation. In her psychosocial formulation of casework, Florence Hollis (1972: 229) stresses that the relationship is basic to all casework treatment for several reasons: "It is a means of communication between client and worker; it is a set of attitudes; and it is a set of responses, expressed in behavior." In her problem-solving approach to practice, Helen Harris Perlman (1957: 65) also explains that "the casework process, like every other process intended to promote growth, must use relationship as its basic means":

> The labors of mind and body involved in problem-solving may feel less arduous when they take place within the warmth and security of a strong relationship; the will to try may be spurred and sustained by the helpfulness and hopefulness it conveys.

At the same time, it is recognized that the relationship is extremely complex since "there are significant non-cognitive elements, such as feelings, attitudes, and inherent patterns of behavior" (Reid, 1977: 600). As client and worker proceed with their interaction, they are influenced by cognitive as well as noncognitive elements:

> Both the client and the worker are constantly reacting to each other in terms of reality and projection and the perceptions and misconceptions which one has of the other. It is no wonder that sometimes workers and clients alike become frustrated with the therapeutic experience (Reid, 1977: 606).

For these reasons, it is important to learn more about the qualities and components of the client-worker relationship that affect the helping process in general and client-worker interaction in particular. It is especially urgent to obtain the views of clients in this area, since research on worker qualities for the most part has not taken into account the client's perspective (Truax and Mitchell, 1971). Therefore, I asked respondents in this study a series of questions on their evaluation of the relationship and its impact on the service, their satisfaction or dissatisfaction with it, and salient client and worker qualities.

TABLE 8–1. Clients' and Workers' Evaluation of Their Relationship (N = 33 client-worker pairs)

Evaluation	By Client	By Worker
Positive	67%	61%
Negative	12	18
Ambivalent or noncommittal	21	21

EVALUATION OF RELATIONSHIP

A crude measure of each respondent's evaluation of the client-worker relationship was derived through inspection of the data. A respondent's evaluation was considered *positive* if he or she consistently expressed satisfaction with the relationship, *negative* if he or she consistently indicated dissatisfaction with it, and *ambivalent* or *noncommittal* if he or she expressed mixed feelings or was evasive about it.

As seen in Table 8-1, about two-thirds of the clients as well as their workers evaluated their relationship in positive terms. Approximately one-third of the respondents described it in negative or ambivalent ways. The relationship was viewed as negative by workers in seven of the ten cases in which clients could not be reached or declined to be interviewed. In six of the eight cases in which both spouses were interviewed, the clients agreed with each other in their evaluation of the relationship; in the other two cases, the wife was dissatisfied while the husband was either satisfied or noncommittal.

In all but two of the client-worker pairs, their evaluation of the relationship was congruent. In the exceptions, the worker was more dissatisfied than the client. In each of these two cases, there were discrepancies in the clients' and workers' expectations. In one, for example, the client apparently could tolerate only limited closeness with another person and was satisfied with how far her relationship with the worker went; the worker, on the other hand, expected much more of herself as well as the client in respect to emotional closeness and therefore was dissatisfied when it did not develop. Similar findings have been noted by other investigators (Beck and Jones, 1973).[1]

QUALITIES OF CLIENTS

Workers easily described the client's qualities and the aspects that they liked most or least about them. They viewed two-thirds of the clients as having mostly positive qualities and one-third as having largely negative

[1] In the 1970 nationwide study conducted by the Family Service Association of America, more than five out of eight client-counselor pairs rated their relationship as "very satisfactory" and only one in twenty as "not satisfactory" (Beck and Jones, 1973; 129).

qualities. The qualities most frequently mentioned by workers are presented below:

Positive Qualities	*Negative Qualities*
Workable	Simplistic
Likable	Not in touch with feelings
Open	Distant
Articulate	Rigid
Flexible	Not verbal
Perceptive	Resistive
Funny	Formal, businesslike
Sensitive	Defensive
Appealing	Not giving emotionally
Ready to help	Not motivated
Motivated	Avoids closeness
Allows closeness	Hard to get to know
Easy to read	Not trying hard enough

On the basis of the workers' responses, there emerges a picture of preferred or nonpreferred clients that is consistent with what has been noted in the literature and in practice: the preferred client is someone who is open, responsive, and capable of emotional involvement and insight, whereas the nonpreferred client is a person who is rigid, resistive, and nonverbal. In describing preferred qualities of clients, workers may be reflecting those qualities that they value in themselves. In addition, these are the qualities most suited to the psychotherapeutic modalities to which most practitioners have been exposed in their education.

Inspection of the workers' responses suggests that the preferred type of client evokes a sense of competence and satisfaction in the workers, whereas the nonpreferred type provokes feelings of self-doubt, inadequacy, and frustration.[2] Two excerpts illustrate this point.

In the first, the worker is talking about a "very responsive" and "well motivated" client who, in her view, had made considerable progress within a few months:

CASE OF MRS. DONNELLY

This is a satisfying woman to work with. Um . . . the frustrations are that with Judy you had to repeat things, you know, because she just really had to take them in a little bit at a time and practice them through herself and then she'd get feedback and then you'd try again and, maybe

[2] This is analogous to the parent-child interactional process (Anthony and Benedeck, 1970).

the first time that you said, "I think that you're a good person," she would hear—maybe perhaps as an outside chance—that "there is some worth to me." The second time you said it she would hear it a little stronger. So, there was a lot of repetitive kinds of things, a lot of testing. . . .

So that was frustrating but that was also normal and to be expected, given her situation at the time. But there were many, many rewards, you know? She's a warm, responsive, with-it person, she's highly motivated, you know, just a very nice feeling there. She just tries so hard.

Mrs. Donnelly's worker went on to exclaim, "Oh, yes, *yes!*" when I noted that she had apparently been getting good feedback from the client.

In contrast, this is how another worker spoke about the case of a "difficult, demanding, rigid" woman:

CASE OF MRS. TALCOTT

I tried to be supportive with her but she turned me off. She expected simple, concrete answers for her complex problems with her husband. . . . She wouldn't let me get close to her. . . . Also, she was reluctant to talk about her problems. . . . I wanted to reach out to her and tried to share my feelings but this backfired. . . . I felt even more frustrated and inadequate. . . . There were many complaints and unreasonable demands from her. I tried to get her to see what she was doing but didn't get far. . . . I felt angry but it was difficult to share this with her since I didn't want to hurt her feelings.

As described by their workers, clients seemed to fall into the two categories of patients delineated by Goldstein (1969; 1973): (1) the YAVIS patient—"young, attractive, verbal, intelligent, and successful"; and (2) the non-YAVIS patient—"typically lower or working class . . . often middle-aged or elderly, physically ordinary or unattractive, verbally reticent, intellectually unexceptional or dull, and vocationally unsuccessful or marginal" (Goldstein, 1973: 5-6). As seen in earlier chapters, most of the clients who were dissatisfied and/or dropped out displayed characteristics of the non-YAVIS patients. Goldstein (1973: 7-17) has demonstrated that the latter have expectations of therapy that are incongruent with those of their middle-class therapists and that these discrepancies in expectations negatively influence the process and outcome of therapy.

WORKERS' SATISFACTION AND DISSATISFACTION

In addition to the problem of lack of congruence in expectations, the findings of the present study suggest that the different qualities of clients also affect the worker's sense of competence and satisfaction and, in turn, the outcome of the helping process.

Workers were regularly asked about their satisfactions and frustrations in each case. They generally responded thoughtfully and freely, as reflected in the following excerpts from a range of cases in which they expressed varying degrees of satisfaction or dissatisfaction.

First are examples of cases in which workers were mostly *satisfied:*

CASE OF MR. AND MRS. CROMPTON

This was a satisfying case. I felt that we worked very well together . . . that we reached treatment goals. . . . I was happy with myself and my work in the case. I realized that there were other issues involved, but I chose not to go into them when Mr. and Mrs. Crompton indicated they were not ready. . . . I was on top of the situation. . . . I wasn't overwhelmed. . . . I felt I had something to give them. . . . They made me feel good about myself. . . . They were both genuine people . . . involved in what we were doing.

CASE OF MR. AND MRS. FORT

I was quite satisfied, despite my initial impression that I wouldn't have any impact on either of them, since I didn't think they would be following through with treatment. . . . But they did and I felt good . . . that I had given them what I could and they responded positively. . . . The Forts stand out in my view as a very sincere couple, willing to take risks in counseling . . . verbal and aware.

Next are cases in which the workers were mostly *dissatisfied:*

CASE OF MRS. FOLEY

I felt so frustrated in not being able to get to know this family better. . . . I didn't know them as people. . . . They weren't open with their feelings. . . . I couldn't get something going with them since they didn't really want to get involved emotionally with me or with each other. . . . I felt bad, because they came for help and I couldn't give it to them.

CASE OF MRS. TALCOTT

There were many frustrations in this case. . . . Mrs. Talcott and I just couldn't get going. . . . We couldn't connect. I kept trying but felt like I was hitting a brick wall. . . . I suspect that's how she felt about me too. . . . Perhaps I'm overly self-critical . . . but I didn't feel so confident in this case.

CASE OF MRS. BOGDANSKY

It was painful to see them suffer, to see mother and daughter trying to communicate but unable to give each other any feedback. I tried to help them with this . . . but they never quite touched, they never quite made it. *That* was frustrating. . . . I tried hard to get them to communicate with each other . . . but I didn't succeed. . . . It's upsetting to see that Laurie couldn't get what she needed from her mother.

Finally, here are some cases in which the workers expressed *mixed feelings:*

CASE OF MISS BECKER

This was a case in which it took a long time for the relationship to develop. Diane was so needy and afraid that it was very satisfying when we got to know each other and she let me get a little closer to her. . . . She got to know me and I shared a little about myself and my family. . . . But it was also frustrating a good part of the time . . . and she found it so hard to risk herself.

CASE OF MISS KRAFT

I am happy with what we accomplished. . . . But I wish that Beth could be even happier with herself than she was. . . . It turned out all right when I accepted the limits of what we could do, of how far she could go. . . . This was frustrating, because I expected more. . . . Well, actually, considering where she came from, she went a long way. . . . As the case went on, I had to do a lot of compromising with myself about treatment goals.

CASE OF MRS. PORTER

My satisfaction was low in comparison to other cases. In relation to the case itself and who Mrs. Porter was, I felt good that she was able to accomplish what she set out to do. . . . She was a formal, businesslike person who knew exactly what she came in here for. This is not my favorite kind of client. . . . She didn't let me in as others do. There are many others with whom I'm able to get involved, who are more open, who let me get closer to them.

What emerges from these excerpts of workers describing their satisfactions and frustrations in different cases? First, there appear to be certain qualities that the *worker* brings to the encounter, including a need for human involvement, for establishing emotional connections with others. Second, there are certain key qualities of the *client* that influence how the worker feels and responds, including sincerity, authenticity, openness, responsiveness, ability to take risks, and capacity to establish object relationships.

All of this reinforces the notion of the transactional nature of the client-worker relationship. Workers, as human beings, are affected differently by different clients. Clients, with their individual or unique attributes, evoke feelings and reactions in the workers that may not be readily detected in the course of their engagement with each other. The interaction between the client's qualities and those of the worker affects the process and outcome of their engagement. In other words, the worker's helping efforts seem to be contingent, to some degree, on the client's personal impact on him or her.

In various cases, it appears that a client and worker make such a good connection with each other that the worker feels satisfied and effective; in others, the connection is missing or incomplete and the worker feels frustrated or ineffective. In this regard, it should be noted that, in most of the ten cases of noninterviewed clients, workers repeatedly expressed feelings of inadequacy and doubt concerning their role, pointing particularly to their failure to establish an emotional connection with the client.

Thus, the client's qualities and responses influence the worker's sense of competence and performance in ways that may be positive or negative. For example, in several of the preceding excerpts, the worker revealed satisfaction in having had an impact on the client's situation. In others, the worker expressed frustration in not having had any impact. In White's terms, the experience of successfully *doing* and having a significant effect on the client's functioning contributes to the worker's competence and self-esteem. As emphasized by White (1963: 150) in his analysis of the ego in psychoanalytic theory, a human being gains strength and purpose through his or her "action upon the environment, feelings of efficacy, and cumulative growth of a sense of competence."

There is a need to explore further the dynamic process through which clients and workers evoke positive and/or negative responses in each other that affect their respective sense of competence and, in turn, the outcome of their interaction. For instance, one wonders if the worker's own feelings of satisfaction or frustration are conveyed to the client and, if so, what they may mean to the client, and how they affect the client-worker relationship and the outcome of the service. Unfortunately, there are minimal data in the study regarding the client's perception of the worker's satisfaction or dissatisfaction, since I did not routinely ask clients enough questions in this area. There were several cases in which clients were aware that their workers felt quite good about client-worker interaction. These clients indicated that they, in turn, were pleased with the workers' positive reactions. As Miss Appel noted, "It was so nice to know that she felt good about me. . . . I must have done something right!"

QUALITIES OF WORKERS

Social workers in general found it difficult to talk about how they thought their clients viewed them, their qualities, and their styles, typically pointing out that they did not usually get this information from the clients. As noted by one worker:

> I think that Miss Norton in general felt very positively toward me. But I couldn't say specifically how she viewed me. As you ask me this question, I realize that these are things that we rarely talk about . . . . Negative things usually come out or I'm aware of them . . . but I usually don't stop to talk with the client about positive things, such as what they particularly like about me.

The reluctance of workers to get feedback from clients concerning their own qualities is noteworthy particularly since, when I talked with them about their orientation toward social work practice, most of them clearly wished that the clients would share their feelings and reactions about their relationship. It may be that workers do not encourage client feedback for fear of what they might learn. This reluctance may also be symptomatic of a larger problem in interpersonal helping:

> It is perhaps the most glaring deficit in the helping relationships that professional counselors, clinical psychologists, psychiatrists, social workers and others rarely, if ever, are given any systematic feedback of their effects on clients (Truax and Mitchell, 1971: 339).

The workers' apparent hesitation to get client feedback is in a sense ironic since, as seen in this study and others, much of what clients have to say about the workers' qualities and effectiveness is generally positive.

Unlike the workers, clients had much to say regarding the workers' attributes. In their initial responses to questions in this area, both satisfied and dissatisfied clients were quite vague and gave overall or superficial impressions. They described their workers in terms such as kind, friendly, likable, knowledgeable, trustworthy, warm, and caring. Dissatisfied as well as satisfied clients were reluctant to ascribe any negative characteristics to their workers.

As the interviews probed further into their views, clients were able to be much more specific and to individualize the workers in sensitive and perceptive terms.[3] The clients' observations on workers' qualities were varied, rich, and complex, so much so that it was difficult to systematize these data in clear and meaningful ways. However, many of the responses were related to the following qualities that have been highlighted by Carkhuff and his associates in their research on the outcome of psychotherapy (Truax and Carkhuff, 1967; Truax and Mitchell, 1971):

Empathy or accurate empathic understanding: Sensitivity to client's feelings; being with the client; ability to convey this understanding.

Genuineness or authenticity: Being himself or herself; being sincere; not being defensive in the therapeutic encounter.

Acceptance or nonpossessive warmth: Accepting and valuing the client as a person, separate from any evaluation of his or her behavior and thoughts; being able to provide a safe and secure atmosphere.

I would add three other qualities that emerged as significant in the present study:

Concreteness: Ability to communicate thoughts and ideas clearly and specifically.

Competence: Proficiency in carrying out his or her professional role; knowledge of human behavior.

Objectivity: Ability to see different points of view; being unbiased.

I found that most of the clients' responses could be classified according to one or more of the above qualities. These qualities or categories are probably overlapping rather than mutually exclusive. Some, such as with empathy, genuineness, and respect, may represent alternative measures of the same variable. At any rate, typical responses in each category—positive and negative—are presented below.

Qualities of Workers, as Described by Clients

POSITIVE	NEGATIVE
Empathy	
Able to put me at ease, relax me. Concerned about me, interested. Understood me, picked up my vibrations. Gave me time to talk about myself. Nice to talk with. Gentle, kind, understanding. Avid, intense listener. Made me feel comfortable. Tuned in to my needs, feelings. Communicated easily with me. Comforted me when needed. Cared a lot about me. A lot of concern for people.	Detached, distant. Cold fish. Didn't relate to me. Didn't hear what I was saying. Didn't get us to open up. Was off in her own world. Didn't seem to care.

[3] This is another example of how the particular method (i.e., a probing type of interviewing) influences the findings.

POSITIVE	NEGATIVE
Genuineness	
Warm, lively, alive. Good sense of humor. Casual, relaxed, easygoing, low-key. Talked about own family, self, own experiences. Shared own feelings. Didn't seem like a social worker. Like a friend, a good buddy. Natural person. It was more than a job. Friendly, pleasant, easy to talk with. Likeable, personable.	Too nice, phony; put on. Too low-key. Too calm and collected. Too reserved. Doing job as a job. Was above it all; almighty; holy. Mechanical; businesslike.
Acceptance	
Let me say what I felt. Didn't accuse, criticize, or condemn me. Respected me. Didn't hold anything against me. Didn't treat me like a child. I could trust her, could say anything. Made me feel equal. Made me feel good. Treated me as an individual. Didn't put me down.	Pushed me when I wasn't ready. Seemed superior to me. I felt inferior. Lectured me. Didn't like me. Got angry when I didn't follow her ideas.
Concreteness	
Talked clearly. I could understand him/her. He/she made a lot of sense. Was down to earth. Came right to the point.	Vague; philosophical. I didn't understand what he/she was getting at. Didn't come straight to the point. Beat around the bush.
Competence	
Knew what he/she was doing. Knew his/her job. Knew what he/she was talking about. Obvious that he/she was very good in his/her work. Well educated. Experienced. Good teacher. Had put it all together. Seemed to know when to ask a question. Always had the situation well in hand.	Didn't know much more than I did. Too quiet; rarely said anything. Just like chattering with a girlfriend; too casual. Gave us no guidance. Too young, new, inexperienced. Seemed like he/she was still in training. Not capable; not professional. Disorganized. No confidence in him/her.
Objectivity	
More objective than a friend. Didn't take sides. Didn't just tell you what you wanted to hear.	Didn't realize I had different ideas. Sided with my wife. Couldn't see my point of view.

OUTSTANDING QUALITIES

The most commonly mentioned qualities were empathy, genuineness, respect, and competence. Nearly every client made at least one positive or negative comment pertaining to each of these. Especially noteworthy was the frequency with which clients offered evaluative comments regarding the worker's competence. In different ways, clients also emphasized the worker's pattern of paying attention exclusively to them and to their feelings and needs. In this sense, they demonstrated the importance of *total attention*, one of the contextual features of the interactional environment postulated by Lennard and Bernstein (1969: 168–170). There were few comments relating to the worker's objectivity and concreteness. There were no comments concerning other qualities or values traditionally associated with good social work practice, such as confidentiality.

The composite picture of the good or ideal worker is that of someone who is warm, accepting, understanding, involved, natural, genuine, competent, objective, and able to share of himself or herself with the client. The worker's human qualities are emphasized by clients more than his or her technical skills. This picture is consistent with the one revealed in other research on client perception,[4] experimental studies of the expected behavior of helping persons,[5] and research on client preference.[6]

Bent et al. (1976: 149) found that clients who were very satisfied with psychotherapy, in contrast to those who were not satisfied, "described their therapists as warmer, more likeable, more active, and more involved." Mayer and Timms (1970: 82–89, 107–110) categorized the major reasons for client satisfaction as: relief through unburdening; emotional support; guidance; and enlightenment or understanding. A review of their data shows that underlying each of these reasons are frequent references by the client to the worker's personal qualities. Sainsbury (1975: 68–69) found that clients gave as their rationale for preferring certain workers such aspects as the worker's "informality," "patience," and "caring." His findings show that, in considering which worker qualities are most closely associated with clients' satisfaction, clients place emphasis "on the worker's personal acceptability, his concern and activity, his trust, and his ability to lessen feelings of shame in seeking aid" (pp. 69–70).

Unlike respondents in the studies by Sainsbury and Mayer and Timms (1970), clients in the present study rarely mentioned the worker's provision of material aid as a reason for their satisfaction. This difference is probably due to the fact that the samples in both the Sainsbury and Mayer and Timms studies included many more clients who were seeking material aid such as financial assistance, whereas the sample in the present study was composed largely of individuals seeking help with personal or interpersonal problems. It will be recalled that in this study too there were some clients who had come to the agency expecting some type of concrete aid. These persons, as discussed in earlier chapters, were those who tended to drop out of treatment. In describing the workers, they generally expressed overall dissatisfaction with the service and tended to focus in particular on the fact that they had not

---

[4] See Chance (1959: 104–105); Sainsbury (1975: 116–117); and Strupp, Fox, and Lessler (1969: 117).

[5] See Kadushin and Wieringa (1960); Thomas, Polansky, and Kounin (1955); and Worby (1955).

[6] For concise reviews of research on client preferences in respect to worker or therapist qualities, see Kadushin (1972: 99–103) and Rosen (1967).

gotten the specific, concrete help they had been seeking. At the same time, they were hesitant to attribute negative qualities to their workers.

In another study of families in treatment at a mental health clinic, Chance (1959: 104) found that clients generally attributed positive characteristics to their therapists. The most outstanding qualities viewed by clients in the practitioners were "leading, giving kindly guidance, advice, help, sympathy, and love." There were very few instances in which the therapists were described in negative terms.

As Chance has speculated, clients may tend to ascribe to workers the kinds of attributes that they themselves value. This may represent transference reactions: as clients become emotionally involved with the workers, they perceive in them — or imbue them with — those qualities or attributes that they need the most. Also, the tendency to ascribe positive rather than negative qualities may represent another instance of the "face-work" in which, according to Goffman (1967), human beings engage to save face in interpersonal relations.

The following representative excerpts illustrate in further detail the flavor and richness of clients' responses in the present study, as they described their workers and their qualities. First are comments from several clients who felt positively toward their workers:

Miss Moore: She was like a friend, but more objective, because she didn't merely tell you what you wanted to hear. I liked her very much as a person. She didn't seem like a social worker. . . . She was very sincere. . . . Didn't act at all like I expected a social worker to be . . . you know, formal, above it all. . . . She talked about herself, about her family. . . . She didn't throw questions at me . . . didn't take notes. She never criticized me for what I had done wrong. . . . I always felt better whenever I went there.

Mrs. Lodano: He was a genuine person. . . . I could best describe him in animal terms as a mongrel dog or maybe a bloodhound. . . . He was casual, relaxed. You didn't think of him as a social worker but as someone you had known for a long time . . . someone who didn't think badly of anyone . . . someone whom you could easily trust. . . . He was very good in his work.

Mr. Mosca: I guess what I liked the most was his low-key approach. He didn't push himself or impose himself on us during the interviews. I liked that. And he just seemed like a genuine individual and I place a lot of stock in people who are genuine and I guess that's what I liked most about him. I sensed that he could feel for us. . . . He would say, "You know, I've been thinking about you," and I know he really meant it. . . . I'm sure he had a lot of other people too that he was thinking about, but it was very sincere thinking.

The clients' recurring references to the workers' human qualities support recent humanistic and existential emphasis on the validity of the workers' natural, emotional involvement in the therapeutic relationship. The clients repeatedly underlined the significance of personal qualities of the worker such as empathy and genuineness, which have been shown to be positively correlated with therapist effectiveness and client improvement (Truax and Carkhuff, 1967; Truax and Mitchell, 1971). According to Truax and Mitchell (1971: 302), "These ingredients of the psychotherapeutic relationship are aspects of human encounter that cut across the parochial theories of psychotherapy and appear to be common elements in a wide variety of psychoanalytic, client-centered, eclectic, or learning-theory approaches to psychotherapy."

Other satisfied clients, like the next one, appreciated their workers' interpersonal skills but also highlighted other qualities such as competence.

CASE OF MRS. GATES

Interviewer: What was it that you liked most about the way the worker was with you?

Respondent: Oh, I think the thing I liked the most was that she never really said much at all, she was quiet and yet always made sure that you got out what you were really thinking. Uh, she was very persistent, she wouldn't let you just sit back and hide in a shell or anything.

I: How did she do that?

R: It was just the way she questioned. It's very hard to describe it but she's very quiet and low-key and personality-wise, I think—it was right for me. Now I don't know if she was the same with everybody else but . . .

I: But you felt for you it was fine?

R: For me, yes.

I: How would you describe her as a person, you know, what was she like?

R: I don't really know except—you know, I think she was very quiet but yet, you know, very dynamic in many senses too. She just seemed very generally concerned and interested and, um, competent.

I: Can you talk a little bit about what it was about her that made you feel that she was competent?

R: That's hard. It was—I don't know, she always seemed to know when to ask a question, she always seemed to know when she needed to probe further, she just seemed to know exactly what she was doing and never hesitated very much. The sessions always went very quickly. You always felt she was in control of the session too. . . . Sometimes it can get a little strained and a lot of tension and everything and yet she always had the situation well in hand. How? I don't know. But she just did.

Next are comments from clients who were dissatisfied with the worker and/or the outcome of the service:

Mrs. Bates: Meeting her as a friend, I think I would have liked her . . . but she was just not professional enough. . . . She didn't hear what we were saying . . . didn't understand us . . . didn't seem to know what we were doing. . . . She was not my idea of a professional person . . . someone that you could trust . . . put your life in their hands. . . . When you go to a professional for help, you have to have confidence in them, you have to feel that they know more than you do, . . . or else, why would you go? I didn't think she knew much.

Mrs. Grover: She was coldish, distant. . . . I wasn't sure she was really concerned about me . . . although she seemed like a nice person. . . . She was too young and didn't seem to know about life. . . . I had the impression I was her first case. I don't know what else to say.

Mrs. Talcott: She was probably well educated . . . that's about all I can say. . . . I'm neutral about her. . . . She wasn't at all helpful. . . . She didn't really know how to help me . . . but I don't want to say more . . . . I know that the human heart is weak . . . and I don't want to hurt her feelings.

While clients who were satisfied emphasized human qualities of the worker such as genuineness or warmth, those who were dissatisfied seemed to stress much more the worker's competence or knowledge, but in negative ways. Perhaps dissatisfied clients find it easier to criticize the worker's technical skills rather than his or her personal qualities.

Some respondents indicated that their views of the worker's qualities changed over time, as seen in these examples of clients who felt that they received a great deal from the service after initially having been so dissatisfied that they had considered dropping out:

Miss Appel: It's funny, when I first went in, she impressed me as a typical social worker person. Well, you know, she was very reserved and cool and unemotional and objective looking—just kind of sat back there and looked at me behind her glasses. . . .

In the beginning, I took her too seriously. I thought of her not even as a person but just as this kind of thing sitting behind the desk, an objective, mechanical-like thing. But after I got to know her, that really wasn't her, you know? She was funny and she was human, and I got to laugh at the things she did.

At times she still continued to get into the social worker's role . . . like she would say to me, "How are you?" and I'd say, "Fine," and she'd say, "No, how are you *really*?" and I'd just burst out laughing because it was just really funny. She sounded so funny, . . . so stereotyped.

Mrs. Crompton: Oh, at first I wasn't sure about her. . . . It's hard to explain . . . but she was young and I wondered whether she really knew the score, about marriage and everything. That was the first thing that entered my mind. Also, she was so quiet. . . . I had expected her to ask me more questions and I thought to myself: *Maybe she doesn't understand, maybe she doesn't know what to ask, maybe she doesn't know anything.* . . .

After I kept going back, somehow I felt better . . . she was still quiet . . . but a *nice* "quiet." . . . She was really interested in me; she made me feel relaxed. . . . I realized that she had been giving me so much, without expecting anything in return.

Other clients, while satisfied with the worker and with the outcome, were able to point to negative qualities in their workers in the midst of their generally positive statements:

Miss Xavier: She was a very friendly, caring person who made me feel good from the beginning . . . but at times I though she was being *too nice*. It was like it was false or put on — her being nice all the time. I never said it to her because I really liked her, but that was the only thing wrong with her. . . . I mean, my life wasn't all that nice and I felt bad about it and I made her feel bad too . . . maybe she should have come out and said so. . . . But I guess she was just trying to make me feel better about myself.

Mrs. Stewart: She had a nice personality . . . with a good sense of humor. . . . The only thing was that she never got excited; she had a very low-key approach, sometimes to the point that I would almost fall asleep.

Mrs. Gates: I don't want to seem like a fink or anything . . . because I liked her. She was very good, efficient. But she came across as too detached, very businesslike, almost like she was saying, "Okay, here are your fifty minutes." . . . But at times she surprised me . . . she was really interested and even called me at home a couple of times to find out how I was.

SOCIAL DISTANCE

In interpersonal helping there has been growing awareness of the importance of understanding and dealing with the difficulties that arise because of the separate worlds of the helper and the client:

Class, color, age, and sex are some of the significant subcultural differences which might separate interviewer and interviewee, increasing social distance and limiting empathy and understanding (Kadushin, 1972: 219).

It is interesting therefore that, in addition to personal qualities such as empathy and professional attributes such as competence, in relating their views on the client-worker relationship many clients referred to characteristics such as age, sex, and marital status. But there was very little mention of religion, socioeconomic status, or race as possible factors in client-worker interaction. Since there were some client-worker pairs in which one was black and the other white, I directly asked about their views regarding racial differences. Both clients and workers in these cases stressed that race did not make any difference in their relationship. Other researchers and clinicians have pointed out that racial differences arouse feelings that have to be recognized and dealt with in order to develop a therapeutic relationship (Gitterman and Schaeffer, 1972). Consequently, my impression was that clients and workers needed to deny their feelings in this area.

In general, clients felt more positively and were more satisfied with the service the closer they were to the workers in respect to characteristics such as age, sex, and family status. Some representative comments follow:

> As a woman, she understood me better.

> It was good that he was of same age.

> Good thing that we were of same generation.

> Her being young—almost my age—made it easier for me.

> She was also a working mother and knew what I was going through.

> She was married . . . knew that marriage isn't easy.

These clients apparently found it easier to relate to the practitioners—and felt understood and helped by them—in part because the social distance between them and their workers was reduced.

In contrast, clients whose social distance from their workers was greater viewed negatively some of the differences in areas such as age and sex:

> It would be better if worker had been a woman.

> She couldn't really help when it came to my daughter. I don't think she had children of her own.

> How could she understand me, since she had never been married herself?

> She was too young, practically a young girl.

> She was too old for me. . . . She was middle-aged.

Mrs. Gates pointed to the negative role of social distance when she described her husband's and her own feelings about their first worker at the agency several years before:

> The first time we went there we were both dissatisfied with the counselor. She was very young, had never been married, acted like a trainee. She didn't seem to understand what we were going through. . . . She didn't seem that concerned about us. . . . I think she was leaving and we were her last case. . . . We didn't get anything out of it.

> The second counselor was also young and at first we weren't too sure about her. But it turned out that she was very interested in us, really knew her job. . . . She was mature for her age. . . . We could talk with her easily.

Practitioners should try to reduce the potentially negative influence of social distance between them and their clients by such means as increasing client-worker mutuality (Gitterman and Germain, 1976) and using the client-worker contract to shift the power balance toward the client (Maluccio and Marlow, 1974).

It should also be noted that, as suggested by the above excerpt from the interview with Mrs. Gates, the correlation between social distance and the level of client satisfaction was not always direct or simple. Some clients in fact indicated that they preferred a worker who was older or younger than they were or of a different sex or marital status. The clients' views in these cases could usually be explained on the basis of the concepts of transference and countertransference. In some cases, in other words, strong and positive transference or countertransference reactions apparently served to counterbalance the potentially negative impact of social distance between client and practitioner. At times, the client viewed the worker as a warm, giving mother figure and responded positively to her despite the discrepancy in their ages. In some instances, the worker's own countertransference reactions stimulated his or her caring responses toward the client.[7]

TRANSFERENCE AND COUNTERTRANSFERENCE

As generally used in social work and other disciplines, the concepts of transference and countertransference refer to the tendency of clients and workers to displace onto each other feelings, attitudes, or responses that they originally experienced in early childhood in their relationships with significant family members (Hollis, 1972: 234). In a number of cases in the study, there was evidence of marked transference and/or countertransference reactions. For example, workers revealed feelings such as competitiveness with a client. Clients, on the other hand, frequently referred to their workers in terms such as these:

She was like a mother.

I knew I could depend on her.

He was always there, like a good father.

Thus, many of the respondents imbued the worker with parental virtues. Workers, in turn, talked about the nurturing responses that clients aroused in them. Some workers pointed out that they needed to watch carefully their responses to a client's dependency on them; they realized that the dependency was gratifying to them but that they needed to avoid perpetuating it.

Workers in general seemed to be aware of transference and countertransference reactions and felt that they had handled them adequately. In some cases, however, there was indication of negative transference and countertransference reactions that interfered with the course and outcome of

---

[7] In a microscopic analysis of therapeutic interviews with a couple in marriage counseling, Fanshel observed that an important reaction took place in the relationship between the clients and the therapist: the clients evoked in the therapist "a response of deep caring and involvement in their fate. Their predicament moved her as a human being and drew from her an empathetic response which was conveyed to them" (Fanshel and Moss, 1971: 318).

the service. In the following situation, the client was very dissatisfied with her
first worker:

CASE OF MISS MOORE

The first counselor I had was not at all helpful. . . . Too cold and distant . . . much older than me. . . . I could see right away that it wouldn't
work out. She made me feel like she was patronizing me, always handing
me Kleenex whenever I cried, whether I wanted them or not. The second
one knew when to do it and when not to do it. Sometimes she gave me
Kleenex and sometimes she went on talking. She knew what to do. . . .
She was closer to my age. . . . She understood me better. She was like a
good friend but also very objective.

Miss Moore was ready to drop out, but the first worker apparently recognized
that there were negative transference and countertransference reactions
operating and arranged a transfer to another worker.

Generally, however, workers were very hesitant to consider a change, and
continued to try hard to help a client. Mrs. Donnelly, for example, had
transferred to a female worker at the Family Service Bureau after terminating with a male worker in private practice because of financial reasons.
Throughout her contacts at the Bureau, the issue of the worker's sex was
crucial, as seen in the following excerpts:

INTERVIEW WITH MRS. DONNELLY

INTERVIEWER: You said that things changed eventually. How did they
change?
RESPONDENT: She, um . . . Oh, when I told her I thought I should
change because I was more comfortable with a male social worker and she
asked me why and I said, "Well, they've been more relaxing, there's no space
of silence . . . we're always talking about something and . . ." I think maybe
that made her think, and the next time it was better. You know, she got more
comfortable with me. I don't know if she was afraid of me or I was afraid of
her. I couldn't figure that out at that time and then, when we got more
familiar with each other, we went on.
I: And how did you feel as it went on? How did you feel about the idea of
having a man versus a woman?
R: It was all in my mind . . . I guess, because she was very good. The only
difference in a male social worker that I had was that he would push you to
give him that extra something, which I expected out of her, and it's not
necessary. You know what I mean?
I: You mean he would ask questions?
R: Yeah, he would ask questions and then when I'd answer questions he'd
say, "Well, how do you feel about this?" and he'd get in a little deeper. This
is why I expected so much out of her, you see, and it wasn't really necessary.
. . . I didn't have that problem. I didn't think that it was that deep.

INTERVIEW WITH MRS. DONNELLY'S WORKER

INTERVIEWER: When Mrs. Donnelly came back to the agency, you said that she specifically requested a male worker. How did this issue work out?
RESPONDENT: Well, you see, um . . . like I said, two or three months after we got going with regular sessions again, I knew it wasn't going well and I didn't know why, so . . . I think it was she who brought it up and asked: "Well, maybe we're not just doing so well together, what about a male worker?" In exploring what it is, you know . . . the whole thing came out that she was really afraid that she would lose face if she truly revealed herself to me. I still think that maybe at some point in her life it would be beneficial for her to have a male therapist. But at that time I think that she used it as a smoke screen.
I: Would you do anything differently in this case, looking at it from this perspective?
R: I don't know whether—if there had been an immediate male available—I would have seen that she was assigned to him. I don't think so. We had an existing relationship—you can second-guess all over the place. She was ready to work, and she would have worked whether it was me or whether it was you.

Mrs. Donnelly and her worker discussed her preference for a male therapist, but did not openly and fully consider its meaning for her. Since her feelings around the transfer to a new worker and a new agency were not worked through to her satisfaction, she continued to view the male worker in an idealized way. In addition, she showed ambivalent feelings toward men, apparently engendered by her experiences with a father who abandoned the family at an early age and a stepfather who had rigid expectations of her. At the same time, she viewed women as inferior.

The practitioner agreed that Mrs. Donnelly would probably benefit from a male worker, but played down the significance of this issue for the client. As a result, the issue was never resolved and Mrs. Donnelly continued to feel that a male worker would have been better for her, even though she could also see that she had received considerable help through the female worker. In fact, several months after conducting the research interviews with them, I invited Mrs. Donnelly and her worker to discuss their feelings about their participation in this study in one of my research courses with graduate social work students. Before the class session was over, Mrs. Donnelly herself raised the issue of the practitioner's sex and continued to maintain that a male worker would have been better by being more active, directive, and forceful.

In the Donnelly case, as in others, the extent to which transference reactions were handled evidently influenced the therapeutic relationship and the course and outcome of the helping process. The case continued beyond a year and included a number of apparently unproductive sessions. Particularly in the early sessions, Mrs. Donnelly seemed to be quite preoccupied with the transfer to a female worker and seriously doubted whether she would be getting competent help. The major transference issue pertaining to the worker's sex was recognized by the practitioner but not fully handled by her. The worker's personal qualities and sensitivity to other needs of the client in large measure compensated for this lack, and the case apparently had a favorable outcome. But it is likely that there would have been less waste of energy and greater movement sooner if the transference issue had been more adequately resolved.

While it is not entirely clear why the worker in the Donnelly case did not pursue the issue, the indication is that she was threatened by it and therefore did not pay full attention to its manifestations and consequences. This of course happens often in practice, as the workers' own feelings and reactions interfere with their recognition and handling of major transference and countertransference issues. As demonstrated by Frank (1974) in his brilliant comparative analysis of psychotherapy, transference and countertransference can have an even more powerful and pervasive impact on client-worker interaction than more obvious expectations or attitudes of clients and practitioners. Therefore, the latter have a special responsibility to devote deliberate attention to manifestations of transference and countertransference, so as to lessen their negative influence and maximize their positive role in treatment.

RELATIONSHIP BETWEEN WORKER QUALITIES AND THE OUTCOME OF TREATMENT

On the basis of extensive research, Truax and Carkhuff (1967: 176–189) have concluded that there is a positive relationship between the outcome of therapy and certain qualities of the therapist, particularly empathy, genuineness, and "nonpossessive warmth." These findings have been supported by subsequent investigations in diverse settings (Korte, 1977). In reviewing much of this research, Truax and Mitchell (1971: 310) concluded:

> These studies taken together suggest that therapists or counselors who are accurately empathic, nonpossessively warm in attitude, and genuine are indeed effective. Also, the findings seem to hold with a wide variety of therapists and counselors, regardless of their training or theoretic orientation, and with a wide variety of clients or patients, including college underachievers, juvenile delinquents, outpatient neurotics, and the mixed variety of hospitalized patients.

The findings of the present study also point to the crucial significance of the worker's personality and of relationship variables in the course and outcome of interpersonal helping. In addition, however, they suggest that the correlation between worker qualities and outcome is not a simple or linear one. Thus, there was indication of client satisfaction and positive outcome even when the key qualities were not perceived by the client as being present in the worker. Additional factors, such as perceived competence of the worker, also influenced the client's views and the change process. Some qualities seemed to be more meaningful in one phase of the helping process rather than in another. A number of clients suggested that factors such as the worker's age or empathy made a positive impression on them initially, leading them to be optimistic about the contact. As the encounter progressed, however, the same clients would not continue to be satisfied unless the worker displayed other qualitites, such as competence. Moreover, the same quality was evaluated differently by different clients. Thus, some clients considered a worker's "low-key approach" as positive, while others saw it as negative. Some clients preferred an older worker, while others felt that one closer in age was better. Some clients reacted negatively to a worker's "formal" or "professional" bearing, whereas others reacted to it positively.

From these findings it appears that a changing cluster of worker qualities influences the client's attitudes toward — and satisfaction with — the worker at different points in their interaction, depending on his or her changing needs, perceptions, and life space. Consequently, there is no easy answer to a recurring question: Which worker characteristics are preferred by different clients, or best suited to their needs? Following an extensive review of research on client preferences, Kadushin (1972: 99-103) suggested that a client's satisfaction results from the interplay of multiple factors such as the nature of the presenting problem and the setting, the qualities of the interviewer, and the characteristics of the client. As Kadushin (p. 103) also observed:

> Both interviewer and interviewee bring their reference group, primary group, and biopsychosocial backgrounds to the interview. The influence of any specific variable brought to the interview is modified in the interaction. The interviewer's own feelings, preferences, and needs pose problems for effective interviewing. . . . The interviewee, in turn, has his own tasks, preferences, and problematic needs in implementing his role.

CLIENT WORKER MATCHING

The complex interplay among different qualities of clients and workers helps to explain why in practice it is difficult to know how to match clients and practitioners as a way of maximizing the benefits of interpersonal helping, even in settings where there are adequate and varied personnel resources. As mentioned in an earlier chapter, the issue of matching qualities of worker and client requires further attention in research as well as in practice

In the present study, most of the clients and practitioners in the sample seemed to be adequately matched, even though in the intake process of the Family Service Bureau there was generally no conscious assignment of applicants and workers on the basis of their styles or qualities. Somehow, clients and workers in most cases seemed to be well suited to each other, perhaps in part because workers intentionally tried to adapt themselves as much as possible to the needs that they perceived in their clients. In cases of grossly poor matching, there was evidence of strong negative transference or countertransference reactions or other problems that could have alerted the practitioner to the need to consider assignment of the client to a more suitable worker. Although in some cases workers were cognizant of this possible need, they usually did not act on it, apparently because a transfer would have represented failure or incompetence.

CLIENT PREFERENCES AND OUTCOME

One reason that client-worker matching is still an obscure area is that, while there has been considerable research on client preferences, there is a paucity of knowledge regarding the *relationship* between client preferences and the outcome of the helping process (Rosen, 1967: 787). For instance, not enough attention has been given to what kinds of workers different clients relate to most effectively. Therefore, I made a special effort to learn from clients what there was about worker qualities that in their opinion influenced the outcome. These findings will be discussed in the remainder of this chapter, along with the views of workers.

Both clients and workers attributed considerable significance to the client-worker relationship and its impact on the process and outcome of the service, although clients, as noted in the preceding chapter, emphasized the role of social networks and life experiences more than that of the relationship. Perhaps it should be expected that workers would assign greater importance to the relationship, in view of their investment in it as well as the emphasis traditionally placed on it in social work. In addition, the client's life situation is not as accessible to the worker as it is to the client.

In response to questions such as "What was most helpful?" or "What were the reasons for changes in your (their) functioning?" most clients and workers initially responded with a general reference to the role of the client-worker relationship. Further probing revealed a number of client qualities, worker qualities, and client and/or worker activities that were identified by both clients and workers as crucial in the outcome of their interaction and in their satisfaction with it. The most commonly mentioned qualities and activities are summarized on page 137.

Many of the same qualities or activities were noted by both clients and workers and described by them in similar terms. The respondents differed, however, in the frequency with which they mentioned different types of factors and in the importance that they assigned to them. Thus, clients tended to call attention mostly to *qualities of the worker,* while workers tended to stress *qualities of the client.*[8] This difference is illustrated by the following excerpt, from the case of a woman who had been involved in long-term treatment:

---

[8] In view of frequent references by practitioners to the client's ability or readiness to work, the findings suggest that, as emphasized in the casework literature, workers

Relationship Factors Influencing Outcome and Satisfaction, as Viewed by Clients and Workers

FACTORS	NOTED BY BOTH CLIENTS AND WORKERS	NOTED BY CLIENTS ONLY	NOTED BY WORKERS ONLY
Client Qualities	Motivation or readiness Being desperate Being eager to change		Latent resources Willingless to take risk Being in tune with his/her feelings Hurting
Worker Qualities	Acceptance Interest Warmth Being supportive	Knowing his/her job Human Understanding Caring Trust Friendliness His/her personality Good as a counselor	
Client and/ or Worker Activities	Unburdening self The three of us working together	Encouraging us Making us feel better Looking for a solution Giving advice, suggestions	Relieving their anxiety Role playing Having them read selected books Giving them assignments

CASE OF MRS. DONNELLY

Client: I don't know, she [the worker] pushed me in the right direction. I don't think I would have thought of all those things, and here, the things were right there . . . like calling up my friends. . . . She was so kind, so interested. . . . She gave me the courage—the push—to do it myself.

Worker: It worked out so well because Judy was ready. . . .

She was ready to work . . . and she would have worked whether it was me or whether it was you or anyone else.

In this case, as in others, the suggestion was that, along with being aware of client qualities such as motivation, workers should give further attention to

ascribed considerable significance to the client's motivation or "workability" (Perlman, 1957: 181-185).

the specific qualities in themselves to which individual clients respond either positively or negatively.

Clients who were dissatisfied with the service and its outcome also highlighted the worker's qualities, but in negative terms, as in the following example of a middle-aged man who viewed his worker as too young and inexperienced:

Mr. Grover: Just being there helped a little, because at least I had a chance to talk and she listened . . . but she didn't do anything else and it was mostly a waste of time. . . . She was too young . . . didn't seem that concerned . . . didn't know what I was trying to say. It looked like she was still learning. . . . How could I have confidence in her? . . . I needed someone more experienced, . . . someone with more knowhow.

While workers referred often to the client's direct participation in the helping process, clients mentioned it infrequently. At the same time, clients, more than workers, identified worker actions on their behalf as significant for the outcome and their satisfaction with it. Many clients indicated that the worker's activities had encouraged them to take constructive steps or had changed their situation enough to enable them to function better:

Mrs. Crompton: Every so often it seemed like my husband and I were arguing and not getting anywhere. . . . Then she [the worker] would raise a question, like: "What do you want to do with your life?" . . . Well, this would jolt us back to reality. . . . She showed that she really cared about us . . . and that we should see what we could do to get along better.

Mrs. Porter: She gave me information on different groups for divorced women and also told me about the Women's Center. It was good to know that there were things available if I need them. . . . I never went to the Center or joined a group. . . . In talking about it, I realized I already had friends I could go to. . . . I began to see them and, oh, they welcomed me.

Mr. Voltaire: My kid was having . . . how do you say it . . . a lot of trouble. . . . Mrs. Jones [the worker] found a good place where she could go after school. . . . Now she is not running around like before. . . . I don't have to worry like before.

Miss Appel: When I went there, I had planned to quit my job, leave the area, go somewhere. . . . I had friends but was afraid to go to them. . . . The counselor forced me to talk about it all. . . . She encouraged me to reach out to my friends and kept asking me how it was going. . . . I found out that I could be close to them. . . . They didn't think bad of me. . . . For a while I was afraid I might lose the job because I had been missing so much work when I was depressed. . . . Then the counselor called my boss and explained what I was going through. . . . From then on he was very understanding. . . . He went out of the way to help me at work.

Other clients, particularly in the group that dropped out, were dissatisfied with the worker's *failure* to take some action on their behalf. As seen in an earlier chapter, many of these were clients who had clearly expected a more directive, advice-giving worker and who interpreted the worker's behavior as reflecting lack of interest or caring:

Mrs. Spaulding: She was nice, but *talking* endlessly didn't help. . . . I was very depressed and needed medication. . . . Finally, I went to the family doctor and he gave me something to sleep. . . . The counselor should have sent me to a doctor sooner. . . . She didn't seem to know what I was going through.

Mrs. Stewart: Before we ended, we talked about a women's group for me. . . . She was supposed to look into it but didn't do it. . . . Maybe it was up to me to take the first step. . . . She kept saying I should get out there more on my own. . . . She was right . . . but I don't know if she cared like she said.

Mr. Molina: She didn't help at all with our kid. . . . We thought she would be going to the school to talk with them . . . or at least call the guidance counselor . . . but she never did. . . . We got the impression that the place pays more attention to the delinquent type, kids on drugs, welfare cases. . . . We didn't go no more when it looked like it didn't matter to her. . . . Well, my wife and I decided we weren't getting anywhere, and that was the end of that.

In contrast to clients, workers generally said very little about their activities, particularly their intervention into the client's life situation. This is very interesting, especially since, from the perspective of clients, certain specific actions of the workers were quite useful in mobilizing their own competence and spurring them on to more successful action on their own behalf. Moreover, while workers often did get involved directly or indirectly in their clients' life situation, they did not regard situational changes as highly as what happened within the more immediate helping relationship. Consequently, as will be discussed in the next chapter, they did not perceive their external actions on behalf of the client as so important for outcome.

In conclusion, the findings show that worker personalities and styles affect client responses, and in turn the outcome of interpersonal helping. Practitioners are of course aware of these influences on their interventive efforts and, in a more or less deliberate fashion, usually try to adapt themselves to the needs of a particular client. In other words, they strive to achieve the "proper kind of working relationship" with the client:

> [This] . . . is a unique interpersonal experience in which the patient feels a quality of warmth, trust, acceptance, and understanding such as he has never before encountered with any human being. . . . [The therapist] must provide the patient with an experience that will act as a prototype of a different kind of human relationship—one that inspires new and constructive patterns toward people (Wolberg, 1954: 317-318).

While attempting to attain in each case situation the ideal relationship described by Wolberg, practitioners also need to remind themselves of the complex interplay of forces affecting client-worker interaction. In so doing, they may be better able to accept their own limitations as human beings, and to discriminate between those situations in which they can appropriately adapt themselves to clients' needs and those in which they should find some way to supplement their relationship with the client or even consider reassignment to another worker.

Chapter 9

Social Networks
and Life Experiences

A distinctive and pervasive theme of social work throughout its history has been the "person-in-situation" configuration, that is, the impact of the interaction between people and their environments on human behavior in general and on the helping process in particular. In the early part of this century, Mary Richmond, a leading social work pioneer, stressed the significance of the client's situation or environment in *Social Diagnosis* (1917), the first systematic exposition of casework. She referred, for example, to the need for a precise definition of the "situation and personality of a human being . . . in relation to the other human beings upon whom he in any way depends or who depend upon him, and in relation also to the social institutions of his community" (Richmond, 1917: 357).

The person-in-situation theme has been sustained and further developed by succeeding generations of social workers, notably Gordon Hamilton and others espousing a psychosocial approach to casework. Hamilton (1951: 3–4) defined a "social case" as "a living event, within which there are always economic, physical, mental, emotional, and social factors in varying proportions. A social case is composed of internal and external, or environmental factors." The interrelatedness between the person and the environment is a recurring theme throughout Hamilton's influential *Theory and Practice of Social Casework,* as reflected in the following reference to diagnosis:

> Diagnosis becomes clearer and more penetrating as socio-economic, psychological, and cultural factors are analyzed in relation to their interrelated meaning for the individual and the family (1951: 183).

Although historically they have embraced divergent theoretical and ideological orientations in their quest for further refinement of their methods, caseworkers have consistently concurred in their emphasis on the person-in-situation configuration. For this reason, Strean concluded an extensive review of writings on social casework with the assertion that all authors

> conceive of the individual as a bio-psychological unit in constant interaction with its environment. Each individual piece of behavior is viewed within a large gestalt of component parts which are in constant interaction (1971: 23).

141

If anything, in recent years the notion of the interrelatedness between people and their environments has generated even more interest among social workers, as seen in applications of general systems theory to social work (Gordon, 1969), reformulations of psychosocial therapy (Turner, 1978), studies of social networks (Collins and Pancoast, 1976), and the emergence of the ecological perspective on social work practice (Germain, 1973; Gitterman and Germain, 1976). Gordon (1959: 10) captured the essence of renewed emphasis on the person-in-situation configuration in his delineation of the central focus of social work as the *"matching of people's coping patterns with the qualities of impinging environment for the purpose of producing growth-inducing and environment-ameliorating transactions"* (italics by author).

In view of the long-standing recognition of the interplay between the person and his or her environment, in the present study it will be interesting to examine client and worker views on the role of environmental factors in the process and outcome of interpersonal helping. In the preceding chapter we reported that workers, in particular, emphasized the role of the client-worker relationship as the major vehicle of help. In this chapter we will see that clients attributed more significance than workers to the role of factors outside of their immediate interaction, particularly the client's social networks and life experiences and events. Thus, clients, more than workers, pointed to the positive impact of friends, relatives, and informal "helping" agents in the community. Both clients and workers mentioned natural life experiences and events (such as a job change) as factors influencing the process and outcome of their interaction; however, clients mentioned more of these in *positive* terms, whereas workers mentioned more in *negative* terms.

SOCIAL NETWORKS

Both clients and workers often indicated that one or more persons in the client's social networks influenced the client in some way while in treatment. Examples included relatives, friends, employers, neighbors; other professional helping agents such as teachers, clergymen, and physicians; and informal helpers such as hairdressers and bartenders. Clients generally referred to these people in positive terms, viewing them as providers of support, care, and encouragement. For instance, this is what one woman said in response to the question, "Was there anyone or anything beyond the service at the agency that helped you to make the changes you have told me about?"

Mrs. Gates: I found a lot of people who became very good friends that I had never felt I could count on and this helped a great deal. As I was going through the divorce . . . as soon as they found out I had problems, a lot of people helped out . . . a lot of people in my church, a lot of neighbors. . . .

They helped in many ways: people in the church were looking for jobs for me, setting up interviews, doing anything they could. . . . My neighbors went out of the way to take care of the kids and just to help me out . . . just to be there. They were marvelous. And they're still there! . . . I know I can count on them and it really gives you quite a feeling of support.

As for the workers, they also brought out that in some cases members of the clients' social network exerted positive influence on their functioning. However, they pointed to the negative impact of such persons as family members and friends more frequently than clients did. Moreover, in some cases workers tended to take a negative view of close relationships that clients described positively. These differences are illustrated in the following comparative excerpts.

CASE OF MRS. PORTER

Client: I'm glad I still had my daughter. . . . Fortunately, she was doing all right in school and everything. . . . She was only eight years old and still needed a lot of attention from me. . . . That made me feel good, like I was needed. . . . Well, oh, I had something to live for.

Worker: We can't discount the influence of Mary, her daughter. . . . Sometimes it was helpful, sometimes not. It was good for her to have a child to focus her energies on . . . but she was also overly preoccupied with her daughter and in this way maybe she avoided focusing on some other concerns.

CASE OF MISS XAVIER

Client: My boyfriend also had a lot of problems, but he was always so concerned about me. . . . He encouraged me to go to the agency. . . . He was there whenever I was down. . . . He helped me to meet new friends and get out of the rut.

Worker: Joan had serious problems in interpersonal relationships. . . . Her boyfriend was always problematic. . . . He constantly put her down.

CASE OF MISS KRAFT

Client: During my worst period, I realized that my parents and my two brothers were really behind me. . . . Well, I was very surprised especially when my parents turned out to be so understanding. . . . They took me back home, and that meant a lot to me. . . . I never knew how close a

Worker: Her parents worked on different shifts. . . . They gave her little support and almost washed their hands. . . . They didn't have the energy to deal with their daughter's problems. . . . Her brothers were supportive, especially the younger one. . . . Betty had some friends

family could be until you go through something like this. . . . My friends also helped a lot. . . . They didn't ignore me. . . . You know, they understood what I was going through and made me feel that life goes on.

. . . but I don't think they were that available or helpful to her.

CASE OF MRS. NORTON

Client: My relatives were always around. . . . Sometimes they bothered me a lot with their own problems. . . . But they also came through when I was really down. . . . It was good to know that I could count on them if I needed them.

Worker: Mrs. Norton had relatives but they were not of much help to her. . . . Two of her sisters were having a lot of problems with their own kids. . . . She had frequent contacts with her sisters and my impression was that they put a lot of pressure on her. . . . Kept calling on her for help.

Thus, clients tended to view positively their relationships with members of their kinship system, whereas social workers tended to define the same relationships as problems and obstacles in the client's functioning. It may be that, as shown in another study of casework treatment in a family agency (Leichter and Mitchell, 1967), clients and practitioners hold different values and beliefs in respect to their kin. In the latter study, it was found that clients viewed their relatives positively and sought closer relationships with them. In contrast, caseworkers regarded the client's wish to interact with his or her kin as problematic, that is, as a reflection of immaturity or dependence; in the course of treatment, consequently, they sought to restrict the client's involvement with relatives. Leichter and Mitchell (1967: 261-262) stressed that practitioners should be aware of their own personal, cultural, and professional assumptions in the area of kinship, and more cognizant of the meaning that relatives may have for a particular client. As they observed, "The extent to which the caseworker has knowledge and understanding of the client's position . . . is most significant in treatment" (p. 262).

A few clients did indicate that friends or relatives were not helpful. Several agreed with their worker that their family members put pressure on them or could not be of help. For example, Mrs. Gates, who had been very positive about the role of her friends and neighbors, also remarked:

My family? Oh, I avoided them. . . . I knew they wouldn't be able to cope too well and so for a long time I didn't even tell them that John and I were getting a divorce. I knew that they would blame me and make things harder.

Mrs. Gates and her worker had talked about her family members and concurred that they would be of little help, in view of their own problems as well as negative attitudes toward her.

Members of the client's social network can not only provide support in the client's life situation but can also be instrumental in encouraging him or her to use the service itself (Mayer and Rosenblatt, 1964). One-third of the clients interviewed brought out that they had friends or relatives who had previous or current experiences in counseling at this agency or others.

Some respondents noted that a friend or relative had been helpful by explaining what would be involved or giving them confidence in first going to the agency or continuing there:

Mr. Crompton: My brother had been to a marriage counselor before he got a divorce. Well, when I told him I was thinking of going too, he explained it all. . . . He remembered how he went the whole route himself. . . . We had a long talk and he told me what would be going on with the counselor. . . . He gave me the confidence that things would work out . . . that I didn't have to be ashamed to go there for help.

Another client indicated that she would have dropped out when the therapeutic process became painful, if it had not been for the support of a friend who was in treatment at a psychiatric clinic:

Miss Kraft: It looked like the counselor and I weren't making it. . . . She kept pushing me but we weren't getting anywhere, and I felt bad and was thinking of not bothering with it anymore. When I went home, sometimes I spoke to my girlfriend about it and she knew what it was like. She went through the same thing with her counselor. . . . She told me it was hard to change, oh, well, to stick it out . . . to think of myself and my future. . . . She told me counselors sometimes go to the heart of the matter and it can be rough. She urged me to keep going . . . and I'm glad I did.

Others felt that their friends had helped them to make better use of the service by providing encouragement or explaining what was involved:

THE CASE OF MRS. DONNELLY

Interviewer: And then, when you started with Mrs. Gray, was there discussion of how you felt about going from one worker to the other?
Respondent: Oh, yeah, yeah . . . she was good that way [unclear] . . . but she was starting from scratch. I think her part was hard but like my girlfriend said to me, "You're going in there to help yourself, you're not going in there to think of her part, or how she feels." . . . At times, I felt bad because I wasn't responding. I felt bad because the instructor or teacher or whatever you want to call it, the speaker—What would you call it?
I: You mean the worker?
R: Yeah, the worker. Here's the worker and I'm not getting across to her and I, when I went home, sometimes I spoke to my girlfriend and I'd say, "I feel

bad that, you know, I'm not . . . I'm trying hard to get together with her but I can't," and my friend said to me, "You know, you're so used to another way that it will be hard to change it," and then I . . .

I: So your friend helped you to see it more clearly in that way?

R: Yeah.

In the above case, the worker did not mention the role of Mrs. Donnelly's friend in encouraging her to stay in treatment. Usually, however, workers were aware of situations in which a friend or relative was helpful to a client in becoming engaged in and using treatment. In several situations, the worker stated that the client would have dropped out if it had not been for the encouragement of a friend or relative.

Workers rarely mentioned the role of informal "care-givers" or "help agents" in the community. In contrast, nearly half of the clients referred to people other than friends or relatives who had been helpful to them. Several clients spoke of the role of others such as bartenders and hairdressers in a particularly interesting way. This was exemplified again by Mrs. Donnelly, a hairdresser:

CASE OF MRS. DONNELLY

Interviewer: Do you think you might refer other people to this agency if the occasion comes up?

Respondent: I have, I have. . . .

I: For what kinds of problems?

R: Well, the usual problems. Either a death in the family, emotional problems that she can't cope with, things which we hear in a beauty salon because they tell you all about it. . . . We hear it all the time. . . .

I: Why do they tell you about their problems?

R: Because they're relaxed. It's the same with a bartender. When I was in Colorado, I read an article in the local paper that in the future they were going to teach hairdressers and barbers and bartenders certain ways to get to the people to give them the right direction for help . . . rather than drinking themselves to death or spending all their savings on hairdos or ending up killing themselves . . . which I thought was very, very good and it hasn't come here yet.

I: No, I haven't heard of it yet.

R: It makes a lot of sense.

I: Yeah, it makes sense. . . .

R: I know a lot of bartenders and they tell me the same thing. They hear the same thing we do. . . . People you don't even know come right over and say, "Boy, I can't go home—my wife's miserable!" or "These kids are driving me crazy!" or "My husband has left me and I don't know what to do about my finances. . . ." And, well, here they are, spending money on their hairdo, and they don't even know about their financial end. So, right there, they're searching for some type of help.

I: Uh, uh. . . . Does it suggest that maybe if beauticians or bartenders could get some training they might be able to do more . . .?

R: I try to direct them to the right place. This agency is the only place I know, and . . . you see . . . me telling them that I went makes them feel at ease because sometimes they feel like they're going to be the only ones. Then they unwind right away and tell me a lot about their troubles.

I: When they know you also went?

R: Yup, and I tell them it wasn't hard and it wasn't easy—so I'm getting to be the "Director of Social Work"—which is good, though. I'd rather see that than have something bad happen to them.

I: I imagine this can be a big help to some of your clients.

R: Well, that's one of the reasons that made me go back to college, because I feel I should have more training, and I started to take courses earlier this year.

As Mrs. Donnelly so vividly illustrated, human beings tend to make use of natural resources in their environment when confronted with life problems or challenges. Her comments support the recent movement in community mental health toward greater involvement and education of informal care-givers such as bartenders and hairdressers (Caplan, 1974: 210–212; Taynor, Perry, and Frederick, 1976).[1]

Other clients in the study sample, particularly some who were dissatisfied with the service, referred to the lack of resources or impoverishment in their social networks. Mrs. Stewart, for example, poignantly brought out her loneliness and isolation:

Mrs. Stewart: Since getting the divorce, I'm trying to bring up the kids as best I can. . . . Sometimes it's rough . . . especially at the end of the day when they go to bed and I have no one to talk with. Even during the day, I get tired of talking to little kids and mediating their arguments over and over. . . . You need to carry on a conversation with adults or you go crazy. . . . On Sundays, when they go with their father, I have nowhere to go to and then it really gets lonely. . . . There is no place that's open, like a library. . . . I have some friends, but I can't keep going to them. They have their own families, their own lives.

Mrs. Stewart was like several of the other clients who were quite dissatisfied with the worker and/or the service; it seemed that she and the others had hoped for direct help in enriching or expanding their social networks. They became frustrated when this did not materialize. In some cases, the problem seemed to be that they had not communicated to the worker their expectations or feelings in this area. In others, there was an indication that the

---

[1] See Baker (1977) for an excellent review of the literature on self-help organizations and informal care-givers and a discussion of their relationship to professional support systems.

workers were aware of the clients' need, but uncertain about how to deal with it.

Perhaps in some situations social agencies should provide leadership in setting up necessary resources or in helping clients with similar needs or problems to develop support groups. At times, these supports may be needed even by clients who have access to significant members of their social networks. Mrs. Donnelly, for instance, explained that, in terminating with individual counseling, she felt that she needed a support group of persons who had recently gone through separation or divorce:

> When I was near the end, I said I would like to have had a group session with people in the same shoes . . . you know, with divorced people, so that I would see the feelings that they had. Mrs. Gray [the worker] said that we all have these feelings—she *said* that—but I didn't know it for a fact. I never talked to anybody who had also gone through it.
>
> I had asked her [about a group] and I had gone to two places—one to the Y, the women's Y, which they had discontinued. But I felt the Y wasn't the place for it. I felt right *here* was the place for it. . . . At that time they didn't have it.

Mrs. Donnelly and other clients expressed, in one form or another, a need for various group services as extensions of the agency's formal counseling program. As Toffler argued in his discussion of "future shock," these clients showed that a variety of informal approaches are required to help people cope with natural life challenges in postindustrial society. One such approach involves the creation of "situational groups" providing mutual support for people who are passing through similar life transitions such as relocation, death of spouse or parent, divorce, or retirement (Toffler, 1970: 384). Since publication of Toffler's book, a growing number of such support systems has been emerging through the auspices of social agencies, self-help groups, or other organizations.

The findings of the present study, however, suggest that there is some reluctance on the part of practitioners to use these informal services or other resources in their clients' social networks as an integral part of treatment programs. One wonders why practitioners give less weight to social networks than clients do. The usual explanation that social networks are not as accessible to the workers as the client-worker relationship seems overly simplistic. In addition to this, it is likely that, as a result of their education and socialization into the profession, social workers tend to view intervention into the client's life situation as less effective or less prestigious than clinical forms of treatment. It may also be that practitioners are jealous of the role and influence of significant members of a client's network.

Whatever may be the reasons for the workers' views, the study's data, particularly those pertaining to the clients' views, reinforce the strong impact of social networks on human behavior that has been postulated by social scientists.[2] Other investigations have also shown that clients are influenced in their functioning and use of casework by members of their social networks (Mayer and Timms, 1970: 52-61; Sainsbury, 1975: 90). These findings, therefore, suggest that more systematic attention should be devoted to the potential use of social networks as instruments of help. Much has been accomplished in social work practice within the rubric of environmental manipulation or modification; but much more needs to be done so as to make more effective the use of people's natural social networks as instruments *of* help rather than simply as influences *on* help (Germain and Gitterman, 1976).

In the past few years, various theorists and practitioners in social work as well as related disciplines have made important contributions in this area.[3] Swenson (in press) has applied the concept of social network to the "life model" of social work practice, stressing in particular the dynamic and inter-related functions of social networks and self-help or mutual aid programs. Collins and Pancoast (1976) have written extensively about the nature and functioning of natural helping networks, which they describe as the "informal counterpart to organized social services." They have emphasized the tremendous potential of natural helping networks in social work practice, highlighting the significance of "central figures" found in many neighbor-hoods — people who play important helping roles, such as the school custodian, the beautician, the grocer, the mailman, and so on. Collins and Pancoast (1976: 29) have concluded that "productive relationships between social workers and these central figures can dramatically extend the effective reach of professional efforts.[4]

To exploit the potential of natural helping networks, practitioners need to become more active in developing closer linkages between the informal and formal helping systems. Both systems can play differential roles and make crucial contributions. Informal helpers, for example, can support agency clients in their efforts to make effective use of available services. Smolar (1976: 163-164) has observed that informal agents such as clergymen, teachers, or neighbors could be called upon to help in developing client confidence in existing programs and institutions. By the same token, professional practitioners can be instrumental in aiding clients to seek and use resources in their social networks. In this respect, it is noteworthy that in the present study many clients indicated that they had initially sought help from the Family Service Bureau because of dissatisfaction with or inade-quacies in their networks; after having been involved in treatment, however,

---

[2] See Bott (1957); Mayer and Rosenblatt (1964); and Mitchell (1969). In an empirical study, Tolsdorf (1976) demonstrated the importance of social networks in day-to-day life.

[3] See Caplan (1964); Collins and Pancoast (1976); Golner (1971); Speck and Attneave (1973); and Swenson (in press).

[4] See Gershon and Biller (1977) for a comprehensive review of mental health programs utilizing paraprofessional and nonprofessional helpers.

they reported more positive feelings toward significant members of their networks and toward the help that they had received from them. The suggestion was that, at least partly as a result of the service, they were better able to identify and/or use supports and resources available in their own environments.

LIFE EXPERIENCES AND EVENTS

In more than half of the cases, a variety of experiences and events in the client's life space were mentioned by clients and workers as possible factors influencing the client's functioning and the outcome of the service. Typical examples included:

work; job change; returning to old job; promotion or raise; reduction in overtime work

resuming college; college graduation; enrollment in "enrichment" courses

resuming or initiating cultural or recreational pursuits such as painting and athletics

involvement in volunteer activities in such settings as hospitals, youth agencies, or charitable organizations

changes in family functioning or structure—e.g., father no longer drinking or spouse leaving

Previous investigators have reported that social workers are less likely than clients to be aware of details about changes and events in the client's life situation (Beck and Jones, 1973: 15). No such difference was found in this study. Workers were generally well aware of what was going on in the client's life outside the office. However, there were other important differences. First, clients mentioned more of these factors in *positive* terms, whereas social workers mentioned more of them in *negative* terms. Second, where clients and workers concurred in viewing a particular life event or experience positively, the former tended to ascribe more significance than the latter to its impact on the client's functioning and on the outcome of the service. Comparative responses in several client-worker pairs illustrate these differences:

CASE OF MR. AND MRS. GATES

Mrs. Gates: I felt real good when they made me a supervisor after being there less than a year. You know, this made me want to go on and live my life, even though we had decided to get a divorce.

Worker: The promotion was a mixed blessing for Carol. It demonstrated that people thought highly of her, but it also put more pressure on her to perform . . . at a time when much of her energy was going into coping with the divorce.

CASE OF MR. AND MRS. FORT

Mr. Fort: For years I had been working overtime a lot of hours. When business went bad, they cut down my hours. . . . They thought I wouldn't like it but they did me a big favor. . . . Well, I began to spend more time with my wife. . . . We did more things together. . . . I was home more with the children. . . and that probably helped us more than anything else.

Worker: There were many things that helped them to change, like the fact that Mr. Fort began to work less hours. Also, Mrs. Fort threatened him. . . . She told him she would leave unless things changed. . . . I think the main thing that happened was that they really worked hard in treatment. . . . They really wanted to change.

CASE OF MR. AND MRS. MOSCA

Mr. Mosca: When I was promoted — almost unexpectedly — my life began to change. . . . Well, I felt better about myself, more positive toward my wife, more optimistic about our relationship and our future together. . . . Yes, we talked about it a little in counseling. . . . Both the counselor and my wife seemed to appreciate what I had accomplished.

Worker: Halfway through our contact, John got a job promotion. . . . That helped him to feel better and more optimistic. . . . However, we didn't talk much about the promotion or what was going on with his job. . . . This wasn't directly related to treatment goals, which had to do more with looking at himself and his relationship with his wife.

Several clients also spoke with great conviction about the value of their participation in volunteer activities:

Miss Appel: Another thing that helped me a lot was working at Crossroads [a crisis intervention center for young people]. I started to do that after seeing the counselor for a few months. Oh, oh, I wasn't sure I could do it. . . . She kept encouraging me and I finally volunteered. . . . You know, it was great. . . . Oh, I enjoyed talking with young people . . . helping them out. . . .

I felt kind of funny at first that I was going to be like a counselor. . . . And it really helped to bring me out. . . . Oh, it made me feel good . . . like I had something to give to other people!

Mrs. Donnelly: Well, I used to go to this orphanage and I used to cut these kids' hair. There were about twenty-five girls, and I used to go monthly and take care of them. I don't know if that helped me or not. Maybe it did because I saw them very emotionally upset there, and I said to myself: "I don't want to be that way." And I wonder if maybe that helped me, I don't know . . . but those kids—they talk to me, they write to me, which is really nice. I'm happy because I like to make friends there too.

In the excerpts just presented, as in other cases, workers also viewed the client's involvement in volunteer and other activities positively. For example, the workers talked about the client's enhanced self-image, the importance of getting positive feedback from significant others, and the meaning of successful experiences in various areas. But the workers in general did not feel that this was as important as whatever was happening within the context of the therapeutic process itself. As suggested in the earlier discussion of the client-worker relationship, workers may need to stress, for understandable reasons, their participation in the helping process as a means of explaining, justifying, or supporting their own contributions.

More than three decades ago, in discussing the role of extratherapeutic experiences in psychoanalysis, Franz Alexander (1946: 40) observed that the experience of success in significant activities encourages new trials and enhances the person's well-being:

> Successful attempts at productive work, love, self-assertion, or competition will change the vicious cycle to a benign one; as they are repeated, they become habitual and thus eventually bring about a complete change in the personality.

The findings of the present study support this notion; clients reported that they felt better and that they coped better as they became engaged in positive, rewarding life experiences. As underlined by ego psychologists (White, 1963) the human being grows through involvement in life experiences or activities providing task fulfillment, crisis resolution, and learning of social skills. Even in work with supposedly "unmotivated" or involuntary clients, it has been found that the experience of success can enhance personal well-being and encourage new trials: "by showing the client that change is possible . . . [the worker] lays the groundwork for subsequent successes, thus instilling hope" (Kirkland, 1977: 9).

TRIGGERING CHANGE

What is it that brings about positive change in a client's situation? What role does the service play in the change process? As I listened to the views of workers and especially of clients, I was struck by one point: over and over, there were indications that some aspect of the service—such as the worker's encouragement—triggered a chain of events that led the client to identify and/or use more effectively significant life experiences or resources in his or her environment. This was graphically illustrated by Mrs. Thompson's case:[5]

> Mrs. Thompson, a recently divorced middle-aged woman, had gone to the agency following frequent suicidal thoughts. She was described by the worker

[5] This example comes from one of the cases in the pilot phase of the study.

as an unhappy, withdrawn person with a long history of depression that had been reawakened by her former husband's abandonment and their subsequent divorce. For the previous seven years, she had been employed as a psychiatric aide in a large state hospital.

In the research interviews, both Mrs. Thompson and the worker indicated that in several of the initial sessions they talked extensively about her dissatisfaction with her job, especially her frustration and discouragement in working day after day with people suffering from chronic schizophrenia. With the worker's encouragement, Mrs. Thompson began to think about changing jobs and eventually applied at a flower shop advertising for a salesperson. She obtained this job and soon found great satisfaction in selling flowers, watching plants grow, and being surrounded by beauty.

In further sessions with the worker, she talked with feeling about her pleasure in making people happy, her eagerness to go to work in the morning, and her sense of satisfaction at the end of the day. While her underlying depression was still evident, there was no doubt that the new work environment was much more positive and rewarding for her than the psychiatric ward where each weekday for seven years she had previously encountered continuing reinforcement of her depression. As her environment changed and she began to feel better about herself, Mrs. Thompson not only continued in treatment but also showed a new readiness to work on other factors involved in her depression.

During the research interview, in considering reasons for the obvious improvement in her functioning, Mrs. Thomson stressed the fact that the worker's encouragement had made her feel that she could get another job and that in fact she was entitled to something more satisfying. She suggested that, without this encouragement and her improved self-confidence, she might never have been able to think about another job. In discussing this case, the worker also recognized the connection between the job change and Mrs. Thompson's improved functioning. Although she had not explicitly viewed a change in employment as a treatment goal, she realized that treatment sessions had helped Mrs. Thompson to feel better about herself and to become more assertive in seeking a better life.

In Mrs. Thompson's case, social work intervention helped to set in motion a process that enabled her to seek and eventually to find a *new environment* that was better suited to her needs and therefore promoted her coping and adaptation (Hartmann, 1958: 27). In turn, her improved functioning and self-image enabled her to continue making use of treatment.

There were many other clients for whom involvement in social work services had a similar triggering effect. Some of them were quoted in earlier sections of this chapter: those who, through encouragement from the worker, sought new friends or reestablished ties with old friends; those who worked through some of their feelings so that they could go on to develop more satisfying relationships with their parents or other family members; those who gained a real sense of accomplishment and satisfaction as they became involved in meaningful volunteer activities while in treatment; and the woman who began to function better as the worker intervened in her job situation by helping her supervisor to understand what she was going through.

In these instances, as in many others, it appeared that, as a consequence of client-worker interaction, the person was helped in ways such as the following: becoming freer to reach out to others, to use available resources, to act positively on his or her needs; modifying his or her attitudes toward others and interacting with significant others in a manner that elicited more positive feedback; and enhancing his or her hope and motivation for change. In many cases, it seemed that clients had acquired new or improved "techniques of effective living" (Strupp, Fox, and Lessler, 1969: 136). In essence, the worker and/or the service served as a catalyst triggering a train of events that ultimately resulted in the client being helped. Workers, however, were not uniformly aware of their positive impact on clients or of the triggering effect of their intervention. Through further research, it would therefore be important to explore more intensely the various sequences in the change process and to derive pertinent practice implications.

In short, the findings show that life experiences, events, and processes can be exploited to provide more effective help. As I have discussed in further detail elsewhere (Maluccio, in press, a), life itself can be viewed as the arena of change. Life experiences can be used to promote the client's competence, facilitate his or her adaptive strivings, and achieve his or her goals. Life transitions, life tasks, and new social roles can provide opportunities for personal growth. Furthermore, human problems, needs, and conflicts can be translated into adaptive tasks providing the client with opportunities for mastery and competence.[6]

The findings also suggest that the client's social environment can be restructured, that is, substantially modified, to promote his or her adaptive strivings and to make better use of natural resources in his or her social networks. While workers in this study were aware of the role of life experiences and social networks in their clients' lives, it was clear that they did not pay as much attention or attribute as much significance to these aspects as clients did.

It was striking that workers said very little in the research interviews about situational intervention, despite increasing emphasis on this in the field as a whole (Siporin, 1972; Siporin, 1975: 302-310; Turner, 1978). The workers talked much more extensively about the therapeutic role of the client-worker relationship than the importance of situational intervention, even though there was evidence that they had used the latter modality. Furthermore, as noted in Chapter 5, workers appeared to be doubtful or apologetic about their involvement in activities outside of the office. Other researchers have also found that there is at best limited worker satisfaction with activities such as brokerage, referral, and advocacy (Rubenstein and Bloch, 1978).

---

[6] For discussion of practice guidelines in using life experiences and activities in social work practice, see Maluccio (1974) and Maluccio (in press, a).

It is obvious that significant resources, changes, and events in the client's impinging environment can have a positive or negative impact on the client's functioning and use of social work services or other treatment programs. In many cases, the helping process could become more effective if the client's life situation were more accessible to the practitioner and if the latter focused on this aspect more systematically and deliberately. As one means of facilitating this approach to interpersonal helping, it is increasingly imperative that practitioners move out of the narrow confines of the office setting and station themselves, as Reynolds (1934) proposed long ago, at the "crossroads of life," that is, at locations such as the workplace, the school, and the neighborhood, where human beings intersect naturally with societal systems and institutions.[7]

[7] See Meyer (1976: 75-79) and Reynolds (1934) for elaboration of this point. In her classic formulation of the functions of casework in the community, Reynolds (1934: 110) observed that this method "is concerned with relating men and women and children to life, and seeks first to understand where they are in adjustment to their own life aims and social group."

Chapter 10

The Agency Environment

It has long been recognized that an agency's environment influences the nature and quality of the services provided by its staff. By "environment" is meant not only the physical setting but also such aspects as purpose and sanction, regulations and procedures, and social climate or atmosphere.

In the problem-solving approach to social work, Perlman has defined the "place" in which the service is offered as a basic component of the casework situation. In the psychosocial tradition, Hollis (1972) and Turner (1978) are among those who have indicated that the agency setting should be viewed as an important part of the therapeutic process. In addition, the role of the agency setting has been emphasized even more strongly in the functional approach. Thus, Smalley (1967: 151) has enunciated the following as one of five generic practice principles:

> The use of agency function . . . gives focus, content, and direction to social work processes, assures accountability to society and to agency, and provides the partialization, the concreteness . . . which further productive engagement.

Although the significance of the agency context as a component of treatment has been noted, the specific nature and extent of its influence have not been understood clearly or considered fully. As Turner (1978: 170–171)[1] has observed, practitioners hold different attitudes about the importance of the agency setting:

> At one extreme is the viewpoint that holds that the process is the critical variable, while the setting is a necessary but noninfluencing factor. . . . At the other extreme is the viewpoint that the setting is far from a neutral factor and cannot be ignored . . . and that therefore . . . [it] must be viewed as an important part of the therapeutic process and hence should be examined, evaluated, and utilized in a planned way.

In light of these divergent opinions, in the present study it seems especially appropriate to examine clients' and workers' views regarding the role of the agency environment in the helping process.

[1] Turner (1978: Chapter 8) has comprehensively analyzed the significant components of the agency setting, such as location and accessibility, and their impact on practice.

In contrast to workers, clients had much to say about the environment of the agency, in response to such questions as the following:

What did you think about the agency as a whole?

What did you think about agency policies and regulations?

Workers, on the other hand, either offered few comments in this area or minimized the significance of the environment.

The responses of clients and workers relate to the following:

1. The "social" environment—that is, agency staff, social climate or atmosphere, and so on.
2. The "physical" environment—that is, location, appearance, condition of the building, and so on.
3. The "operational" environment—that is, agency policies, procedures, regulations, and so on.

"SOCIAL" ENVIRONMENT

Over two-thirds of the clients offered positive comments about the agency's social environment or climate. Some typical remarks were:

> We got a very warm reception.
>
> Everyone was friendly.
>
> Very pleasant people.
>
> They were all ready to help you.
>
> The lady at the front desk was so pleasant.
>
> Mary [the receptionist] made you feel at home.
>
> The people are so nice, especially the lady downstairs [the receptionist].
>
> They always seemed so glad to see me.
>
> You didn't feel like a cog in a wheel.

Several more detailed quotes from clients follow:

Miss Kraft: It was good the way they handled it. Well, you didn't have to go through a lot of rigmarole like in a hospital. You didn't have to talk to many different people . . . fill out a thousand forms. . . . You didn't have to wait forever to see the counselor once you got there. They made you feel good. . . . They were paying attention just to you.

Miss Becker: It was a friendly place. . . . After going there a few times, I got to know Mary [the receptionist]. . . . She and I never talked about my problems . . . but she was very friendly. . . . She was always glad to see me . . . and it made me feel so good that after a while I didn't mind going there.

Mrs. Donnelly: The waiting room when you first go in—I thought that was excellent. You know, being in my own business, we have a lot of people we have to contend with and sometimes it is hard to control them. But here, the fact that they have the waiting room . . . They have things to do, which is good—you know, it calmed people down a little bit before they went upstairs. . . .

They were very, very nice, especially the girl at the desk when you first go in. In fact, when she called me [to ask about participation in the study], I remembered everything right away and I said, "I know who this is!" and she said, "Yup," she says, "I'm from the Bureau." Oh, I recognized her voice because I talked to her on the phone before and she has a very friendly voice. She is a very, very likable person and she's just the receptionist. You see, right there, it's like they have an open door. . . . If I had gotten a cold feeling, I probably wouldn't have gone upstairs or never finished.

Miss Appel: In the beginning I wondered why they were always so nice to me . . . why everyone I met in the hall smiled at me. . . . I thought that maybe they felt bad for me . . . but then I realized that they really liked me . . . especially the woman at the front desk.

Even people who were dissatisfied with the service or its outcome had favorable impressions of the agency as a whole. For example, one of the clients who dropped out said:

Mrs. Norton: They were very nice, not like other places I've been to. In my life I've been to a lot of welfare places and hospitals where you feel like they don't want to talk to you nohow. . . . Here they treat you like a real person . . . like someone who has feelings. . . . They don't act like you're there just because it's free.

As with other dissatisfied clients, Mrs. Norton had a positive impression of the agency's social climate, even though this was not sufficient to counteract her disappointment in not having her expectations met.

As seen in the above excerpts, clients expressed a variety of favorable comments about the agency's staff and climate. A recurring theme was the clients' comparison of the agency with other community systems such as hospitals and welfare agencies; clients contrasted the agency's warm climate with the impersonal or dehumanizing quality of larger bureaucratic organizations. Other key themes pertained to the friendliness of staff members, their readiness to be of help, and the feeling that clients were regarded as individuals.

Workers, on the other hand, had little to say about the agency's social environment, frequently indicating that they had not considered its meaning for clients or discussed it with them. The only exception was in relation to the receptionist: most workers brought out that she played a significant role with clients and that clients often commented positively about her. Perhaps practitioners in general tend to take the agency's environment for granted.

ROLE OF THE RECEPTIONIST

As suggested in some of the above quotes, most clients singled out the receptionist as a prominent member of the agency's staff. They pointed in particular to their pleasure in knowing her and their feeling comfortable in relating to her. As explained in Chapter 3, at the time of the study the receptionist was a warm and caring person who related easily and spontaneously to people and who was very effective in meeting clients and making them feel at home. Her work area was located directly across from the waiting room, facilitating interaction between her and the clients while they were waiting for their appointments. Many clients felt that she was very interested in them and that they could talk easily with her about such matters as current events or, in a few instances, about some of the changes and experiences in their lives from week to week.

Moreover, as indicated by Mrs. Donnelly in one of the excerpts above, quite a few clients explained that they readily decided to participate in the study when the receptionist called them about it. As one of them put it: "Mary had been so nice to me. How could I say no to her? . . . Well, I knew I could trust her." Thus, the receptionist influenced the decision of some clients to participate in the study, and perhaps also the quality of their responses in research interviews.

In general, clients demonstrated a high level of acceptance of the receptionist. As these findings imply, the role played by the receptionist in the helping process demands further attention. It is obvious that, in entering a new system such as a social agency, an applicant or client forms initial impressions that can influence his or her attitudes toward the service. Yet, as various authors have suggested, receptionists at times are set up in such a way as to be barriers to service (Cumming, 1968: 115). Others have observed that the receptionist or secretary in a mental health setting is an essential part of the success or failure of the program:

> Secretaries are forced by necessity to function as part of the therapeutic team in community mental health centers. They talk first with prospective patients, family, and interested members of the community on the phone. They often see the patient and family first, and must obtain detailed information about the patient. The secretaries usually make and change appointments, handle fee dispositions, and transact with the patients and family in the waiting room (Nyman, Watson, and James, 1973: 368).

Despite the significance accorded to the functions of the receptionist or secretary, very little empirical research has been carried out in this area. In one of the few available studies, Hall (1974) carefully analyzed the reception process in several British social agencies. He concluded that receptionists have a marked impact on the delivery of services, since they perform a variety of functions, including: (1) being the first point of contact with the agency at the time of the initial interview; (2) offering support and encouragement through their informal relationship with the clien'.; and (3) acting as the client's advocate or controlling the client's access to the social work staff (Hall, 1974: 124-128). The evidence from Hall's study confirmed that "one of the many elements which may affect decisions about who receives what services is the person who looks after the telephone or sits behind the reception desk" (p. 139).

The roles of the receptionist and other staff members such as secretaries should therefore be examined and developed more systematically as a part of the agency's services. An agency may consider how to enrich the reception process and maximize its potentially positive impact. Training programs may be introduced to facilitate the integration of receptionists or secretaries into the therapeutic team (Nyman, Watson, and James, 1973). Ways may be found to enhance the roles of the cadre of clerical and maintenance staff, which is often an underused resource in various agencies:

> Usually, it is one of the secretarial staff to whom a client first speaks. If indeed the helping process does begin at this point, then it is essential that this first contact be a facilitative one. I have often thought that some of our most effective crisis managers have been our unrecognized receptionists and switch-board operators (Turner, 1978: 188).

IMPACT OF AGENCY'S SECTARIAN AFFILIATION

Another important component of the agency's social environment was its sectarian affiliation. Nearly half of the clients made reference to this aspect through comments such as:

> I went there because it's part of the Church.

> They helped me even though I'm not Catholic.

> They're guided by religion.

> It was better to be in a place that's Catholic.

> They understand better because they are a Catholic organization.

> Being a Catholic society, they're not out to make a profit.

Most of the comments about the religious affiliation reflected a positive view of the agency as an extension of the church. Thus, the agency's religious affiliation was another factor that influenced some people to become involved with it, to use the service, and to have positive expectations from it. For instance, as noted in Chapter 4 in connection with discussion of the referral process, some clients indicated that they chose the Family Service Bureau specifically because they felt more comfortable in a Catholic setting. As implied in some of the above quotes, these clients expected that in such an environment they would be better understood and more effectively helped. As Mrs. Mosca suggested, for some clients their identification of the agency and the worker as members of their reference group facilitated their becoming engaged in treatment:

> At first I wasn't clear why he was asking some of these questions about our life together. . . . Not that they were strange questions. . . . Well, they were private matters between me and my husband. . . . But I didn't mind so much, being that this was a Catholic place. . . . I figured they know what they're doing.

The clients' comments about the meaning of the agency's religious affiliation support Jerome Frank's (1974) thesis that human beings bring to the helping situation a variety of expectations and attitudes that may be mobilized in the process of healing. This is particularly true when the helping person is viewed by the client as a member of his or her reference group:

> Despite the stubbornness of maladaptive attitudes, the psychotherapist, as a socially sanctioned expert and healer and a *member of the patients' reference groups,* may be able to mobilize forces sufficiently powerful to produce beneficial changes in them" (Frank, 1974: 45) (italics mine).

In other cases, the Bureau's religious affiliation or the client's related expectations interfered with the helping process. Mrs. Talcott, for example, had gone to the agency wanting to "save my marriage at all costs," and was shocked when the worker mentioned the possibility of a divorce in joint sessions with her and her husband. She soon withdrew. In the research interview, she expressed her firm conviction that a Catholic agency should help couples to reconcile by emphasizing that divorce is contrary to church teachings. Mrs. Talcott could not understand why, in her view, the worker not only did not try to do this but openly presented separation or divorce as one of the alternatives for consideration in the course of treatment. The discrepancy between Mrs. Talcott's expectations and the worker's response contributed to their mutual frustration and her premature withdrawal from the service.

Other clients, as will be seen later in this chapter, equated payment of a fee for the service with the need to sacrifice in order to get help and improve one's situation. In these instances, there was the suggestion that the agency's religious aura played into the clients' feelings of guilt and need to atone for their sins through suffering or sacrifice.

In contrast to the clients, practitioners rarely referred to the agency's religious affiliation and its possible positive or negative impact on client expectations and the course and outcome of treatment. It is likely that workers did not attribute special significance to the sectarian component because the agency serves persons of all denominations; in accordance with stated agency policy, workers are expected to practice their profession freely and to avoid imposing their own values on clients.

The clients' responses suggest, however, that the agency's sectarian affiliation did have a special meaning for them that may have affected the helping process. In this agency setting, as in others, the sponsorship under which an organization operates should be appreciated as one of the factors influencing the client's use of treatment as well as the worker's involvement. Perhaps the most crucial point here is that an agency's affiliation or sponsorship can have different ramifications for different clients. Furthermore, a client's image or expectations of an agency may be quite different from those of the worker. In other words, the diverse value orientations of clients affect their perception of the agency and, in turn, the therapeutic process:

> Because of these value differences, some clients will be able to relate to certain settings more easily than others, depending on their view of significant others and their perception of and comfort with the process of seeking help outside their own significant network (Turner, 1978: 176).

By being attuned to the particular meaning of the setting and its sponsorship to a given client, practitioners are better able to deal with the client's expectations and values and their influence on the helping process.

"PHYSICAL" ENVIRONMENT

As practitioners and theorists have increasingly realized in recent years,[2] the agency's physical environment is another feature that may affect client-worker interaction.

In giving their impressions of the agency as a whole, at least two-thirds of the clients offered remarks about the physical setting. Most of these were negative comments about the location and physical appearance of the agency, the size and condition of the waiting room and offices, and the lack of parking. These comments came from satisfied as well as dissatisfied respondents. It may be that some persons found it easier to criticize the physical environment than the workers or other staff members with whom they had developed a personal relationship.

Some typical remarks about the physical setting were:

Location	Appearance	Office
I was leery about going there.	An old building.	Tiny offices . . . I felt closed in.
Parking very bad.	Looks like it needs a coat of paint.	Office looked cold; no rug or pictures.
Didn't like going to the area.	Physical surroundings terrible.	Office small. . . . Oh,
Hard to get there.	Looked rundown.	just a desk and a

---

[2] See Germain (1976); Seabury (1971); and Turner (1978).

Location	Appearance	Office
Not greatest location in the world.	Very plain sur- roundings.	few chairs. Office seemed empty.

All of these comments pertained to the main office of the agency, which was located in an area of the inner city awaiting redevelopment. The location was more accessible to city residents than to suburban residents, who constituted a substantial proportion of the clientele. At the time of the study, several buildings around the agency's office had been torn down. The clients' negative evaluation of the physical surroundings was not exaggerated. The building was indeed in poor shape. Since the agency was due to move even-tually to another location, it may be that the administration was reluctant to invest in extensive maintenance or renovation.

Most clients in the study sample had been involved with the main office. The few clients who had been seen at the agency's small suburban branch of-fice were pleased with the location and "homey" atmosphere of the office but dissatisfied with the lack of privacy. They explained that the office was located in a converted large house along with other professional offices and that there was no waiting room. In addition, they feared that their discussion with the worker could be overheard in the next room.

While declaring their dissatisfaction with the quality of the physical en-vironment in the main office, over one-third of the clients also proceeded to explain it as something they had expected in view of the agency's nonprofit status and its identity as a charitable organization. Some representative remarks follow:

Mrs. Mosca: It was poorly kept, an old building, but that's what you can ex-pect for this type of agency. . . . You know, a charitable agency. They can't have a fancy place or location.

Mrs. Gates: As a subsidized agency, it's always working on a minimal budget. They can't afford really adequate facilities.

Mrs. Crompton: The building isn't too appealing. . . . It's very plain . . . . Well, you know, they can't do much about that, since the fact of the matter is that most people who go there are poor, elderly, or on welfare. . . . They couldn't afford to pay for anything more elaborate.

One wonders how the helping process was influenced by the client's negative views about the physical environment of the agency or perception of it as an organization for the poor or those on welfare. The clients in the three excerpts above were middle-class persons who suggested that they had selected the Family Service Bureau at least partly because they could not af-ford more expensive treatment from other sources such as private practi-tioners. In general, they reported that they were satisfied with the service and its outcome. While these clients were concerned about inadequacies in the agency's physical environment, in the long run this factor did not seem to matter to them enough to affect the outcome. For one thing, as with most other middle-class respondents, they tended to disassociate themselves from the charity cases, which they perceived as constituting the bulk of the clientele. Mrs. Lodano, for instance, was one of the suburban residents who questioned whether she belonged in this particular agency, although she and her husband had found the service to be very helpful:

> Well, oh. . . . Someone from the suburbs usually wouldn't go there. . . . We couldn't afford anything else at the time. . . . Oh, I felt a little odd whenever we met someone who was obviously poor in the waiting room. . . . My husband felt like me. . . . We didn't really belong there. Those people had more serious problems. . . . They were really poor.

I asked Mrs. Lodano and several other clients why they continued with the service and why they found it effective despite their strong negative feelings regarding the physical setting. In response, they generally referred to their strong attachment to their worker and conviction that he or she was helpful. It appeared that other variables, such as the worker's competence and the strength of the client-worker relationship, counteracted the potentially negative influence of the agency's physical environment.

Other clients, from diverse socioeconomic backgrounds, felt even more strongly about the environment and noted ways in which it affected the helping process. For example, after expressing his understanding that realistically the agency had limited resources, Mr. Mosca stressed the significance of adequate facilities:

> I don't know if they can afford it, but they should do something about the physical surroundings. The only thing I could hope for would be to have the facility in a decent location. . . . The physical setup makes an impression on people. . . . I think they could do a better job if the facilities are improved. . . . People would feel better about going there. . . . Well, maybe the counselors themselves would feel better.

Some respondents suggested that certain qualities of the physical environment affected the way they felt about themselves:

Miss Becker: I liked the location because it was close to my job . . . but the building was something else. They should do something about it . . . fix it up a little bit. . . . You know, it made me feel worse about myself, because I couldn't afford anything better. If they changed it, maybe the social workers would like it better.

Various clients who had been in treatment elsewhere also compared their workers' offices unfavorably with those of their former psychiatrists or private social work practitioners. Mrs. Donnelly was especially critical of the office:

> I thought that initial time when she says hello is good. . . . She shakes your hand or she shows some sign of affection. . . . Then you go in the

room and the room is completely different from what she's showing you. You know, and it's cold and . . . it was kind of hard, but I felt, well, they didn't have the money because it was an association. . . . It was affiliated with the church and it was just a sideline for the church. That's why I overlooked it. I didn't realize that it was that important until I sat here and in Mr. Smith's office and then remembered what his office looked like.

In Mrs. Donnelly's case, she and the worker at first found it very difficult to become engaged with each other, partly because, as discussed in Chapter 8, there had been a strong transference reaction in her relationship with the therapist in private practice. In a sense, through her negative evaluation of the office, Mrs. Donnelly seemed to be conveying her continuing feeling that the private practitioner was better than the one at the Bureau. As she went on with the latter worker, Mrs. Donnelly eventually felt that she had been helped, and both she and the worker expressed satisfaction with the service. But at the same time there were indications that the size and appearance of the office contributed to Mrs. Donnelly's sense of discomfort and inability to relax for several sessions, especially in the beginning phase.

Over one-fourth of the clients were similarly critical of the size and appearance of the worker's office. As the following quotes illustrate, they expressed concern about the influence of the office on the helping process:

Mr. Crompton: The office was small and very crowded. You know, whenever my wife and I went in together, it was hard even to move around. . . . Well, we laughed about it. . . . I don't think that the office has a lot to do with counseling, but I felt strange in there. . . . Oh, I kept thinking that maybe I should go somewhere with better offices. . . . Sometimes we wasted time talking or thinking about the office.

Miss Moore: The room was very small—just a desk and some chairs. The social worker put in some plants and tried to make it homey . . . but it was still an office. . . . The room looked empty, like I felt for quite a while. . . . Sometimes, well, it made it hard to get going.

In contrast, a few clients responded positively to physical features such as the small size of the office:

Mrs. Crompton: The place was not what I had expected. It was sort of plain. . . . The office was very tiny, with just enough room for a desk and three chairs. That was good. . . . It made you feel like you didn't have to pretend. . . . If there had been a lot more in the office, you might have looked at the other things. . . . It might have distracted you.

In light of the many critical remarks about the office, practitioners should be more sensitive to its meaning for the particular clients. At the same time, administrators as well as practitioners should consider ways of improving the office and the messages that it conveys to clients. Mrs. Donnelly made some suggestions along these lines:

> Um . . . I think I would change . . . the room, the colors, you know, put things on the wall to make it feel like it could be a house. Or, maybe, a lamp or something which you would see in a house. Um . . . I would make it not so cold.

While these suggestions are rather obvious, social workers seem hesitant to implement them. It appears that "we . . . fail to make use of the information available from others on the effects of color, lighting, furniture arrangement, and amenities on providing the kind of setting that is desired" (Turner, 1978: 193).

Our reluctance in this area may be due to more than the realistic factor of limited financial resources. Before making a substantial improvement in regard to the office or other features of the agency's physical environment, we may need to change some of our underlying attitudes. For example, since historically most social agencies have been developed to meet the needs of the poor, we as social workers may still be preoccupied with the value of parsimony and ambivalent about providing comfortable physical facilities for our clients—and for ourselves. Furthermore, we may not fully appreciate the impact of the physical setting on the helping process, because of our traditional emphasis on other components such as the client-worker relationship:

> It is so easy to be comfortable with the familiar that we fail to appreciate how our setting is seen by others or how it affects them. . . . It appears that often we are prepared to overestimate our ability to develop and maintain a therapeutic relationship and to underestimate the usefulness, knowledge, and experience of interior decorators (Turner, 1978: 192-193).

The findings discussed thus far were drawn from the majority of clients who were satisfied with the service. The indication is that the physical setting has a differential impact on clients, depending on such factors as their personality and expectations, the quality of the client-worker relationship, and the degree of satisfaction with the service. This is also evident in the views of dissatisfied clients. Several did not say anything about the environment or indicated that they paid little attention to it:

Mrs. Cain: I don't know about the agency's setup. . . . Well, it's not easy to be aware of your surroundings when there are other things on your mind that are so paramount. . . . Maybe now if I went in there I might see things or react to the place differently, but I don't think that I was really looking for that kind of thing at that time.

Mrs. Norton: I never paid much attention to the agency. . . . You know, I was more concerned with my problems.

Other dissatisfied clients, like the following, had strong feelings about the physical environment:

Mrs. Bates: Oh, I have nothing to say about the people. . . . You know, the people were all very polite from the time I called and so on. . . . Oh, the location and the agency itself. . . . It is in a very bad section of town where we had evening appointments and you are leery of going there — of going in and out of the building at night in that section of town. . . .

The building itself, like I say . . . the first impression — it is a very dreary building and it does give you a kind of creepy feeling when you're *already* creepy when you're going for help, you know. . . . You're leery, wondering what to expect and when that is what you're confronted with — a dreary place — I think it has a little bit of effect on you.

For some of these clients, the physical environment was apparently another source of dissatisfaction that reinforced or supported their negative attitudes toward the service, the worker, or the agency. These clients' negative perception of the value of the agency may have hastened their premature or unplanned termination.

Workers were aware that clients might have feelings about the agency's physical environment, particularly its location. In general, however, they indicated that they rarely discussed this topic in treatment sessions and that it was something about which they were not likely to get feedback. Several workers suggested that they were so used or resigned to the agency's physical condition that they paid little attention to it. Others noted that they were tolerating the poor physical facilities in anticipation of the agency's move to better quarters. In addition, some workers' comments reflected their conviction that the physical environment is not as important as the personal relationship with the worker. As one of them put it:

As with most people, Joyce didn't think about the agency, but about me as the worker. Well, . . . maybe the physical environment made some impression on her initially — but, as we went on, there was no indication that it mattered to her.

But the issue of the impact of the physical environment on the helping process and its outcome should not be glossed over. Most clients remarked about it, although their responses reflected a variety of views. Moreover, it is noteworthy that for many clients the poor quality of the physical environment accentuated the stigma of going to this particular agency, which they already perceived as a setting for poor or lower-class clients. This evidence supports the assertion that "space, design and decoration in our agency settings communicate messages about their status and worth to users of service and affect self-esteem and psychic comfort" (Germain, 1976: 20).

In view of these results, it is surprising to find that little attention has been devoted to this matter through research or writing, especially within social work:

Even though, conceptually and historically, emphasis has been placed on the effects of physical settings on psychosocial behavior, it is remarkable that the literature on this critical topic is almost non-existent. This absence of data is even more interesting when it is known that there are indeed many data available from other fields, such as industry (Turner, 1978: 191).

There has been limited consideration of the agency's physical environment in basic social work texts (Hollis, 1972: Siporin, 1975).

Yet, the findings of environmental psychologists and others demonstrate that the physical environment is a significant determinant of human behavior.[3] Through his naturalistic research, Barker (1968) has highlighted the unique properties of "behavior settings"—such as a social agency—and their influence on the functioning of human beings operating within them. Moos (1976) has imaginatively analyzed a range of environmental determinants of behavior, including physical space, building design, and social climate. Ittelson, Proshansky, and Rivlin (1970) have shown that the physical setting is one of the major variables contributing to the effectiveness of therapeutic programs in a psychiatric hospital.

In one of the few pertinent studies conducted by social workers, Seabury (1971) analyzed the physical setting in six different social work agencies, ranging from a private practitioner's office to a large public welfare center. He found that there were different space arrangements in such areas as waiting rooms and interviewing offices. The various physical patterns conveyed different messages to clients. Although both the family service agency and the public welfare center were large, bureaucratic organizations, the latter had a distant and dehumanizing atmosphere, while the former conveyed a sense of cheerfulness, comfort, and warmth. Similarly, the hospital social service department presented a most unpleasant appearance, while private offices and private agencies seemed most comfortable. As a result of this evidence, Seabury (1971: 48) speculated that "there is a distinct relationship between the arrangement and atmosphere of a setting and the class of clientele."

Seabury further stressed that the optimal arrangements of the physical setting in any agency should be based on its functions and the needs of its clients. At the present time, however, there are few guidelines to assist agencies in this effort. Consequently, it has been proposed that social workers collaborate with other professionals such as architects to improve service delivery.[4] Further research in this area is essential to clarify the specific role that the environment of an agency may play in treatment, and to devise ways of maximizing the positive impact of the physical setting.

"OPERATIONAL" ENVIRONMENT

In giving their impressions about the agency as a whole, clients also commented extensively about the agency's policies, regulations, and procedures,

[3] An excellent collection of research studies in environmental psychology is that of Proshansky, Ittelson, and Rivlin (1970).
[4] See Wittman and Wittman (1976).

particularly the scheduling of appointments and the charging of fees. Nearly half of them expressed some dissatisfaction with the scheduling of appointments, manifesting a desire for greater flexibility in respect to frequency, duration, and location of counseling sessions.

USE OF TIME

A number of clients raised questions about the duration and frequency of interviews. Two representative comments follow:

Mrs. Gates: Maybe they should see less people per day. In some meetings I remember that the discussion was hot — you and the counselor were really going good — and then the darn phone rings and it's time for her next appointment. She would continue for a little while longer but then had to end. You know, I don't blame her . . . she had other people waiting. . . . The next week she would start with where you left off . . . but by then it was hard to remember.

Mr. Crompton: Sometimes one hour wasn't long enough. . . . A few times I felt cheated, because we were talking about something pretty important and then suddenly it was time to go.

Suggestions from clients included having more evening hours, allowing for longer sessions occasionally, and having more than one session during each week when necessary. The clients' responses suggest that, as postulated by Lennard and Bernstein (1969: 23), scheduling of sessions is a formal contextual feature of the client-worker interactional environment. The way it is handled in each client situation may influence the quality and outcome of the helping process.

In contrast, workers offered few comments in the area of scheduling, except for the recognition that for some clients it would be helpful to have more evening hours to accommodate people who are employed during the day. It was evident that workers were accustomed to the traditional hour or fifty-minute period that, through the influence of psychoanalysis, has become the prototype for all interviews by social workers, psychologists, psychiatrists, and others engaged in interpersonal helping (Aldrich, 1966: 341-342). Rigid adherence to the fifty-minute hour is strongly defended by psychoanalysts and some psychiatrists for therapeutic as well as pragmatic reasons. For instance, in supporting the use of a regular time allotment for therapy, Menninger (1958: 39-40) has observed:

> The hour is our time unit in general use, perhaps because it does involve some kind of natural span . . . and is a feasible unit fitting into the working day. While there have been many experiments of speeding up analytic sessions to two a day or increasing the length to two hours at one session, no such practice has generally taken hold.

Although more recently there has been experimentation with marathon sessions and flexible scheduling, the fifty-minute hour continues to reign supreme.

Unlike psychoanalysis, in fields such as social work there is usually some flexibility in scheduling of appointments, in recognition of the different needs and qualities of people seeking help. The responses of clients in this study suggest the need for even more flexibility in this area. As Turner (1978: 58) has explained, workers should reexamine their reliance on the once-a-week, one-hour contact as the norm:

> Not every client can tolerate a one-hour interview, while some persons can function effectively in a two or three-hour interview. Some people need a week between interviews to make maximal use of the interview process; others get more benefit out of a more frequent type of interview. Clearly, some of the variables that affect these differences are the level of internal stress, frustration tolerance, intellectual ability, physical condition, and the type and nature of service and problem.

HOME VISITS

At least one-fourth of the clients commented about the locale of interviews, indicating that home visits would have been desirable at least occasionally, while only one worker remarked about the value of home visits. There seems to be a difference in clients' and workers' perspectives on home visits, as seen in the following example:

CASE OF MISS BARNES

Client: The place is far from my home. . . . It's hard to get there . . . especially with the baby. . . . You know, sometimes I would get going so late that I would have to cancel. . . . Oh, maybe they should come out to the house sometimes . . . when you can't make it to the office. . . . I never asked her about it. . . . Well, I didn't think they could do it.

Worker: When she canceled office appointments so often I thought of home visits. . . . I didn't do it, feeling that she didn't want me to go to her home. . . . She seemed to be more comfortable coming to the office. . . . Besides, there was no privacy at her home.

Although the value of the home visit for diagnostic or therapeutic purposes has long been recognized in social work (Hollis, 1972: 257–258), practitioners may be reluctant to use it because of logistics (e.g., lack of privacy or excessive time required) or because it does not have as much prestige as clinical activities in the office.

FEES

Clients from the lower socioeconomic group said very little about fees. Most middle-class clients, however, spoke positively about the Bureau's system of charging service fees on a sliding scale, describing it as reasonable and appropriate. Several suggested that paying a fee contributed to their satisfaction and self-image and to their use of help:

Mrs. Donnelly: I think it's good, I really do. . . . Because if you didn't pay a fee, you wouldn't be as attentive. For some reason, when people pay for things, they respect them more and they try to do what's right. But if we just went in for free, I don't think that would help. . . . I know, cause I've had that experience dealing with the public myself. When you give them something free, it didn't mean nothing. When they pay three dollars, four dollars, or five dollars — *wow!* — they'd say *that stayed in good*, or, *I didn't like it.* They have some initial respect for what their money was spent for.

Miss Appel: Paying something is good . . . even though I could only afford two dollars weekly. . . . It's more like it's yours. Maybe it has to do with charity, but with me paying it, it made me feel like I was doing something on my own. It made me feel more independent.

Mr. Crompton: You should pay something. If you're interested enough, you should make some sacrifice. When you go to a doctor, you have to pay. I felt good about paying. It gives you a sense of pride because you're not begging, you're not getting something for nothing.

Apparently, clients responded to the fee, as to other aspects of the service, on the basis of their own needs and qualities, but in general viewed it as a worthwhile thing. In many cases, the ability to pay a fee signified the person's active participation in the problem-solving process and contributed to his or her sense of competence and self-worth. The clients' responses also reflected the importance placed on money in our society, and the presumed relationship between the quality of a service and the amount paid for it.

In addition, the payment of fees enabled some of the clients in the middle socioeconomic group to separate themselves from the charity cases that they associated with the Family Service Bureau, and thus to deal with the stigma that they felt. For others, the fee symbolized the sacrifice that they expected they should make as a condition of getting help. In this regard, they seemed to be reflecting professional as well as cultural values and expectations. As a leading psychoanalyst has noted, there is the belief in psychiatry that "the analysis will not go well if the patient is paying less than he can reasonably afford to pay. It should be a definite sacrifice for him, for *him* and not for someone else" (Menninger, 1958: 32) (italics by author).

Social workers in the study also commented about the positive value of the fee and their impression that clients were receptive to it. But, as with other aspects of the agency environment, they indicated that they rarely discussed the fee or the client's views about it, except in initially setting it or in the few situations in which the client later brought it up because of financial problems.

In psychiatry, fee charging has been extensively considered and strongly defended as a sine qua non of effective therapy (Menninger, 1958: 32-36). In social work, in contrast, there has been very little examination of this issue for various reasons: the limited number of social workers in private practice; the historical development of social work as a profession committed to the poor; and the ideological controversy over the role of fees in the provision of social services. The views of social workers have ranged from the conviction that social agencies should provide services free of charge to the belief that everyone should pay on a sliding scale (Goodman, 1971). There is empirical evidence that clients are willing to pay a fee, while social workers are concerned about the appropriateness of fee-charging (Shireman, 1975).

While the controversy over fees has been with us for a while, there has been very little about it in the social work literature. This is now likely to change, however, as a result of the recent emergence of private practice as a growing component of social work programs (National Association of Social Workers, 1974). Gradually, there will probably be greater acceptance of fees in the field as a whole. At the present time, it is incumbent on practitioners to pay more attention to the issue of fees and their significance for particular clients.

INTERVENTIVE MODALITIES

As indicated in the preceding chapter, some clients expressed a need for interventive modalities other than individual or family counseling. Particularly noted by clients was the potential value of therapy groups and various group services as extensions of the agency's formal counseling program. Mrs. Donnelly, for instance, stressed the importance of support or peer groups, especially in preparation for — or following — termination of contacts with the worker.

Workers also brought out the need for other modalities such as formal or informal groups, which were available at the Bureau only to a limited degree at the time of the study. In nearly a third of the cases, workers indicated that they had been active in efforts to help the client to find and use such resources elsewhere in the community. Often these efforts were unsuccessful or consumed a great deal of time. Since people respond to different approaches differently, it seems that in any agency setting it would be desirable to have available a variety of interventive modalities. This would enable practitioners to respond more flexibly to the unique needs of particular clients, especially as they change over the course of treatment.

EVALUATING THE QUALITY OF THE AGENCY ENVIRONMENT

Especially from the perspective of clients, the findings of this study indicate that an agency's environment is an important component in the process of a person's becoming engaged with the worker and using the service. It is noteworthy that the clients' impressions of the Family Service Bureau persisted to the point of the research interview, which occurred after the termination of the service, in many cases long after they had initially been exposed to the agency.

Obviously, client-worker interaction occurs within a broader context that includes the agency with all of its physical, social, and operational features. As Lennard and Bernstein have pointed out (1969: 205), "The adequacy or inadequacy of treatment environments is not independent of the larger context of which they are a part."

Consequently, an essential task in service delivery is to evaluate the quality of an agency's environment as one of the critical components of the helping system. This means, first, that a practitioner needs to evaluate the quality and meaning of the agency's environment for each client. Second, and perhaps more important, numerous questions should be asked at a broader level, such as the following:

> Does the setting give a first appearance of concern, competence, comfort, of a place where an individual, family or group will find the kind of understanding and wise help that is sought? Or does the setting give the message of incompetence, lack of respect, lack of privacy, lack of comfort that could well deter persons? (Turner, 1978: 191).

On the basis of the answers to such questions, an agency's staff and administration would be better able to effect necessary changes, making the environment more attractive and more supportive to clients and practitioners in their respective roles.

Part IV

Learning from Clients

How did the client view the objectives of our work together? I don't really know. . . . You keep asking *me this question and it makes me think about my approach.*

I think that Ann [Norton] in general felt very positively toward me. But I couldn't say specifically how she saw me. . . . As you ask about this, I realize that these are things we rarely discuss with our clients. Negative things usually come out . . . but normally I don't stop and talk about positive things, such as what they liked about me.

I often wish I knew what my clients think of me—and what we're doing together. . . . Maybe I should ask them!

From interviews with workers in this study.

Chapter 11

Summary and Discussion of Major Findings

If we truly listen to the people whom we serve, "learning from clients" can be much more than a simple slogan. It can be a productive and rewarding means of contributing to refinement of theory and practice in the area of interpersonal helping. Toward this end, we have presented in this book the thinking of a group of clients and their social workers regarding their shared experiences as participants in a therapeutic endeavor in a family service agency. By focusing on what clients think and comparing their views with those of their workers, we have identified crucial theoretical issues and derived pertinent practice implications.

To proceed further with this learning process, we will summarize in the present chapter the major findings and consider in a more systematic fashion their significance for theory and practice, for education, and for research. In so doing, we will highlight issues and raise questions that serve to reexamine social work practice and some of its underlying assumptions. In addition, we will discuss how the findings help in clarifying key concepts, identifying pertinent variables and their relationships, and suggesting ideas for further study in the area of client perception of services.

SUMMARY OF MAJOR FINDINGS

Interpersonal helping has been conceptualized in this book as an interactional phenomenon in which client and practitioner come together to form a new social system that follows these interrelated phases: *getting engaged, staying engaged,* and *becoming disengaged.* The study focused on exploration and comparison of client and worker views regarding each of these phases as well as the outcome. Data were derived primarily through in-depth, personal, face-to-face interviews with a small, randomly selected sample of clients and their social workers soon after termination of service at the Family Service Bureau. Most clients interviewed were white, Catholic, middle-class women seeking help with personal or interpersonal problems. Data analysis was done through qualitative methods.

The major findings will now be summarized in relation to each phase of the helping process and its outcome.

THE BEGINNING PHASE: GETTING ENGAGED

Clients and workers agreed on the nature of the presenting problems, which had to do mostly with personal or interpersonal conflicts. Most clients had access to a variety of formal and informal "helping" agents in their social networks; as these were perceived by the client as inappropriate or inadequate, he or she went to the agency. Prior to going there, clients were usually given limited information about the agency and were vague about its functions or services. Most of them expected that treatment would quickly solve their problems.

Clients vividly recalled their initial session with the worker, especially their own feelings and reactions. Workers, on the other hand, did not relate as many details about their feelings or those of the client and, instead, tended to describe their observations of the client's problems and their efforts to engage each person in a treatment relationship. There was the suggestion that, for the workers, the *content* of the interaction in the initial session was more significant, more lasting in their memory, than the *process*. For the clients, the reverse was true.

As described retrospectively by clients and social workers, the process of getting engaged follows a series of interrelated but distinct events: (1) the experiencing of inner distress or external pressure by the person; (2) the person's trying to cope by reaching out to significant others; (3) the referral to an agency by self or others; (4) the evoking of expectations in the person, mobilizing him or her to get to the agency; and (5) the initial encounter with the worker.

Each of these events, in turn, includes various prominent variables affecting its course and transition to the next stage. Thus, the person's distress or pressure from an outside source needs to be of sufficient magnitude that it propels him or her to take action (e.g., "I was so upset that I had to do something about it"). The severity of the person's experience with distress or with external pressure leads to a variety of coping efforts, which typically involve reaching out to (or being reached by) formal and/or informal sources of help. When the formal or informal helping agents are perceived by the person as inadequate or inaccessible, a referral to an agency ensues. The referral evokes expectations that, although they are generally unrealistic, stimulate sufficient hope to enable the person to go through the referral process, despite its attendant anxiety, and to get to the agency.

In the initial session, a great deal of client-worker activity is directed toward a decision as to whether or not they should *get engaged*. This decision is influenced by their success in coping with various tasks that seem to be critical in the beginning phase: (1) opening up the prospective client's life space; (2) assessing need and appropriateness of service; (3) establishing an emotional connection; (4) mobilizing the prospective client's motivation; and (5) reaching a beginning working agreement.

Each of these tasks involves complementary functions and responsibilities for both parties. For example, "opening up life space" is dependent on the client's willingness to share of himself or herself, as well as the worker's readiness to provide encouragement and support. In most cases in the study sample, client and worker were able to resolve these tasks satisfactorily, and therefore went on with subsequent contacts. In some cases, the prospective client agreed to go on even though the tasks had not been adequately resolved. In these instances, the person's distress or pressure from external sources continued to be sufficiently strong as to force him or her to go on despite dissatisfaction with the worker and/or the initial encounter.

THE MIDDLE PHASE: STAYING ENGAGED

Through the initial session, clients and worker agreed, more or less explicitly, to have further meetings. What happened as they continued their engagement?

To begin with, the problem focus was increasingly expanded and clients seemed to be able to share more of their life space as their interaction with the worker proceeded. In addition, there was a high degree of congruence between clients' and workers' problem definitions.

Clients and workers agreed that the main problem-solving activity in which they had engaged was *talking*, but disagreed about its value: whereas workers viewed it as an important medium, many clients wondered what it had to do with their problems. An exception to this was a small number of college-educated clients, who remarked about the utility of talking in solving their problems.

A related theme was common questioning by clients about the role of *listening* on the part of the worker. While they expressed their gratification in having the worker listen to them, they were puzzled as to how this was supposed to help them. Another recurring theme was the client's expectation that the worker play a more active role in the helping process through expressing opinions, giving advice, and offering suggestions. This was evident among respondents from both the lower and middle socioeconomic groups.

Despite the marked differences in clients' and workers' orientations toward problem solving, most clients not only went on to stay engaged in treatment but also indicated in the research interviews that they had gotten help and that they were satisfied with the service. In a few situations, it was evident that clients and workers went on with each other in order to save face (Goffman, 1967) rather than out of conviction that the service was useful. In the majority of cases, however, other factors seemed to be instrumental in helping clients and practitioners to overcome disparities in their perceptions and expectations as their respective worlds met and often clashed. The key variables were the client-worker relationship, the interactional environment, and the contracting process. The latter was especially prominent. Although workers and clients reported that they were not consciously or systematically involved in contract negotiation and renegotiation, their recollections suggested that much of their activity and energy went into this area. They were often involved in efforts to define their tasks and roles, to deal with their divergent expectations, and to explain or clarify their ideas in such areas as problem definition, desired goals, and treatment methods.

In about two-thirds of the cases, there was evidence of ongoing negotiation and renegotiation between clients and workers that served to facilitate their interaction. In the remaining one-third, incongruent perceptions or expectations and other issues around contracting also emerged over and over. However, they were not handled adequately. Instead, in these cases there were indications of inability or reluctance on the part of client and/or worker to share their questions or differences openly with each other, resulting in considerable mutual frustration. As differences between clients and workers were not reconciled and there was insufficient complementarity between them, in the majority of these cases the clients eventually withdrew.

Two typical patterns emerged in these unsuccessful client-worker transactions. In one, the client and worker were aware of their differences in respect to choice of target problems or treatment objectives, but did not explicitly discuss them. In the other, they discussed their different views, but did not openly confront the issue of whether they should continue or not. They simply went on for a while with their contacts, despite their obvious dissatisfaction.

The Ending: Becoming Disengaged

Termination occurred by plan in most cases, with clients and workers concurring in giving as the main reason one of the following: (1) achievement of goals; (2) client's readiness to function independently; or (3) limited productivity of further sessions. While most clients indicated that they were the ones who took the initiative to end, most workers viewed it as a mutual decision.

Termination was planned in two-thirds of the cases and unplanned in the other third. Most clients in the "planned termination" group were middle-class persons who were generally satisfied with the worker and the outcome of the service, while those in the "unplanned termination" group were mostly persons from the lower socioeconomic group who had been pressured to go to the agency or who were dissatisfied with the service and the worker.

In the majority of cases in the planned termination group, the client and worker concurred in their decision to terminate, were actively involved in discussing their ending, and made plans to do so gradually. In various ways, the workers actively tried to use the termination experience for therapeutic purposes. In many of these cases, there were also indications that, by the time they explicitly considered it, both had been thinking about termination and even hinting at it.

In cases in which termination was unplanned—that is, in which the client withdrew—clients ended either because they felt that they had gotten what they were looking for or because they were dissatisfied with the service. Often, there was evidence of lack of openness between client and worker and lack of clarity or agreement in respect to their roles, goals, and expectations. These were cases in which problems in client-worker interaction were evident as early as the initial session. In contrast to those in the planned termination group, clients and workers in these cases had a vague sense of what would be happening in treatment, were unable to establish an emotional connection between them, did not actively engage in contract negotiation, and ended the first session with marked vagueness and uncertainty about future plans. Thus, there were various predictors or "early warning signals" that should have alerted the worker to the need to clarify the focus of the service and/or confront the client's ambivalence.

The termination phase provoked multiple and intense reactions in workers as well as clients. Most clients, especially those who ended by plan, expressed their feelings openly and directly about termination, bringing out such themes as dependence on the worker, investment in the relationship, ambivalence about ending, and loss of support. Workers, on the other hand, described extensively their *clients'* feelings, but were hesitant to bring out their *own* reactions to termination. Their feelings emerged indirectly, however, through frequent references to their disappointment in not having helped the client further, dissatisfaction with the degree of change that had taken place in the client's situation, concern over the client's continuing problems, or doubts about his or her capacity to deal with future life crises. These responses occurred even in cases in which client and worker agreed that mutually formulated goals had been achieved and that the client was ready to terminate.

THE OUTCOME

There was agreement between clients and workers that the former had received some benefit from the service in over two-thirds of the cases and no benefit in slightly less than one-third. Clients and workers also agreed on the main areas of improvement, which generally involved a change in either "self or other individual family member" or in "family relationships."

Different perspectives of clients and workers surfaced over and over. Most clients felt that they had received help and gave evidence to support their conviction that they were functioning adequately, that they were strong enough to cope with life challenges, and that they had significant resources in themselves and in their environments. Workers, on the other hand, stressed the clients' problems and weaknesses, highlighted their underlying conflicts, and raised doubts about their capacity to cope in future life situations. The workers' more pessimistic outlook was evident even in cases in which they acknowledged that there had been positive changes in the clients' functioning.

Furthermore, although most clients and workers concurred that the former had derived some benefit from the service, there were striking differences in their *satisfaction* with the outcome. Most clients were satisfied with it, whereas in most cases workers were dissatisfied or ambivalent. Clients and workers in cases of unplanned termination were less likely to be satisfied than those in cases in which termination was planned. The practitioners did not seem to be aware of the impact of treatment as seen by the client. Also, the workers had high expectations of the service and of themselves. It seemed that clients were satisfied with having obtained help in relation to specific "problems in living," while workers were concerned with overall "cures" or broad changes in an individual's situation or personality structure.

Clients and workers also differed in regard to what they perceived as the major influences on the outcome. Workers ascribed more importance to the client-worker relationship, while clients emphasized the role of external factors such as life experiences and events and resources in their social networks. In addition, clients more than workers reported that the agency environment affected the course and outcome of the service in positive as well as negative ways.

The client-worker relationship was generally evaluated positively by both parties. Client-worker interaction was influenced by a number of qualities that clients and workers perceived in each other. Workers described two-thirds of the clients as having positive qualities and one-third as having negative qualities. The preferred client was someone who was open, responsive, and capable of emotional insight, while the least-liked client was presented as rigid, resistive, and nonverbal. The preferred client seemed to evoke a sense of competence and fulfillment in the worker, while the non-preferred client provoked feelings of self-doubt, inadequacy, and frustration.

Initially, clients talked in generic terms about the workers, describing them as kind, friendly, likable, warm, caring, and so on. As I probed further, however, they were able to spell out their views in more discriminating terms. The most commonly mentioned qualities were empathy, genuineness, respect, and competence. Various worker qualities, such as empathy and genuineness, were especially important in influencing the client's views as well as the change process. However, there was no simple or linear correlation between worker qualities and outcome of the service.

From the clients' perspective, some qualities were more important at some points of the helping process than others. A number of clients suggested that the worker's age or empathy made a positive impression on them initially, sufficiently so that they became engaged with the worker and were optimistic about the contact. As the encounter progressed, however, the same clients would not continue to be satisfied unless the worker displayed other qualities, such as competence.

In addition, the same quality was evaluated differently by different clients. Thus, some clients considered a worker's "low-key" approach as positive, while others viewed it as negative. Some clients reacted negatively to a worker's "formal" or "professional" bearing, while others reacted to it positively. It may be that a changing cluster of worker qualities influences the client's attitudes toward—and satisfaction with—the worker at different points in their engagement, depending on the client's changing life space and consequently changing needs and perceptions.

There was also some indication that the factor of social distance between client and worker was correlated with client satisfaction with the service; in general, clients felt more positively and were more satisfied with the service and its outcome the closer they were to their workers in respect to characteristics such as age, family status, and sex.

The complex interplay among different qualities of clients and workers suggested that in practice it is very difficult to arrive at optimal matching of clients and practitioners, even in agencies where there are adequate and varied personnel resources. In a few cases in the study, however, there was evidence of grossly poor matching and strong transference or counter-transference reactions that could have alerted the practitioner to the need to consider reassignment to another worker. While workers in these cases were cognizant of this possible need, they usually did not act on it, apparently because of fear that a transfer might have been considered a sign of failure or incompetence.

Clients and practitioners agreed on certain features of their interaction that influenced its outcome, specifically, *client qualities, worker qualities,* and *client and/or worker activities.* They disagreed, however, on the relative importance of these features, with clients tending to emphasize *qualities of the worker* and workers stressing, first, *activities,* and, second, *client qualities.*

Clients and workers also identified a number of "external" influences on the outcome and on their satisfaction with it, namely, the client's social networks, the client's life experiences and events, and the agency environment. Clients, more than workers, pointed to the positive influence of friends, relatives, and informal helping agents in the community. Clients tended to view positively their relationship with members of their kinship system, whereas social workers tended to define the same relationships as problems and obstacles in the client's functioning.

Although the majority of these clients had initially sought help from the agency because of dissatisfaction with people or resources in their environment, after having been involved in treatment they reported more positive feelings toward significant members of their networks. The suggestion was that, at least partly as a result of the service, they were better able to identify and/or use available supports and resources.

Both clients and workers mentioned natural life experiences and events (such as a job change) as factors influencing the outcome of their engagement; however, clients mentioned more of these factors in *positive* terms, whereas workers mentioned more of them in *negative* terms.

Clients and workers also referred to the positive influence of the agency's social environment (especially the role of the receptionist) and the negative influence of its physical environment (particularly its location). But workers did not assign as much importance to the environment as the clients did; they suggested, instead, that the client's personal relationship with the worker was more meaningful than the affiliation with the agency as an institution. Unlike workers, many clients also commented about the agency's "operational environment," that is, its policies, regulations, and procedures. In general, clients recommended greater flexibility in relation to such aspects as timing and location of interviews and use of diverse treatment modalities.

DISCUSSION OF CENTRAL THEMES

In social work, as in other fields, the interpersonal helping process is generally regarded as a complex phenomenon. However, in our efforts to reduce it to understandable and manageable proportions, we tend to over-simplify what happens as client and worker interact with each other. The study on which this book is based has served as another reminder of its complexities and subtleties.

Client and worker perception and use of interpersonal helping in general—and their interaction, in particular—are influenced by a multiplicity of factors, including not only what they bring to it but also their different roles and statuses and the agency setting—in short, the field of forces and totality of events existing in their respective "life spaces" (Lewin, 1935). As client and practitioner come together, they form a new social system that is fragile and temporary. They are then expected to become sufficiently involved with each other to do something about the problem or need that brings the person to the agency.

As clients and workers share their views in this investigation, a variety of discrepancies emerge in respect to role expectations, orientation to problem solving, significance of critical points in their engagement, satisfaction with the course and outcome of the service, and sources of influence on the outcome. Crucial differences occur especially in the beginning and ending phases. In a sense, client and worker start from divergent perspectives, gradually converge as their engagement proceeds, and again move in different directions as it comes to a close. Within the context of systems theory, client and worker may be seen as farthest apart in their views in the beginning and ending phases, when their newly emerging social system is most fragile and the boundaries between them are less permeable. In the middle phase, in many cases, the reciprocity between client and practitioner is strengthened, leading to fewer differences between them and/or reducing the impact of any differences. In those cases in which client and worker are unable to develop mutuality as a new system, there is considerable evidence of dissatisfaction and divergence, even during the middle phase.

This brings up a recurring question in the field, namely: What are the sources of discrepancies between clients and workers that have been repeatedly observed in practice as well as in research? In response, we have typically looked at discrete factors such as socioeconomic status, client motivation, worker competence or experience, or theoretical orientation. The findings in the present study suggest that, to learn more about the sources of client and worker differences and dissatisfaction, we should move from a linear to a transactional view and examine the interplay among the multiple forces and events in their life spaces. A principal yet neglected source is found in the structural context of their separate statuses, which embody different role demands and expectations. The client's and worker's efforts to achieve role complementarity (Spiegel, 1968) or reciprocity of expectations (Goldstein, 1973; Lennard and Bernstein, 1969) are affected by the cognitive discrepancy as well as the discrepancy of goals resulting from the different structural contexts in which they operate. These discrepancies may be more influential in the beginning and ending phases, when the client-worker system is more vulnerable than in the middle phase.

The differences and dissatisfactions between clients and practitioners may also involve "sociological ambivalence," that is, the incompatible normative expectations assigned to a status, a role, or a set of roles in a society. For example, the combination of expressive and instrumental functions assigned to the role of social worker or therapist may in itself lead to conflict and sociological ambivalence in the practitioner (Merton and Barber, 1963: 91–120.

The findings indicate that much client and worker activity throughout the helping process is directed toward coping with these discrepancies, particularly disparities in their expectations concerning roles, methods, and goals. Thus, there is empirical support for the theoretical notion that reduction of expectational discrepancies is a necessary functional requirement of interactional systems (Festinger, 1957; Lennard and Bernstein, 1969: 159).

Strains and differences between clients and social workers are apparent in nearly all cases. In cases in which they are able to cope with their disparities and achieve more congruence or mutuality in their expectations, clients and practitioners not only go on interacting with each other but also use their interaction and the service as a whole productively. In cases in which there is a continuing lack of congruence or clarity, clients and workers become increasingly dissatisfied and frustrated with each other (Lennard and Bernstein, 1969). A substantial number of these cases then results in a breakdown of the interactional system through withdrawal of the client from the service. Thus, there is a direct relationship between the nature and handling of client and worker expectations and the outcome of the service as well as their satisfaction with it. In this connection, it is noteworthy that a substantial proportion of the evidence on client and worker dissatisfaction and discrepancies comes from "involuntary" clients, that is, persons who have been pressured to go to the agency by someone else. The conflicts between clients and workers and the negative outcome in these cases stem, at least in part, from the clash in expectations between them. In effect, these persons never assume the role of *client,* partly because of their perception of the service as irrelevant to their needs and wishes.

Despite the pervasive discrepancies between clients and workers in a variety of areas, the interpersonal helping process seems to work out well in most cases. Many clients report that they get help, that they are able to function better, and that they are therefore satisfied with the service and its outcome. As a matter of fact, from the perspective of clients, the findings of this study should be gratifying to practitioners, since they provide evidence of the positive outcome of treatment. How is it that in the majority of cases clients and workers are able to overcome obstacles such as clashes in expectations and derive some benefit from the service?[1] In addition to the possibility that some people go on with each other mainly to save face (Goffman, 1967), several prominent variables emerge in this connection.

First, the *client-worker relationship,* which comes up over and over in the responses of both clients and workers, seems to be a critical factor that serves to counteract or overshadow the possible negative impact of other variables such as differences in their expectations or orientations toward problem solving. Disparities between clients and workers are minimized as their relationship grows.

A second prominent variable is the *interactional environment* of client and practitioner, that is, the context and patterns of interaction that characterize their functioning as a social system (Lennard and Bernstein, 1969: 18–25). Various properties of the interactional environment, such as the worker's total attention to the client's needs and feelings, appear to be instrumental in reducing the impact of cognitive differences or disparities in expectations between them.

Third, the *contracting process* also plays a noticeable role in workers' and

[1] Some researchers doubt that there is a causal relationship between treatment and outcome; the link may be in the mind of the client, who is probably inclined to rate "the outcome of treatment favorably simply because of the investment of energy, time and sometimes money" (Schuerman, 1976: 325). However, as discussed later in this chapter, the views of the clients suggest that certain aspects of the service act as catalysts that trigger the change process in such ways as helping the client to identify and/or make better use of resources in himself or his environment.

clients' efforts to cope with their differences. Although they do not always explicitly recognize it, throughout their interaction clients and practitioners are frequently involved in recurrent efforts to define their tasks and roles, to deal with their divergent expectations, and to explain or clarify their ideas in such areas as problem definition, goal formulation, and selection of interventive strategies. In those case situations in which these efforts are successful, the contracting process contributes to complementarity and reduction of cognitive dissonance between the participants. In cases where this is not so, the consequent incompatibility between clients and workers seriously interferes with maintenance of their system.

In light of the different life spaces of client and practitioner and the inevitable differences in perspectives between them, the contract is an ongoing process that is useful in achieving or restoring complementarity or equilibrium in the action system of client and worker (Lennard and Bernstein, 1960: 179-180). The contracting process may in fact be viewed as a major contextual property of therapeutic interaction, with manifold functions: (1) clarifying reciprocal expectations and enhancing mutuality between client and practitioner; (2) resolving issues and overcoming blocks that arise in client-worker interaction; (3) engaging the client's cognitive powers; (4) speeding up the helping process in cases in which the service is appropriate; and (5) helping to terminate as early and as positively as possible cases in which the service is inappropriate.

Thus, the contract emerges as a much more complex concept than is reflected in the social work literature; it is not only an *event* or a *product* but also a dynamic, ongoing *process* that influences the quality and outcome of the client-worker engagement in ways that need to be explored and understood further. For example, the usual mode of arriving at a working agreement early in the client-worker encounter may be insufficient and inappropriate. Also, we need to appreciate that in practice the contract apparently serves not only *instrumental* functions (such as clarification of mutual tasks) but *expressive* functions (such as provision of attention and interest by the worker to the client). Therefore, contract negotiation is not only a prerequisite for effective interpersonal helping but may be "therapeutic" in and of itself.

Going on with other findings from the study, we see that another major theme is the marked discrepancy in the satisfaction of clients and workers with the outcome. In the majority of cases, both agree that the service has been helpful and that treatment goals have been achieved. However, while most clients are satisfied with the outcome, in most cases workers are either dissatisfied or ambivalent. Furthermore, as noted earlier, clients are satisfied in having obtained help in relation to specific "problems in living," while workers are concerned with overall "cures" or broad changes in an individual's situation or personality structure. Similar findings have been noted by other investigators (Sacks, Bradley, and Beck, 1970).

It is apparent that somehow clients leave with a certain reduction in the rather high expectations that they initially bring to the agency. In contrast, as they get involved with the client, practitioners seem to *increase* their expectations and, at the point of termination, are dissatisfied with what has been accomplished. This suggestion should be explored through further research. It may be that the interactional environment affects clients and workers differently. Whereas clients are helped by the therapeutic context of the interaction, workers are more attuned to its content and thus become more aware of, and concerned about, underlying problems and conflicts in the lives of the people whom they are trying to help.

In addition to revealing disparities in their satisfaction with the outcome, clients and workers differ in regard to the perceived sources of *influence* on the helping process and its outcome. Workers, more than clients, emphasize the role of the client-worker relationship as the major vehicle of help. Clients, more than workers, note the positive impact of friends, relatives, and informal "helping" agents in the community. Both clients and workers point to natural life experiences and events as factors influencing the outcome of their engagement; however, clients relate more of these in *positive* terms, whereas workers mention more in *negative* terms. Similarly, clients attribute greater significance to the agency's social and physical environment.

The responses of clients in this area highlight a number of facets: their satisfaction in participating in meaningful life activities; the importance of rewarding work and appropriate job changes; the pleasure of giving of themselves to others through volunteer service; and, in short, the satisfaction of doing. Within the framework of ego psychology, the suggestion is that, through purposeful involvement in significant natural life activities, many clients are able to experience their impact on the environment and thus to enhance their competence and their self-image (White, 1963). While workers tend to look upon them as reactive participants in interaction with the environment, clients emerge as *active* organisms who view themselves as capable of autonomous functioning, change, and growth.

The clients' more positive perceptions of life experience and resources in their social networks are impressive, particularly since they indicated that they originally came to the agency after perceiving significant members of their social networks as inadequate or inaccessible. The marked change in their perception seems to be due in part to the *triggering* effect of the service. In many instances, the service or its individual aspects—such as specific interventions by the worker—appear to set off a train of events that ultimately result in the client being helped. Some examples are opening up a client's life space, freeing the client to use personal or social resources, or encouraging the client to seek a new environment by such means as a job change. In those cases in which the outcome is positive, the interpersonal helping process apparently serves as a catalyst by supplying something that enables people to identify and mobilize resources within themselves and/or within their ecological context. There should be further exploration of the "triggering effect" and the various sequences and features of the change process. As some clients speak, for instance, there is the suggestion of an almost regenerative quality to their functioning: as they have the experience of coping more effectively and gaining some mastery over their environment, they go on to rekindle dormant capabilities and develop new coping patterns.

In view of the widespread emphasis on human strengths and potentialities that has been a hallmark of the social work profession, it is noteworthy that practitioners in this study seem overly concerned with weaknesses or other negative qualities in their clients. Furthermore, workers do not appear to be consistently aware of the impact of their intervention on the client or of the triggering effect that I have described.

These differences in client and worker perspectives on satisfaction and influences on the outcome may be explained, to some extent, on the basis of the preoccupation with psychopathology that is part of socialization into the profession. The traditional emphasis on pathology in social work education, especially in the area of clinical practice, does not encourage a view of clients as active human beings who are capable of organizing their own lives.

But this explanation in itself is simplistic. In addition to this, here again it seems that the different roles, statuses, and frames of reference of clients and workers lead to different perceptions and behaviors. Workers, who have limited access to the client's world outside of the office, focus on the interactional environment, that is, the immediate context of client-worker engagement. They are more conscious of their investment in the helping relationship and understandably may need to emphasize its relative importance. Clients, on the other hand, experience and appreciate the role of the overall social environment in their functioning. While recognizing the importance of the helping relationship, they seem to put it into a more realistic perspective, as they realize that there are many other factors in their life space that influence their use and perception of the service. Intuitively, clients appear to appreciate the impact of multiple experiences and systems on their functioning and on their engagement with the worker.

Finally, another significant theme is the transactional nature of the client-worker relationship. There has been extensive examination of the impact of practitioners' personal styles on clients (Truax and Mitchell, 1971). In the present study, too, there was evidence of a relationship between certain elements of the workers' styles, such as personality, values, and predispositions, with client satisfaction and outcome of the service. Clients seemed to respond more positively to workers who were genuine and empathic, who spontaneously involved themselves as human beings with them, and who played active roles in client-worker interaction. At the same time, the findings suggest that there should also be examination of the impact that *clients* have on workers. This is an area in which very little research has been conducted. Yet in the study workers clearly come through as human beings who have personal needs and qualities and who are deeply affected by their clients and by what happens in their transaction with them. Workers talk openly and honestly about their own feelings of satisfaction or frustration in each case situation. There are indications that the client's responses to them elicit positive or negative reactions that influence their sense of competence and role performance in a variety of ways. The workers' helping efforts are thus contingent upon the clients' personal impact on them. We need to appreciate and explore further the process through which workers are affected by their clients and the ways in which they can cope more effectively with their own reactions. The paucity of research in this area illustrates how the "ideology" of treatment has prevented us from learning what actually goes on in casework situations or in other forms of interpersonal helping.[2] For instance, as a basic part of this ideology, we have tended to consider the workers' human reactions as nonrational, unconscious, and inappropriate (Reid, 1977); but they are very real and influential features of the human transaction between clients and workers and should therefore be accepted, analyzed, and understood.

IMPLICATIONS FOR RESEARCH

As this study shows, users of our services have a great deal to say that can be valuable in our efforts to build theory and improve practice in the area of interpersonal helping. Much could be learned through further research exploring the client's perception of critical questions. Various implications for further study have already been noted in the preceding discussion of the central themes reflected in the findings. I would like to suggest some additional ones at this point.

First, there should be programmatic research on clients' use of resources and supports in their natural social networks and environmental contexts, including the interaction between this aspect and the person's use of treatment services as well as the triggering effect of social work intervention. In particular, the informal helping system represents an important topic for research.

Going beyond emphasis on clients, there is a need for research involving people who do not come to the attention of social agencies or other helping systems, particularly research focusing on how human beings cope with natural life tasks or problems in living.[3] Especially in view of growing evidence that their functioning improves without formal or professional intervention, there could be more research involving applicants who are placed

[2] I am grateful to John E. Mayer, who suggested the possible influence of the ideology of treatment on casework research in a personal communication, dated February 1, 1977.

[3] An excellent example of pioneering research in this area is the series of coping studies carried out with children and adolescents by Murphy and her collaborators (Murphy et al., 1962; Murphy and Moriarty, 1976).

on the waiting list of social agencies and mental health centers (Sloane et al., 1975). Such a new orientation toward research could lead to substantial changes in social work theory and practice, which are still heavily influenced by research based on pathology.

Second, there should be further controlled and intensive investigation of the client-worker engagement as an interactional phenomenon involving a newly emerging social system. There could be in-depth study of mutual and/or differential tasks faced by clients and workers in each phase of their interaction, the ways in which they cope with these tasks, and the consequences for the process and outcome of interpersonal helping. There could be efforts to document the contextual properties of the client-practitioner interactional environment and their impact on interpersonal helping (Lennard and Bernstein, 1969). Furthermore, various leads could be pursued in respect to specific phases of the helping process, particularly termination. It could be hypothesized that client and worker tacitly begin termination long before its actual occurrence. Also, in view of the indication that the quality of the initial phase influences the nature of termination, it would be interesting to investigate the relationship between beginning and ending phases. It might be speculated, for example, that the type and timing of termination can be predicted from the nature and quality of client-worker engagement in the initial session(s). Further research in this area could lead to greater understanding of the termination process and to practice principles enabling clients and workers to end earlier, more efficiently, and with a more positive impact on their functioning and coping.

As a part of research on the client-worker interactional phenomenon, it would also be productive to conduct further exploration of client-worker discrepancies in relation to aspects such as problem definition, selection of target problems and goals, and evaluation of outcome. What are the sources of failure and success in client-worker interaction? Why are some clients and workers able to become successfully engaged with each other while others fail to one degree or another? As one possible approach, a group of clients and workers could be brought together to engage in discussion and analysis of their experiences and perceptions.[4]

Third, there should be intensive examination of the relationship between (1) characteristics of the client, the worker, and the service, and (2) the client's use of the service, the outcome, and clients' and workers' evaluation and satisfaction in diverse practice contexts. Many previous studies have been concerned with linear relationships, such as the connection between worker

---

[4] Writing from the theoretical perspective of symbolic interactionism, Blumer (1969: 41) stressed the value of bringing together a small group of informed observers in exploratory research:

> Such a group, discussing collectively their sphere of life and probing into it as they meet one another's disagreements, will do more to lift the veils covering the sphere of life than any other device that I know of.

qualities and the effectiveness of the service,[5] or with simplistic questions, such as whether clients are satisfied or not with treatment.[6] The findings in the present study reveal a much more complex picture. Thus, there is no simple or direct relationship between social class and client perception or use of service; clients from varied socioeconomic backgrounds prefer an active social worker who is willing to offer opinions and advice. Moreover, particular techniques such as advice-giving have diverse meanings for different clients. Similarly, there is no simple connection between a worker's qualities and a client's satisfaction. Satisfaction is not a unidimensional variable but a many-faceted phenomenon: many clients express satisfaction with the overall service, but dissatisfaction with specific features of it or with certain qualities of the worker.

In order to improve service delivery, we need to explore the phenomenon of interpersonal helping in depth. We might ask questions such as the following: What is the interrelationship among such factors as the nature of referral (voluntary or involuntary), the worker's style and qualities, client and worker satisfaction, and outcome? What is the differential impact of various worker qualities on the client and on the helping process? What are client perceptions of other social work services, such as group treatment? A promising approach would be to probe more deeply into the factors accounting for successful social work services through intensive investigation of satisfied clients.

In short, we need to undertake further research into the complex field of interacting forces affecting the process and outcome of the client-worker engagement as well as their perception of it. A pervasive, critical question is: Under what conditions do certain factors combine to produce particular outcomes? The use of client feedback in research is one effective means of obtaining further documentation that can help us to answer this question.

IMPLICATIONS FOR PRACTICE

Presenting implications for practice on the basis of qualitative research is questionable, since inferences and generalizations cannot be offered with any degree of confidence. There should be caution particularly in generalizing the findings to practice in other settings. Nevertheless, some observations are in order, especially in areas in which the evidence is overwhelming and/or consistent with previous investigations. At the very least, speculations based on the findings may serve to produce new ways of thinking about practice and service delivery. In the long run, however, whether the study's findings

[5] See Truax and Carkhuff (1967) and Truax and Mitchell (1971).

[6] For instance, the simplistic quality of many satisfaction studies conducted in community mental health centers has been highlighted in a survey by McPhee, Zusman, and Joss (1975).

will stand up or not remains to be seen through more rigorous and extensive research.

First, in each case situation it is urgent to focus on the crucial tasks with which clients and workers are confronted in the initial phase of their interaction, in view of the evidence that there is a direct link between events in this phase and the course and outcome of the interpersonal helping process as a whole. For example, because of natural differences in their roles, approaches, and expectations, in early sessions it is especially important that client and social worker engage in an active process of negotiation regarding the goals, rules, and methods of their emerging social system.[7] This, of course, has long been emphasized in social work practice. Thus, we have extensively considered the impact of the *prospective client's* expectations on his or her use of agency service and the importance of socialization of the person into the client role during the intake phase of casework. Perlman (1975) has investigated the relationship between the ways in which consumers approach social service agencies and the outcomes that they experience. He has concluded (p. 63) that consumers appear to adjust their behavior toward the agency and to use its services "in accordance with at least two criteria: (1) how close will the organization come to meeting their needs as they define them and (2) how high a price will they be required to pay."

The findings of the present study show that, in addition, we should devote similar attention to the *worker's* expectations and views. In some cases the worker's apparent preoccupation with pathology and expectation of cure may reinforce the client's problems and dependency. In other cases, the worker's preference for clients with qualities such as responsiveness or verbal facility may lead to feelings of rejection and even premature termination when the clients do not meet these criteria. In his discussion of psychotherapy, Goldstein (1962: 120) has thoughtfully observed that

> since therapist prognostic expectancies are communicated to and influence patient behavior, therapists would do well to become more aware of the channels and cues through which this expectational transmission takes place.

Another researcher has demonstrated that social workers need to assess their expectations and those of their clients and how these might affect the helping process:

> A client's choice as to whether to seek help, how to present his request, how to make use of help if it is offered, is guided by norms which the social worker may not know about and may not share. The social worker has perspectives and acts on cues which are not visible to the client and which the social worker may not make explicit (Rees, 1974: 276).

In addition to awareness and assessment of expectations, practitioners need to pay attention to their socialization into their own roles in each case

[7] For a thoughtful discussion of explicit guidelines on the negotiation process in the initial psychiatric interview, see Lazare, Eisenthal, and Wasserman (1975).

situation. In the majority of cases in the study, clients and workers come through as actively engaged in a necessary process of mutual socialization into their newly emerging social system. By this I mean that they constantly struggle with defining their relationship in respect to major dimensions such as allocation of responsibility, differentiation of their respective roles, selection of focus and strategies of intervention, and discussion of timing. Consequently, in talking about *role induction* into counseling or therapy, we should not think simply in terms of induction of the prospective clients, as we usually do (Siporin, 1975: 212-216). Perhaps more important, we should also think about induction of the worker, who needs to be socialized into the prospective client's norms or ways of thinking, feeling, and perceiving. Socialization, in other words, is a reciprocal undertaking between client and worker rather than the one-way process that is usually portrayed in the literature.

Socialization of the worker is especially crucial in case situations of persons who do not possess the qualities generally preferred by practitioners, namely, the "unmotivated," "non-YAVIS" clients described by Goldstein (1973: 5-6), who are mostly from lower socioeconomic backgrounds and who probably constitute the majority of people coming to the attention of social workers.

Other practice implications are in the area of greater explicitness and openness on the part of clients and practitioners. Despite traditional social work emphasis on openness, there is repeated evidence of defensiveness, "game playing," hinting at and avoidance of issues in the course of client-worker interaction. Workers in particular have a responsibility to provide the leadership and to set the tone, so as to encourage explicitness, establish a conscious focus, and reduce cognitive dissonance. There could be, for example, more explaining to clients concerning interventive methods that may be puzzling to them (e.g., talking). Similarly, there could be ongoing clarification of mutual expectations about the purposes and methods of treatment, particularly in those cases in which there is evidence of confusion, ambivalence, or inappropriate expectations on the part of the client and/or worker. The contract is one of the tools that may be used to promote role learning on the part of both client and worker, and to facilitate the change process.

There should be another look at the issue of engaging people in the helping process, especially those who are described as "involuntary," "hard to reach," or "unmotivated." In many of these cases, much more could be accomplished through reduction of social distance between client and practitioner, provision of needed tangible services and supports, opportunities to enhance the person's hope and motivation, and teaching of interpersonal skills and other coping patterns. One promising formulation is that of "structured learning therapy," through which Goldstein (1973) proposes a research-based, educationally oriented treatment approach that is specifically designed to match interventive strategies to the characteristic styles and expectations of unmotivated or "unresponsive" clients. Structured learning therapy offers practical guidelines that are based on a combination of modeling, role playing, and social reinforcement.

In many cases of so-called unmotivated clients, the worker's expectations need to be changed. Often, engagement of the person in the traditional sense may not be possible or even desirable: perhaps in these cases the worker's efforts should be directed not toward engaging the "client" in the helping process, but toward engaging some other system or resource in the environment on his or her behalf.

With "voluntary" as well as involuntary clients, there should be more systematic collaboration between professional helpers and informal helping systems. The use of natural helping networks in the treatment process should be actively supported by agency staff and administration.[8] Members of the client's environment and other informal helpers could be used as therapeutic agents (Guerney, 1969). In work with.population groups such as Puerto Ricans, for instance, we are becoming aware of the importance of faith healing and other forms of indigenous therapy that have profound cultural roots. These approaches could be tapped even more systematically as a means of providing more effective service through collaboration with the formal helping system (Delgado, 1977).[9]

Further attention should be given to the role of the agency's social and physical environment in the helping process. Specific questions that could be raised include: How does the physical environment influence client-worker interaction? How can the roles of the receptionist and other staff members be exploited more systematically and enriched as an integral part of the overall service to individuals or families? In other words, there should be careful evaluation of the quality of the agency's environment and its impact on people in general as well as of its meaning and influence in each case situation.

There should also be careful consideration of the role of each client and his or her life space in the helping process. In each case, we should identify ways of maximizing the client's role and participation. In this regard, it may be worthwhile to highlight again the finding that workers tend to view clients as reactive organisms with underlying weaknesses and limited potentialities, while the latter present themselves as active, autonomous human beings who enhance their competence and functioning through use of personal and environmental resources. From the client's perspective, it appears that much could be achieved through interventive approaches emphasizing such aspects as the client's own action and natural life processes; the spelling out and carrying out of mutual client and worker tasks;[10] the use of social networks and

---

[8] For practice guidelines on the use of natural helping networks, see Collins and Pancoast (1976) and Swenson (in press).

[9] See Harwood (1976) for an excellent study of spiritualism as a community mental health resource among Puerto Ricans.

[10] For discussion of practice guidelines in using tasks, see Maluccio (in press, b); Pincus and Minahan (1973); Reid and Epstein (1972); and Reid and Epstein (1977).

environmental resources as instruments of help; and the provision of opportunities for the client to have a meaningful impact on the environment.

As social workers often see in their daily practice, a client's experience of managing his or her own life or accomplishing developmental tasks is in itself therapeutic (Kurtz and Kyle, 1977; Kurtz and Wolk, 1975). Social workers also know through experience that what goes on outside of the office affects not only a client's functioning but also the process and outcome of interpersonal helping. Yet the client's ecological context is not easily accessible to the worker, especially when the service is confined to the office setting.

Without direct exposure to the client's environment, the practitioner cannot adequately evaluate its quality or significance in the person's functioning or treatment. Such an evaluation is crucial, since there is considerable evidence of significant interplay and even interdependence between the formal helping system of an agency and relevant social networks and informal influences in the client's life. This suggests that practitioners should make active efforts to become aware of events and resources in the client's broader environment and to focus on them more explicitly in the course of treatment. As the client's life and environment become more accessible to the worker, the latter could more effectively aid him or her in seeking or creating and using significant environmental opportunities.

These approaches would require fundamental changes in organizational arrangements and service delivery. There would have to be, for instance, provisions for encouraging and facilitating the worker's involvement in the client's natural life context through such means as home visits, rather than having to rely primarily on the office setting. In addition, as noted, there would need to be more active collaboration between the formal and informal helping systems. And there should be more emphasis on understanding, changing, and using the client's environment. The latter emphasis is exemplified by emerging formulations of "community counseling." Lewis and Lewis (1977) stress that the environment frequently needs to be changed as a means of helping people to solve their problems. To identify and achieve the necessary environmental changes, the client and counselor engage in a mutual exploration, asking the following questions:

1. To what extent is the individual capable of resolving the issue through personal change?

2. What resources in the environment are available to help the individual grow?

3. To what extent does the solution really rest in the environment instead of in the individual?

4. How can the counselor and/or the counselee act to bring about the necessary changes in the environment? (Lewis and Lewis, 1977: 11–12).

As the findings of the present study suggest, through careful analysis and intervention, the client's social environment can be restructured or modified to facilitate adaptive strivings and to maximize the use of natural resources existing in the social networks.

In addition to greater emphasis on the interaction between people and their social systems and the need for environmental change, workers should revise their orientation toward clients and their overemphasis on the power of professional roles. More specifically, clients need to be viewed truly as partners in the helping endeavor and in decision making. Practitioners need to demystify therapy and reduce their expectations of themselves:

> They do not have to be magicians or the repositories and purgers of their clients' illness to help their clients to solve problems. This view may decrease the workers' sense of frustration or failure, which comes from the inability to meet their or their clients' unrealistic expectations (Frey and Edinburg, 1978: 91).

In the present study, the workers' high self-expectations were especially evident in relation to decision making around crucial issues. In talking with clients and workers, I was struck by the frequency and complexity of decisions confronting them throughout their interaction. In some of the research interviews, even months after termination, the workers were still agonizing over issues dealing with diagnostic impressions and treatment objectives or methods. While some of the agony was appropriate or inevitable, much of it seemed to be unnecessary and even counterproductive, since clients themselves could have participated more actively in deciding the issue in question. In some cases, they *should* have been the ones to decide it. In assuming major responsibility in critical areas, the workers not only made it more difficult for themselves, but also lost opportunities to help clients to exercise their own decision-making powers.

IMPLICATIONS FOR EDUCATION

In addition to changes in practice and service delivery, the views of clients and social workers point to various implications for retraining of practitioners and for education of students. As a group, the workers in this study were well educated, highly experienced, and sophisticated in relation to social work theories. In a sense, they were *too well* trained or educated: in their approach to practice they reflected some of the biases, values, and untested assumptions that characterize social work.

By examining the clients' perspectives on interpersonal helping, we are compelled to raise basic questions about the underlying bodies of knowledge in social work, the ways through which we transmit this knowledge to students, and the process of socialization into the profession.

Above all, we need to reexamine the pervasive emphasis on pathology—especially psychopathology—in our theories and in our teaching. The preoccupation with pathology manifests itself in numerous forms: in the workers' determined quest for specific causes of their clients' difficulties; in their tendency to uncover underlying or dormant intrapsychic conflicts; in their dissatisfaction with the outcome of the service and their accomplishments or those of their clients; and in their persistent doubts about their clients' capacities to cope with future life challenges.

One wonders how practitioners could help but react and function precisely as they did in this study. Thus, in casework they are taught to engage in a process of assessment of the clients' functioning that is essentially a search for problems, weaknesses, and limitations in the clients. Although there is also appreciation of the clients' strengths and resources, the latter are not emphasized. Recently, there has been extensive discussion of "problem-oriented recording" (Martens and Holmstrup, 1974) but no consideration of another perspective that might be designated as "strength-oriented recording," in which the focus would be on identifying and mobilizing strengths and resources in the clients and their situations. There is no doubt that the former approach leads to a mind set in the worker that reinforces a concern with pathology and diverts him or her from careful attention to the client's actual or latent strengths.

Practitioners, moreover, are effectively conditioned by the emphasis on pathology that permeates most theories of human behavior or personality development and most approaches to interpersonal helping. As Leichter has observed in her review of the literature on the family, there is an "overly solemn and grim emphasis" in the research on which these theories and therapeutic modalities are based:

> The therapeutically oriented literature, for example, while necessarily concerned with problems and pathologies, has virtually ignored the lighter side of family experience, the fun and exhilaration that can occur even in difficult circumstances. Even the recent search for "strengths" in the family has at times been heavy-handed. Humor has often been taken as a clue to hidden pathology rather than as a basis for integration and solidarity, while ritual has been viewed as a form of obsession rather than a pleasurable activity associated with sentiments of continuity (Leichter, 1974: 216).

As the findings of the present study suggest, there is a need to shift the focus in social work education from pathology to human strengths, resources, and potentialities. If this shift occurred, students and practitioners would be more likely to view clients as proactive human beings who are capable of organizing their own lives to one degree or another. Workers would then be better able to place emphasis "not on exploring pathology, but on finding, enhancing, and rewarding competence" (Minuchin, 1970: 129).

Along with deemphasis on pathology, there is a need to redirect social work education toward teaching ways of helping human beings to create or build on resources in their own ecological context and to develop their competence in transacting with the environment. Various approaches are emerging that should be useful in this regard. These include: the ecological perspective on social work practice, with its focus on the mutuality and dynamic interaction between people and their environments;[11] task-oriented modalities, with

[11] See Germain (1973); Germain (in press); Gitterman and Germain (1976); and Whittaker (in press).

their emphasis on formulation of client and/or worker tasks and stimulation of the clients' own cognitive powers and processes;[12] and educationally oriented practice models such as "relationship enhancement,"[13] which highlight the teaching and learning of interpersonal skills and other coping strategies as means of preventing as well as treating problems.

Most of these approaches also involve the provision of resources and concrete services that are required to help clients to make their environment more nurturing and more conducive to their growth and self-fulfillment. This suggests that educators need to stress a more active orientation toward the environment; they need to give more weight to nonclinical activities such as advocacy, situational intervention, and environmental manipulation—all of which have traditionally been neglected or have had limited prestige in the hierarchy of treatment modalities.

At the same time, in education there should be more emphasis on accountability to *clients.* This involves, among other aspects, teaching students to act not only on the basis of their professional judgment and knowledge, but also on the basis of the client's definition of the "problem" and his or her ideas about what will be helpful. In essence, it involves teaching students to respond flexibly to clients on the basis of their needs, expectations, and interests.

These are some of the implications that are suggested by the study's findings and that also undoubtedly reflect my own biases. The most crucial additional point is the importance of inculcating in students the need for ongoing professional development and incorporation of new knowledge as responsible, autonomous practitioners. In light of rapidly changing social conditions and practice demands, this should be viewed as a lifelong process requiring continuing educational opportunities.

Perhaps more important, this process can be furthered through learning to use client feedback as a prominent method of reexamining and improving our theory and our practice. Client feedback, therefore, is a topic that merits—and will get—more extensive treatment in the next and concluding chapter.

[12] See Maluccio (in press, b); Reid and Epstein (1972); and Reid and Epstein (1977).
[13] See Guerney (1977).

Chapter 12

A Plea for Client Feedback

In concluding this book, I recall how I approached the research on which it is based with considerable trepidation. Despite the positive experiences reported by previous investigators in similar studies, I had numerous concerns and questions. Would clients be willing to participate? How would they receive me? Would social workers be threatened by the study? Would the research process have adverse effects on the clients and, besides, did I have any right to intrude upon their lives? What would be the quality of data that I would be gathering?

These and other initial questions and concerns challenged me to approach the entire research enterprise with considerable caution. For example, I met in advance on various occasions with members of the agency staff and administration, to share with them details of the study's design and methods and obtain their criticisms and suggestions. In contacting and interviewing each client, I tried to be sensitive to any indication of discomfort and was prepared to stop the research process if at any point there should have been any question that it might be hurting anyone. And I adhered rigidly to confidentiality in relation to the responses of workers and clients.

As the research progressed, I was glad that I had taken these precautions. But I also realized that my concerns were for the most part unfounded. Furthermore, in proceeding with the research interviews, I increasingly appreciated that clients and social workers were much stronger, more self-confident, and more cooperative than I had imagined. They tackled difficult questions, shared their views thoughtfully as well as spontaneously, and in many ways truly engaged with me as partners in our efforts to understand the interpersonal helping process.

All of this was very gratifying. It was especially exciting to see how much clients themselves had to say about the service. They were eager to participate and not only responded to my questions but shared additional experiences and insights. Many of them expressed surprise—along with pleasure—that someone would be interested in their views. Several of them remarked: "No one ever asked me what I thought about the counseling!" Other clients suggested that the research interviews helped them to review their experience with treatment and to consolidate their gains. For instance, this is what Mrs. Donnelly said when I asked her at the end whether she had any further thoughts or suggestions:

I'm just glad we had this session because it made me gather all my thoughts for the past two days and . . . some things I realized here just talking which I didn't realize before, which is good . . . for me too, not only for you. I can see more and more that I'm doing all right.

In research, we tend to think that the collection of data has a negative impact on the subjects. In this investigation, on the contrary, it was evident that there were positive consequences for the clients who participated in it. In relating their feelings, ideas, and perceptions, many of them in fact seemed to gain personal satisfaction. It was as if their sense of competence was reinforced and their self-esteem enhanced through participation in the research.

The study also had a profound impact on me as the researcher. I learned to appreciate more than ever before the complexity of interpersonal helping as a social phenomenon. At the same time, in recognizing how workers and clients interacted with each other in essentially human ways, I began to demystify my concept of social work treatment or intervention. I also gained further respect for practitioners, as I increasingly realized how they were called upon to give of themselves to other people with diverse needs, qualities, and expectations. I began to see that practice demands, interventive methods, and professional skills are vastly more complex than the way they are often portrayed in our literature and in our classrooms.

In addition, while listening to clients and workers, I was challenged over and over to think differently about interpersonal helping. As a part-time practitioner primarily engaged in social work education and research, I was most impressed with how the study influenced me to reassess my own approach to practice, to reexamine basic theoretical notions, and to open up different ways of thinking about social work and its consumers. Thus, the study demonstrated the dynamic interplay between practice and research. In presenting and discussing the findings in earlier chapters, I have tried to indicate the kinds of issues and questions that were stimulated in this process. It may be worth repeating here the most compelling themes that emerged: the influence of the interactional environment on the process and outcome of client-worker engagement; the dynamic potential of the contract as a basic feature of the service; the role of clients as partners in the helping process; the impact of life experiences and social networks on the client's functioning as well as on the service; the relationship between professional and informal helping systems; and the value of viewing and treating clients as active and striving human beings rather than as creatures laden with pathology and bound by psychic and/or environmental determinism.

Of course, it may be that, prior to initiating the study itself, I had been ready to raise these questions and to engage in a critical reexamination of social work theory and practice in general, and my own orientation in particular. Perhaps the research provided me with the necessary impetus and framework for such an undertaking. At any rate, getting this kind of feedback was most worthwhile and stimulating and I recommend it to others who are involved or interested in interpersonal helping. As a result of my experiences, I would therefore like to make a plea for client feedback as an integral part of the service provided by every social worker. As I hope this book has demonstrated, expanded client feedback can have multiple uses and purposes in social work and other fields.

PURPOSES OF CLIENT FEEDBACK

At the individual worker level, obtaining feedback from each client can serve as a useful device for monitoring one's practice and improving one's skills. By being tuned into their clients' perspectives, workers might be better able to determine for themselves which methods or techniques are effective, what they need to modify in their approach in order to make it more relevant to client needs and qualities, and what questions they need to ask about their underlying assumptions regarding human behavior and interpersonal helping.

Individual practitioners can obtain the views of their clients following termination or periodically throughout their contacts with each person. These informal studies can be especially useful to social workers as they increasingly move toward self-directed practice and as they are called upon to evaluate their performance and account for their effectiveness, now more than ever before.

Furthermore, as workers are more aware of the frequently positive impact that they have on their clients, they may be able to lessen their self-doubts and enhance their sense of competence and self-image as practitioners. In so doing, they might become more comfortable in changing the traditional client-worker relationship. In particular, they might be able to shift the power balance between them and their clients and promote more active participation of the client in decision making on his or her own behalf. As vividly demonstrated in a recently published account of their work together by a social worker and a client (Fibush and Morgan, 1977), clients and practitioners can learn from each other and change and grow through their shared experiences.

At the agency level, the systematic gathering of clients' impressions and perceptions can serve as a means of monitoring services and as an essential component of program evaluation and planning. In the analysis of the functioning of any human service organization, the input of its consumers or clients adds greatly to the perspectives of its staff and outside consultants (Giordano, 1977). Consumer input is becoming even more urgent as demands for accountability are increasing and as the results of evaluative research are raising further doubts about the effectiveness of services in diverse practice contexts.

The clients' views can help to maintain accountability, identify service gaps or deficiencies, influence policy formulation and decision making, and initiate changes within a specific agency or the broader service delivery system. To achieve these purposes, client feedback surveys should incorporate much more than simple rates of client satisfaction. Clients should be encouraged to give their views in depth on a variety of aspects: what they think they need; what there is about the service that they find helpful or not; and how they think the service could be improved.

The role of client feedback in evaluating programs and implementing changes in service delivery has recently been demonstrated in a variety of agency settings.

In a study of veterans' perceptions of their care in a general hospital, it was discovered that there was considerable dissatisfaction with key aspects of the service, such as the quality of staff members' interactions with patients. The findings pointed to the "necessity of sensitizing and training various levels of staff in certain areas, such as human relations" (Rosenberg, 1977: 34).

Reporting on consumer feedback research at a community mental health center, Landsberg (1977: 369) has described it as an important tool for program evaluators, administrators, program planners, and community boards:

> The technique permits the agency to gather detailed programmatic information from the direct consumers of mental health services. It is especially valuable in that it represents a method of soliciting the opinions of service users who may not be reached or represented through formal community groups or boards.

As a result of the input of consumers, the above center established a number of new services, including a specialized aftercare program that was more responsive to the needs of former mental hospital patients (Landsberg, 1977). Other researchers have used consumer feedback as a means of evaluating the effectiveness of psychiatric hospitals and community mental health clinics (Ellsworth, 1975).

Partly in response to the impetus provided by the Family Service Association of America, numerous family service agencies have revised and strengthened their programs through follow-up studies of clients' views (Riley, 1975; Dailey and Ives, 1978). In one of these studies, it was also found that staff members who participated were stimulated to examine and improve their practice:

> Interviewers found themselves enriched by looking at service in a different part of the city and with a somewhat different clientele from their usual daily work. Seeing and hearing the evaluation of service from the client's point of view added a new dimension to their individual practice (Dailey and Ives, 1978: 244).

Consumer feedback research is being carried out even in settings such as foster care in which until recently it would have been unthinkable because of concern over its impact on children. In one such investigation, foster children were asked to evaluate their placement. The children proved to be reliable respondents who provided important information useful in evaluating child welfare services. The researchers concluded:

> In the absence of data about the effect of certain styles of parenting and environments . . ., we are left with decisions which have to be based on current descriptions of the options. The child in placement has a firsthand view of these options and is most affected by them. Our data suggest the importance of each child's individual participation in placement decisions and . . . opinions about what constitutes supportive caretaking (Bush, Gordon, and LeBailly, 1977: 500).

METHODS OF CLIENT FEEDBACK

To accomplish the purposes that I have outlined, an agency is not necessarily required to undertake extensive or expensive research. Individual practitioners can learn a great deal through informal or limited studies involving some of their clients. Perhaps more important, they can build into the helping process ways of obtaining consumer feedback systematically at key points throughout the service.

There are various guides from which practitioners can select and adapt specific questions suited to particular client-worker interactions in their agencies. Thus, Beck and Jones (1973) have devised a well tested, comprehensive mail questionnaire useful in client follow-up studies, particularly in family service agencies. The interview guide from the present investigation (Appendix B) includes a range of questions especially pertinent for in-depth exploration of clients' views and feelings about each phase of the helping process. And Lazarus (1971: 253–271) has described an extensive "patient's therapy report" schedule. The latter is designed for evaluation and analysis of each therapy session by the patient and includes a range of topics, from subject areas covered during the session to the patient's assessment of the outcome. Although this schedule is too elaborate to be given routinely to clients, it does suggest numerous specific questions that workers can adapt to their purposes in a more informal way. There is, for example, an excellent series of questions pertaining to the patient's assessment of the quality of the therapist's functioning during the session (p. 269).

Along with a worker's examination of his or her practice, agencies should conduct broader and more formal studies. Even limited research efforts can be productive, as long as certain basic conditions are present: (1) There is attention to methodological issues, such as obtaining proper samples of clients and providing for reliability and validity of data. (2) The agency climate is such that staff and administration are ready to ask questions of clients without feeling overly threatened by their eventual responses. (3) Data collection instruments and procedures are carefully designed so that clients can feel free to express their views spontaneously.

Various questionnaires or interview guides, such as the ones discussed above, may be employed for the purpose of agency studies. Another interview guide is provided by Strupp, Fox, and Lessler (1969: 149–165). This one is particularly suited to psychotherapy and includes parallel forms for patients and therapists. In addition, the Family Service Association of America has produced a manual on conducting client follow-up or outcome studies (Beck and Jones, 1974). This manual contains very useful, practical guidelines for data collection and analysis, along with sample instruments and forms. In a later supplement to this manual, Beck (1977) reports on the experience of various agencies with client follow-up research and provides revised instruments and instructions.

In light of my experience with the present study, I recommend in particular the use of qualitative methodology in consumer feedback research. This type of methodology is especially suited to the study of complex human phenomena such as interpersonal helping. In order to understand in depth the intricate processes of human behavior and human interaction, it is necessary to "obtain information relevant to the various attitudinal, situational, and environmental factors that compose the real world for those under investigation" (Filstead, 1970: 6–7). Therefore, researchers must emphasize the subject's own perception, understanding, or feelings: "It is the observer's task to find out what is fundamental or central to the people or world under observation" (Lofland, 1971: 4). As Blumer (1969) has stressed, qualitative research is valuable in achieving two complementary objectives: (1) developing a close and comprehensive acquaintance with a segment of social life, and (2) sharpening the method of inquiry so that it arises out of, and remains grounded in, the empirical phenomenon being investigated.[1]

A central feature of much qualitative research in the social sciences is use of the focused or open-ended, in-depth interview as a major method of data collection. One of my purposes in undertaking the present study was to explore the advantages and disadvantages of focused interviews in social work research. Some observations about my experience may be of interest to others.

Of special importance in the study was the pattern of *probing* in order to stimulate respondents to explicate their views and impressions. As reflected

---

[1] The applicability of qualitative methodological strategies to different spheres of human life has been tested through a variety of excellent studies in such areas as deviance (Polsky, 1967), the sociology of medicine (Becker et al., 1961), and the social-psychological impact of spinal paralytic poliomyelitis on children and their families (Davis, 1963). In addition, qualitative approaches such as participant observation and other field methods have, of course, been used extensively in anthropological and sociological research.

In social work, strategies of qualitative methodology have been used in numerous studies. Researchers have used the interview method in studies of client perception of services (Mayer and Timms, 1970), adoption (Fanshel, 1972), and casework (Leichter and Mitchell, 1967).

throughout the chapters on the findings, this approach influenced data collection, since it often stimulated both clients and workers to go from their initial, generic responses to more precise and discriminating comments. My experience demonstrates that the interviewee's initial response to global questions tends to be vague or stereotyped, and that further probing is necessary to bring out the richness or subtleties of his or her views. At the same time, the form and substance of probing stimuli can also contaminate the data, as I found out particularly in the pilot phase of my investigation.

Despite some of the limitations, the study has reinforced my conviction about the role of qualitative methods — such as focused interviews — in social work research. Over and over, in listening to clients and workers, I was challenged to raise for myself questions about theory and practice and to pursue different ways of thinking about interpersonal helping in general. Furthermore, some of the details that respondents brought out as they were encouraged to recall the process of client-worker interaction would not have come out if I had employed a quantitative or survey approach. On the other hand, the latter method would have had advantages such as use of a larger sample and opportunity for quantification and statistical analysis of data.

Future formal studies in this area could be strengthened through a combined approach using survey techniques with a large population of clients and workers, along with qualitative methods with a small subgroup. This would achieve the dual purpose of illuminating in some depth the complex interplay of factors involved in client and worker perception of their engagement, and carrying out a more rigorous analysis of at least some of these specific factors.

NEW ROLES FOR CLIENTS

In addition to its potential contribution to improvement of theory and practice, further emphasis on client feedback can lead to the creation of new roles for consumers in education, research, and practice.

Clients can effectively serve as resource persons or collaborators in formal and informal educational programs: through their special insights, they can help students and practitioners to appreciate the richness of the interpersonal helping process. We should therefore feel freer to bring clients into the classroom, as a means of enriching our teaching and learning. Shachter (1976) has discussed various imaginative modes of instructor-client collaboration in classroom teaching. In addition to client input through the use of audiovisual aids, *real* clients can be invited into the classroom to share their views and examine the interpersonal helping process with students and instructors.

Soon after completing the present study, I involved several of the participating clients and workers in classroom sessions in my courses on casework and research methods. I usually asked a client and her worker to join us together in a class. The resulting experiences were most productive and exciting. The client and worker typically engaged in a stimulating examination of their respective perceptions of the helping process, revealing agreement as well as discrepancies in key areas. The students and I could appreciate the complexities and subtleties of the client-worker relationship, as we saw them interacting before our eyes. Furthermore, we were most impressed by the competence and strengths revealed by clients in the way they presented themselves in these sessions. In short, these shared experiences were very effective in stimulating teaching and learning.

There can also be new roles for consumers in the area of research. Current as well as former clients, for example, might be called upon to participate in formulation of research projects. This is something that I did not do, other than in a minimal way in the pilot phase. It will be recalled that, prior to initiating the research interviews, I involved the social workers in examining the research design and methods. At the time, however, it did not occur to me to ask some clients to serve in a similar consultative capacity. In retrospect, this would have been most appropriate and useful in such ways as clarifying some of the research questions.

In addition, clients themselves might be employed to obtain the views of others who are active with an agency. In a children's psychiatric center, selected consumers serve as "client representatives" and routinely collect data on client satisfaction with the service. They also provide on an ongoing basis their evaluation of the center's effectiveness in meeting community needs (Wursmer, 1977).

Clients could also play more active roles in service delivery. In the psychiatric center mentioned above, the same client representatives serve as consumer advocates by identifying obstacles to effective service in specific case situations as well as proposing changes in policies and procedures in the agency's programs (Wursmer, 1977).

In conclusion, client feedback studies can be of benefit to us in relation to education, research, theory building, and service delivery. By regularly obtaining the views of those whom we serve, we may be able to achieve a better understanding of interpersonal helping — an understanding that will lead to improvement of services. In so doing, we would be truly involved in *learning from clients* through a mutually rewarding process of interaction and growth.

APPENDIXES

Appendix A

Further Notes on Methodology

PILOT PROJECT

As a basic part of this investigation, I carried out a pilot study at a small, sectarian family service agency in another city. Its purposes were to test and refine the research approach, particularly the interview, and to help in delineating the critical dimensions in client and worker perception of service.

OBTAINING THE SUBJECTS

To obtain subjects for the study sample, I collaborated with the Executive Director of the agency. The Director identified the case that had been closed most recently by each of the six social workers at the agency.

Initially, the Director sent a letter to each of these six clients, explaining the purpose of the study and soliciting their participation. (See sample letter below.) The Director soon after followed up with telephone calls to the clients, asking whether they would be willing to participate in the study. In response to this procedure, only two of the six clients agreed to participate. The others indicated that they did not have enough time.

Sample Letter to Clients *

Dear _____ :

Because our agency is interested in improving its services, we are cooperating with an independent researcher from the University of Connecticut in a study of the opinions and views of those who have recently had some contact with us.

I will be calling you within the next few days to ask if you could help us by permitting Mr. Anthony Maluccio, the researcher, to talk with you at your convenience.

I want to assure you that any information you provide will be treated in strictest confidence. Your name will not be used in any way, nor will anyone at the agency or anywhere else be able to connect your name with anything you might say.

---

*Adapted in part from Mayer and Timms (1970: 151).

I look foward to talking with you over the telephone and hope that you will be able to help us with this study. Thank you very much in advance for your cooperation.

Sincerely,

_____

(Executive Director)

In view of the high refusal rate and the fact that the above procedure was both slow and time consuming, in consultation with the agency staff we decided to try a different approach. I asked the agency's receptionist to call directly, without any prior letter, four other clients who had recently terminated at the agency. The receptionist briefly explained the purpose of the study and asked for the client's participation.

The new procedure proved extremely successful, as all clients thus contacted agreed to participate. A major reason for this success seemed to be the clients' personal relationship with the receptionist, particularly their trust in her and their wish to please her. In the main phase of the study, consequently, I followed the revised procedure and relied on the Bureau's receptionist to get in touch with clients and invite their participation. (See "Instructions to Receptionist" later in this Appendix.)

INTERVIEWING CLIENTS AND WORKERS

After each client agreed to participate, I was given his or her name. Then I interviewed each of the six clients in the sample at a location chosen by him or her. All six clients chose to be interviewed in their homes. Within a few days I also interviewed the appropriate worker. By plan, each of the six workers on the agency's staff had one case in the pilot study. All interviews with clients and workers were tape recorded.

All except one of the workers had received the M.S.W. degree and were highly experienced. There were three women and three men among the workers. As for the sample of clients, there were five women and one man. All six of the clients had voluntarily sought help in connection with personal or interpersonal problems. Duration of agency contact varied from two months to over three years, and the number of treatment interviews ranged from four to over sixty.

EXAMINING THE RESEARCH PLAN

Once the interviews were completed, the research plan was critically examined through various means, in addition to my own review:

1. Soliciting each client's and each worker's criticisms, suggestions, and

reactions to the research approach soon after the interview was ended and after I explained the nature of the pilot study.

2. Holding a meeting with the six workers involved in the pilot study to engage in a joint, critical assessment of the research approach.

3. Having an experienced social work researcher and educator listen to all interviews to compare his judgments with mine and obtain his critique of the interviewing approach.

BENEFITS OF PILOT STUDY

The pilot study proved to be extremely useful in several ways. First, as noted, the procedure for obtaining client participation was streamlined and made more effective. Second, I substantially modified the interview guide by including a number of key questions asked of all respondents in essentially the same terms and by clarifying the wording of certain questions. Third, I eliminated from the study various rating scales on such aspects as "satisfaction with outcome," since both clients and workers repeatedly observed that they seemed inconsistent with the free-flowing and spontaneous tone of the research interview itself. I had asked clients and practitioners to fill out these scales at the conclusion of the interview but several of them pointed out that they seemed superfluous and false, especially following the open give-and-take that had occurred within the interview.

In addition to helping in assessing and revising the data collection instruments, the pilot study served to highlight the strengths and weaknesses in my approach as the interviewer, leading to a number of important changes. For example, it was evident that I tended to influence the results by engaging in discussion of interesting points or showing more enthusiasm in response to some comments of clients or workers than to others. In preparation for the main study, I was thus helped to modify my style so as to be more objective, and to establish a climate in which respondents would be more likely to express their views freely and spontaneously.

Analysis of the substantive findings from the pilot interviews with clients and workers was also helpful. A variety of themes emerged that were useful in developing the content and sequence of the interview guide. It was also encouraging to see that there was substantial agreement between my judgements on key themes and those reached independently by the experienced social worker who studied all of the interviews.

Above all, the pilot study provided me with much-needed experience in the analysis of qualitative data gathered through open-ended interviews. The complexity of data analysis in this type of research became dramatically evident, stimulating me to employ a more focused interview than originally planned. As an example, in view of the themes that emerged, I organized the interview guide (and thus the interview itself) on the basis of the different phases of the interpersonal helping process. This facilitated the formulation of various categories that later aided tremendously in the classification and analysis of data.

INSTRUCTIONS TO RECEPTIONIST

On the basis of the experience in the pilot study, in the main phase of the research I arranged to have the Bureau's receptionist contact by telephone the clients who had been randomly selected for inclusion in the study sample. The receptionist was given these instructions and requested to follow them as closely as possible:

Introductory Statement

This is _____, the receptionist at _____.
(agency)

We're calling to see if you could help us with a research project in which we're trying to find out what people think about our services and how we can improve them. The project is being carried out by Mr. Maluccio, an independent researcher from The University of Connecticut. Since you recently had some contact with us, we would appreciate it very much if you could talk with him at your convenience. Whatever you have to say will be confidential—strictly between you and him. No one here at the agency will know what you as an individual have to say.

Would it be all right if we give your name to Mr. Maluccio so that he can talk with you about this soon? We hope that you can do this. The ideas of people such as yourself are very important to us, since you are the ones who know what it's really like to come here.

If client says yes:
Fine. We'll give Mr. Maluccio your name and he'll call you within the next few days. Thanks very much for your help.

If client hesitates:
Could you think about this and would it be OK if we have Mr. Maluccio call you later and you can tell him directly one way or the other?

If client asks a lot of questions:
You're raising some very important points and I'll be glad to have Mr. Maluccio call you about this. All right?

If client absolutely refuses:
I appreciate what you're saying. Thanks very much for thinking about it anyway.

The following letter was sent under the receptionist's signature to the few clients in the study sample who could not be reached by telephone:

Sample Letter to Clients*

Dear_____:

Because our agency is interested in improving its services, we are cooperating with an independent researcher from The University of Connecticut in a study of the opinions and views of those who have recently had some contact with us. Since we have not been able to reach you by telephone, we are writing to ask if you would help us by permitting Mr. Anthony Maluccio, the researcher, to talk with you at your convenience.

We want to assure you that any information you provide will be treated in strictest confidence. Your name will not be used in any way, nor will anyone at the agency or anywhere else be able to connect your name with anything you might say.

Please return the enclosed postcard as soon as possible to let us know whether or not you would be willing to talk with Mr. Maluccio. If you have any questions, feel free to call me during office hours.

We would appreciate hearing from you soon, and hope that you will be able to help us with this study. Thank you very much in advance for your cooperation.

Sincerely,

_____

(Agency Receptionist)

LIMITATIONS OF THE STUDY

The major limitations of the study concern: (1) the interview as the chief instrument of data collection; (2) the retrospective nature of the study; and (3) analysis and interpretation of data. There may also be some question about the small size of the study sample. However, since I gathered a great deal of material through in-depth interviews, I believe that samples of 33 clients and 11 social workers are adequate for an exploratory study of this type.

USE OF RESEARCH INTERVIEW

A major problem inherent in use of the interview in research is the likelihood of a variety of potential sources of bias, distortion, or error. This is especially true of the type of nonstandardized, in-depth interview used here: the data are dependent on so many factors related to the interviewer, the

*Adapted in part from Mayer and Timms (1970: 151).

interviewee, or the interview situation that serious questions may be raised about their reliability and validity.

Partly to compensate for these limitations, I carried out the pilot study discussed earlier, which was quite helpful in refining the interview format, questions, and procedures. In addition, since I served as the interviewer, I hoped that my prior experiences in clinical and research interviewing in a variety of social work settings would help to establish the appropriate climate and desirable interaction with respondents that could contribute to reliability and validity. The use of *one* interviewer also helped to control for variations in interviewer bias. Since respondents were able to share their views freely and spontaneously, I have reason to believe that the interviewing approach was successful.

To cope in part with the problem of validity, I examined the consistency of statements relating to attitudes or matters of a comparable nature (e.g., the client's attitudes toward the worker). There was a high degree of consistency in the responses of individual clients and also between spouses in those cases in which both marital partners were interviewed. In regard to reliability, I built into the interview a modification of the traditional test-retest procedure through such means as asking similar questions at different points of the interview. This helped to determine the reliability of each respondent at least in a crude way.

RETROSPECTIVE NATURE OF THE STUDY

To a considerable degree, the study focused on clients' and workers' attitudes, views, and feelings in regard to social work service *at the time* of their involvement in it.

Since the research interview occurred some time after termination of treatment, the accuracy or precision of the respondents' reports may have been influenced by factors such as problems in recall or the respondent's circumstances at the time of the interview. For example, if the client's current situation was markedly positive or negative, he or she might in retrospect have viewed the experiences with social work services in a more or less favorable light than was warranted.

As a means of coping with this problem, at least in part, I interviewed the client and worker as soon as possible following termination of treatment.

DATA ANALYSIS AND INTERPRETATION

As discussed in Chapter 2, a formidable task in qualitative research consists of organizing, interpreting, and reporting complex and multiple data as objectively as possible. One basic danger is the researcher's tendency to fit data into neat, oversimplified, or fancy categories reflecting preconceived theoretical notions as well as the desire to formulate richly meaningful theoretical propositions. The patterns, meanings, and relationships that a researcher sees in a set of qualitative data are at times obscure to another reader.

I am not sure that much can be done to cope with this limitation, since the analysis of qualitative data involves a largely artistic process in which the researcher's personal qualities and preferred theoretical notions combine to create an individualized interpretation of one segment of reality. I would say, however, that, in terms of the type of qualitative analysis advocated by Blumer (1969: 35-40), my familiarity with the subject under study and prior experience as a practitioner and teacher of casework could be considered a strength in this research project.

Owing to lack of resources, it was not possible to include a reliability check that had originally been planned and that had been built into the pilot study. I had planned to have experienced social workers study a random sample of taped research interviews, thus crosschecking my observations on key dimensions such as the level of client satisfaction with different aspects of services. However, as discussed earlier, I was able to have an experienced social worker study all of the interviews in the pilot phase of the study, and it was encouraging to find substantial agreement between his judgments and mine on key themes and variables. Ultimately, however, my interpretations must stand the test of replication.

In short, the study's limitations are basically those of typical qualitative studies. In examining and interpreting the findings, there should therefore be caution in generalizing to social work practice in other settings.

COMPARISON OF CLIENTS IN STUDY SAMPLE WITH AGENCY'S OVERALL CLIENT POPULATION

In Chapter 3, I explained that clients in the study sample were in most respects comparable to the agency's overall client population, that is, all clients whose cases were terminated during 1975. The data on which this comparison was made are summarized in Table A-1.

TABLE A-1. Characteristics of Interviewed Clients and All Agency Clients Terminated in 1975*

	INTERVIEWED CLIENTS	ALL AGENCY CLIENTS
	(N = 33)	(N = 679)
Age	%	%
30 or under	43	53
31-40	24	28
41-50	18	11
51-60	9	3
Over 60	6	5
Sex		
Female	73	70
Male	27	30

TABLE A-1.   (Cont.)

	INTERVIEWED CLIENTS	ALL AGENCY CLIENTS
	(N = 33)	(N = 679)
Race/Ethnicity	%	%
Black	6	16
White	94	72
Hispanic	0	12
Annual Family Income		
Under $3,000	12	23
$3,001-$5,000	21	11
$5,001-$9,000	31	22
$9,001-$12,000	21	16
Over $12,000	15	28
Duration of Agency Contact		
3 mos. or less	40	37
3-6 mos.	28	30
6-12 mos.	28	24
Over 12 mos.	4	9
Number of Interviews with worker		
1	4	20
2-5	24	41
6-12	28	32
13 & up	44	7
Primary Focus of Service		
Marital relationships	34	15
Parent-child relationship	26	14
Other family relationships	23	27
Environmental problems	6	9
Out-of-wedlock pregnancy	11	9
Other	0	26

*Data on religion and marital status were not available for all agency clients.

NONINTERVIEWED CLIENTS IN STUDY SAMPLE

In Chapter 3 we saw that, in 12 of the 37 cases in the original study sample, the clients were not available for interviewing or declined to participate in the study. Demographic characteristics of these clients are summarized on the next page.

Demographic Characteristics of Noninterviewed Clients in Study Sample*

No.	Sex	Race†	Age	Marital Status	Religion‡	Highest Grade Completed	Occupation	Socio-economic Class**	Position**
1	F	B	53	Married	P	6	None (Welfare Recipient)	V	77
2	F	W	39	Married	RC	10	Waitress	V	69
3	M	B	26	Separated	P	12	Laborer	V	65
4	M	W	55	Widowed	RC	12	Typist	IV	44
5	F	B	45	Separated	P	6	Housekeeper	V	70
6	F	W	18	Single	RC	12	Office Clerk	IV	44
7	F	W	30	Single	RC	12	Secretary	IV	44
8	F	B	39	Divorced	P	10	None (Welfare Recipient)	V	69
9	F	W	25	Separated	Unknown	6	None (Welfare Recipient)	V	77
10	F	W	32	Married	RC	B.A. degree	Teacher	II	22

*Data not available in two cases.
†B = Black; W = White.
‡P = Protestant; RC = Catholic.
**Based on Hollingshead (1957).

Appendix B

Guide for Research Interview with Clients*

As the interviewer, I introduce myself to clients as an independent researcher from the University of Connecticut.

The interview begins with a brief explanation of the purpose of the study, which is presented as an attempt to improve the help provided by a family service agency by examining how clients and workers view the service after they have finished with it. It is also emphasized that: (1) the agency has agreed to cooperate because of its interest in improving services; (2) responses will be held in strictest confidence; (3) the researcher has not been told anything about the client except the name and the fact that he or she has had contact with the agency; (4) obtaining the client's frank views is extremely important; (5) the interviewer will follow an outline.

After obtaining some brief identifying information on each client (see schedule below), the interviewer explores the client's perception of the service and its outcome by asking open-ended questions and following up the client's responses to each question with more specific, probing inquiries. Interviews are tape recorded.

While the sequence, content, and format of the questions are adapted to each situation and flow naturally from it, the interviewer is guided by a variety of content areas germane to the study. There is an effort to cover each area in depth.

Following is the outline of specific content areas, along with description of the overall objective in each area and possible guide questions. The interviewer begins each section with a general question, which is asked in essentially the same form of all respondents and is followed up by other questions as appropriate.

*In developing the guides for interviews with clients and social workers, I have drawn from a number of previous investigations, particularly those of Beck and Jones (1973); Mayer and Timms (1970); Silverman (1969); and Strupp, Fox, and Lessler (1969). I am grateful to these researchers for the suggestions that their work provided.

220

I. Identifying Data on Client

Overall Objective:
The major purposes will be to obtain basic information about the respondent and his or her family situation and to help in making the respondent become involved and feel at ease in the interview situation.

	CLIENT	CO-CLIENT (e.g., spouse)
Age:		
Sex:		
Race:		
Religion:		
Marital status:		
No. and ages of children at home:		
No. and ages of children out of home:		
Other members of household:		
Highest grade completed:		
Occupation:		
Ethnic background:		
Annual family income:		
Residence (town or section of city):		

AT THIS POINT CLIENT WILL BE ASKED FOR PERMISSION TO TAPE THE INTERVIEW: e.g., "Would it be all right if I use the tape recorder now? It helps me to remember what you say and saves me the time of writing everything down."

II. Referral to Agency

Overall Objective:
To explore the client's view of (1) his or her "presenting problem" or reason for initial contact with agency; (2) the referral process—i.e., expectations, feelings, impressions, and evaluation of the process; and (3) other actual or potential resources in his environment that were or could have been used.

Reason for Referral:
COULD YOU TELL ME A LITTLE ABOUT THE DIFFICULTIES WHICH BROUGHT YOU TO THIS AGENCY?* How long had they been going on? What did you think were the main causes or reasons for them?

*Questions in capital letters were those asked of everyone in the same way. The other questions in each section were asked or adapted as appropriate.

Availability of Other Resources:
WHAT DID YOU TRY TO DO ABOUT THESE DIFFICULTIES PRIOR TO GO-
ING TO THE AGENCY? Did you talk about it with anyone else? (Look into contact
with informal helpers such as friends or relatives and other agencies or professionals.)
If *yes*, how did it work out? If *no*, why not?

Referral Process:
HOW DID YOU HAPPEN TO GO TO THIS PARTICULAR AGENCY? Who re-
ferred you to it? What did you know about the agency? Did you consider other agencies? How did you feel about going to the agency? With whom did you initially talk at
the agency?

Expectations:
AT THAT POINT, WHAT DID YOU THINK IT WOULD BE LIKE GOING TO
THE AGENCY? What did you hope would be done to help you? What kind of help
did you hope they would give you? What kinds of people did you think typically go to
this agency? With what kinds of problems?

III. BEGINNING PHASE

Overall Objective:
To explore the client's impressions and reactions at the point of initial encounter with
the worker and the agency — e.g., the "intake" phase.
NOW I WOULD LIKE TO ASK YOU ABOUT YOUR ACTUAL EXPERIENCES
AT THE AGENCY.

Client's Initial Feelings:
HOW DID YOU FEEL IN FIRST GOING TO THE AGENCY? What could have
been done to help you with these feelings? Did you share these feelings with anyone? If
so, how did he/she react?

Agency Procedures:
HOW WERE YOU RECEIVED AT THE BEGINNING? How did the agency staff
relate to you? What did you think about the way they related to your difficulties?
What did you like most? What did you dislike most? What could have been done differently?

Characteristics of Agency:
WHAT DID YOU THINK ABOUT THE AGENCY AT THE BEGINNING? For example, its location, appearance, waiting room, atmosphere, etc.? What could be
changed to make people feel more comfortable in going to an agency such as this?

Initial Session with the Worker:
WHAT WENT ON IN THE FIRST SESSION? What did you talk about? What did
you like? Dislike? Did you feel you and the worker understood each other? Did the procedures or questions followed by the worker seem to relate to your problem? What
were your hopes or expectations? Did you discuss these with the worker? How did the

initial session fit in with what you were expecting or looking for? What was most helpful? Least helpful? What could have been done differently?

Conclusion of Initial Interview:
WHAT WAS DECIDED AT THE END OF THE FIRST INTERVIEW? How did you and the worker arrive at this decision? How did you participate in the decision? Did the decision seem related to what you were concerned about? What were you most satisfied with? Dissatisfied with?

IV. MIDDLE PHASE

Overall Objective:
The purpose in this section will be to engage in in-depth exploration of the client's views concerning the helping process during the middle phase—i.e., the ongoing contacts with the agency and the worker following intake and preceding termination. There will be emphasis on the client's perception of the total process, the relationship with the worker, the worker's qualities, the kind and quality of interaction and communication, the subjects covered in the interviews or other contacts, and the client's satisfaction or dissatisfaction with various aspects of the service.

Problem Definition:
AS IT WENT ON, WHAT DID YOU THINK WERE YOUR DIFFICULTIES OR NEEDS? . . . WHAT DID THE WORKER THINK? What did you and the worker think were the reasons for your difficulties? If you disagreed, what did you do about it?

Helping Process:
WHAT WENT ON AFTER THE FIRST SESSION? How often did you meet with the worker? Where did you meet? Was anyone else involved? For how long did you continue?

What were you and the worker trying to accomplish? What did you do in your contacts with the worker? What did you talk about? What was it like talking with the worker? How did it make you feel? What did the worker think should be done about the problems? What did you think about this? How do you think problems should be resolved?

Qualities of Worker:
WHAT WAS THE WORKER LIKE? How would you describe him/her as a person? In what ways was he/she like or unlike . . . [informal confidants or other professionals seen by clients]? What qualities in the worker did you like most? What qualities did you like least? Was he or she the kind of person you had expected? If yes, how? If no, why not?

Relationship with Worker:
WHAT DO YOU THINK ABOUT THE WAY YOU AND THE WORKER WERE WITH EACH OTHER? How did you get along with each other? What did the worker think of you? How well do you think that the worker understood you and your difficulties?

What did you like most about the way the worker was with you? What did you dislike (or like least)? What could you and the worker have done differently in the way you got along with each other?

Agency Policies and Procedures:
WHAT DID YOU THINK ABOUT AGENCY REGULATIONS AND POLICIES? (For example, fee, locations of interviews, frequency and duration of interviews.) Was there anything about the agency or its policies that made it difficult for you to use the services? (e.g., fees, waiting period, location of agency, appointment hours, etc.) What change should be considered in the way the agency gives service?

Communication with Others:
WHILE YOU WERE GOING TO THE AGENCY, DID MEMBERS OF YOUR FAMILY (OR FRIENDS, RELATIVES, ETC.) KNOW THAT YOU WERE GO-ING? If *no*, how come they didn't know? If *yes*, how did they feel about your going? Did you ever tell them what you did at the agency? How did they react?

V. ENDING PHASE

Overall Objective:
To examine the client's reactions to — and perception of — the termination phase, particularly the reasons for and process of termination.

HOW DID YOU HAPPEN TO STOP GOING? What would you say were the main reasons? Who made the decision to stop? How did you feel about stopping? Was there anything about the way you and the worker stopped that you think should have been handled differently?

Were there any arrangements made to come back to the agency or to go elsewhere for services? If other services were recommended, what did you do about it? Since leaving this agency, have you gotten help (or thought about getting help) from any other place or person? Would you consider going back if you should need help in the future? Would you refer someone to the agency? If so, with what kinds of difficulties or needs?

VI. OUTCOME

Overall Objective:
(1) To obtain the client's evaluation of the service;
(2) to identify changes in the client's coping patterns, functioning, and overall life situation; and
(3) to explore the client's perception of possible reasons for any changes or influences on the helping process and its outcome.

Evaluation of Service:
IF YOU LOOK AT YOUR TOTAL EXPERIENCE AT THIS AGENCY, HOW DID IT WORK OUT FOR YOU? What was most helpful in your experience at this agency? What was least helpful? What was there that bothered you or made you feel

uncomfortable? How satisfied are you with the service that you received? Was there something you wished to get that was not available? Was there any other kind of help that you needed?

Changes in Functioning:
SINCE YOU STARTED GOING TO THIS AGENCY, WHAT CHANGES HAVE THERE BEEN IN HOW YOU'VE BEEN GETTING ALONG? [Positive or negative changes].
    [Follow up if necessary with questions in regard to:]
    —How you and other family members get along with each other.
    —How you get along with others outside the family.
    —How you feel about your "problems" and how you handle them.
    —Have you made any decision or taken specific actions in regard to your problems? [If client has encountered new "crisis," how has he or she coped with it?]

Reasons for Changes:
WHAT DO YOU THINK ARE THE MAIN REASONS FOR THESE CHANGES?

How do you feel the services provided by the agency influenced these changes? How has going to the agency made any differences in your life? Did anything not related to the agency influence these changes?
    [Explore the following if it has not already come out in response to previous questions.]

Life Situation of Client:
WHAT WERE THE MOST IMPORTANT THINGS GOING ON IN YOUR LIFE WHILE YOU WERE GOING TO THE AGENCY? What was happening in your life? Who else helped you with your problems?

VII. SUMMARY

Overall Objective:
The purposes in this concluding section of the interview include: (1) to explore the client's overall impressions and perceptions; (2) to provide the client with an opportunity to bring out new points or expand on previously mentioned points; and (3) to get some sense of the client's attitudes toward seeking help.

LOOKING BACK, WHAT WOULD YOU SAY IN GENERAL ABOUT YOUR CONTACT WITH THIS WORKER AND THIS AGENCY? What would you change or keep the same? What were the main ways in which they were helpful? What else do you think you could have gotten from them? How could they have been more helpful or do things better?

What are you most satisfied with? What are you most dissatisfied with? WHAT OTHER SUGGESTIONS DO YOU HAVE FOR IMPROVING THE AGENCY'S SERVICES?

DO YOU HAVE ANY OTHER IMPRESSIONS OR IDEAS THAT WE HAVEN'T TALKED ABOUT?

THANK YOU VERY MUCH FOR YOUR HELP. AFTER I LISTEN TO THE TAPE, I MAY FIND THAT I FORGOT TO ASK YOU SOME QUESTIONS. IF THIS HAPPENS, WOULD IT BE ALL RIGHT IF I TALK WITH YOU AGAIN SOME TIME?

Appendix C

Guides for Research Interviews
with Social Workers

There are two types of interviews with each social worker: (1) the interview concerning a specific client, and (2) the interview concerning the worker's orientation toward social work.

GUIDE FOR INTERVIEW WITH SOCIAL WORKER
ON EACH CLIENT

Within a few days after the interview with a client, his or her social worker is interviewed. The interviews with workers follow essentially the same process and format as those with clients (Appendix B).

Although workers are already familiar with the nature of the study, the interview begins with a brief explanation of its purpose, which is presented as an attempt to find ways of improving services by exploring how they are viewed by clients and social workers. It is also emphasized that: (1) the study is not intended to evaluate each worker's performance; (2) responses will be held in strictest confidence; (3) the researcher has already interviewed the client but cannot reveal any of the client's responses; (4) obtaining the worker's frank views is very important; and (5) the interviewer will follow an outline.

Identifying data on the worker are gathered in the first interview with him or her and recorded on a schedule (see Section on the next page). The rest of the interview is tape-recorded.

As with the research interview with clients, the interviewer explores the worker's perceptions by asking open-ended questions and following up with more specific, probing inquiries. Similarly, although the sequence, content, and format of the questions are adapted to each situation and flow naturally from it, the interviewer is guided by a variety of pertinent content areas and possible questions. These are outlined on pages 228-233.

The content areas and sample questions closely parallel those in the "Guide for Research Interview with Clients" (Appendix B). In each area, the overall objective is to explore the worker's perceptions of the helping process and his or her understanding of the client's perceptions.

I. Identifying Data on Worker

Age:_____   Sex:_____

Race:_____

Religion:_____   Marital Status:_____

Education:_____

    Highest Degree:_____ Date:_____

    Major:_____ School of Social Work:_____

Employment:

    Present agency — Date:_____ Position:_____

Prior Employment — Agency settings and duration:

_____

_____

_____

II. Referral to Agency

Reason for Referral:

COULD YOU TELL ME A LITTLE ABOUT THE DIFFICULTIES THAT LED
THE CLIENT TO THE AGENCY?* How long had they been going on? What did the
client think were the main reasons or causes?

Availability of Other Resources:

WHAT DID THE CLIENT TRY TO DO ABOUT THESE DIFFICULTIES PRIOR
TO GOING TO THE AGENCY? Did he/she talk about it with anyone else? Was there
any contact with other agencies or professionals or informal helpers such as friends or
relatives? If yes, how did it work out? How did the client feel about it? If no, why not?

Referral Process:

HOW DID THE CLIENT HAPPEN TO GET TO THIS PARTICULAR AGENCY?
Who referred him or her? How did he/she feel about being referred here? What did
he/she know about the agency? Did he/she consider other agencies or helping persons?
How satisfied was the client with the referral process? How about you?

Expectations:

AT THE POINT OF REFERRAL, WHAT DID CLIENT THINK IT WOULD BE
LIKE COMING TO THE AGENCY? Prior to actually coming here, what did he/she
expect to get?

III. Beginning Phase

Initial Feelings:

HOW DID CLIENT FEEL ON FIRST COMING HERE? What could have been done

*As in the interviews with clients, questions in capital letters were those asked of
everyone in the same way. The other questions in each section were asked or adapted
as appropriate.

to help him/her with these feelings? How did you initially respond to this person? What were your impressions? How did you like him/her? What did he or she like/dislike most?

Expectations:
WHAT DID CLIENT THINK IT WOULD BE LIKE COMING TO THIS AGENCY? . . . WHAT EXPECTATIONS OF YOU AND/OR THE AGENCY DID HE/SHE SEEM TO HAVE? Were these expectations discussed? How did you handle them?

Agency Procedures:
HOW DID CLIENT FEEL ABOUT AGENCY PROCEDURES? For example, how did he/she feel about the way he/she was received?

Characteristics of Agency:
WHAT DID CLIENT THINK ABOUT THE AGENCY AT THE BEGINNING? For example, its location, waiting room, atmosphere, etc.

Initial Session:
WHAT WENT ON IN THE INITIAL SESSION? What kinds of things did you talk about? What did the client like? Dislike? What did you like? Dislike? How did you view the client's problem or need? What did you think needed to be done to help the client? Did you feel you and the client understood each other? How do you think that the initial session fit in with what the client was expecting?

Conclusion of Initial Session:
WHAT WAS DECIDED AT THE CONCLUSION OF THE INITIAL SESSION? How did you and the client arrive at this decision?

How satisfied were you with the way the initial session worked out? What were you most satisfied with? Dissatisfied with? How did the client view the initial session? What was the client most satisfied with? Dissatisfied with?

IV. MIDDLE PHASE

Problem Definition:
AS THIS CASE WENT ON, WHAT DID YOU SEE AS THE MAIN PROBLEMS OR NEEDS? . . . WHAT DID CLIENT SEE AS THE MAIN PROBLEMS OR NEEDS? If you and the client had different views, how did you handle them? How did this work out?

The Helping Process:
WHAT WENT ON AFTER THE FIRST SESSION? . . . WHAT DID YOU SEE AS THE TREATMENT OBJECTIVES IN THIS SITUATION? What did client view as major objectives? How did you arrive at these objectives? How was client involved? How did you deal with any discrepancy between your expectations and those of the client? How did you decide what to work on and the methods to be used?

HOW DID YOU TRY TO ACHIEVE THESE OBJECTIVES? What did you and the client do? How did the client feel about what you were doing? How did client think the difficulties should be resolved? How did client respond to the treatment methods? What did the client seem to understand about your role and what you were trying to do? Do you think that the client was aware of what you were trying to do?

Qualities of Client and Worker:

WHAT WAS THE CLIENT LIKE? What did you like most about her/him? What did client like most or find most helpful about your approach and your qualities? Dislike most and find least helpful? How did you fit in with the client's expectations of you as the worker?

Relationship with Client:

WHAT DO YOU THINK ABOUT THE WAY YOU AND THE CLIENT WERE WITH EACH OTHER? How did you get along? How do you think the client viewed the relationship? How do you think that the client viewed you?

Agency Policies and Procedures:

WHAT DID THE CLIENT THINK ABOUT THE AGENCY AS A WHOLE? (For example, such aspects as fees, location, frequency, and duration of interviews.) How did these or other agency policies or procedures influence the helping process? What could have been done differently to help this particular client?

Communication with Others:

WHILE CLIENT WAS COMING TO THE AGENCY, DID MEMBERS OF HIS/HER FAMILY (OR FRIENDS, RELATIVES, ETC.) KNOW ABOUT IT? If so, how did they react? What did client tell them about the contact here?

V. Ending Phase

HOW WAS THE CASE TERMINATED AND WHY? How did the client feel about termination? How satisfied were you with the decision to terminate and the process of termination? How satisfied do you think the client was? Were arrangements made for the client to return here or go elsewhere? Was there anything about the way you and the client terminated that might have been handled differently? Do you think that the client might come back if further help were needed later on? Do you think the client might refer someone else to the agency? If so, for which types of problems?

VI. Outcome

Evaluation of Service:

ON THE WHOLE, HOW DO YOU THINK THINGS WORKED OUT IN THIS CASE? . . . HOW DO YOU THINK THE CLIENT FEELS ABOUT THIS? What do you see as having been most helpful in the client's experience with the agency? Least helpful? Was there anything that might have been done differently? Was there any other service he or she wanted or needed?

Changes in Functioning:
SINCE THIS CLIENT BEGAN AT THE AGENCY, WHAT CHANGES HAVE THERE BEEN (POSITIVE OR NEGATIVE) IN HOW THE CLIENT HAS BEEN GETTING ALONG? (For example, relationship with family members and others, coping patterns and overall functioning, feelings about himself or herself.) Do you think the client feels that there have been changes—and if so, what changes?

Reasons for Changes:
IF THERE HAVE BEEN CHANGES, WHAT DO YOU SEE AS THE MAIN REASONS OR CONTRIBUTING FACTORS? . . . WHAT DO YOU THINK THE CLIENT VIEWS AS THE MAIN REASONS?

How do you feel that the services provided by the agency influenced these changes? Do you think that coming to the agency made any significant difference in the client's life? And how do you think the client sees this? Was there anything not related to the agency that influenced these changes?

[Explore the following if it has not already come out in response to previous questions]:

Life Situation of Client:
WHAT WERE THE MOST IMPORTANT EVENTS OR EXPERIENCES IN THE CLIENT'S LIFE WHILE HE OR SHE WAS ACTIVE WITH THE AGENCY? What was going on in the client's overall life situation? How did these events or experiences help or interfere with the helping process? Did anyone else help the client? In what way?

VII. SUMMARY

LOOKING BACK, WHAT WOULD YOU SAY IN GENERAL ABOUT THIS CASE? . . . What would you change or keep the same? How satisfied were you with the way things went? How satisfied do you think the client was? What did the client find most satisfying? What was the client most dissatisfied with? How could you or the agency have been more helpful to him or her?

HOW DID YOUR EXPERIENCE WITH THIS CLIENT COMPARE WITH YOUR EXPERIENCES WITH OTHER CLIENTS? WHAT PARTICULAR SATISFACTIONS AND/OR FRUSTRATIONS DID YOU HAVE IN WORKING WITH THIS CLIENT? What did you find most rewarding? Most frustrating? Why?

DO YOU HAVE ANY OTHER IMPRESSIONS OR IDEAS THAT WE HAVEN'T COVERED?

THANKS VERY MUCH FOR YOUR HELP.

GUIDE FOR INTERVIEW WITH SOCIAL WORKER
CONCERNING ORIENTATION TOWARD SOCIAL WORK*

After completing the research interviews with workers that pertained specifically to their clients in the study sample, I held a brief informal interview with each of them to obtain some idea of his or her orientation toward social work. In this interview, I followed the guide below and took brief notes on the worker's responses.

INSTRUCTIONS TO RESPONDENT:

I AM INTERESTED IN YOUR VIEWS ABOUT SOCIAL WORK TRAINING, THIS AGENCY, AND YOUR APPROACH TO PRACTICE. FOR THIS REASON, I WILL ASK SOME GENERAL QUESTIONS TO WHICH THERE ARE NO RIGHT OR WRONG ANSWERS. PLEASE INDICATE BRIEFLY WHAT COMES TO YOUR MIND IN RESPONSE TO EACH QUESTION.

I. Relevance of Training

    A. How did your social work education prepare you for your current work?

    B. In thinking about your social work training, what would you say has been most relevant or helpful in your work here?

II. Preferred Theories and Practice Approaches

    A. What theories do you find most helpful in your work with people?

    B. What is your preferred approach to practice? (e.g., What would you say about your style in working with people? What do you see as the best way to help people?)

*Several of the questions in this interview were suggested by Silverman (1969: 44-58).

III. EXPECTATIONS OF CLIENTS

A. What do you expect from clients in order to be able to help them?

_____

_____

_____

IV. AGENCY

A. Could you briefly describe the goals and purposes of this agency?

_____

_____

_____

B. How do agency characteristics (e.g., policies, procedures, physical features, etc.) influence your professional functioning in *positive* and/or *negative* ways?

a) Positive Ways:_____

_____

_____

b) Negative Ways:_____

_____

_____

Appendix D

Sample Schedule for Extracting Data from Research Interviews

The schedule on the following pages was completed in one of the cases in the study. It illustrates the method used in extracting and categorizing significant data from research interviews with clients and workers. First, however, some details about the case may be of interest to the reader.

CASE OF JOYCE MOORE

Miss Moore is a bright and articulate twenty-year-old white woman from a middle-class background who was in treatment for over six months. She had been referred to the Family Service Bureau by a priest for help in connection with her out-of-wedlock pregnancy. She had dropped out of her junior year in college soon after learning that she was pregnant.

Miss Moore was the middle of three children. Her siblings as well as her parents were very supportive of her throughout the pregnancy and encouraged her to seek and use counseling. She also had numerous friends who provided continuing support.

The social worker was a middle-aged, white woman with several teenage children of her own. Clients described her as a warm and outgoing person with an open, informal approach. She evidently made them feel quite comfortable with her.

Miss Moore and the worker agreed that the service had been helpful to her. Miss Moore was quite satisfied with the helping process and its outcome, whereas the worker was dissatisfied, since she felt that she had not been able to help the client further in relation to her conflicts with her parents.

Case of Joyce Moore

Category	Client	Worker
I. BEGINNING PHASE Problems/Themes	My out-of-wedlock pregnancy and planning for baby's adoption. Had mixed feelings about adoption.	Out-of-wedlock pregnancy. Plans for adoption of baby.
Referral	Priest referred me to agency. He explained about counseling. Boyfriend and other friends also thought it a good idea. My father didn't want me to go to shrink—but okay since it was Catholic.	Referred through priest.
Expectations	Help with adoption. Find good home for baby. Also, I knew it would be awful period for me—that I needed to talk with someone.	Initially, get help to have baby placed in good home.
Initial Encounter	I was scared. The first social worker was older person who did not impress me. It was like talking to a grandmother. I couldn't open up with her. Would have dropped out but she soon retired and I got transferred. Second worker was much better. . . . I liked her. . . . Was more at ease with her.	I was the second worker. Transferred to me following retirement of first worker, whom she had seen for a few interviews. . . . We got along well from the beginning. I liked her.
II. MIDDLE PHASE Problems/Themes	We got away from the pregnancy—into feelings about marriage, my family relationships, our family problems.	Plans for baby. Conflict over adoption. Unhappy kid who wanted to talk about her problems beyond the pregnancy. Family relationship problems, relationship with boyfriend, sexual identity conflicts.

Case of Joyce Moore (Continued)

Category	Client	Worker
Activities	Mostly I talked. She listened a lot.	There was a lot of talking on the part of both of us.
Contracting	As we got away from pregnancy and into family problems, sometimes I couldn't say more. I didn't want to talk—like I was blocked. She helped me to get over this by being honest with me. She brought things up each week but also told me to feel free to bring up what's on my mind. Told me okay if I didn't want to talk about some things sometimes.	I was unsure whether to pursue issue of homosexuality. We explored it to the point I felt it wasn't a great problem for her. I never said to her, "Do want to get into it or not?" But the issue kept coming up. I'm not sure I handled this area very well, or adequately. . . . Maybe I should have discussed goals more with her.
Client/Worker Relationship	When I met the second worker I immediately knew she would be great. Made me more comfortable. She went into what *I* wanted in the first session. Made it clear not selfish of me to think of myself and have baby adopted. We got very close and I almost didn't want to stop.	She verbalized very well. Related very well. We got along fine.
Client/Worker Qualities	Worker was like a friend but more objective . . . not tell you what you want to hear. I liked her as a person—she didn't seem like a social worker. She was very friendly—talked about herself—about her daughter—was much warmer than I had expected. . . . Didn't throw questions at me—didn't penalize me—never took notes. I always felt better after leaving there. Only time I didn't like her was after baby was adopted. . . . It was like *she*	No idea as to how she saw me. Maybe as older sister, or mother? I think she liked my not being critical of her, since she was so self-critical.

Worker's Role/ Style	A few sessions poor—when we got into family problems. . . . I was uncomfortable and couldn't say much . . . but it helped. First worker not helpful at all and I could see it right away. Wanted to tell her so but didn't know how and not close enough to say it. Made me feel like patronizing . . . always handing me Kleenex when crying—but I didn't want them. The second one knew when to do it and when not to. Sometimes she acknowledged crying—sometimes she went on talking. . . .	I don't really know how she saw my role. No discussion between us about this. We talked about my being direct, but not too much; I took it for granted. That's how I am.
III. ENDING PHASE Reasons/Process	After baby had been placed and we had talked about my family problems and feelings about boyfriends, I was ready to go on my own.	Mutual decision. Ended after baby was placed and her main need taken care of. We stretched sessions out to every other week.
Significance	I didn't want to stop going because it was like a security blanket. I knew in my mind that I was okay but the support was gone all of a sudden. Kind of scary. Nothing could be done about it—if she keeps going she is not doing her job.	I was comfortable that issues around the pregnancy and the baby were resolved. She was squared away in her thinking.
Continuing Problems	I was getting along okay by then.	Still had problems in family relationships.
Future Plans	We made arrangements to keep in touch. She told me no need to have a problem to call her. I'll be calling her sometime.	We arranged for her to call me after she gets back to college to see how she is doing.

Case of Joyce Moore (Continued)

Category	Client	Worker
IV. OUTCOME What happened?	Helped me realize things about myself, about my parents, that my father wasn't as bad as I thought. How to assert myself more with parents. It's amazing—I know what I want out of life now. I have grown up a lot—closer to my father, better relationship with parents—know myself more.	Good things happened with her. She was satisfied with her decision to have baby adopted. Was more comfortable with herself. There were changes in her relationship with parents. More in touch with her feelings. Gained insight into herself.
Client/Worker Satisfaction	I felt pretty good about everything . . . all the help I got.	Frustrated that I couldn't keep case open, have chance to get deeper into family conflicts. Once baby was born and placed for adoption, the issue resolved and we didn't go into things further. I'm dissatisfied with that—I'm satisfied that she could share her feelings and I felt good about her decision for adoption.
What Helpful/ Not Helpful	Having someone like her to go to every week. . . . I needed it—was good . . . regular . . . consistent. Would have been good to have some home visits [later in pregnancy] but I didn't want to inconvenience her.	I don't know. Maybe my acceptance of her, helping her get in touch with her feelings. Resolving issue of pregnancy and baby's adoption relieved a lot of pressure for her and her family.
Client/Worker	She helped me become aware of things—presented different views that I never would have	She had a lot of courage.

thought of. Couldn't have done it without her. . . . Sounds so cliché . . . but it's the truth . . . for example, how it's not selfish to think of yourself.

Agency	Room very small—just a desk and chairs—She put in some plants and tried to make it homey . . . but still an office. . . . It made me feel more empty. I felt strange walking up the stairs—everyone saw me and knew why I was there—but they seemed nice. Everyone made me feel at home. Receptionist very good—made me feel so good. . . . Talked with me . . . was friendly. Fee was reasonable. I kept up with it . . . maybe it was too low. Felt so good about service that every now and then I contribute to United Way.	Don't recall that we said anything about agency. She liked her [the receptionist]. We never discussed the fee other than when we first set it.
Life	Family also helpful. 100 percent behind me. My sister called regularly from West Coast to make sure I was okay. Some problems with mother who had wanted me to keep baby.	Relief of anxiety once the baby was placed. Positive changes in family relationships.
Social Networks	Had good friends who helped me pull through. Had a girlfriend to whom I went often. Also boys who took me out when pregnant . . . paid attention to me—provided male support. Another male friend would send me flowers. Found out that most of those who had been my friends continued to be.	Her father stopped drinking. Her family was very supportive . . . even though they put a lot of pressure on her. She had many friends who were very helpful—both male and female. Everybody liked her.
Other		

Appendix E

Research Interviews with Mrs. Donnelly and Her Social Worker

The full transcripts of research interviews in a "successful" and an "unsuccessful" case are reproduced, respectively, in this Appendix and in the next one. My purpose is to illustrate in further depth the kind of material that I collected as well as the method that I employed. The interviews are preceded by a brief summary of background information in each case. A postscript highlighting key issues and themes follows each set of client and worker interviews.

Judy Donnelly was a white, middle-class, divorced woman in her early thirties who had completed one year of college and was self-employed as a beauty parlor operator.

Several years earlier she and her former husband had gone to the Family Service Bureau for marital counseling, following referral by their parish priest. They had been married for four or five years and had apparently been dissatisfied with each other since early in the marriage. They had no children.

The Donnellys' initial contact with the Bureau terminated after a few sessions. Evidently Mrs. Donnelly was eager to continue in joint sessions, while Mr. Donnelly saw no purpose to counseling and therefore withdrew. Soon after, the couple decided to divorce. While in the midst of divorce proceedings, Mrs. Donnelly went into treatment with Mr. Smith, a social worker in private practice. Her main reason for seeking treatment was that she was having difficulty coping with her sense of failure and guilt concerning the divorce and with the negative reactions of members of her extended family as well as that of her husband.

Mrs. Donnelly continued in treatment with Mr. Smith for several months and then decided to return to the Family Service Bureau because she could no longer afford the cost of private treatment. She requested a male practitioner, but none was available. She was then assigned for intake evaluation to Marie Gray, the same worker she and Mr. Donnelly had seen earlier. Her presenting request was for help to cope with the depression that she was feeling as the divorce was becoming final.

After the intake evaluation, Mrs. Donnelly remained in treatment for over a year with Mrs. Gray. She was seen weekly until the latter part of this period.

Following some initial difficulty in becoming engaged with the worker, Mrs. Donnelly found the service very helpful to her. She and Mrs. Gray agreed that the "case" had been successful and emphasized that there had been significant improvement in Mrs. Donnelly's functioning.

Mrs. Donnelly was eager to cooperate in the study and highly motivated to present her views. She participated thoughtfully in the research interview, which lasted somewhat over an hour. At her request, the interview took place in my office. She impressed me as an open, relaxed person who expressed herself clearly and directly, even though at times she struggled to find the "right" words.

The interview with Mrs. Gray took place in her office two days later and lasted a little over an hour. Mrs. Gray was also very interested in the study and involved herself fully in the interview. This was the third interview I held with her in connection with her cases, so that she was by then well acquainted with the process and format of questions.

Like Mrs. Donnelly, Mrs. Gray was in her thirties. She was an experienced practitioner who had been with the Bureau for several years and who specialized in work with families involving children and adolescents. She was an easygoing, warm person who readily made clients feel at ease with her. As she explained it, she used a task-oriented approach to practice in which she encouraged clients to define explicitly their goals and expectations and to become actively involved in achieving desired changes. She provided much support for clients and tended to allow and encourage them to move at their own pace and in response to their own needs rather than being too directive with them.

RESEARCH INTERVIEW WITH JUDY DONNELLY

Interviewer: [Following various introductory remarks, including explanation of the study's purpose] The first thing is . . . Could you tell me a little about the difficulties that initially brought you to the Family Service Bureau?
Respondent: When we first went there a few years ago, I had made a decision to get a divorce and my husband was still living with me but we didn't know the procedures . . . plus I had a business at that time and I didn't want to upset my business, so I thought if I talked to somebody, it would help me both ways, which it did.
I: What did you try to do about these difficulties before you went to the agency? Did you talk with anyone, for example . . . ?
R: Well—not really—we didn't want to talk to our friends or relatives.
I: Why?
R: They're too close to you—they take sides—you need someone who can be objective.
I: When you decided to seek help, how did you happen to go to this particular agency?
R: Well, at that time, of course I wasn't divorced so I was a Catholic and I was going to church and they recommended them to me.

I: Did you know anything about the agency before going?

R: No, but when you go there they have little brochures that you can read, and I found out all about it.

I: What did you hope they would do for you before you went there?

R: Well, I hoped, I thought they were going to make my mind up for me, but then I realized, you know, that you have to make your own mind up and they just give you suggestions or let you decide, which is very good.

I: Now, if we could talk about the first sessions that you had, I imagine you called and you made an appointment. How soon after. . . .

R: That was, um, I think about a week or two. . . . I don't remember exactly but it wasn't very long.

I: Ah . . . when you . . . if we could talk a little bit about that first session . . . how did you feel in going there?

R: Very uncomfortable. Matter of fact now, when I went the first time several years ago, the first session was with my husband. I dragged him with me, and then we only went three sessions and he decided not to go. Then, the second time, when I went by myself, I was confident and I knew I wanted to go so I wasn't as uptight. But the first session I was because he was with me.

I: Is that why you were uncomfortable?

R: I think so, because I didn't know whether he wanted to continue or what the situation was.

I: How were you received at the agency in the beginning?

R: Very well. They have a very friendly group of people there, and that makes you feel comfortable right away.

I: And in that first session, do you remember what went on, what did you do, what did you talk about?

R: I'll talk about the first session we had . . . when my husband was also there. . . . Well, at that time, the first thing that came into my head was communication. We had a span where we were not communicating in our marriage and we asked Mrs. Gray, the social worker, to help, and she just suggested that it was something that we would have to work out. We had exercises every week to try to work on and it was only three sessions and my husband didn't want to continue.

I: So, you went for three sessions together. And later, when you went back yourself the second time, for how long did you go there?

R: Myself? For about a year.

I: About a year . . . was that on a weekly basis?

R: Right, then in the end it was like once a month—the last three months.

I: Now, could we talk about all of those contacts that you had, particularly the ones that you had yourself with the worker? There are several questions I would like to ask you. First, what went on in those contacts, in those sessions when you went there?

R: Well, what do you mean, "What went on"?

I: What did you do, what did you talk about?

R: Well, I don't know, she . . . it's hard to explain . . . when I went there the first time, I was kind of, I was . . . I wasn't talkative to her. I thought she was very young and . . . it was going around in my head, how could she know all the scores. . . . (**I:** Uh, huh.) That was the first thing that blocked my mind, and then, later on, when we got to know each other, I came out and said it to her . . . that I wasn't too confident (**I:** Uh, huh), which was really the best thing because, you know, she gave me trials days . . . she said you'll have a chance to try things out [unclear] . . .

I: What was there beyond her age which made you feel uncomfortable?

R: Oh, she was *very* quiet and . . . I thought she was going to ask me questions and she didn't and I thought, *Wow! maybe she doesn't know anything,* which wasn't true.

I: Uh, hmm. . . . Now, as it went on and you became more comfortable in those contacts, what did you do during those meetings, what did you discuss?

R: Well, uh . . . I had remembered an exercise that Mr. Smith had given me to relax myself . . . in the morning . . . at night . . . so, by then . . . I wasn't as nervous, I was more relaxed and when you're more relaxed, of course, you can talk, you can express yourself. . . . The thing that she tried to make me understand about the marriage was that it wasn't just my fault, I was blaming myself an awful lot and the fact that, you know, he didn't want to come in and get help was one of the reasons why we're having problems in our marriage. . . .

I: What did the worker think were your problems as it went on?

R: Well, I didn't have confidence in myself. . . . Now, I still don't know why I didn't have the confidence in myself, you know, I felt, maybe I wasn't doing enough because I had my own business. I felt guilty, thinking that this was one of the main reasons I wasn't a good wife. . . . And, instead of us getting closer we got further into trouble.

I: What did *you* think were the problems as you went on talking with the worker?

R: When I first went in, I thought it was all my fault and I felt guilty because I was the one that was seeking the divorce. I was pushing it and I thought, well, I shouldn't be doing this, you know, we all have guilty feelings sometimes. (**I:** Uh, huh.) Later, I realized my husband and I just weren't happy together.

I: What did the worker try to do in order to help you with these kinds of problems?

R: Well, one of the things was that she wanted me to get back to my old friends that I had and tell them that I was sorry that I hadn't seen them in the last six months or year, and . . . even if I never went over to their house . . . she said just relieving you of the guilt was a good thing, and that was one of the things that I did. The second good thing was that I had to start mixing with people, . . . I was withdrawing because I was divorced. I didn't want to go anywhere, didn't have anybody to go with, and, uh . . . I thought *that* was a problem there. She helped me—I started taking tennis and then I started voluntary work and through the voluntary work I met people my age, so . . . she helped me a lot. Things that I probably would have sat back and thought about . . . but wouldn't do on my own. . . .

I: Why not, what was different about having a worker?

R: I don't know, she pushed me in the right direction. I don't think I would have thought of all those things, and here, the things were right there. . . . It was just that I didn't use them. You know, I felt, at one time, that I would like to call my friends up like couples and say, "Hi, how are ya? I just want you to know I'm divorced and that's why I haven't been over," but I'd never have the guts to do it. You see what I mean? (**I:** Oh.) She was so kind, so interested . . . she gave me the courage—the push—to do it myself.

I: Ah . . . if we could talk about the worker for a moment, ah . . . , what was she like? How would you describe her? What kind of person was she?

R: She was very humble. She was a very clean person, clean looking. I don't know, she was a quiet nice but a quiet nice that I didn't understand. (**I:** Uh, huh.) You know what I mean? Dead silence. . . . I was just getting nervous about the silence, which I think is why it took us a little longer to get going.

I: How did it feel in those early contacts before you got to know her when she was so quiet?

R: I felt uncomfortable and, lots of times, when we started our session, she would say nothing—just say, "Hi, how are you?" and we would look at each other and I felt . . . I didn't know what to do next after that. I guess she thought I should have spoken and I thought, well, *she should ask questions.* . . .

I: And then, eventually, I think you said that you were . . .

R: Eventually, things changed. I don't know. . . . She didn't come down a peg but . . . she made me feel relaxed. I don't know how to explain that; we started talking about things I like to do and then, why don't I go and do them . . . things I hadn't done for seven or eight years.

I: How did things change? Was there any discussion in those early sessions of why she was like that . . . ? Like you were saying that you went in and you expected her to ask questions and [both laughing] she expected you to start and neither one did it?

R: Um, yes, I think that's when the ice was broken. She, um . . . oh, when I told her I thought I should change because I was more comfortable with a male social worker and she asked me why and I said, "Well, they've been more relaxing, there's no space of silence . . . we're always talking about something and . . ." I think maybe that made her think, and the next time it was better. You know, she got more comfortable with me. I don't know if she was afraid of me or I was afraid of her. I couldn't figure that out at that time and then, when we got more familiar with each other, we went on.

I: And how did you feel as it went on? How did you feel about the idea of having a man versus a woman?

R: It was all in my mind . . . I guess, because she was very good. The only difference in a male social worker that I had was that he would push you to give him that extra something, which I expected out of her, and it's not necessary. You know what I mean?

I: You mean he would ask questions?

R: Yeah, he would ask questions and then when I'd answer questions he'd say, "Well, how do you feel about this?" and he'd get in a little deeper. This is why I expected so much out of her, you see, and it wasn't really necessary. . . . I didn't have that problem. I didn't think that it was that deep.

I: What were the things or the qualities that you liked most about the worker at the Bureau? About her and her approach?

R: Oh, she was . . . not shy, she was modest, in a way. In other words, through all the sessions, she was giving me things and I didn't realize it, which, I think, was nice about her. She'd give me ideas and I didn't realize that it was all going to add up in the end. When we started to meet less often, I had more time to think about her. In a nice way, she was like a mother. She gave but she didn't expect anything in return and was so humble about it, but yet was happy that you were going ahead . . . on your own.

I: From what you were saying, you didn't really realize this until the end?

R: I didn't see it. . . . I didn't see it at all. And, for a while there . . . I thought it was a waste of time and I was really thinking of dropping out, but now I'm glad I didn't.

I: Would it have helped if somehow she had made you more aware of what was going on between the two of you, and what she was doing?

R: Well, she did do that in a way. . . . She was very outspoken about it, and she said: "I'm here to hear what you've got to say, but, I also am here to direct you." It was a long time before she said that.

I: Do you think it would have helped if that had come sooner?

R: Yeah, I think it would have been out in the open. I would have been open a little more because, you see, it was a change for me. I didn't want to change . . . really, from Mr. Smith to another worker . . . but financially I couldn't afford it. Okay, that was one of the reasons. . . . And then, you know, I had to change a whole new way of doing it. How come that they're not all the same?

I: How come that there are two different approaches? (**R:** Yeah, yeah.) How much discussion was there at the beginning, you know, of your going from one worker to another?

R: Oh, Mr. Smith asked how I felt when I was leaving and I said, "I like you very much but I couldn't afford it . . . and . . . I said, "I am going to miss you, but this is a decision I have to make since I'll be taking care of myself," and I left. I guess, he . . . he . . . he was supposed to write to her but he talked to her on the phone and gave her my records.

I: And then, when you started with Mrs. Gray, was there discussion of how you felt about going from one worker to the other?

R: Oh, yeah, yeah . . . she was good that way [unclear] . . . but she was starting from scratch. I think her part was hard but like my girlfriend said to me, "You're going in there to help yourself, you're not going in there to think of her part, or how she feels." . . . At times, I felt bad because I wasn't responding. I felt bad because the instructor or teacher or whatever you want to call it, the speaker—what would you call it?

I: You mean the worker?

R: Yeah, the *worker.* Here's the worker and I'm not getting across to her and I, when I went home, sometimes I spoke to my girlfriend and I'd say, "I feel bad that, you know, I'm not . . . I'm trying hard to get together with her but I can't," and my friend said to me, "You know, you're so used to another way that it will be hard to change it," and then I . . .

I: So your friend helped you to see it more clearly in that way?

R: Yeah. . . .

I: What do you think could have been done, now that you look back on those early sessions? What do you think could have been done to make it more useful for you so that you didn't have to go through as much as you did?

R: Well, I thought that Mr. Smith probably would have made her understand me better and that it wasn't like we were sitting there, facing each other and challenging each other. You know, that's how I felt it was at first. Um, you have to know what upsets the people that you're talking to. Those are the things that you have to pick up if you're a social worker . . . and probably you can't pick it up in one session, but you can figure it out and [unclear] . . . the only time I like quiet is when I'm reading. (**I:** Oh.) It's just annoying. Maybe a radio would help, I don't know. You know, we're in a very small room, and I don't know. . . . It was kind of bare. There was one painting up there that one of the children had done and then . . . I don't know, it was kind of *coldish,* and I don't know if it would have been a radio that would have made me feel at home. . . . It wasn't *her* because she was a very welcome person, she was very nice, you know, friendly. It's just that the atmosphere you're sitting in, I think, you know . . . it's not so great.

I: And then the silences made it uncomfortable for you?

R: But that part was only me, I'm sure. . . .

I: But that's important because you felt that way. . . .

R: Now a good example is in here—because of the carpeting, there is a lamp, you won't recognize but we would . . .

I: Later, we'll be talking more about the place itself. . . . Ah, for now, what were the things . . . ah . . . We were talking about some of the things that you liked about the worker and her approach. What were some of the things that you liked the least beyond what you've already said?

R: What I liked the least. . . . It was, well, I already told you . . . um . . . sometimes she got perturbed when I didn't remember [unclear] . . . and sometimes I found myself doing that on purpose, almost like I didn't want to communicate with her, which I didn't realize until the end. I could have helped myself better if I hadn't done that.

I: You mean you didn't answer her questions or . . .

R: Well, no, sometimes she might say, "All this week I want you to try to do this, go out of your way to extend yourself to certain people, go out of your way to do such and such." I had done all this. Then, when we came back into the session to talk about it, I didn't open up.

I: Why was that?

R: I don't know why, maybe because I didn't feel comfortable.

I: So you still, as you went on . . .

R: I did that just a couple of times, and then we talked about it. I guess she was getting pretty fed up that she was giving me all these sessions and I wasn't coming back and responding and I was getting upset too, you know, and then we got down to the bottom of it.

I: How did you and she do this?

R: Well, she would say, "Well . . . Mr. Smith thinks you can talk and for some reason you don't because you're not . . . we're not talking this out." The way she said it really made me think a little bit. You know, maybe I better communicate with her — or at least talk — and it was funny because I was there to help myself and I was afraid to . . . [Long pause]

I: What was the worker like? You talked already a little bit about that, I wonder if you'd tell me a little bit more about how was she like or unlike the previous worker that you had?

R: I don't know. One thing I felt was . . . she didn't give me enough conclusions. You know what I mean, like after you have a session you usually go home and think and try to use something they give you. After a session with Mr. Smith I had felt like it had drained me, but yet there were still little pieces I could carry home with me. When I was with her, I didn't feel that drained. I felt like I was just talking to my girlfriend. Can you see the difference?

I: Yes, there's an important difference there. . . .

R: And that's maybe why I didn't think of it as being as helpful as when I was going to Mr. Smith.

I: Oh, so because of that you didn't think it was as good?

R: Yeah, I'd think . . . well, she's not as deep, not that intuitive. . . .

I: Anything else, any other differences that you saw?

R: No, they were both friendly, um . . . the male, uh . . . social worker . . . if I was just sort of a minute late he got very upset about that and Mrs. Gray . . . she never really said anything about that.

I: About your being late?

R: Yeah, I guess because I traveled far to get there.

I: You've talked with a couple of social workers and also with your friends, what is it like talking with a friend versus talking with a social worker . . . ?

R: Well, it's a lot closer because I feel . . . your friends know you better . . . but the social worker knows how to understand you, how to be . . . how not to be prejudiced, to be objective.

I: The social worker?

R: Yeah, aren't they supposed to?

I: How do you mean?

R: They can tell if you're nervous, they can tell, um . . . if you're communicating and getting along, they can [unclear] . . .

I: So you feel that one difference between friend and social worker . . .

R: Sure, when you're with a friend you're much closer, and they can sense right away because they've been with you longer—that if your feelings are hurt you don't know what to say or you can't say it. With a social worker, it's not the same. They're not with you long enough. . . .

I: They're not with you long enough to really get to know you?

R: Yeah. . . .

I: Any other similarity or difference between the social worker and a friend?

R: No, they're trying to make it as friendly as they can, which is good. I think that's excellent.

I: In what way do you feel it's good?

R: They want you to come here and help yourself; I think that's good. **(I:** Uh, huh.) I think if she was very cold to me, I don't know, I wouldn't have liked it. I know that because I [unclear] . . .

I: Now, while you were going to this agency, uh, . . . from what you said, you talked with at least one friend—at least one friend knew that you were going. How did she react to your going there? How did she feel about it?

R: Well, she felt that I should have gone because this one friend is still going, so we're both in the same situation. You see, she . . . it was her second divorce, and she was upset about this . . . going through it twice . . . and she wanted to know why. I sent her myself to a clinic. I thought she was a very bright girl; she was too smart for herself, and she was the one that told me to think of myself and not to feel bad for the social worker. Otherwise, you're not helping yourself.

I: What did you think about this?

R: She put the question in my mind, and that's when I said to Mrs. Gray that maybe I'd work better with a man . . . and that's when things came out in the open between me and Mrs. Gray.

I: Now, after that point, how did you get along with Mrs. Gray?

R: I think it was good that I said that because we got along better. When we had a meeting that would drag she would say it—"What's wrong?"—"You're not concentrating on what you're supposed to—how was your week?" She would push to get back into things, which was good.

I: Aside from the worker, what did you think about the agency as a whole?

R: They were *very* good.

I: What other impressions do you have?

R: I was very impressed because, in the waiting room sitting there all those weeks, I saw a lot of other people really disturbed. Young kids—the way they handled them—you know, they gave them toys to play with, something to amuse them; they were fantastic. . . . If somebody was late, they weren't rude, they would just say, "She'll be a few minutes, or he'll be a few minutes." I think they were very, very good. They handled that front situation, the first situation, very well.

I: What do you mean? In the waiting room when you first go in?

R: The waiting room — I thought that was excellent. You know, being in my own business, we have a lot of people we have to contend with, and sometimes it is hard to control them. But here, the fact that they have the waiting room. . . . They have things to do, which is good — you know, it calmed people down a little bit before they went upstairs.

I: How were the other staff members that you saw?

R: The only contact I had was with the woman on the phone, which I would assume was the receptionist. They would change sometimes . . . when I went upstairs, they had a different girl when I came down. It was all charity work, she told me when I asked them why they changed so much. They were very, very nice, especially the girl at the desk when you first go in. In fact, when she called me, I remembered everything right away, and I said, "I know who this is!", and she said, "Yup," she says, "I'm from the Bureau." . . . I recognized her voice because I talked to her on the phone before, and she has a very friendly voice. She's a very, very likable person and she's just the receptionist. You see, right there, it's like they have an open door. If I had gotten a cold feeling, I probably wouldn't have gone upstairs or never finished.

I: It sounds like that initial impression is very important. . . .

R: That helped me a lot! Maybe that's just one person, but I think that's very important.

I: How about the physical surroundings and the location of the agency?

R: That was really a bad location — there were all those kids on the street. In fact, I said that to her . . . "Where should I park my car?" I was kind of afraid to park my car right there because they were all hanging around there, and she said, "No, just say hello to them and they won't bother you." So I said, "Well, gee. . . . " I didn't like that area — I hope they can relocate.

I: Did you pay a fee for the service?

R: Yup, they went according to your pay.

I: What do you think about the idea of paying a fee?

R: I think it's good, I really do.

I: In what way?

R: Because if you didn't pay a fee, you wouldn't be as attentive. For some reason, when people pay for things, they respect them more, and they try to do what's right. But if we just went in for free, I don't think that would help. . . . I know, 'cause I've had that experience dealing with the public myself. When you give them something free, it didn't mean nothing. When they pay three dollars, four dollars, or five dollars — *wow!* — they'd say *that stayed in good,* or, *I didn't like it.* They have some initial respect for what their money was spent for.

I: They would be more attentive?

R: I really believe that.

I: Anything else about the agency as a whole?

R: No, the only impression that I thought, um . . . when I was near the end, I said I would like to have had a group session with people in the same shoes . . . you know, with divorced people, so that I would see the feelings that they had. Mrs. Gray said that we all have these feelings—she *said* that—but I didn't know it for a fact. I never talked to anybody who had also gone through it.

I: Did you mention this to Mrs. Gray?

R: I had asked her, and I had gone to two places—one to the Y, the women's Y, which they had discontinued. (**I:** Oh.) But I felt the Y wasn't the place for it. I felt right *here* was the place for it.

I: Oh, and they didn't have it available?

R: At that time they didn't, and now, I recently sent somebody over there, somebody else, who told me they had group therapy, and she expressed that she hated it. Maybe because she hasn't been through it. . . . I would probably hate it at first too.

I: How did you happen to stop your sessions at this agency?

R: We both agreed. Um, we decided that as soon as I felt I could make my own decisions, that I could handle everything myself without getting too emotionally upset . . . um, you know, that I could leave. And that was funny; after all that time . . . I really felt bad in leaving. I was glad, and then I felt bad at the same time. You know, I was going to miss her in my life because I had grown fond of her but then . . . I had to leave some time—I couldn't go there forever.

I: Did you share these feelings with her?

R: Yes, I told her I felt bad leaving because I had grown to like her—you see—then we were getting closer after the early sessions, after we broke that spell or . . . I don't know what it is . . . the lapse, I felt much closer, much better.

I: How did she feel about your leaving?

R: She also felt that it was time for me to leave and she felt that somebody else might need her much more . . . that I was doing well (**I:** Uh, huh.), that it was time for me to make the decision to go. And, she always said, "Once you leave, if you ever have any real emotional problems, you always can come back, just call." So it wasn't that you went forever, and I think with that in your mind the chances of going back are probably one in a million.

I: How do you mean?

R: Well, because, um, she, in her way, gave you the confidence that you can do it, right? And, then just knowing you can go back, you just try to be self-sufficient, see?

I: Oh! Do you think that if anything came up you might go back to this agency or a similar person?

R: Oh, yeah, I would go back to the same agency . . . if it was still there.

I: Now you mentioned that you referred someone, one of your friends . . .

R: Yeah, and they started right away in the group therapy, which they didn't like. This person is a very shy person and she is not outgoing. She is going through a divorce and she had many problems because of her children and other things.

I: What was it that she didn't like about the group sessions?

R: Well, she said first of all they were all women and she wanted very much to know the male point of view. . . . (**I:** Uh, huh.) Now I don't know what she wanted to know for, maybe because she wanted to know how her husband felt, his feelings or what . . . I don't know, and she had gone just a couple of times, and now she won't go. So, I thought, I told her to go back, maybe she should have her own individual worker — *I* said, I didn't feel I wanted to talk to anybody till the end. (**I:** Oh.) Maybe they would try a new approach if she asked them, I'm sure they would schedule you with somebody, you know.

I: Do you think you might refer other people to this agency if the occasion came up?

R: I have, I have. . . .

I: For what kinds of problems?

R: Well, those same problems. Either a death in the family, emotional problems that they can't cope with, things which we hear in a beauty salon because they tell you all about it. . . . We hear it all the time. . . .

I: Why do they tell you about these problems?

R: Because they're relaxed. It's the same with a bartender. When I was in Colorado, I read an article in the local paper that in the future they were going to teach hairdressers and barbers and bartenders certain ways to get to the people to give them the right direction for help. . . . Rather than drinking themselves to death or spending all their savings on hairdos or ending up killing themselves . . . which I thought was very, very good, and it hasn't come here yet.

I: No, I haven't heard of it yet.

R: It makes a lot of sense. (**I:** Yeah, it makes sense.) I know a lot of bartenders, and they tell me the same thing. They hear the same thing we do. . . . People you don't even know come right over and say, "Boy! I can't go home — my wife's miserable!", or "These kids are driving me crazy!", or "My husband has left me and I don't know what to do about my finances. . . ." And, well, here they are, spending money on their hairdo and they don't even know about their financial end. . . . So, right there, they're searching for some type of help.

I: Uh, huh . . . does it suggest that maybe if beauticians or bartenders could get some training they might be able to do more? . . .

R: [Interrupting] I try to direct them to the right place. This agency is the only place I know and, you see, me telling them that I went makes them feel at ease because sometimes they feel like they're going to be the only ones. Then they unwind right away and tell me a lot about their troubles.

I: When they know you also went?

R: Yup, and I tell them it wasn't hard and it wasn't easy—so I'm getting to be the "Director of Social Work"—which is good, though. I'd rather see that than have something bad happen to them.

I: I imagine a lot of times this can be a big help to some of your clients.

R: Well, that's one of the reasons that made me go back to college, because I feel I should have more training, and I started to take courses earlier this year.

I: Well, if we could just take a few more minutes. (**R:** Sure!) Uh, if you could look at your total experience at this agency now that you're through with it, how helpful would you say it was for you?

R: The whole thing? I thought it was really good and it was something I needed very much at that time. I'm glad that it's in the past. . . . I don't know, it's something you suddenly need but then, when it goes by you, you're glad it's in the past. I don't know if it's the feeling that I don't want to feel that I'm so weak that I needed a crutch—I don't know if it's that feeling—which it probably was or if it's a feeling that [unclear] . . . I don't know, it was something that I needed at that time. I'm glad I went, but I'm also glad it's over. . . . I'm glad I can make my decisions, that I can control things better.

I: Uh, huh, what would you say was most helpful about going there at that time?

R: I think the thing that we were talking about—getting over the divorce—was most helpful . . . and then, when I got that over with, I wanted more out of life. You see, who are you going to talk to? You can't talk to your parents because they know both of you and they're going to side with one of you, and you don't want them to side. You can't talk to a sister or brother—in my situation, my brother was younger than I. I couldn't talk to an in-law, right? I'm divorcing their son. It was very hard. Who were you going to talk to? And the only one I had spoken to was a friend that had experienced it, that's why I went to her. Just like I say to my customers when they ask me—well, they feel better when I tell them, because I've had the experience, so they feel relaxed. . . .

I: Uh, huh . . . what would you say was least helpful about the sessions as a whole?

R: Going that far—it's far from the office. Traveling was a pain. I thought that made me want to hurry to get things done; that was a pain. Uh, least helpful in the sessions? Well, when I first started, I thought it was kind of hard to get started. I mean you sit there, just facing each other . . . it's kind of hard.

I: It's hard. . . .

R: I thought that initial time when she says hello is good. . . . She shakes your hand or she shows some sign of affection. . . . Then you go in the room and the room is completely different from what she's showing you. You know, it's cold and . . . it was kind of hard, but I felt, well, they didn't have the money because it was an association. . . . It was affiliated with the church and it was just a sideline for the church. That's why I overlooked it. I didn't realize that it was that important until I sat here and in Mr. Smith's office and then remembered what his office looked like.

I: And you can compare?

R: I can compare three of you now, isn't that funny?

I: Yeah, well, this is interesting. . . . Now if you could think a little bit about another area. Since you started going to that agency, what changes have there been in your life, in your functioning, in the way you get along with other people, that kind of thing?

R: Well, that's a hard question. . . . Yeah, for a while there I thought I was doing good because I was very quiet before I said anything. Before I would just say what I meant, get it out; now I'm more cautious. That taught me a lesson because, you know, I think of all the bad eight years I had, because I mean, I'd say what was on the top of my head. Um . . . I tolerate people more, which I never did before, I know that for a fact because some people have said that—"That's not you sitting there, biting your tongue!" You know, I was a very impatient person. Those two things I can remember. I can't remember everything. I know there are other things too. Um, I don't know, it's more compassion for me to my friend that's in trouble where before, if they were divorced and they had trouble, I didn't understand it. I didn't know what it was like to have problems. Now . . . I think twice about that. I might even extend myself to them to help.

I: So it seems that you made a number of important changes. Any other changes in your life?

R: Just that I can take care of myself . . . [laughs] That's a good change. I'm happy about that, (**I:** Oh, sure.) which I was scared, and I didn't think I could. And especially the times now when I have a lot of pressures—like at work—and I can handle it pretty good.

I: What do you think there was beyond the help that you got from the social workers? Was there anything or anyone else that was helpful to you in accomplishing these changes?

R: I don't know. . . . It—if the charity work helped or not—I don't know. I couldn't say that right now.

I: What kind of charity work did you do?

R: Well, I used to go to this orphanage, and I used to cut these kids' hair. There were about twenty-five girls, and I used to go monthly and take care of them. I don't know if that helped me or not. Maybe it did because I saw them very emotionally upset there, and I said to myself: "I don't want to be that way." And I wonder if maybe that helped me, I don't know . . . but those kids—they talk to me, they write to me, which is really nice. I'm happy because I like to make friends there too.

I: Uh, huh. . . . How about your friends? You mentioned in particular one friend with whom you seemed to be close. Was that helpful in any way to you?

R: Yes, she was very helpful. But now, it's funny, she's still going for treatment, and now I don't talk to her, I don't see her. I don't understand if maybe she's really wrapped up in her sessions, or what.

I: Have you tried to see her?

R: Oh yes, I've called her and everything, and she's usually busy studying so I wonder if, her being . . . you know, there's a saying that you can go too deep and sometimes it's not good for your own good, and she's withdrawn now, and she is one person that I would not expect it . . . and *she* was the one that helped me!

I: Anything else in your life situation, for example, at work . . . ?

R: Well, that has helped because I don't have my own business, and it helped me to make the decision to sell it.

I: Oh, you sold your business?

R: Yes, and that has helped a lot. I have less responsibility, I don't have that much on myself anymore, which may be a reason why I was having trouble before.

I: Do you still work in the same field?

R: Oh, yeah. . . .

I: When you were going to these sessions with the worker, was there a discussion of your business, selling it or not selling . . . ?

R: Yeah, yeah, yeah . . . We talked about that. That was good. That was something I had to make my mind up. And then, we went through the procedure of applying for jobs. (I: Oh, I see.) You know, and all that which was really nice. It was like having a friend there all the time. (I: Uh, huh.)

I: Now, a couple of final points, first, again . . . if you look at your total experience at this agency from this perspective, what would you say about it in general, for example, what would you change, if anything?

R: Um . . . I think I would change . . . the room, the colors, you know, put things on the wall to make it feel like it could be a house. Or, maybe, a lamp or something which you would see in a house. Um . . . I would make it not so cold. And, I would keep the reception area — I would keep that. Um, the social workers — both of them were wonderful. But then, in the end, I would give people a choice . . . if I wanted to go into group therapy . . . I would change that. I think that's very important.

I: You'd give them a choice?

R: Yeah, 'cause when you're divorced or there is a death or, I don't know what other reasons you could go for, whatever those reasons are, nobody wants to feel alone, and that's the feeling you get when you're in a room that's kind of cold. You feel like you're the only one in the world that's doing this.

I: And a group would help?

R: Maybe at the end if they felt you were capable of handling group therapy, or if they asked you, I think that's a good idea. In a group there would be other people, maybe somebody there who you'd have future contact with — which is good when you're in that feeling.

I: Uh, huh . . . anything else?

R: Nothing that I can think of.

I: I think you mentioned earlier that you would do the initial session a little differently. . . .

R: [Laughing] Right, right . . . in the beginning. That, but that's something between just you and them. It might have . . . it might not be with everybody else.

I: Do you have any other thoughts or suggestions or ideas that we haven't covered?

R: No, I'm just glad we had this session because it made me gather all my thoughts for the past two days and . . . some things I realized here just talking which I didn't realize before, which is good. (I: Oh) For me too, not only for you. I can see more and more that I got help . . . that I'm doing all right.

I: Well, I'm glad that it all worked out. . . . You said earlier that you'll be going to college?

R: Yeah, I just started summer school . . . at a community college near me.

I: Are you working toward a degree?

R: Yes, my Business Administration degree. They only have the two-year degree there, and then you can go to another college.

I: Yeah, well, thank you very much.

R: Gee, I'm *glad* I came!

I: Well, I really appreciate it.

RESEARCH INTERVIEW WITH MARIE GRAY, SOCIAL WORKER IN THE DONNELLY CASE

Interviewer: [Introductory remarks reviewing purpose of the study] To begin with, could you tell me a little about the reasons that led Mrs. Donnelly to this agency?

Respondent: [Reading from the case record, the worker reviews a history of marital difficulties in connection with which several years earlier Mr. and Mrs. Donnelly had sought help at the Family Service Bureau. After a few sessions, they indicated that things were going along better with them and withdrew from treatment. More recently, Mrs. Donnelly returned to the agency requesting help for herself because of being "depressed" while in the midst of divorce proceedings. She had been in treatment with a social worker in private practice but wanted to transfer to a social agency since she could no longer afford the cost.]

I: What difficulties did she want help with when she came back to this agency?

R: She wanted to focus on her basic lack of self-confidence, her ambivalence toward her parents, her intense, competitive, hostile feelings toward men. She was having a hard time relating to people, but a very hard time relating to men. And that's actually what brought her back, to see if she could feel better about herself.

I: What did she seem to expect from you and the agency in relation to some of those problems?

R: To help her work on these. After having been in treatment with the private practitioner, she had pretty clearly established in her mind where she was at and where her goals were and what she needed to work on, so she sort of brought the contract with her to negotiate with me. And my perception was that it was pretty correct — I didn't differ with her assessment and I did get in touch with Mr. Smith [the private practitioner], and he shared with me his assessment — and it seemed to be pretty appropriate to continue along the focus that they had set together.

I: What did you see as the problems as things went on during the most recent contact?

R: Well, low self-image, a lot of things that got started in her childhood that she had been trying to work out through her behavior in her adult life. After her parents got divorced while she was still an infant, she rarely saw her father. She lived with her mother and her grandparents for the first few years of life. Then her mother married and Judy acquired a stepfather and more children were born, half-brothers and sisters. And apparently the family tried to provide her with all the good things that families provide but they stressed excelling and competence, they stressed doing very well. . . . They were strivers, achievers, and expected her to be so also, and she wasn't allowed to complain about this. Nor did they ever give her any support to help her, you know, any credit — no icing on the cake — She would achieve and they would sort of accept it as, "Well, that's what is expected of you, we're not going to give you any praise for that," so she was very competitive.

I believe that she was entering latency age when her mother married. She and her mother had been pretty close and she had come to take discipline from her mother and her grandmother and grandfather, and all of a sudden there was this new stepfather on the scene who apparently wanted to take over as a father, and wanted her to obey his rules. The mother felt that she married this man, she was going to share her life with this man — that included her child — so that the father, her new husband, of course, would be able to discipline the child. But Judy resented this deeply and so it got into a competitive thing, a rivalry, I guess, for the attention and affection of the mother. Judy resented deeply having her stepfather tell her what to do.

Now this is all in retrospect, but even up through high school — she loves him, she cares a great deal about him, she worries about him when he's in ill health. He drinks too much in his later years, she's very worried about that, you know. And she knows he cares about her, but there is a lot of things left to be desired in that relationship. So . . . she sort of emerged into adulthood feeling that she had to compete and that people to compete with were men and that in order to be any good, you had to prove that you were not only as good as a man, but better. And, you know, it wasn't a friendly ego-building rivalry—it was hostile, and this is really the basis of what happened in her marriage.

I: How did Mrs. Donnelly see her problems as she went on working with you in the most recent contact with the Bureau?

R: Well, you see, a lot of that had gotten started with Mr. Smith, and so she was pretty aware of some of this. I think through our contact she gained a greater appreciation of what it means to be—she got back to her childhood—and tried to think of what it meant when you really worked hard on an assignment and got an "A" and you came home and said, "I got an 'A,'" and it was just sort of, "Eh . . . so you got an 'A.'" You know, she apparently spent all her time on her homework and she tried too hard to please, to achieve, to meet whatever the expectations were—and apparently she did very often. She never got any positive feedback. And then, of course, that translated to her as, "I guess I didn't do well enough, I guess I should have gotten an 'A +' or a commendation." There was something that she felt she wasn't producing, and it meant that she was defective.

I: What did you do in relation to these problems as the contacts went on? What did you try to accomplish with her?

R: Take a look at what she was doing with her life and . . . you know, if what she was doing with her life is what she wanted to do . . . what she felt would make her happy or whether she was still living by the same rules that were set up for her when she was a child.

When I was working with her both the first and the second time, she was the owner of a beauty salon. She was a very talented beautician and nothing would do but that she had to *own* her own salon. She wasn't going to be bossed around by any man. So . . . she did buy this salon and, um . . . it was a small, struggling business and she had employee problems. It's hard if you're a small salon, apparently, to attract and hold good people. It was in a small, little, rural-suburban town where people were the kind that were set in their ways and didn't want the new fashions and she couldn't charge competitively with a big-city salon, so it was always sort of a marginal operation. She didn't really care too much for the business end of it.

The shop that she had, it was almost like she had a tiger by the tail, you know—she was a part of being a salon owner at twenty-seven or twenty-six, very young, like she was the youngest person in the whole group of salon people to own your own salon, and, you know, she got some approval and some recognition for that, but she wasn't enjoying what she was doing. Yet she didn't know how to get out of it. She recognized within herself that she really enjoyed doing creative things with her skills, but that didn't necessarily include the bookkeeping, the ordering, and the hassling with employees. But, to give up owning the salon and go back to being an employee—she thought that she would lose face and, you know, that she would be a failure to herself, a failure to her family.

And so one of the things that she did the second time around with counseling was to sell the salon. Now she works for somebody else and she is, in fact, much happier. You know, she came to terms that she should be able to set her own expectations for herself based on what makes sense to her, not some nebulous idea in her mind about what her parents or stepparents or her friends or society think that she should be achieving.

I: Sounds like there was a lot of discussion then during the contacts regarding her involvement in business. . . .

R: Oh, yes! I learned a lot! She taught me a lot. She really, um . . . in some ways if she can harness some of her competitiveness, some of her striving, I think she has the potential of making herself very happy. But what she would do, she just buried herself in the business, she had no social life, she didn't go out. All the money that she made had to be poured back into the business. She was living on a shoestring. She was exhausted working six-seven days a week, you know. When the salon was closed, she'd be doing the bookkeeping, cleaning up, she'd be hiring, she'd be interviewing people. And when she was getting ready to sell the salon . . . what she did was to take a part-time job on top of it. By the end of therapy, she had sold her business and given all that up, and she just kept one job employed by somebody else. She just had to keep pushing herself—she had this need to achieve, to some mythical level that she had arrived at in her own mind.

I: Were these the kinds of things that she also wanted to talk about or work on?

R: Oh, yeah! Yeah, these all came from her.

I: Now, could you talk about your relationship with Mrs. Donnelly. What do you think about the way it worked out, particularly during the second series of counseling sessions?

R: It was terrific. We had a very good relationship. That doesn't mean it wasn't stormy sometimes. Um . . . oh, I don't know, maybe three or four months after she came back into therapy, I knew something was going wrong, and she just wouldn't tell me and finally she came out and said there was a part of her that didn't want me to know some of the less lovely things about her—that she didn't want me to think badly of her. She thought that if she was really honest about some of the things she was thinking or that she had done, that I would like her less or that she would lose my respect. But she did finally get up the courage to get that out, and from then on things really began to move.

I: When Mrs. Donnelly came back to the agency, you said that she specifically requested a male worker. How did this issue work out?

R: Well, you see, um . . . like I said, two or three months after we got going with regular sessions again, I knew it wasn't going well and I didn't know why, so . . . I think it was she who brought it up and asked: "Well, maybe we're not just doing so well together, what about a male worker?" In exploring what it was, you know . . . the whole thing came out that she was really afraid that she would lose face if she truly revealed herself to me. I still think that maybe at some point in her life it would be beneficial for her to have a male therapist. But at that time I think that she used it as a smoke screen.

There was a part of her that really liked and respected me, and she wanted me to like and respect her. It was very important—feeling that she could be accepted. But, of course, if she was holding back and felt that was getting my acceptance, then she really didn't feel truly accepted anyway. You know, there always would have been the question, "What would she really have thought if she had really known about me?" But, once that came out, and once that got settled, the question of male versus female worker really was sort of laid to rest. And she understands and I understand that it might be very beneficial . . . a preventative or strengthening experience sometime to have a therapy relationship with a male worker. I don't rule out that at all because she is still just at a very tentative stage of working out male-female relationships on different levels—in business, friendship, dating kinds of things, family kinds of things.

I: It would seem that when you were facing that critical point, that she was able to bring out some of these feelings, and these were discussed between the two of you about what was happening? (R: Oh, yeah.) And did you say that she seemed to initiate that kind of discussion?

R: It was no secret—we knew each other at that point well enough to know what was going poorly and what was going well. We knew each other well enough—there was no façade anymore and we couldn't con each other or weren't into the conning of each other. You know, we certainly knew if it had been a good session; we knew if it had been a nonproductive session. I knew her well enough to know if she was holding back.

I: So that was pretty clear?

R: But at that point she didn't know me well enough to know what I could expect—and it was so innocuous. You wouldn't believe what she would worry about—*nothing.* I expected some huge revelation, like she'd been dealing in white slavery—*nothing! nothing!* And that was just another indication to me how she really worried. She was just extremely scrupulous—just on the minutest little thing. She could blow it all out of proportion and just focus all her attention on that. She just basically didn't like herself and she just didn't really feel that people liked her; that her parents liked her or accepted her as she was. She just arrived at adulthood not really feeling that she could like herself and expecting other people not to really like her. But, of course, she had a hand in this too! She would set herself up and come on like gangbusters and she did get very annoyed, and I can just imagine how she handled some of these male beauticians. You know, there was a part of her that just had to prove that she was better and then when people left her, walked out on her, or were hurt by it, then she couldn't understand. That reinforced her feelings of being not such a nice person.

I: What do you think were the things or qualities that she liked the most and the least about your approach, and you as her worker?

R: Well, originally what she liked least was that I was a female and she wanted a male. Um . . . I think that eventually she really began to believe that I could accept her as she really was. I think she knew that I was open and honest and that I would tell her what I was thinking. She trusted me, you know.

I: Anything else?

R: No, every time you ask the question about what they liked the least, all I can think of is that's the—that very information is the type of information that we are least likely, as workers, to know. That it's hard unless there's been some real showdown issue between worker and client. There may have been something about me that annoyed her extremely, but I didn't ever see any indication of it.

I: It would be difficult for her to find, to bring it out, I would imagine. . . .

R: Unless there was some real big issue that it focuses on but as far as, did she like me, did she think I was helpful—she's the kind of client that gives a lot of feedback, you know. She's very generous in saying "Thank you," or "The discussion was really helpful," or "I don't know what I would have done if we hadn't had this discussion," or "I appreciate you taking the time to talk with me on the phone," or "I get treated so well when I'm here." This is another client who responded very well to this whole agency. (I: Uh, huh.) You know, I think that we present ourselves pretty well, right from the front door on up with clients. Judy was very fond of Mary [receptionist]. Very rapidly Mary gets to know people by their names, so she can say, "Mrs. D" or "Miss J," and sometimes the client says, "Oh, please call me by my first name." So Mary says, "Well, I'm Mary," so that they feel at ease, they feel that they're going to be responded to, that they're important.

I: Did she also bring out some of these impressions about the agency and the other staff members?

R: To the extent that she said to me several times, "Gee, Mary is awful nice," or "The people down at the desk are really nice," or "Everybody seems so friendly"—things like that. . . .

I: Uh, huh . . . how did she feel about the fee after having come back partly because of financial reasons?

R: Oh, she thought it was very modest because, based on her income, her fee was three dollars and fifty cents. She never, never was concerned about the fee. She was seen twenty-nine times the second time and the total charge was $101.50 for service—a real bargain! And, she recognized it. She had been paying fifteen dollars to twenty dollars before.

I: How did the case happen to terminate?

R: She was ready, and I'll tell you why I felt that. She was ready, I thought, quite a while before she actually terminated. She was willing to take a few risks in relationships and other situations and to see how she functions. She knew that you can talk, talk, talk for twenty-nine sessions but if you're not really going to plunge in and see how you function, you can talk about how you'd handle future relationships but unless you're willing to engage yourself in a present relationship, you're not going to see. And that's the point that I feel we reached.

We gradually began declining sessions back last Fall. She was ambivalent about becoming too dependent on me. There was a part of her that really wanted to be dependent and there was the other part . . . that competitive, striving, achieving part and dependence was very scary to her, you know. She was a lady that canceled quite a few appointments, but not from disinterest or whatever. What I figured out and what I checked out with her later was some of the times that she canceled, that was sort of her signal that, "Hey, I'm all right this week, I'm doing pretty good, I don't need you," you know? So, finally when I realized that that was in the wind, we moved to an every other week and then I think we went a couple of times once a month. She was reluctant to let go but she wanted to try some of these things on her own, and I think we reached the point where allowing her to come in every week and talk about it was encouraging her to postpone. She was getting out there and seeing what she could do.

I: Was she trying things out during this period — her relationships with people and so on?

R: Ah, yes . . . that was the slowest to come, but she did do that. What she did was, soon after we began seeing each other for the second time, she volunteered her time at a children's home as a beautician. She gave haircuts to the kids, which she really liked. The first few times it was rough because those kids have a lot of people come in and out of their lives and they're slow to open up and they don't show much appreciation, but she stuck with them and she became a person that they became used to seeing. They began to joke with her and open up and invite her to stay to dinner, and that was a real boost to her. She'd come in and talk with them about the latest hair styles and what shape face they had — what kind of haircut she'd suggest or how they might take care of the haircut she gave them. And . . . she really liked that.

She also enrolled in tennis lessons, found a roommate to share her expenses, and that arrangement went on for over six months, and when she realized that the roommate was not working out, she had the courage to say, "It's not working out." She only had a one-bedroom apartment, and it made it very cramped. Plus, it was an older woman — a woman whose children were all grown and had grandchildren, so it was almost like sharing your apartment with your mother. So, that didn't work out but she took some action. She was going to have to move because she wasn't making enough money to keep the rent so she rented out her bedroom — but she didn't lose her apartment. She began going out for an occasional evening, she went to Cape Cod to treat herself for a weekend, and she sold her business. So . . . she did do some things.

I: It seems like a lot went on!

R: Oh yes! Also, just before we terminated, she joined a church group. Uh . . . she hadn't been particularly associated with any religion, I guess she was more Catholic than anything else, but in her town there's a very active Episcopal group, a discussion group, and she thought maybe she'd like to join the Episcopal Church, and she started to go to meetings there, and there were a few other people who were also interested — so, they had a small group and that allowed her some social contact and also allowed her to study some things that she was interested in.

I: It sounds like she did quite a few things during the course of treatment. . . .

R: The thing is, the real biggie, is whether she is going to feel comfortable in a heterosexual relationship. That's the real big thing. When Mr. Smith referred her back here, he was afraid that what she was going to do, the minute her divorce became final, she was going to leap into an all-consuming type of other relationship, and that she was just going to latch onto the first man that asked her out. She steered clear. She just hardly ever, ever went out. She did, I guess, date briefly one of the men that she employed, but that didn't work out. He had all kinds of problems, ended up hospitalized, and it was more of a sympathy thing. I don't think that she felt that she could just accept a date from somebody who didn't need anything from her, or that she wasn't there to be a shoulder to cry on. I don't think that she felt that she could meet somebody on equal terms, and that she would want to choose him because he was nice and he would want to choose her because she was nice, and that was the next big step.

I: Did she still have some problems in that area at that time?

R: Yeah, but I believe that she had begun to think about joining a singles group, there are so many of them around and — I've heard a few good things and a lot of not-so-good things, but at least she was trying to explore where some other young single people were and how she might meet them. But that would be the really big thing and I wouldn't be a bit surprised if, after she has dated a few people, depending on how the relationship went, that I would hear from her again because she has managed to get away and spend a little bit of money on herself and selling the business — that was not the trauma she thought it was going to be. She sold it in one of the papers and, for a change, she felt good — not that she was a failure.

I: Why do you think you might hear from her?

R: Because the relationship thing was really the big unresolved issue. She was staying on, ready to start dating, but said, "I don't need anybody." You know that when you hear that, it means that a person really isn't making an effort to meet others.

I: Did you make any arrangements for any kind of follow-up?

R: Well, yeah . . . within the context of this being a closed case, she had had the follow-up; but she might, at some time in the future, check back with me, depending on how things are going.

I: Was there any discussion at the time that you terminated of anything else that you might use at that point, like some kind of group experience?

R: She looked pretty consistently for a women's group and I think that it would have been a good thing for her, or a mixed discussion group, but she called the Women's Center and, apparently, it was temporarily closed or whatever. The closest women's discussion group that we could find was in another city, and she felt it was too far away. Not exactly consciousness raising, but a group that would be composed of women in all different life situations. At the time, she was looking maybe to sit down and have a chance to develop relationships with other women who were trying to struggle to keep their own businesses going . . . but not just other professional women.

I: There was no group here at the agency that she could join?

R: No, not really. . . . . There were some groups but they weren't appropriate for her, since they were more like treatment groups. She didn't need to be locked into another treatment activity associated with this agency at the time. She didn't need any more treatment. She had thought about calling the Y and seeing what they had there, and then the church discussion group came along and there were other women in that group, and I really think she could use that kind of experience. I think that would be good for her.

I: Do you think she might refer someone to the agency?

R: She already has.

I: Oh, she has?

R: She already has, several people.

I: For what kinds of problems?

R: Her sister-in-law is in the process of divorcing her former brother-in-law; in other words, the wife of her former husband's brother, who was having similar problems. Judy could see a lot of herself a few years ago in what her sister-in-law is experiencing now, and she referred her. The client is being seen here, although not by me. And I think she referred a couple of other people here that I didn't pick up on.

I: So she has a good feeling about the agency?

R: She sure does! She sure does!

I: Well, if you look at this case as a whole, the ways things worked out, particularly the more recent contact, how do you feel it has worked out?

R: Very well, very well. . . . I'm very satisfied with it.

I: What do you think has been most helpful to Mrs. Donnelly?

R: That she's made friends with herself. She really didn't like herself very well. And, the ways that she was trying to work out this problem were the kinds of ways that were compounding it. She couldn't let herself be human.

She couldn't see that she could make a mistake and the sun wouldn't stop shining and the floor wouldn't open up—she couldn't accept her own humanness—because her parents couldn't.

I: Earlier you talked a little about some of the changes in her functioning since she started coming here. Any other significant changes in her functioning, in her coping, that you can think of?

R: She lost some weight. How did she look when you saw her? She used to be quite overweight and when I last saw her, she was doing very well.

I: A little on the plump side. . . .

R: She always took an interest in her appearance, that was her business, you know. Very up to date with the styles, hair coloring, and skin creams and everything. Oh, that's another thing—she was going to start a small beauty product demonstration job. She wanted to—you know how the Avon lady goes around—well, there's a company that has a fairly high-priced line of skin creams and makeup and what they want is beauticians to supervise other beauticians who go out and, for a fee, make up a woman. She felt that that would be just the size of something that she would like to do.

I: In addition to her regular job?

R: Last I knew, she was only working—she wasn't quite working full time at this new salon. What happened was that some of her customers from her own salon wanted to know where she was going to go, and at that time she didn't have any place to tell them, so a friend of hers who owns a salon offered to employ her or rent her a chair in this other salon. So some of her ladies that she had done for years followed her to this new place and she could build up as much of a following as she wanted, but also there was part of her that still wanted to be in there in the business. It was sort of like Avon, a manager of people. It wasn't as expensive as buying into your own business again. That's another change she wanted to make in her life.

I: What was there beyond the help that she got here that you think might have been useful to her in relation to some of these changes?

R: The selling of the business. I don't think that would have come about. We talked about that endlessly and, before she finally decided that she was going to sell the business, she went to the Retired Businessmen's Association for help. I mean, she really explored all avenues to see what was the most appropriate, and we talked about that. We talked about small business loans and she went for additional training in New York last summer to see if it could improve the business a little bit. This wasn't anything that she did lightly. I mean, hours upon hours of discussing the business and how she would feel and what it would mean to her employees and what it would mean to her family, her friends, and her customers. There were no really significant people in her life. That was her problem—she isolated herself so much—she had a few friends, but she lost touch. While she was married, she and Mr. Donnelly had some friends as couples, but she was pretty embarrassed or ashamed. She just felt funny about continuing her relationship with married couples after the divorce, so she let some people drift away. Um . . . she was a very sensitive woman and once she's stung, she's twice as cautious. Apparently, some of her friends had done minor slights or fairly insignificant things, and Judy just wrote them off. She has one friend that, apparently for seven years at a time they don't speak, and they resolve it, and then they go back, and this happened twice! That's fourteen years we're talking about! So that was another problem, that there wasn't significant others, you know? And when she chose a roommate, she chose another lady that was pretty isolated, years older than she was, who pretty much worked and ate her meals out and went into her bedroom and shut the door and that was it. So, she didn't have anyone that was helpful to her. She had the business.

Toward the end of treatment, she had tried to reestablish a couple of friendships — and make a couple of new friends. And, she was more involved with her sister-in-law, who was also in the process of divorce. So, she was getting out a little bit more, and she did go to Cape Cod with one of her friends, which was the first thing she had done purely social in years. She goes to New York a couple of times a year to these hair shows, you know, for training, and then maybe she'll get to go out to dinner or see a show, but to just say, "I'm going to have a weekend off," and not have it connected with work or have it justified in terms of further learning. . . .

I: How do you think she feels about the way things worked out?

R: I think she's very satisfied. She was finally ready to terminate and she realizes that I'm not going to drop off the face of the earth, you know, and when you terminate, that doesn't mean that she can never knock on our door again.

I: Would you do anything differently in this case, looking at it from this perspective?

R: I don't know whether — if there had been an immediate male available — I would have seen that she was assigned to him. I don't think so. We had an existing relationship — you can second-guess all over the place. She was ready to work, and she would have worked whether it was me or whether it was you or anyone else.

I: She was motivated?

R: Ah, yes!

I: Looking again at the case as a whole, what particular satisfactions and/or frustrations did you feel in it?

R: This is a satisfying woman to work with. Um . . . the frustrations are that with Judy you had to repeat things, you know, because she just really had to take them in a little bit at a time and practice them through herself and then she'd get feedback and then you'd try again and, maybe the first time that you said, "I think that you're a good person," she would hear — maybe perhaps as an outside chance — that "there is some worth to me." The second time you said it, she would hear it a little stronger. So, there was a lot of repetitive kinds of things, a lot of testing as to really how much she could trust me or whether, you know, I was telling her what she wanted to hear.

She *loved* criticism because, of course, she expected this, anything critical. If I said something like, "Have you ever looked at the other side of this or did you think of why you did this?"—she'd jump on that because that was right up her alley, which made me leery about doing it. She'd take *that* to heart—if there was one negative thing in a session and a hundred positive—she'd go off saying, "Well, during this session I learned that . . . ", you know? So that was frustrating but that was also normal and to be expected, given her situation at the time. But there were many, many rewards, you know? She's a warm, responsive, with-it person; she's highly motivated, you know, just a very nice feeling there. She just tries so hard, you know.

I: You were getting good feedback?

R: Oh, yes, yes!

I: Very good—anything else that you can think of about this situation?

R: You always ask that—really, I can't. . . . I would say for that period of time when this case was closed, it was appropriate to close and she'd done beautiful, beautiful work and I think that she, that she richly deserves everything I expect she's achieved, but I think there's a way to go yet, you know. I really think that she's got to do quite a bit more work on heterosexual relationships and, you know, not just in her head but experimentally to see how she can do with others. I think somewhere along the line she's going to be hurt, because the world isn't populated by lovely people all the time and I have a hunch that maybe she'll choose inadvertently—because of her own needs—somebody that might not be so good for her once in a while. Based on everything else she was able to do, I have every confidence that she'll work that out too.

This is a case that is closed and she doesn't need any more counseling now and I think it would be inappropriate for her to be in counseling at this time. But, in the future, I can well see, maybe the next time around it should be with a male worker. I could see right now that a nontherapy women's discussion group would be good for her. But, I don't think that everything was resolved—and whose work is ever completely done?—but I guess it's just a myth. I have a clearer sense of what some of the things are that she will probably be giving some attention to in the future. That's all that I can say.

I: Thank you very much.

R: Okay!

POSTSCRIPT

The interviews with Mrs. Donnelly and her worker illustrate a number of themes that have been discussed in the book. These include: the client's expecting the worker to play an active role through such means as giving advice or asking questions; the client's and worker's ongoing struggle to understand each other, to negotiate a contract, and to achieve mutuality in the face of such influences as discrepant outlooks and transference or counter-transference reactions; the impact of their respective human qualities and styles on the helping process and on each other; the client's greater emphasis on such aspects as the agency environment and the positive role of resources in her social networks; the client's typical method of indicating readiness for termination through canceling appointments; and the practitioner's continuing concern over the client's underlying problems and conflicts.

Going from the substantive to the methodological area, there is also evidence of some of the complexities inherent in in-depth interviewing for research purposes. For example, the interviewer in a sense needs to be fully involved with the interviewee, while at the same time remaining sufficiently detached to avoid contaminating her responses. I found that it was not easy to maintain this balance. Thus, at times I responded by encouraging Mrs. Donnelly with such comments as "that's an interesting point." On other occasions, I did not hear what she was saying or did not know how to handle it and therefore did not probe into potentially important areas, as when she asked me why social workers use different approaches.

While reflecting some common themes, this case is also atypical in some respects. First, unlike most of the other cases, the worker appreciated the importance of life experiences and events in the client's environmental situation. Thus, she concentrated on Mrs. Donnelly's involvement in her business, and the issue of selling it became a focal point of treatment.

Second, while Mrs. Donnelly was typical of many clients who had sought help through other professionals prior to coming to the Bureau, unlike others she experienced considerable difficulty in transferring from one practitioner to the other. There was evidence of marked transference and possibly countertransference reactions that interfered with the helping process and that consumed much energy as she and Mrs. Gray tried to become involved with each other, especially in the early phase of treatment. In particular, Mrs. Donnelly's preference for a male worker persisted throughout the contact. In fact, as I previously noted, she continued to feel that a male practitioner would be better and more effective when I brought her and Mrs. Gray into one of my courses to discuss their participation in this research project.

Despite some of these complications, Mrs. Donnelly clearly felt that the service had been helpful to her, and she and Mrs. Gray agreed that there had been substantial improvement in her functioning and in her coping capacities. While satisfied with the service and its outcome, Mrs. Donnelly was also able to express her dissatisfaction with certain qualities of the worker, such as her being quiet and her not being directive. This illustrates the point that *satisfaction* is a complex rather than a unidimensional variable. A client may be satisfied with the service and its outcome and yet be dissatisfied with certain aspects of the service and/or the worker. Conversely, a client may be dissatisfied with the outcome but satisfied with the worker. Simplistic studies of client satisfaction tell us very little about the process through which clients and practitioners become or do not become successfully engaged with each other. As the Donnelly case suggests, there is much more that we need to understand about interpersonal helping in our efforts to adapt interventive strategies and worker styles and qualities to the needs and expectations of individual clients.

Appendix F

Research Interviews
with Mr. and Mrs. Bates
and Their Social Worker

Mr. and Mrs. Bates are a white, Catholic, middle-class couple in their forties with a twenty-year-old son who is away at college, a nearly seventeen-year-old son, and a ten-year-old daughter at home. Each of the children was adopted as an infant through a Catholic agency. Mr. Bates is a management consultant for a large corporation while Mrs. Bates has not been employed outside the home. The Bates family has moved around the country frequently because of the father's periodic reassignments by his company. They moved to this state from the Midwest less than a year before going to the agency.

Unlike most of the clients in the study sample, Mr. and Mrs. Bates were quite sophisticated in relation to mental health services: throughout the past ten years, they had been involved on and off with numerous agencies, clinics, and private psychiatrists in connection with Bob, their middle child. According to the parents, Bob has long been an emotionally disturbed child who frequently engages in destructive behavior such as slashing furniture, who has difficulty communicating with them or his siblings, and who does not function socially or academically in school. At one point soon after he entered adolescence, Bob was hospitalized briefly in a psychiatric center, apparently because of his destructive, antisocial behavior. The parents felt that they and Bob had been helped by the professional persons with whom they have been dealing over the years; however, they were frustrated by Bob's continuing problems and the professionals' failure to "cure" him.

Soon after moving to this state, Mr. and Mrs. Bates again sought help for Bob, at the suggestion of his former psychiatrist, who had referred them to a well known, private mental health clinic in the area. After deciding that they could not afford the cost of treatment at this clinic, Mr. and Mrs. Bates obtained the names of several other clinics and agencies and chose to go to the Family Service Bureau because of its Catholic affiliation as well as lower fees.

At the Bureau the Bates family was assigned to Kathleen Donovan, an experienced, white social worker in her thirties who had been with the agency for several years and who specialized in family therapy. Miss Donovan was a pleasant, outgoing person who used an informal, relaxed, personal approach in working with people. She was extremely supportive with clients and involved herself actively with them. She believed in being honest and direct with clients and felt that she worked best with those who were able to express their feelings openly.

In going to the Bureau, Mr. and Mrs. Bates specifically requested help in communicating better with their son. They met with the social worker for five sessions, most of which included their daughter in addition to Bob. Following the fifth session, they dropped out of treatment without explicitly discussing termination with Miss Donovan.

As will be seen in the following interviews, Mr. and Mrs. Bates were disillusioned with the service and particularly the worker, although they emphasized that they had received some help. On her part, Miss Donovan as the worker was very upset with the outcome, feeling that this was a "disastrous" case and that she had not provided adequate help to this family. Consequently, I classified this case as one of the "unsuccessful" ones, in view of the clients' and especially the worker's dissatisfaction with the service and its outcome.

The research interview with Mrs. Bates took place first, in her home. The next day I interviewed Mr. Bates in his office, and two days later Miss Donovan in her office. Each interview took approximately one hour. The clients as well as the worker were most cooperative with the research.

RESEARCH INTERVIEW WITH MRS. SYLVIA BATES

Interviewer: [Introductory remarks explaining purpose of the study] The first thing that we're interested in has to do with the main reasons that led you to this particular agency. How long ago was it that you first went there?
Respondent: Oh, it's been, I would say, four or five months ago . . . but we haven't been going again for a while . . . at least a month.
I: Now, when you first went there, what were the main reasons?
R: Uh, actually finances. We probably would have considered private therapy had it not been for the cost.
I: I see. What were the concerns or difficulties that led you to consider therapy to begin with?
R: Uh, we have been in therapy before with our son. Bob is — it's actually, I guess it's more or less considered a problem of adolescent adjustment.
I: Is this your oldest one?
R: No, this is the middle child. And it's, uh, we had had him in therapy for several months before we moved to this state and really should have continued because we had been advised to continue in the therapy. But we felt we were doing well and we would do without it for a while or try . . . so, uh,

really the problems have been with him since he has been a very small child and what we have found out before is . . . it's mainly that he seems to have been born with no fear of consequences. . . .

I: How do you mean?

R: Since he's been a very small child, yes, we have been in therapy since he was small—I think this is about the third time—and it's really just a matter of talking things out once in a while and making us get back to the point of realizing that this is his problem and you have to deal with it.

I: How does he show his problems, or how has he shown them?

R: Yes, uh, he is a very poor student, although he is very intelligent. Uh, it's a—well, you can kind of imagine a child that doesn't fear consequences from the time he's been very small. I mean you tell him to be home at a certain time and he just will come home when he feels like it, or if he wants to do something very badly he just does it, you know, he just doesn't fear any . . . and the same with school. If he's lazy and doesn't feel like working, he doesn't think ahead to the fact, you know, there's just no . . . Oh, I don't know. . . .

I: Now how did you happen to go to this particular agency after you decided that you should follow up with some therapy, as you were saying?

R: Uh, we had dealt through the school first. We asked people at the school because we're new in the area, of what was available and they recommended the clinic [an outpatient psychiatric clinic]. It was recommended to us as one of the best in the area, but what they were charging we couldn't afford it. So from there there were the smaller agencies and because we are Catholic we chose the agency [the Family Service Bureau].

I: I see. Did you know anything in particular about the Bureau before you went there?

R: No. Only that I can say this—uh, our children are adopted, and they are adopted through a Catholic agency. . . .

I: Oh, in another part of the country?

R: In another area.

I: I see, I see. Um, you mentioned that prior to coming here you had had contact with other agencies.

R: Um, hm . . . yes. . . .

I: A clinic? In connection with your son?

R: Yes, a mental health clinic.

I: I see. How did that work out? What were your impressions and your experiences there?

R: Our son was actually committed to this place for five months a few years ago. Uh, we feel that it did a great deal of good.

I: You were . . . you had counseling also at that clinic yourself?

R: Yes, we wound up after they had worked with him, then we went into the family counseling so that we could learn to understand his problems and that he could understand his problems and that he could understand how we felt also. . . . We had a caseworker and a psychiatrist. . . . And these are student psychiatrists, I should mention . . . and they report to a psychiatrist.

I: How did it work out for you?

R: Good . . . pretty good . . . they helped us to communicate better with our son. This is very important. Well, oh, the idea of communicating and so on with our son because we do get uptight, we are rigid, and he is so completely the opposite, and we know these are our problems. We knew it when we came but we will hit a point where we all get so hostile about the thing and we don't communicate and it evidently takes a certain party, a third party, for us to get us all communicating again.

I: I see. Now, at the time you first went to the Bureau, what did you hope they would do in your situation to be of help? What were you expecting, in other words?

R: Uh, actually it's a matter of knowing that you've reached a point of hostility where something has to be done, you know? We reached a point where we were getting very hostile with our son and he in turn was getting very hostile with us again—which we had had before and once the hostility starts, then we also start with the problems where he would destroy things or steal money from us or, you know, his little ways of getting back with his hostility which builds up. That type thing. So you just reach a point where you know something—you have to do something about it and you—where else do you turn other than therapy with that type of problem?

I: Did your son also go to the agency?

R: Yes, he did, uh, huh. . . .

I: Now when you first went there, if you can try to recall the first time that you had a session at this particular agency, how did you feel, do you remember? You yourself?

R: Um, well, when you finally decide to go to a counselor, you go with a great deal of anticipation that you're going to get help and then on the other hand, uh . . . whether . . . when you meet the counselor you wonder whether this person is going to be able to help you because here you do have to have a meeting of personalities also if you're going to be helped. I can't explain it . . . but if you clash, you're not going to open up . . . you won't feel like getting involved.

I: How were you first received there?

R: In what way do you mean?

I: When you first went there, what impression did you have? What were your initial impressions even before you got too far in talking with your caseworker?

R: Uh . . . it's hard to say . . . it's hard—people—'cause you try to—I try to bring the building away from the people and that building is very drab and, you know, you're going up three flights of stairs and down a dingy hallway to get where you're going—which kind of turns you off to begin with.

I: How do you mean?

R: It does, it turns you off because already you're—you feel creepy, you know.

I: What is it about it that turns you off?

R: Well, it's a very, very old building. It's painted gray, if I'm thinking right—the hallways, there's pipes all over that show—I mean it's just an old—the hallways are narrow and it's just a very drab, drab, dreary place and uh . . .

I: How did that affect you especially at the beginning, when you were first going there?

R: It gives you just a little bit of a feeling of wondering, although I don't—if you think about it—it's not right—but it gives you the feeling of, if this is what the building is like, you know, what kind of reception or what kind of help are you going to get? Is it going to—you kind of almost put it with the building, you know, is it all going to be this dreary type, you know, thing?

I: I see . . . now how about the people themselves, aside from the building and the atmosphere, how did they impress you?

R: The people were all very friendly and you know, very willing to help. The caseworker, the particular caseworker that we had, I don't feel that my son related to her very well, and I think this is why we didn't stay with it. We got to the point . . . I can't say it didn't help somewhat because we did open up again and be able to start talking again but we decided to stop it and start just at home on our own because, well, if you could picture my son is like six foot three and he's got shoulders, you know . . . a yard wide . . . and she was calling him Bobby—his name is Bob, you know, and we kept saying *Bob*, and she would say *Bobby*. Well, this turned the boy off at that age, you know.

I: And your son didn't like being called Bobby.

R: Yes, he personally took a disliking to her which meant that he wouldn't open up and I think—I felt that it was because he—I heard him tell her two or three times, "My name is Bob," and she kept calling him Bobby.

I: Oh, oh.

R: Nothing against her, I mean she was a fine person,—and she did succeed in getting us to talk again—but I felt it would have been done easier had it been someone we related to a little better.

I: Yeah, now if you could go back to that initial session that you had, was that you and your son and also your husband . . . meeting with the worker, or was it just one of you?

R: No, it was all three of us to begin with, and later on she suggested that we also bring our daughter the next time because we all lived in the home and it was a family problem.

I: How did that first session work out? What did you do in that first session, what did you talk about?

R: Before my daughter was brought in?

I: Yes, the first one you had at the Bureau.

R: Simply the fact of what the problems were that we felt were causing — you know, what was causing our problem. What was upsetting us and making us hostile and as I recall, my son did not talk very much and he never did, other than in one session, reach a point here where he did much talking, I mean . . . again, I say, I think it's because he did not relate to her.

I: Did you ever bring this up with the worker?

R: No. My husband and I are both people that can't say something that's going to hurt someone's feelings, you know? So we just never mentioned it.

I: Did you discuss it between the two of you?

R: Yes, we did.

I: But you decided not to bring it up?

R: That is why we decided not to go anymore, because we felt that we didn't relate that well to her and that our son wasn't and so therefore we felt the help could not go any farther than the point we had reached.

I: Later, I'll be interested in knowing more about why you ended. For now, how did you conclude that first session?

R: Um, hm. . . . We made plans to bring our daughter in. . . . Our other son was away at college.

I: Was that the worker's suggestion or . . . What did you think about that?

R: I was a little leery of it because she had never been included in therapy before and she was not our problem and the problem was not between she and her brother either (**I:** I see.) . . . and I just felt a little leery that this would upset her to bring her into it.

I: Did you mention that to the worker, that you — in that session, that you felt a little leery about bringing her in?

R: Well I did say, "Do you feel that this is necessary?" and she said that she felt that it was because it was a family problem and we did all live in the same home.

I: I see. . . .

R: So, you know, once you — when you go to seek help you are desperate, you will do what you are asked to do if you can go along with it at all. . . . There is no sense of paying for it if you're not going to follow what they say.

I: Now after that, you went back — was it at that point the whole family including your daughter — and then how many times did you go back?

R: We probably went . . . I would say roughly six times all together.

I: All of you each time?

R: Yes.

I: Um, hm . . . and during those — if you could think about those subsequent times, subsequent contacts, that you had, how did they work out? And what are your impressions now in thinking back about them?

R: Uh, I tried to discuss this with my husband before you came so I could get his impressions too and I would say that the first time we went we weren't too impressed. The second — we said "Well, give it another chance," you know. We went the second time and still were not completely impressed; my husband wanted to quit at this point and I said I really think we should give it three times, at least, before we make a judgment of whether it's going to help or not, and so the third time was a very good session. My son talked at this point and everybody, you know, was talking so we were at this point very enthused about it and then when we went back it seemed to go steadily downhill again and I really can't give a reason.

I: Oh, what seemed—how about that third session—it seemed to have worked out well, what do you think, what was there about it that made it more successful than the others?

R: I can't really say other than the fact that this is the only time that she did get Bob to talk.

I: Uh, huh.

R: And this was, you know, really good for us. When we have a problem with him, we have to know what he's thinking . . . in order to, you know, to feel that we're being able to solve the problem.

I: So in that session, uh, she was able to get him to talk.

R: Right.

I: Now, do you remember what did the worker think were the causes of your problems?

R: Well, communication, which we have known was a problem. Uh, also she seemed to feel that by bringing in my daughter that we had more or less built a fortress, the three of us, and left Bob out, you know? Which . . . I can see . . . by over the years the things that he has done to all of us, you know, with his problems, you kind of get so you are a protective force against something that is hurting everybody, you know. But that's not good so, I mean, this was pointed out to us, which hadn't ever come up before.

I: Oh, you hadn't been aware of that before?

R: No.

I: Oh, I see.

R: So I can say we did learn this in this therapy, and it's something that we can work with. If you don't know what a problem is or what your problem is, which is something an outsider can pick up, you don't know what to do about it.

I: So it sounds like that particular part was helpful to you.

R: Yeah.

I: What were the goals that you were working toward in those sessions, you and the rest of your family and the worker? Did all of you ever talk about what you were trying to accomplish?

R: Uh, yes, yes we did. We didn't actually refer to it in terms of goals, but as I think of it we did discuss what we were looking for and this is mainly that for all of our children that we want them to turn out to be good human beings that can fit into society, this is all we ask, you know? We don't care if they're a doctor or ditch digger, you know, we want them to be happy people. This is the thing, it's our worry over the problems you have of how the child is going to turn out, and these were our goals as far as I can see in the therapy.

I: Now how about the worker; what seemed to be her goals in the process?

R: I think she—it was mainly to get us talking, that's all that seemed to be—what I considered to be her goal.

I: Was there anything that could be done to clarify goals?

R: Well, I would say . . . usually, when you go in to get help you really don't think of a goal—of what you want to reach—you go because you're desperate, you have a desperate situation that you don't know how to handle and this is—you just go—*I want help.* You don't really have a goal of what you want to accomplish there or anything, I think it's just "I want help" and "What do I do?"—Just desperate . . . you know. . . .

I: You have that general idea that you want help.

R: Right. . . . You should make things clearer after a few sessions of talking about goals; but to begin with, I think you just need to talk out all the things that are bothering you and, you know . . . it can get to a goal after you have really gotten the emotional part over with, because I feel, when people go the first few times, you're very emotional. Also, maybe you're a little afraid to talk and so I just—I really don't think it would be a good time to talk about goals, the first few times.

I: That's an important point—so there is something about those initial sessions . . . there is a need to go through a certain process before you can talk about specifically what are we going to do here. During those early sessions did you feel that you were getting what you were looking for in terms of talking, for example?

R: With this particular worker?

I: Yes.

R: No, 'cause like I say, that first—or it was about the third?—the first couple of sessions we didn't feel we were getting anyplace.

I: What do you feel, in retrospect, what do you think could have been done to help you to feel more comfortable and feel that you were getting something?

R: I can't . . . it's hard to say because I feel that it really has to be a confidence in your worker and a clicking of personalities, you know? And you can't—you can't buy that.

I: Yes, yes. . . .

R: You don't know when you walk in whether you're going to relate to that person or not, you know.—So it's really such an individual thing that it's hard to put it into stereotype, you know?

I: How would you describe the worker you had at the Bureau? How would you describe her as a person?

R: I don't know—She was a very nice person. Meeting her as a friend, I think I would have liked her . . . but she just wasn't professional enough.

. . . She didn't hear what we were saying . . . didn't understand us . . . didn't seem to know what we were doing. . . . She was not my idea of a professional person. . . . I mean it just didn't relate . . . the smoking of cigarettes one after the other and, you know, not picking up on the fact that a big boy like that doesn't like to be called Bobby. . . . As a *caseworker*, she was not my idea of a caseworker — although as a person she'd be a very lovely person.

I: But as a caseworker she wasn't what you had expected?

R: No, she was not someone that you could trust . . . someone that I felt I could put my life in her hands . . . that I could open up to and feel confident that she knew more than I did, you know? And you do have to have this, when you go for professional help, you have to have confidence in them, you have to feel that they know more than you do or else, why would you go? I didn't think she knew much.

I: Did you have these feelings from the beginning? Did they change as you went on?

R: No, I think we felt like this from the beginning, and it stayed. And that's why I say, you know, we tried — we kept trying it, thinking that maybe we're not giving it enough chance, we're not giving her enough chance.

I: So that was one reason you kept trying?

R: Right, right — but then we just finally reached the point where we just didn't feel we were relating to her, and it was no use of spending our money to continue going.

I: What did you like most about the way this particular worker was with you and what did you like the least?

R: I don't know, that's very hard — what I liked the least was the fact that we weren't able to relate to her but — What I liked most, the only thing I could say is that she was a friendly person, other than that I can't think of what I could say.

I: How about the agency? Do you have any other impressions about the agency itself rather than the specific worker?

R: Oh, I have nothing to say about the people, you know, the people were all very polite from the time I called, and so on. Oh, the location and the agency itself — it is in a very bad section of town where we had evening appointments and you are leery of going there — of going in and out of the building at night in that section of town. If we had not been going as a family group, I would have never gone there by myself.

I: Oh, I see . . . yeah. . . .

R: The building itself, like I say . . . the first impression — it is a very dreary building and it does give you kind of a creepy feeling when you're *already* creepy when you're going for help, you know . . . . You're leery, wondering what to expect and when that is what you're confronted with — a dreary place — I think it has a little bit of effect on you.

I: How about the fee? What thoughts do you have about the fee?

R: I can't feel that it wasn't in line with what—it's based on your income, and so I feel that it's just right as far as I'm concerned.

I: Now while you were going to that agency, did you talk with anybody else, either your relatives or friends or neighbors about your going there?

R: Yes, I—I talked to my mother about it and I had also talked to a close friend about it.

I: How did they react to your going there and your experiences as you shared them with them?

R: Very open. . . . I think today this is not something you have to hide like you used to; it's an open thing, I think—which is pretty wonderful—I think before many people didn't go because it was so taboo, you know, and today I think with most people you can talk about the fact that you have gone one time or another, and it's not a taboo subject.

I: Now, if we could go back to your ending at this agency—you had started to talk a little bit about that before—could you tell me a little more about how you got to the point of stopping?

R: Uh, we talked about—after about the last two or three times, my son on the way home would make the remark, "I don't know what we're going there for, I don't know what you're spending the money for—we're not ac-complishing anything," and we still wanted to try, but we realized also that we were not really accomplishing anymore once we reached the point where we had the good session. And so it was just—a decision based on the fact that we felt we had reached a point where we could not be helped there anymore. . . . We realized that she couldn't help us.

I: Did you share that decision with the worker or . . . how did you actually stop?

R: No. . . . We didn't tell her so. . . . I just called the agency and left a message that we had decided to stop. I called the agency and I was asking for the caseworker and she was not available—so I told the office worker that we had made the decision that we didn't want to come anymore and if the caseworker would like to discuss it with me, to give me a call, and she didn't call back so I assumed that she understood why we didn't want to come.

I: Looking back, do you think that—is there any different way in which you would have ended—anything differently that either you or the worker or together should have done in ending?

R: Uh, not really, because I think we realized and I think she realized that she had reached a point where she couldn't help us anymore. I felt that in the last couple sessions.

I: Oh, you had that feeling?

R: Yes, uh, huh. . . .

I: Why was that? Did you share your feelings with the worker?

R: No . . . oh, it probably would be a good idea to be shared. Although, see at the point we made the decision, we wouldn't pay seventeen dollars to go back and share it with her, you know? So, I could have shared it with her over the phone or whatever or — but, see, we wouldn't make the decision there, maybe some people would but we wouldn't make it there in front of her; my husband and I had to talk this over.

I: I see . . . what would you have done if the worker had said something like, "I sense that the two of you have questions about continuing here?"

R: Well . . . that would have brought it out then, and my husband and I probably would have discussed it in front of her rather than on our own.

I: Have — since you've stopped — have you thought about going back there or going to any other similar person for help?

R: No, no, because we have — our son is going to be seventeen in another week. We feel that from the time he's been small that we have, you know, we've tried everything. We feel that we have reached a point where we know what we have to do, we have learned from — I'm not saying we didn't get anything out of going to the Bureau — we have learned that we have to keep the communication open in our home. We do it on our own now; we set aside a time that if we start feeling the hostility, that it's okay — it's time to sit down and talk — what is bothering you and so on, and so therefore we feel that we have reached a point where we can help ourselves.

I: So you've learned certain ways of coping with it. Would you refer someone to this particular agency and, if so, with what kinds of needs or problems?

R: I would if they couldn't get into other places like, for instance, the [mental health] clinic.

I: I see.

R: Um, because I do feel when you have your regular professional, a psychiatrist on the staff at least, if you can't work right with one staff member you go to another, or they check things out with the psychiatrist.

I: It sounds like you would feel more comfortable in a place where there would be a psychiatrist. . . .

R: Yeah, I think a caseworker can work with you when she knows what the problem is — but to identify the problem, I think you really need a professional.

I: I see. So in a way, do you differentiate between a psychiatrist as a professional and a caseworker as not a professional?

R: I don't say they're not professional — I think they *are* in their field — in what they do — but they're limited, you know. . . . They may have more knowledge in another area than the psychiatrist — but I really feel to get to the bottom of the problem, if you have a very deep problem, you do need somebody that's trained in psychiatry.

I: Now, if you could look at your experience as a whole at this agency from the beginning to the end — I wonder what you would say about it in general? How do you feel about it in general?

R: Like I said, we eventually dropped out . . . but I feel that we were helped because, well, we started talking again with each other . . . that had been one of our problems. . . .

I: Yes, you mentioned that before.

R: So in a way I feel we were helped.

I: Is there any other ways in which you feel you were helped?

R: No, there was no other way we were helped.

I: Since you went there, have there been changes in your family functioning?

R: Yes, yes there have, uh, huh.

I: Could you tell me a little bit about these changes?

R: Well, it renewed what we had, like I say, we had already found out before, so therefore it just brought us up to date on the fact again that he is not going to change, he is a lax type of person and we have to remember that we're rigid and we can't expect so much of him, you know, we have to let him kind of roll on his own instead of, you know, being on his back all the time about doing things the way *we* think they should be done. We may not be right either.

I: Is there anything other than your contact with the agency that helped you to achieve some of these changes that you mentioned?

R: I can say that at the other clinic we went to, they recommended to us a book and it . . . P.E.T., you probably know the book. . . .

I: Oh, yes.

R: Uh, that helped us a great deal, and we have used it since then — you know, we refer to it, and this does again refresh us too. I think something like this you can read it and put it aside and you never see it again and that's it, you forget it — but this, we do bring it out and refer to it quite often, and it has helped us.

I: Is that something that you think might help other people, you know, to have certain books or articles that they might refer to from time to time?

R: Right, but I think it takes kind of either a wise psychiatrist or caseworker to know which book to get because one says one thing and one another, you know, and I think it has to fit in with your type of person and what your problem is. . . . And then again it has to be whether the people will accept it, because you can hand a person a book and if they won't read it, it's not going to help either.

I: Looking at your experience as a whole again, oh . . . what would you change now that you've gone through it?

R: With this agency . . . ?

I: Yes, with this agency. . . .

R: Uh, I don't think I'd change anything because we chose this agency for the reasons I gave you, you know. It was a monetary thing when we couldn't afford a psychiatrist. I wouldn't change the fact that we hung on as long as we did because we did get something out of it, and then again I wouldn't change leaving when we did because I had gotten what we could out of it.

I: I see. Is there anything from the standpoint of the agency that could have been changed or that could have been done differently so as to be of more help to you and your son?

R: The only thing that I would possibly suggest is that maybe when a caseworker herself can feel that she's reached where she can't help someone, that possibly she suggest: "Why don't we try another one here?"

I: Oh, you mean another worker?

R: Another worker here . . . you know, because then, if you're not relating to this particular worker, you're not going to say to her, "Look, I don't relate to you and I don't want to work with you." . . .

I: Do you feel that would be hard to say for most people?

R: Right, for most people, so you just kind of drop it and go out — where possibly if we had picked up with another worker that we could have related to better . . . maybe things might have been — you know, we might have been able to stay longer and have gotten more help.

I: Well, that's an important point.

R: The worker must sense when it's not going right. . . . And they have to sense it, they work with people all the time. They have to sense when they're not relating to them after a few times, you know.

I: So, you're suggesting that . . .

R: Right, and she might suggest that you try. Most people wouldn't hurt her feelings by telling her. But if she were to bring it out as her professional judgment it would be better.

I: Did your son also think about a different worker?

R: No, he didn't suggest another worker; he just simply kept saying that he didn't like her. He said, you know. "I don't think she's helping us and I don't like her and I'm not gonna talk to her."

I: As far as your son is concerned, do you think that a male worker might have done better at that point in his life?

R: Probably, probably. At that age I would think he would relate more to a male.

I: So that might be something else to be considered in a situation such as this.

R: Right, it had been, you know, the caseworker and the psychiatrist that we had worked with before were males — young males that Bob really related to, and that does make a difference with a young boy.

I: Did your son ever make any comment about that, about the sex of the worker?

R: No, he never — the sex he never said anything about, but it was just more or less the personality type thing right off the bat. He was not going to relate to, you know.

I: Well, this has been very helpful. Can you think of any other impressions or ideas that we haven't gone over?

R: No, I really can't. No, because the Bureau is like other agencies we have dealt through. You know, I told you we adopted our children through a similar agency. . . . Another time we had taken a foster son and we found them through the years to be a very fine agency. I'm certain that they do help many people, just because we didn't relate to a caseworker had nothing to do with the agency itself, or the caseworker, as far as that goes.

I: Well, thanks. . . . I really appreciate this and appreciate your time.

R: Fine, if I can help anybody, you know, in any way, that's—I'm more than happy to.

RESEARCH INTERVIEW WITH MR. LOUIS BATES

Interviewer: [Introductory remarks explaining purpose of the study] To begin with, could you tell me a little bit about what difficulties first led you to this particular agency?

Respondent: Okay, well . . . we had—Bob had been under treatment and had been a patient at the Mental Health Clinic in Illinois, which is a state-run clinic for people who have some kind of a problem. [Mr. Bates reviews his teenage son's history of psychiatric treatment and hospitalization since he was young, in connection with various problems including being "hyperactive," "poor adjustment in school," "conflicts" with his peers, siblings, and parents, and delinquent activities such as stealing].

. . . When we came here, we wanted to continue with some kind of counseling. . . . It had been suggested by the psychiatrist in Illinois. . . . We contacted some place . . . I'm not sure of the name. . . . Sylvia called . . . Oh, yeah, the psychiatric clinic. . . . We tried to make some contact there where we could get counseling for Bob and I forget what the situation was there but I don't think they could take us on or because of my income or something, we weren't eligible, I forget why. She then called the State Attorney's Office, I think it is, where they have the open line and they refer you to whatever services you need or what help you're seeking, and they gave us the names of two or three other organizations—one of them being the Family Service Bureau. So, we contacted them and they were agreeable to take us on and could set up an appointment. So we made the appointment and started counseling there.

I: Before you started, what did you hope they would do for you and your family?

R: Naturally, every time you go to a counselor you hope that a cure will follow. . . . You expect to move toward solution of the problems as they do in medical treatment. . . . You know, normally with any medical or physical problem that you have, if you have a need—an ache or a pain or something that seems to be malfunctioning, you go to a doctor and he gives you treatment and you start immediately toward some kind of cure. . . . But with psychiatric problems it's not the same. Even though you know this, you still expect some kind of cure. . . . The average person wants immediate help, immediate relief. . . . So I think that the typical person, you know, the average person probably doesn't go seeking that kind of help with the right expectations; they think they're gonna get at your—get some kind of an immediate response or turnaround. . . . That's why counselors have never really met our expectations. . . . Every time my wife and I go to a new clinic, we have high hopes . . . but we're always disappointed. . . . We usually feel that we're getting the runaround and that the counselors aren't really helping. . . . We feel like this even though we understand counseling a little bit after having been to so many places in the past ten years.

I: Your expectations are not met?

R: No . . . and how could they be? Actually, each time that we've ever had anything to do with any clinic or psychiatrist and so on, it seems that it's just a long-drawn-out process of talking about something, but nothing ever happens. I think I understand that a little bit better now, having lived through a number of years of seeking that kind of help and so on and probably went into many situations with too high an expectation. In fact I'd be the first one to say to my wife, "I don't think they're helping us, let's go someplace else." I'm pretty sure that I'm always the one that initiates changing horses, if you will, trying to get better help. But in this case with the Bureau here we made the appointment and we went to see the particular caseworker or whatever she's called, and excuse me for the terminology because that's not clear to me.

I: Oh, that's all right.

R: But we went to see her and she kind of took the attitude toward Bob—kind of little-boy thing, you know, like "Bobby this" and "Bobby that."

I: How old is your son?

R: Sixteen and he's as big as I am, so he's over six feet and got shoulders, you know . . . a yard wide and so on and he's a swimmer and he's a very athletic young guy and so on and so on and I don't . . . I think he kind of immediately built up a resentment to the way she was kind of approaching her conversation with him and he just . . . he wouldn't give her the time of day, so to speak, you know . . . uh, in the way of a sensible answer. She'd ask him a question and if she got an answer at all it was kind of a smart-alec one; so it just didn't work out too well.

I: Do you remember what happened at the conclusion of the first session that you had there?

R: On the way home, I said to Bob, you know, "What do you think? How do you feel about this meeting?" and he said, "I think it's a waste of time" and that type of thing, very negative.

I: Very negative. . . . How about in the session itself? What did you and the worker decide or conclude at the end of that first session?

R: There were never any conclusions that I can recall except that, you know, "Do you feel we're helping you at all?", "Do you want to make another appointment to come back?", and we did.

I: You made another appointment?

R: Yes, we did, we went back on about four different occasions. Now the reason I felt it was worthwhile to go back is that the one thing it had accomplished at least, we were talking again.

I: What do you mean?

R: Because on the way to the family center [the Bureau] that first time, Bob and I weren't even speaking. I could ask him a question and he would just—there was a lot of hostility and resentment kind of thing and he was back, you know, to doing things around the house again . . . like destroying things . . . taking out his anger on something rather than telling us.

I: I see. . . .

R: So that's the conditions when we left home on the first night to go down there but on the way back we were able to talk about at least the caseworker, whether we thought she was going to be able to help us and we were communicating, at least he was giving me his feelings. So when we got home later that night, after Bob had gone to bed and gone to sleep, I said to Sylvia, "I think it's helping," and she said, "Why?" and I said, "Because at least we're talking now, we had *something* to talk about with Bob and he was communicating." So I felt that that much was worthwhile.

I: What was there about that session, do you think, that enabled you as a family to talk more, as you were saying?

R: I think it's the factor of someone, some outside influence, some additional person, you know, getting involved and then, you know, being able to hear out both sides.

I: I see. How did it work out as you went on in the session with the worker?

R: So, as we progressed through the next two or three interviews that we had there at the family center, we just felt it was kind of rehashing the same thing and so on and that we were kind of spinning our wheels, we were back to where Bob and I were able to communicate and Sylvia and I were better able to communicate with him so we felt, you know, that we were really where we wanted to be. At least we were talking to him again and on a level of where we were getting more than just the smart answers—we were getting his feelings about some things and he would say if he didn't agree with us and that type of thing. But I'm afraid that eventually we'll get back to where we were before.

I: Have you thought of going back there or somewhere else in view of that?

R: No, we haven't talked about it up to this moment, I guess. I'm thinking that, you know, we've gotta do something.

I: What do you think about the possibility of going back to that particular agency?

R: I would go back, I guess, to that particular agency, and I think I would go back to see the same worker. I would have no qualms about it but I think — I don't think that Bob would have any, you know, weight there. I think — I don't think Bob would like it there. . . . Some other place would be better . . . where he would get along better with the counselor. [Mr. Bates goes over some of the problems his son has experienced throughout his life.]

I: When you went to the Bureau, what did the worker there think might be the reason for these difficulties?

R: Kathleen [the worker] was never given the opportunity, I don't think. She didn't want — she took off the first time saying that she didn't want to rehash a lot of things that we had been through before and so on and not wanting to cover old ground or, you know, start from scratch. She wanted to be able to talk to see if we could communicate.

I: What did you think about that way of doing it?

R: I thought it was okay because it has been rehashed so many times at all the places we've been. . . . It just seemed that maybe it didn't need to be rehashed.

I: If you could think in particular of the worker that you had at this agency, how would you describe her as a person?

R: Well, you know, are you saying a physical description as well as —

I: I mean her qualities, what was she like, you see, in your contacts?

R: Okay, I think that, you know, I would describe her as a very sincere, dedicated type person wanting to help other people. . . . Having the capabilities to generate conversation and listen to both sides of the story and she did never display any, you know, prejudice or preconceived ideas, and so on. She didn't come on as a "I know what the problems are" or, you know, "I understand everything . . ." or "Bob, your parents are right," or "Your parents are wrong." She remained very neutral, and it's too bad that Bob didn't feel that way.

I: What were the qualities that you liked the most in this particular worker and the qualities that you liked the least?

R: Okay. Uh, most would be the, you know, her sincere attitude toward wanting to help. I didn't perceive that as being "put on," I really feel that she is in her profession because she wants to be and that she wants to help other people. I'd say that's her strong point. . . . Her weakness? I feel that it would be maybe in the fact that as a woman and in that situation she was maybe too relaxed or too informal at the first session to take on the air of a professional to some people. You know, she wore slacks and a blouse and she smoked five cigarettes within probably the first few minutes and stuff, which felt kind of — of course, maybe in her business that's what's expected . . . that relaxed way. . . . Maybe it's a way of downplaying who is the pro in the room. . . . Maybe that's really part of the overall training, you know, I'm not knocking it. . . .

I: So you were expecting a more professional person. What do you mean by that?

R: I guess, you know, I would expect to go into a more professional scene . . . at least at the beginning. . . . Later on, the counselor might be more casual . . . after you get to know each other. You might let your hair down a bit and say, "Since we're going to meet evenings, if you want to dress casually," or whatever.

I: Now to move away from the worker herself, what did you think about the agency in general?

R: Yeah, the location of the Bureau in the downtown area is poor . . . inconvenient. We were going there on evening appointments because of my work schedule, and the neighborhood there is not the best in the world to go in. When you get there for an appointment there is a receptionist but after she gets the people in and directed to different counselors, she leaves, so they lock the front door because of the neighborhood, I guess, and then when you leave, after your session, you have to go out by a side door into an alley. . . .

I: I see.

R: Okay? And then you get out there, say eight-thirty-nine o'clock at night, and start walking down that alley. You wonder if you're gonna make it to the street in that particular neighborhood, it's kind of tough. You know, they're in a fairly old building. . . . But they don't have money for better facilities, because it's a subsidized type organization. . . . They're probably on a minimum budget . . . through the United Fund or through the Archdiocese or wherever the funds are coming from. . . . The facilities aren't too good. . . . Makes you wonder if you should go there.

I: Anything else about the agency itself?

R: No, as far as the people that worked there, I think those that we met were all professional people.

I: What was it that they did or that they showed that made you feel that they were professional people?

R: Well, I think, you know, when you walk in the door and someone asks if they can help you and then they find out your name and they know the minute you say, "Well, I'm Louis Bates," and they say, "Oh, yes, you have an appointment with so and so. Won't you have a seat? We'll call you in about five minutes, she has someone else with her," or something like that. The minute they take off on that vein, you feel like, you know . . . I'm not just a cog in a wheel. I'm somebody that they know and they're expecting. It shows they're capable of dealing with people. On the other hand, if you go in a place and they say, "Do you have an appointment?", or "We don't know if they're in yet," or what have you, you get turned off, you feel like they don't care.

I: Any other impressions about the agency or the staff?

R: Well, we had very little contact with anyone other than the counselor. It was a matter of just coming in and finding out if the person we had the appointment with was back, and so on.

I: Could you tell me a little bit about how you happened to end, how you happened to get to the point of ending, and how it actually took place?

R: I think that, you know, we were communicating again with Bob. We were talking and, as I say, from that standpoint that was good and that's part of — that's certainly why we went there. Ah, so since we were talking, you know, we decided to quit going. We were in hopes that we would be able to keep the level of communication going by working at it, and that worked out okay for the first couple of weeks.

I: Did you discuss the idea of ending with the worker?

R: My recollection is that this decision was made like during one of these two-week periods when we would have gone back by my wife and myself. And, in fact, she called Kathleen and told her, you know, that we wouldn't be coming back. As far as I know, that met with Kathleen's approval, or at least I don't think that she made any effort to say, "Yes, You're making a mistake now," but that's all secondhand information. Whatever my wife answered on that was what happened.

I: Looking back at this, is there anything that you think could have been done differently about the ending part of it?

R: No, I don't think so. I think Kathleen's role was that she felt, you know, what we really wanted to do was open up communications with Bob, and if that's what she was striving for and if she felt that we had met that objective at this point, then we were there. 'Cause I don't think she ever approached the problem as trying to find what Bob's real problems were and solve them. I don't think that was her approach.

I: Looking at that experience as a whole . . . do you have just a few more minutes?

R: Sure.

I: Looking at the experience as a whole at this agency, how did it work out for you?

R: Looking at the experience as a whole, I think I was helped. . . . I went from a rotten relationship with my son to one in which we were at least talking. . . . Also, I found out things about myself and it changed me . . . in my attitudes toward life . . . being too strict with my children . . . too concerned about my business.

I: How did the service help you?

R: Oh, well, going to a place like that . . . you find . . . it can't help but improve youself. You do have to talk about some of the things that you like or dislike and that in talking about them you manage to find out how self-centered you are or how one-way you are or how as a parent perhaps, the child is always in a lose situation, you know, the dad makes all the decisions and never discusses it, you know, a dictatorship type thing and you find out through discussing these things, you know, what . . . how wrong this is. I mean not that they ever come out and say you're a dummy, you know, or anything, but in the discussions then they ask you, "Well, what do you think about that?" You know, that you make all the decisions for the family, how do you think they feel? Well, for a minute you start thinking about how you feel about it—you've got a pretty bad situation so I feel it's helping—it's helped me. I feel definitely that my ability to live and deal with other human beings in both the family environment, the business environment—is better. So I feel, you know, there's been a benefit both for Bob and myself, and I'm sure that Sylvia must feel some of that too.

I: Was there anything further that you think the agency could have done to be of help to you and your family?

R: Are we talking strictly about the Bureau?

I: Yes, this particular agency.

R: I can't really say that I feel, you know . . . I don't honestly have anything to say as far as that goes. Even if they had an unlimited budget and totally unlimited resources, and so on, I don't think I could have asked them to do anymore for us—Maybe they could have been available within a more reasonable period of time. Uh, I think from the time we made contact there, it was probably about ten days before they were able to give us an appointment—but from that point on, we could have appointments on a weekly basis, or every two weeks, whatever we wanted . . . which was good.

I: Do you have any other impressions or suggestions?

R: I can't—I couldn't really say . . . the only thing that I could ever hope for would be to have the facility someplace in a decent surrounding and maybe, from the standpoint of their own staff and their own ability to help, I guess the physical surrounding has something to do with it.

I: How do you mean?

R: Well, the physical surroundings make an impression on people when you go to a place like that to get help with some problems . . . I would think especially with little children, small children. If they had a playroom facility or that type of thing at least kids could relax a little bit in and think that that's a nice place to go and it might help in what they were able to do with this kid. I don't know if that makes sense—if it makes a difference to adults—I understand how it is working on budgets and where funds come from, if you don't have the money, you can't have the facility.

I: Speaking of money, what do you think about the fee you paid at this agency?

R: Well, the fee was pretty reasonable—from the standpoint of comparison with others in the area.

I: What do you think about the idea of paying a fee for this type of service?

R: Well, it's good . . . you should pay what you can afford, as long as it's not exorbitant. You should contribute what you can . . . after all, you're there to help yourself.

I: Looking back, what would you say in general about your contact with this agency? What would you change, if anything?

R: Well, that's hard to say. Like I said before, it helped us to communicate with Bob. . . . Too bad he didn't like Kathleen. . . . We could have used more help. . . . Maybe sometimes they should change the counselor. . . .

I: Did you discuss this possibility with the counselor?

R: Oh, no . . . that's hard to do. Also, who am I to say . . . ? After all, they're the professionals.

I: Do you have any other idea or impressions we haven't talked about?

R: No. . . . We covered a lot.

I: Well, thank you!

RESEARCH INTERVIEW WITH KATHLEEN DONOVAN, SOCIAL WORKER IN THE BATES CASE

Interviewer: [Introductory remarks reviewing purpose of the study] What was it that led this family to come to this agency? What kinds of problems did they have?

Respondent: What they said to me?

I: Yes, from what they said to you initially.

R: Uh, they were referred here, if I remembered correctly, by the [psychiatric] clinic. They were given names from the agency that they saw wherever they lived before, I don't remember offhand, and who to contact in this area if they should feel the need, and I think they contacted the clinic first and the clinic generally does not take on too many—you know, they have kind of a closed intake and they referred them. I think she had probably some other places too.

I: Do you remember, from what they said, at that early point in the contact, how did they feel about being referred to this agency?

R: Okay, I gathered. I didn't take the initial intake call, Tony. Someone else did; but in talking with them when I actually saw them, they indicated that they felt okay.

I: How do you think they felt about the referral process, before they got to you as the ongoing worker?

R: I didn't get any great feeling about it, Tony. At least they weren't coming across to me that way.

I: Now in the first session, you saw them after—there was an intake call, and then you saw them for—would that have been an intake interview?

R: Yea.

I: In that initial session, how did they feel in coming here?

R: They didn't express any particular feelings or concerns that I can recall . . . except maybe for Bobby. . . . I think that's the boy's name.

I: What was he saying? What was bothering him?

R: Uh, it was at the point I think we were talking about referring back to their previous experience with counseling. . . . I don't remember exactly, Tony, and how Bobby was resentful about having been hospitalized when they were living somewhere in the Midwest.

I: This bothered Bobby?

R: Yeah, he was afraid to come for counseling. . . . He had some fear that the same thing would happen again . . . that he would be hospitalized again.

I: Is this something the boy expressed?

R: Uh, huh. . . .

I: What did you try to do about it?

R: I tried to focus on it, but the parents weren't eager to get into it . . . and so we didn't pursue it.

I: How about the parents, what expectations did they seem to have of the agency and of you in the initial interview?

R: That initial interview, and it pretty much remained true throughout my brief contacts with them, and that was—that was one of the big problems I think we had—one of them—They wanted to use me as a vehicle that Bobby could talk with his father and work things out with his father.

I: Oh, huh.

R: Father was expressing concern around this.

I: Now is this something that you got a sense of that, or did they say that that was what they wanted you . . . ?

R: They expressed that.

I: I see. How did they put that?

R: Pretty much in those terms and in fact, uh, they said, uh, toward the end of that first interview, that they felt fairly confident about coming here because Bobby had related fairly well to me and was talking, which he was not doing at home, and this is one reason why they had come back for treatment.

I: How did you view the problems in that situation, do you remember? What did you see as the main difficulties?

R: The main difficulties, hm? Okay—Mr. Bates was the one who was running the show pretty much and doing the talking, and he kind of decided generally what was to be done in a very nice way. They were not expressing any feelings except ones that they'd gone through or what they thought they should, but not in any real great depth, and that was the difficulty I had with him right along. I couldn't really get them involved or really to express any great feelings.

I: You—oh, I see—you were trying to help them to express some feelings. . . . About what?

R: Their problems, and what was going on and what was happening. They were leaving it kind of in my lap. Again, Mr. and Mrs. Bates especially weren't too involved in expressing their feelings. . . . Also, they were surprised when I asked to see the little girl. They did bring her in—they were very surprised, and most of the interaction and the verbalness was on the part of Mr. Bates with me.

I: Uh, huh—how was that initial interview concluded? What was decided?

R: Well, as I said, they felt fairly comfortable and at that point, I—at the first interview I was doing a lot of searching around for it in terms of what had happened to them, what had gone on in their previous treatment, because they'd been involved for quite some time. Why now at this point they'd come back for treatment, what had happened in the interim, what about the move here, you know, that had triggered this—what they expected from me and what they wanted, you know. Some kind of beginning general feeling as to where they were.

I: How satisfied were you with how that first interview went?

R: So-so. . . .

I: So-so . . . ?

R: It was okay, you know.

I: Was there anything that you would have wanted to have different?

R: Ideally?

I: Yeah. . . .

R: I would have wanted to have them get more into their real feelings. They talked, but a lot of it was recounting on their part. I really couldn't get any kind of depth or any kind of real feeling that was coming through. . . . You see, one of the problems that I had with this family right straight through, one of the problems was—that they were very middle class, very nice, and they were presenting things in a very nice, middle-class way, even when talking about being very angry they couldn't get as angry.

I: Now how satisfied do you think they were with the way that initial session went?

R: Okay, I think. . . .

I: Did they—do you remember whether they gave you some indication to that effect, or was it what you sensed?

R: Yeah, as I said earlier, I think, they felt fairly comfortable and confident because Bobby had talked some, I had gotten Bobby to talk some.

I: Was that something that they responded to?

R: Mmmmm . . . they liked it.

I: Now after that, see, you saw them jointly for roughly how many times, do you remember?

R: I saw Bobby and the parents that first time and asked to see the little girl also with the family, and I saw them probably about only three more times.

I: Did you ever see any of them individually or . . . ?

R: No.

I: In regard to those subsequent contacts, there are several questions that we will be going into. First, what—as it went on, as the case progressed, what did you see as the treatment objectives in that situation?

R: Actually, I limit it—my treatment objective—Tony, but beginning with the second interview I tried to get at who these people were and what they wanted and to get something out of them as to where they were. This was so difficult and was so lacking, I thought, you know, but I felt I needed to know—what they were instead of just coming in and presenting, you know, Bobby and his father having difficulty getting along.

I: You mean what they were like as people?

R: What they were like, how they felt, how they interacted, what was going on.

I: What did they see as the objectives of coming here as the sessions went on?

R: Well, in the second session I remember very clearly I tried to put this into more effect and it was pretty disastrous, you know, they were withdrawn and everything was just kind of blah. . . . I was not concentrating on Bobby purposefully and obviously they were not very happy about it and I wasn't very happy about it and we weren't getting anyplace in that second session. So, the next session, uh, that they came in and they didn't present anything when they first came in, they just kind of presented themselves—so I decided that this had to be discussed in some detail, you know, and I told them I was very unhappy with the way the last session had gone, you know, I did not think things had gone well, I didn't think I was doing what they wanted me to do, I didn't think they were reading what I wanted—whatever have you that I expressed my feelings—that the time before the little girl had been involved too, that there was a coalition of them, you know, in terms of Bobby being the problem and their being outside of the problems, and I found myself in many ways maybe aligning up with Bobby, you know, because of that, and I didn't like it. They agreed that they were unhappy too with the session.

I: How did they respond? They agreed?

R: Right, and that they were unhappy because I had not again focused on Bobby in drawing him out and having him work out things with his father primarily.

I: What happened as you brought out those dissatisfactions that you and they had? What went on from that point on?

R: I didn't get very far. They agreed that they weren't happy and that I wasn't doing as they wanted, that they did feel that they had to do more in terms of opening up and responding more to feelings and what was going on in terms of the family aligning against Bobby—it opened up a little bit but again it was largely intellectual, letting me in a little bit more in terms of what happened with Bobby and that is—they told me about his adoption and his rejecting of Mr. Bates as the father . . . But they wouldn't go very far in that, saying it was no problem and it really hadn't been any problem, except on Bobby's part. Mr. Bates said he had no problem with this and, besides, it had been taken up with before in their treatment previously and really they didn't need to go into it so they closed me out there.

I: That was what they said—the parents or the boy also?

R: The parents. Bobby was not really going along with this. He was trying to get in but they would not really allow him to.

I: So they didn't want to go back to those issues. Did they explain why?

R: They felt that was irrelevant, but maybe it would be all right to take it up with Bobby because it was his—had been his concern—at one time and maybe was still his concern.

I: Was there any discussion of why you were trying to bring that stuff up?

R: Yeah, and they agreed that maybe some of this was valid to some extent and, as I said, when they terminated at the clinic previously they were just getting into this, and their therapist thought it was most important and they thought it might be good too. Mrs. Bates particularly picked up on this, the first time she'd really been at all aggressive and did express some feelings. Uh, again she was giving me some clues, some indication, very indirect and coming up bleak and in some way what was going on between she and her husband—very oblique and very defensive at the same time too. It's like, you know, it was coming out against some of her will that she didn't want it to.

I: So it sounds like you had the feeling there was a lot going on there, that they were reluctant to bring out.

R: Yeah, and I think by this time Mr. Bates was saying that he was not going to change, that they wanted him to change, that he had lots of ways of functioning—rigidity—and wanting to have things very structured and very planned and such—and he knew it caused a problem but he was not about to change, he couldn't change.

I: Now from what you're saying, it seems as if there was some discrepancy between what you were trying to work toward and what they were trying to work toward. What did you try—as it went on—how did you try to bridge that gap?

R: I tried to bring it out and find a common ground that we could work on and um . . . as I said, particularly in terms of responding to what we—what we were generally doing. They would agree in general. But in specifics, they disagreed, you know, in terms of—say particularly the relationship between Mr. Bates and the rest of the family in terms of how some of his ways of functioning bugged them.

I: They disagreed about that?

R: They agreed that it was so, but they didn't want to go into it.

I: How did things work out as the case went on?

R: I really didn't get to know them. Not only because they were reluctant to reveal themselves but also because, well, as it worked out . . . the problem was . . . I could only see them every other week and I don't function very well that way, I lose the continuity.

I: Why was it every other week?

R: Mr. Bates was out of town every other week so it's impossible to meet weekly.

I: I see, it was hard to maintain continuity. Mm, was this matter of continuity discussed in the session?

R: Yeah, but I felt uncomfortable with it.

I: How do you mean?

R: I had, at the same time, some trouble with Mrs. Bates from the very beginning. At one point, I discussed this with her and the family situation too because she was so quiet and so subservient. She would occasionally, occasionally — not always — oftentimes she would let things go with her husband, but occasionally she would step in and try to smooth things out or explain things out and I had some trouble with this. It bothered me; at one point I discussed it with her. She agreed, you know, but just couldn't go much further into this at all.

I: Yeah. What was it that bothered you about that?

R: I had no idea where she was or what was going on *at all*. I could sense things were going on all over the place but I had nothing to tie onto because she was like a nonentity, until the last when we began to touch upon something in terms of her frustration and her anger — *very, very* minutely.

I: It was hard to get anything from her?

R: Extremely hard.

I: Did you feel that they were getting — and I'm referring now in particular to the parents — that they were getting some of what they were looking for?

R: No, I don't really think so, and again, I think I saw them four times. The second time I discussed this and the fourth time I discussed this. I initiated it. Then I think it was after that they were through, and I was relieved.

I: When they were through?

R: Yeah. . . .

I: How come?

R: Because I, um, I didn't think we were getting anyplace, I think we had — I think we came to an agreement — that's the only way they could come to the agreement — they weren't getting anyplace, not really.

I: Did you discuss that with them — you know — your feeling that you really weren't getting anywhere? Was this discussed with them?

R: Yeah . . . the last time I saw them, this came up again and the frustration that I would pick up on some things they were saying and um . . . they would express dissatisfaction with this. I can remember, too, one thing that sticks in my mind now that I'm thinking about her talking about it, that last session — Mrs. Bates got quite upset, quite disturbed at that time, a little — as much as she could get, because I was trying to help Mr. Bates and Bobby work out something on a practical basis, you know, concrete sort of a thing and . . . well, I had the feeling she was getting a little frustrated around this but wouldn't go any further with it, maybe just generally frustrated. The indication was that she didn't want to get things stirred up — like the relationship between Mr. Bates and Bobby. That's the sense I got from her, yeah.

I: Did you indicate to her in any way that that's the message you were getting?

R: Yeah, I did, yeah.

I: How did she respond to that?

R: She agreed.

I: She agreed, oh . . .

R: One more thing I should mention is that I could have had a great relationship with Bobby. I think he responded well to me, and they indicated in the first interview that "he's talked more with you today than he's talked with anybody for years" — over a period of time — but my feeling was that a heck of a lot of good it does for Bobby to talk with me if, at this point, he has all this trouble with the family. My job is to help the family to talk together, but Bobby said in that first interview that he wished I were a man and he wished I were a big man. Uh, Bobby feels he cannot compete with his father. The only way he could possibly compete with his father would be physically. Bobby is a big guy and so is the father . . . but he can't do this because his father's got a bad back and Bobby feels that he can compete on the physical basis with other guys or he wished that I were a guy and a *big* guy so he could really work this out and get close to somebody this way.

I: He was really looking for something then. Did you think about the possibility of a transfer to a male worker?

R: We don't have a big guy on the staff.

I: Oh . . . but how about the idea of simply having a male worker, aside from the size. Is that something that, as you think back, might have been worthwhile in this particular case?

R: It was impossible, timewise, at that point anyway . . . within this agency. You know, I did respond to it, it would not be possible within this agency and could we therefore work together as I am, a woman and so on and so forth. Of course Bobby indicated from the very beginning he wasn't interested in going anyplace anyway.

I: Oh, he didn't want to. How did you think this family viewed the relationship with you, particularly the parents?

R: Probably I had less of a relationship with them than I had with any other client. That's my feeling — and I think they felt that same way.

I: How do you mean, less than with other clients? In what way?

R: No real great feeling one way or the other.

I: Oh, you mentioned that dissatisfaction earlier, your frustrations . . .

R: Huh?

I: You mentioned earlier that you were frustrated, so there was some feeling there on your part. . . .

R: Yeah, because I wanted to get to know them and I didn't think they were showing themselves at all — really — as human beings with needs and feelings.

I: What do you think . . . ?

R: Of course, part of that is me. I—I do better with a live client—a case in which you're getting some feelings of some extent in some way or another.

I: How do you mean?

R: With people who are more open than they were. Even if it's just anger—you know, you aren't doing as I want. . . .

I: What do you think . . . given the kind of situation that you had . . . was there anything that you think they found helpful about you and the way you were with them?

R: I don't know. . . . I didn't want to take the family on in the very beginning.

I: Oh?

R: And I wonder how much that affected me. . . . I didn't want to take it on not because of the family but because it's late evening and I—you know, I work most of the day Tuesdays and I'm tired.

I: Oh, and the sessions with the Bateses were late in the evening?

R: Yeah, it was the last appointment in the evening. . . . Families do take more of your energy—so I held off and hesitated and took them on only because they'd been waiting for quite a period of time and they needed to be seen and I thought, well, you know, I do have that seven o'clock slot. But I wish I hadn't.

I: Oh, I see. From the beginning you had some reluctance to take them. . . .

R: Right.

I: What do you think Mr. and Mrs. Bates thought about the agency in general?

R: In terms of that, the only indication I had was, uh, they didn't have enough room.

I: Here, in your office?

R: Mmmm. . . .

I: I see.

R: And, I don't know, I just had the feeling that they had some concern about the physical setup of the office. Maybe they didn't, I don't know.

I: Was this ever discussed with them?

R: Yeah, in the beginning, because I was uncomfortable the first time that all four of them got in here. I tried to get the family room, which I did after that . . . then it worked out better because it's a larger office.

I: How about the fee? How do you think they felt about the fee?

R: I don't know, they didn't say a word about it and I think that was set before I saw them. Occasionally somebody will ask a fee on the intake phone and it'll be computed, and I think that was done with them. I'm not sure, but anyway, I always bring it up in terms of the fee whether it was set in advance or any question that concerns them about that, and I don't recall their saying anything.

I: Now, how did the case terminate?

R: Yeah, she called in and left a message saying they were canceling their appointment and would not be back at the agency for service. It came in when I was available to talk, but the phone call never got through to me and so obviously they didn't want to talk with me.

I: Oh, oh. . . .

R: That doesn't happen very often but once in a while — you get a very clear feeling — I was gonna call them, call back and check back with her but then I thought — *I don't know, I don't think I'll get anyplace,* you know? And, I think this is the way they have to cope with it and I'll let them cope with things as they want to, so as to say to them that it's okay.

I: How did you feel about the way the case terminated?

R: I never like it that way. I never like to have things left up in the air. It would be rare that I wouldn't call back, but I made a very conscious decision in terms of this family. That this is the way they wanted it. They may be able to cope with it in time.

I: In retrospect, would you do anything different about the way things terminated?

R: No, I don't think so, I don't think so.

I: Now, if we could look at the case as a whole, how do you think it worked out in general? You've been talking about this already. How do you think the case worked out?

R: I don't feel that there was any change, that they got any help from me. . . . Somehow, we didn't hit it off. I didn't feel I cracked the door or made any impact. I don't think I was damaging to them. . . . To my way of looking, it was a disastrous case. . . . This family came in here with serious problems and I didn't give them any real help. . . . I think it was just one of those things that happens once in a great while. I think they got the wrong person.

I: Oh, you mean in you as the worker?

R: Yeah, uh, huh. . . . Maybe some other people would have done better with them.

I: What kind of a worker do you think might have been more appropriate?

R: I think somebody that could swing with the way they were . . . not open. . . . I was too threatening with them because I was pushing a little bit too much.

I: Did you ever talk with them about another worker?

R: I think to some extent that was brought up somewhat, but I can't say that for sure.

I: If you were to do it over, would you still push them?

R: Probably, but I can't really say. I mean, it was so hard to get feedback from them.

I: How do you think Mr. and Mrs. Bates see how things worked out?

R: I don't think it was what they wanted — the type of therapy they wanted.

I: Did they say anything about that or was that the kind of feeling you got from them?

R: You know, they wanted me to relate to Bobby. Also, I think she in particular wanted me to relate to the other things that were going on but couldn't follow through.

I: Oh, things that were—that might have been going on between Mr. and Mrs. Bates as a couple?

R: Oh, I know there were—she had said something earlier, how frustrated and angry, you know, she got at her husband because he had to have things so one, two, three, four . . . if he decided to go swimming tomorrow at nine o'clock, come hell or high water, things were packed and all the kids were ready at nine o'clock . . . and he agreed to that.

I; Oh, he agreed with that?

R: He agreed to that. That's the way he is . . . but he said I'm not gonna change it, that's the way I am.

I: That's right, you mentioned that.

R: You have to take me as I am and work around it. Don't get me wrong, he was a very likable guy and I liked him, but this was bugging his family up the wall and he was saying, "I can't," or, "I won't," or both. . . . But, you know, they told me not to go any further. . . .

I: And when they tell you, what do you do? . . . Well, in view of some of the things that we've been discussing, would you do anything differently in this case as you look back at it now?

R: I might have terminated with them myself and sent them elsewhere. I might have been even stronger in terms of our difficulties in what they wanted and the bind they were putting me in and sent them off early.

I: Uh, oh, I see.

R: Rather than hoping, you know, that there was a way in—just biding time a little bit. . . .

I: Anything else that you might have done differently?

R: Not really, I don't think.

I: As you think back, Kathleen, why didn't you do those things that you are suggesting now?

R: Well I felt, you know, there was still an opening on this other level with Bobby and his father in terms of practical, concrete things.

I: Oh, so you were trying along those lines, or you thought there might be some hope there. . . .

R: Okay . . . now I could have responded to Bobby. I could have done something with him. He was the most open, but I didn't see it as being productive for Bobby in the long run and I could feel myself—I didn't want to get caught into the whole thing again with identifying with Bobby or taking any kind of sides or anything like that. Most dissatisfying, I think, was the fact that I could not really get them involved in working on their feelings, their mutual needs and frustrations.

I: How did your experience in this particular situation compare with other clients?

R: Yeah, it's been a long time since I've had a client that I've had so much trouble with, a long time. . . . It's been a long time since I've had such a disastrous case—I mean, to my way of looking at it.

I: You feel it was a disastrous case?

R: Yeah, because I didn't feel they were doing anything different or made any kind of impact.

I: It sounds like a very difficult situation to work with. I think we've covered . . . we've covered pretty much what I have on the outline. Is there any other impression or idea that you have or anything that you could elaborate on?

R: No . . . only that I think they came here for help, and I don't really feel that I gave them the help that they came for.

I: It sounds like you're still bothered by that. . . .

R: Yeah. . . .

I: I guess we all have cases like this. . . . Is there anything else that you can think of on this case?

R: I don't think so, I think that covers it all.

I: Well, thanks very much, you've been helpful about this.

R: Do we get any feedback about what the clients think?

I: Do you mean the individual clients?

R: Yeah, yeah.

I: Oh, no. I'll share the overall findings in a general way . . . but, like I said before, whatever individual clients or workers say is strictly confidential. It sounds like you would want to know what this family thinks?

R: Yeah, you know . . . we could find out what they think went on or how to change it. . . . Maybe we should be more open.

I: Well, that's an important point. . . . Any other impressions or thoughts?

R: No . . . can't think of any.

I: Well, thanks very much.

POSTSCRIPT

The Bates case is typical of the "unsuccessful" cases, that is, cases in which clients and/or workers were dissatisfied with the course and outcome of the interpersonal helping process. It is obvious that Mr. and Mrs. Bates were unhappy about the service, although they were guarded in their criticisms and they did point to some help that they received in the area of communication with their son. The worker was even more explicit in expressing her sense of failure and dissatisfaction, as she described this case as one of her more "disastrous" ones.

As with the other unsuccessful cases, a recurring theme was the lack of mutuality or complementarity between clients and worker in respect to key issues such as definition of the target problems and formulation of treatment goals. The parents persisted in identifying the problem as primarily their son's and wanted help in improving their communication with him. The worker, on the other hand, evidently viewed Bob's difficulties as symptoms of family dysfunctioning or underlying intrafamily conflicts and therefore attempted to direct treatment activities toward identification and resolution of family or marital problems. Thus, the worker tried to shift the focus of treatment away from the *son* as the identified patient and toward the *family* as a unit. This effort was exemplified by her request to bring the daughter into the sessions, whereas the parents felt that she was not involved in the specific problems for which they were seeking help.

In addition to the discrepancies in the clients' and workers' problem definition and goal formulation, there were differences in relation to problem-solving approaches. Thus, the parents in a sense wanted the worker to take on the son directly and solve his problems, while the worker resisted assuming this role and insisted on the parents' active involvement.

As with the other unsuccessful cases, the marked clash in expectations and goals between clients and worker provoked considerable frustration and dissatisfaction on the part of each of them. Much of their energy went into efforts to cope with these discrepancies and achieve some mutuality. The issues were out in the open and the worker repeatedly brought them up and tried to handle them with the clients. When these attempts did not succeed, the client and worker became disengaged in an unproductive fashion, without having the opportunity to deal constructively with termination. In a sense, it was easier for all of them to end without a final confrontation.

It is important to consider why the clients and worker in the Bates case were not able to overcome their disparities sufficiently to go on or to terminate more constructively. This is crucial since there were other cases in which clients and practitioners were able to overcome the negative impact of similar discrepancies through such means as the client-worker relationship and contract negotiation. In the Bates case, it appears that no clear contract was ever established. Furthermore, the client-worker relationship was not strong enough to overcome clashes between clients and worker. For one thing, the clients were disappointed by this particular worker, whose informal style and personal qualities were not suited to their needs and expectations. At the same time, the worker was frustrated by the clients' inability to express their feelings openly and in depth. Initially, there may also have been some negative feelings toward the agency on the part of the clients, since the Bureau was actually their second choice. As they entered the agency system, it may be that their doubts and hesitation were exacerbated by the agency's poor physical environment as well as certain qualities in the worker that for them raised further doubt about her competence or professional qualifications.

At any rate, the Bates case illustrates the complex interplay of factors that at times result in a strongly adverse effect on the process and outcome of interpersonal helping—factors such as disparities in role expectations, problem definition, and goals between clients and practitioner; the lack or insufficient level of complementarity between clients and worker in respect to their qualities and styles; and the quality of the agency environment. The case also illustrates practitioners' typical reluctance to accept their realistic limitations in certain cases or the fact that one cannot be equally helpful and effective with all kinds of people. Perhaps the most crucial lesson to be derived from this case is that there are times when workers and clients need to face the difficulties in their interaction, to accept the reality of the inadequate complementarity between them, and to consider termination or reassignment to another practitioner within the agency or referral to some other resource.

Bibliography

ALDRICH, C. KNIGHT. *An Introduction to Dynamic Psychiatry.* New York: McGraw-Hill, 1966.

ALEXANDER, FRANZ. "Extra-Therapeutic Experiences," in Franz Alexander and Thomas M. French, Editors, *Psychoanalytic Theory.* New York: Ronald Press, 1946.

ANTHONY, E. JAMES, and BENEDECK, THERESE, Editors. Parenthood—Its Psychology and Psychopathology. Boston: Little, Brown, 1970.

ARGELANDER, HERMANN. *The Initial Interview in Psychotherapy.* New York: Human Sciences Press, 1976.

ARONSON, H., and OVERALL, BETTY. "Treatment Expectations of Patients in Two Social Classes," *Social Work,* 11 (January 1966): 35-42.

BAKER, FRANK. "The Interface Between Professional and Natural Support Systems," *Clinical Social Work Journal,* 5 (Summer 1977): 139-148.

BARISH, SAMOAN. "Listening and the Art of Clinical Acuity," *Clinical Social Work Journal,* 5 (Fall 1977): 219-228.

BARKER, ROGER G. *Ecological Psychology.* Stanford, Calif.: Stanford University Press, 1968).

BECK, DOROTHY FAHS. "Potential Approaches to Research in the Family Service Field," *Social Casework,* 40 (July 1959): 385-393.

BECK, DOROTHY FAHS. *Patterns in Use of Family Agency Service.* New York: Family Service Association of America, 1962.

BECK, DOROTHY FAHS. *How to Conduct a Client Follow-up Study: 1977 Supplement.* New York: Family Service Association of America, 1977.

BECK, DOROTHY FAHS, and JONES, MARY ANN. *Progress on Family Problems—A Nationwide Study of Clients' and Counselors' Views on Family Agency Services.* New York: Family Service Association of America, 1973.

BECK, DOROTHY FAHS, and JONES, MARY ANN. *How to Conduct a Client Follow-up Study.* New York: Family Service Association of America, 1974.

BECKER, HOWARD, et al. *Boys in White.* Chicago: University of Chicago Press, 1961.

BENT, RUSSELL J., et al. "Correlates of Successful and Unsuccessful Psychotherapy," *Journal of Consulting and Clinical Psychology,* 44 (February 1976): 149.

BLENKNER, MARGARET, HUNT, J. McV., and KOGAN, LEONARD. "A Study of Interrelated Factors in the Initial Interview with New Clients," *Social Casework,* 32 (January 1952): 23-30.

BLUMER, HERBERT. *Symbolic Interactionism—Perspective and Method*. Englewood Cliffs, N.J.: Prentice-Hall, 1969.

BOATMAN, FRANCIS L. "Caseworkers' Judgments of Clients' Hope: Some Correlates Among Client-Situation Characteristics and Among Workers' Communication Patterns." Unpublished Doctoral Dissertation, Columbia University, 1975.

BOGDAN, ROBERT, and TAYLOR, STEVEN J. *Introduction to Qualitative Research Methods*. New York: Wiley, 1975.

BOLMAN, W. M., FOX, EVELYN F., and NELSON, M. A. "The Termination Process: A Neglected Dimension in Social Work," *Social Work*, 14 (October 1969): 55-63.

BOTT, ELIZABETH. *Family and Social Network*. London: Tavistock Publications, 1957.

BOUNOUS, RONALD C. "A Study of Client and Worker Perceptions in the Initial Phase of Casework Marital Counseling." (Unpublished Doctoral Dissertation, University of Minnesota, 1965.

BRIAR, SCOTT. "Family Services," in Henry S. Maas, Editor, *Five Fields of Social Service*. New York: National Association of Social Workers, 1966, pp. 21-28.

BUSH, MALCOLM, GORDON, ANDREW C., and LeBAILLY, ROBERT. "Evaluating Child Welfare Services: A Contribution from Their Clients," *Social Service Review*, 51 (September 1977): 491-501.

CANNELL, CHARLES F., and KAHN, ROBERT L. "Interviewing," in Gardner Lindzey and Elliot Aaronson, Editors, *The Handbook of Social Psychology*, Second Edition, Vol. 2. Reading, Mass.: Addison-Wesley, 1968, pp. 540-551.

CAPLAN, GERALD. *Support Systems and Community Mental Health*. New York: Behavioral Publications, 1974.

CHANCE, ERIKA. *Families in Treatment*. New York: Basic Books, 1959.

COLLINS, ALICE H., and PANCOAST, DIANE L. *Natural Helping Networks: A Strategy for Prevention*. New York: National Association of Social Workers, 1976.

COTTRELL, LEONARD S., JR., "The Analysis of Situational Fields in Social Psychology," *American Sociological Review*, 7 (June 1942): 370-382.

CRUTHIRDS, C. THOMAS. "Management Should Be Accountable Too," *Social Work*, 21 (May 1976): 179-180.

CUMMING, ELAINE. *Systems of Social Regulation*. New York; Atherton Press, 1968.

DAILEY, WILDA J., and IVES, KENNETH. "Exploring Client Reactions to Agency Service," *Social Casework*, 59 (April 1978): 233-245.

DAVIS, FRED. *Passage Through Crisis—Polio Victims and Their Families*. Indianapolis: Bobbs-Merrill, 1963.

DAVIS, INGER P. "Advice-giving in Parent Counseling," *Social Casework*, 56 (June 1965): 343-347.

DELGADO, MELVIN. "Puerto Rican Spiritualism and the Social Work Profession," *Social Casework*, 58 (October 1977): 451-458.

DUBOS, RENÉ. *Man Adapting*. New Haven, Conn.: Yale University Press, 1965.

DUBOS, RENÉ. *So Human an Animal*. New York: Scribner's, 1968.

EDGERTON, R. B. *The Cloak of Competence: Stigma in the Lives of the Mentally Retarded*. Berkeley, Calif.: University of California Press, 1967.

ELLSWORTH, ROBERT B. "Consumer Feedback in Measuring the Effectiveness of Mental Health Programs," in Marcia Guttentag and Elmer L. Struening, Editors,

Handbook of Evaluation Research, Vol. 2. Beverly Hills, Calif.: Sage Publications, 1975, pp. 239-274.

ERIKSON, ERIK H. *Identity and the Life Cycle.* New York: International Universities Press, 1959.

ESTES, RICHARD J., and HENRY, SUE. "The Therapeutic Contract in Work with Groups: A Formal Analysis," *Social Service Review,* 50 (December 1976): 611-622.

EWALT, PATRICIA L., and KUTZ, JANICE. "An Examination of Advice-Giving as a Therapeutic Intervention," *Smith College Studies in Social Work,* 47 (November 1976): 3-19.

Family Counseling of Greater New Haven. "Client Survey." New Haven, Conn.: Family Counseling of Greater New Haven, 1974, mimeo.

FANSHEL, DAVID. "A Study of Caseworkers' Perceptions of Their Clients," *Social Casework,* 39 (December 1958): 543-550.

FANSHEL, DAVID. *Far from the Reservation.* Metuchen, N.J.: Scarecrow Press, 1972.

FANSHEL, DAVID, and MOSS, FREDA. *Playback—A Marriage in Jeopardy Examined.* New York: Columbia University Press, 1971.

FARLEY, O. WILLIAM, PETERSON, KIM. D., and SPANOS, GERALD. "Self-Termination from a Child Guidance Center," *Community Mental Health Journal,* 11 (Fall 1975): 325-334.

FESTINGER, LEON. *A Theory of Cognitive Dissonance.* Evanston, Ill.: Row, Peterson, 1957.

FIBUSH, ESTHER, and MORGAN, MARTHA. *Forgive Me No Longer: The Liberation of Martha.* New York: Family Service Association of America, 1977.

FILSTEAD, WILLIAM J., Editor. *Qualitative Methodology: First-Hand Involvement with the Social World.* Chicago: Markham, 1970.

FISCHER, JOEL, Editor. *Interpersonal Helping: Emerging Approaches for Social Work Practice.* Springfield, Ill.: Thomas, 1972.

FISCHER, JOEL. "Is Casework Effective?", *Social Work,* 18 (January 1973): 5-20.

FISCHER, JOEL. *The Effectiveness of Social Casework.* Springfield, Ill.: Thomas, 1976.

FOOTE, NELSON N., and COTTRELL, LEONARD S. JR. *Identity and Interpersonal Competence.* Chicago: University of Chicago Press, 1955.

FRANK, JEROME D. *Persuasion and Healing,* Revised Edition. New York: Schocken Books, 1974.

FRENCH, THOMAS M. *The Integration of Behavior: Basic Postulates.* Chicago: University of Chicago Press, 1952.

FREY, LOUISE A., and EDINBURG, GOLDA M. "Helping, Manipulation, and Magic," *Social Work,* 23 (March 1978): 88-92.

FRIEDMAN, HENRY J. "Patient-Expectancy and Symptom Reduction," *Archives of General Psychiatry,* 8 (January 1963): 77-83.

GERMAIN, CAREL B. "An Ecological Perspective in Casework Practice," *Social Casework,* 54 (June 1973): 323-330.

GERMAIN, CAREL B. "A Theoretical View of the Life Model: Eco-Systems Perspective," in *The Ecological Approach and Clinical Practice.* West Hartford, Conn.: University of Connecticut School of Social Work, 1976, mimeo.

GERMAIN, CAREL B. Editor. *The Ecological Perspective in Social Work Practice: People and Environments.* New York: Columbia University Press, in press.

GERSHON, MICHAEL, and BILLER, HENRY B. *The Other Helpers: Paraprofessionals and Nonprofessionals in Mental Health.* Lexington, Mass.: Lexington Books, 1977.

GIORDANO, PEGGY C. "The Client's Perspective in Agency Evaluation," *Social Work,* 22 (January 1977): 34-40.

GITTERMAN, ALEX and GERMAIN, CAREL B. "Social Work Practice: A Life Model," *Social Service Review,* 50 (December 1976): 601-610.

GITTERMAN, ALEX, and SCHAEFFER, ALICE. "The White Professional and the Black Client," *Social Casework,* 53 (May 1972): 280-291.

GLADWIN, THOMAS. "Social Competence and Clinical Practice," *Psychiatry,* 30 (November 1967): 30-43.

GLASER, BARNEY G., and STRAUSS, ANSELM L. *The Discovery of Grounded Theory.* Chicago: Aldine, 1967.

GLISSON, CHARLES. "The Accountability Controversy," *Social Work,* 20 (September 1975): 417-419.

GOFFMAN, ERVING. *Interactional Ritual.* New York: Anchor Books, Doubleday, 1967.

GOFFMAN, ERVING. *Frame Analysis.* Cambridge, Mass.: Harvard University Press, 1974.

GOIN, MARCIA K., YAMAMOTO, JOE, and SILVERMAN, JEROME. "Therapy Congruent with Class-linked Expectations," *Archives of General Psychiatry,* 13 (August 1965): 133-137.

GOLDSTEIN, ARNOLD P. *Therapist-Patient Expectancies in Psychotherapy.* New York: Pergamon Press, 1962.

GOLDSTEIN, ARNOLD P. "Maximizing the Initial Psychotherapeutic Relationship," *American Journal of Psychotherapy,* 23 (July 1969): 430-451.

GOLDSTEIN, ARNOLD P. *Psychotherapeutic Attraction.* New York: Pergamon Press, 1971.

GOLDSTEIN, ARNOLD P. *Structured Learning Therapy.* New York: Academic Press, 1973.

GOLNER, JOSEPH H. "Home Family Counseling," *Social Work,* 16 (October 1971): 63-71.

GOODMAN, NATHANIEL. "Fee-charging," in Robert Morris et al., Editors, *Encyclopedia of Social Work,* 16th issue. New York: National Association of Social Workers, 1971, pp. 413-415.

GORDON, WILLIAM E. "Basic Constructs for an Integrative and Generative Conception of Social Work," in Gordon Hearn, Editor, *The General Systems Approach: Contributions Toward an Holistic Conception of Social Work.* New York: Council on Social Work Education, 1969, pp. 5-11.

GOTTESFELD, HARRY. "Professionals and Delinquents Evaluate Professional Methods with Delinquents," *Social Problems,* 13 (Summer 1965): 45-58.

GOYNE, JAMES B., and LADOUX, PAULETTE. "Patients' Opinions of Outpatient Clinic Services," *Hospital and Community Psychiatry,* 24 (September 1973): 627-628.

GRAHAM, HENRY M., and BLUMENTHAL, DAVID L. "Why We Failed—As Clients See It," *Family Service Highlights*, 16 (1955): 91-92.

GUERNEY, BERNARD G., JR., Editor. *Psychotherapeutic Agents: New Roles for Non-Professionals, Parents and Teachers*. New York: Holt, Rinehart and Winston, 1969.

GUERNEY, BERNARD G. JR. *Relationship Enhancement*. San Francisco: Jossey-Bass, 1977.

GURIN, GERALD, VEROFF, JOSEPH, and FELD, SHEILA. *Americans View Their Mental Health*. New York: Basic Books, 1960.

HALL, ANTHONY S. *The Point of Entry: A Study of Client Reception in the Social Services*. London: Allen and Unwin, 1974.

HAMILTON, GORDON. *Theory and Practice of Social Casework*, Second Edition. New York: Columbia University Press, 1951.

HARTMAN, ANN. "To Think About the Unthinkable," *Social Casework*, 51 (October 1970): 467-474.

HARTMANN, HEINZ. *Ego Psychology and the Problem of Adaptation*. New York: International Universities Press, 1958.

HARWOOD, ALAN. *Rx: Spiritist as Needed. A Study of a Puerto Rican Community Mental Health Resource*. New York: Wiley, 1976.

HEINE, RALPH W., and TROSMAN, HARRY. "Initial Expectations of the Doctor-Patient Interaction as a Factor in Continuance in Psychotherapy," *Psychiatry*, 23 (August 1960): 275-278.

HELLER, KENNETH, and GOLDSTEIN, ARNOLD P. "Client Dependency and Therapist Expectancy as Relationship Maintaining Variables in Psychotherapy," *Journal of Consulting Psychology*, 25 (August 1961): 371-75.

HERZOG, ELIZABETH. *Some Guidelines for Evaluative Research*. Washington, D.C.: Children's Bureau, U.S. Department of Health, Education, and Welfare, 1959.

HOLLINGSHEAD, AUGUST B. *Two-Factor Index of Social Position*. New Haven, Conn.: privately printed, 1957.

HOLLIS, FLORENCE. *Casework—A Psychosocial Therapy*, Second Edition. New York: Random House, 1972.

HORENSTEIN, DAVID, HOUSTON, B. KENT, and HOLMES, DAVID S. "Clients', Therapists', and Judges' Evaluations of Psychotherapy," *Journal of Counseling Psychology*, 20 (March 1973): 149-153.

HOSHINO, GEORGE. "Social Services: The Problem of Accountability," *Social Service Review*, 47 (September 1973): 373-383.

HYMAN, HERBERT H. *Interviewing in Social Research*. Chicago: University of Chicago Press, 1954.

INKELES, ALEX. "Social Structure and the Socialization of Competence," *Harvard Educational Review*, 36 (1966): 265-283.

ITTELSON, WILLIAM H., PROSHANSKY, HAROLD M., and RIVLIN, LEANNE G. "The Environmental Psychology of the Psychiatric Ward," in Harold M. Proshansky, William H. Ittelson, and Leanne G. Rivlin, Editors, *Environmental Psychology: Man and His Physical Setting*. New York: Holt, Rinehart and Winston, 1970, pp. 419-439.

JANCHILL, MARY PAUL. "Systems Concepts in Casework Theory and Practice," *Social Casework*, 50 (February 1969): 74–82.

JENKINS, SHIRLEY, and NORMAN, ELAINE. *Beyond Placement—Mothers View Foster Care.* New York: Columbia University Press, 1975.

JONES, E. "Social Class and Psychotherapy: A Critical Review of Research," *Psychiatry*, 37 (November 1974): 307–320.

KADUSHIN, ALFRED. *The Social Work Interview.* New York: Columbia University Press, 1972.

KADUSHIN, ALFRED, and WIERINGA, C. F. "A Comparison: Dutch and American Expectations Regarding Behavior of the Caseworker," *Social Casework*, 41 (December 1960): 503–511.

KIRKLAND, JANET MOORE. "Motivating the Unmotivated." Paper presented at 1977 National Association of Social Workers Professional Symposium, San Diego, Calif., November 19–22, 1977, mimeo.

KISCH, ARNOLD, and REEDER, LEO G. "Client Evaluation of Physician Performance," *Journal of Health and Social Behavior*, 10 (March 1969): 51–58.

KOGAN, LEONARD S. "The Short-term Case in a Family Agency—Parts I, II and III," *Social Casework*, 38 (May, June, July 1957): 231–237, 296–302, 366–374.

KORTE, OSCAR G. "The Perception of Four Relationship Factors as Related to Outcome Scores in Social Casework Treatment." Unpublished Doctoral Dissertation, Columbia University, 1977.

KURTZ, JOHN J. and KYLE, DAVID G. "Life Satisfaction and the Exercise of Responsibility," *Social Work*, 22 (July 1977): 323–324.

KURTZ, JOHN J. and WOLK, STEPHEN. "Continued Growth and Life Satisfaction," *The Gerontologist*, 15 (April 1975): 129–131.

LANDSBERG, GERALD. "Consumer Feedback Research in a Community Mental Health Center," in William Neigher, Roni J. Hammer, and Gerald Landsberg, Editors, *Emerging Developments in Mental Health Program Evaluation.* New York: Argold Press, 1977, pp. 367–375.

LAZARE, AARON, EISENTHAL, SHERMAN, and WASSERMAN, LINDA. "The Customer Approach to Patienthood," *Archives of General Psychiatry*, 32 (May 1975): 553–558.

LAZARUS, ARNOLD A. *Behavior Therapy and Beyond.* New York: McGraw-Hill, 1971.

LEICHTER, HOPE J. "Some Perspectives on the Family as Educator," *Teachers College Record*, Vol. 76, No. 2 (December 1974): 175–217.

LEICHTER, HOPE J., and MITCHELL, WILLIAM E. *Kinship and Casework.* New York: Russell Sage Foundation, 1967.

LEIGHNINGER, ROBERT D. JR., "Systems Theory and Social Work: A Re-examination," *Journal of Education for Social Work*, 13 (Fall 1977): 44–49.

LENNARD, HENRY L., and BERNSTEIN, ARNOLD. *The Anatomy of Psychotherapy.* New York: Columbia University Press, 1960.

LENNARD, HENRY L., and BERNSTEIN, ARNOLD. *Patterns in Human Interaction.* San Francisco: Jossey-Bass, 1969.

LERNER, BARBARA. *Therapy in the Ghetto.* Baltimore: Johns Hopkins University Press, 1972.

LEVINGER, GEORGE. "Continuance in Casework and Other Helping Relationships: A Review of Current Research," *Social Work*, 5 (July 1960): 40–51.

LEVINSON, HILLIARD L. "Termination of Psychotherapy: Some Salient Issues," *Social Casework*, 58 (October 1977): 480–489.

LÉVI-STRAUSS, CLAUDE. *The Raw and the Cooked*, translated by John and Doreen Weightman. New York: Harper Torchbooks, 1970.

LEWIN, KURT. *A Dynamic Theory of Personality*. New York: McGraw-Hill, 1935.

LEWIS, JUDITH A., and LEWIS, MICHAEL D. *Community Counseling: A Human Services Approach*. New York: Wiley, 1977.

LIEBERMAN, FLORENCE. "Clients' Expectations, Preferences, and Experiences of Initial Interviews in Voluntary Social Agencies." Unpublished Doctoral Dissertation, Columbia University, 1968.

LINN, LAWRENCE S. "The Mental Hospital from the Patient Perspective," *Psychiatry*, 31 (August 1968): 213–223.

LOFLAND, JOHN. *Analyzing Social Settings*. Belmont, Calif.: Wadsworth, 1971.

MALUCCIO, ANTHONY N. "Action as a Tool in Casework Practice," *Social Casework*, 55 (January 1974): 30–35.

MALUCCIO, ANTHONY N. "Promoting Competence Through Life Experiences," in Carel B. Germain, Editor, *The Ecological Perspective in Social Work Practice: People and Environments*. New York: Columbia University Press, in press (a).

MALUCCIO, ANTHONY N. "A Task-Based Approach to Family Treatment," in Cathleen Getty and Winnifred Humphreys, Editors, *Perspectives on the Family: Readings in Theory and Practice*. Philadelphia: Lippincott, in press (b).

MALUCCIO, ANTHONY N. and MARLOW, WILMA D. "The Case for the Contract," *Social Work*, 19 (January 1974): 28–36.

MARTENS, WILMA M., and HOLMSTRUP, ELIZABETH. "Problem-Oriented Recording," *Social Casework*, 55 (November 1974): 554–561.

MAYER, JOHN E., and ROSENBLATT, AARON. "The Client's Social Context: Its Effect on Continuance in Treatment," *Social Casework*, 45 (November 1964): 511–518.

MAYER, JOHN E., and ROSENBLATT, AARON. "Clash of Perspective Between Mental Patients and Staff," *American Journal of Orthopsychiatry*, 44 (April 1974): 432–441.

MAYER, JOHN E., and TIMMS, NOEL. *The Client Speaks—Working-Class Impressions of Casework*. Boston: Routledge and Kegan Paul, 1970.

McCOY, TOMMIE, et al. "Clients' Reactions to an Outreach Program," *Social Work*, 20 (November 1975): 442–444.

McKAY, ANN, GOLDBERG, MATILDA E., and FRUIN, DAVID J. "Consumers and a Social Service Department," *Social Work Today*, 4 (November 1973): 486–491.

McPHEE, CAROL B., ZUSMAN, JACK, and JOSS, ROBERT H. "Measurement of Patient Satisfaction: A Survey of Practices in Community Mental Health Centers," *Comprehensive Psychiatry*, 16 (July-August 1975): 399–404.

MEIER, ELIZABETH G. "Interactions Between the Person and His Operational Situations: A Basis for Classification in Casework," *Social Casework*, 46 (November 1965): 542–549.

MENNINGER, KARL. *Theory of Psychoanalytic Technique*. New York: Harper and Row, Harper Torchbooks, 1958.

MERTON, ROBERT K. *Social Theory and Social Structure*, Enlarged Edition. New York: Free Press, 1968.

MERTON, ROBERT K., and BARBER, ELINOR. "Sociological Ambivalence," in Edward

A. Tiryakian, Editor, *Sociological Theory, Values, and Sociocultural Changes.* Glencoe, Ill.: Free Press, 1963, pp. 91-120.

MERTON, ROBERT K., FISKE, MARJORIE, and KENDALL, PATRICIA L. *The Focused Interview.* Glencoe, Ill.: Free Press, 1956.

MEYER, CAROL H. "Practice Models—The New Ideology," *Smith College Studies in Social Work,* 43 (February 1973): 85-98.

MEYER, CAROL H. *Social Work Practice,* Second Edition. New York: Free Press, 1976.

MEYER, HENRY J., BORGATTA, EDGAR F., and JONES, WYATT C. *Girls at Vocational High: An Experiment in Social Work Intervention.* New York: Russell Sage Foundation, 1965.

MINUCHIN, SALVADOR. "The Plight of the Poverty-Stricken Family in the United States," *Child Welfare,* 49 (March 1970): 124-130.

MITCHELL, J. CLYDE, EDITOR. *Social Networks in Urban Situations.* Manchester, Eng.: University of Manchester Press, 1969.

MOORE, EDITH E. "Matching in Helping Relationships." Unpublished Doctoral Dissertation, University of Toronto, 1977.

MOOS, RUDOLF H. *The Human Context: Environmental Determinants of Behavior.* New York: Wiley, 1976.

MOSHER, DONALD L. "On Advising Parents to Set Limits For Their Children," *Social Casework,* 46 (February 1965): 86-89.

MOSS, MIRIAM S., and MOSS SIDNEY Z. "When a Caseworker Leaves an Agency: The Impact on Worker and Client," *Social Casework,* 48 (July 1967): 433-437.

MULLEN, EDWARD J., DUMPSON, JAMES R., et al. *Evaluation of Social Intervention.* San Francisco: Jossey-Bass, 1972.

MURPHY, LOIS B. et al. *The Widening World of Childhood: Paths Toward Mastery.* New York: Basic Books, 1962.

MURPHY, LOIS B. and MORIARTY, ALICE E. *Vulnerability, Coping and Growth.* New Haven, Conn.: Yale University Press, 1976.

NATIONAL ASSOCIATION OF SOCIAL WORKERS. *Handbook on the Private Practice of Social Work,* Second Edition, Revised. New York: National Association of Social Workers, 1974.

NEIGHER, WILLIAM, HAMMER, RONI J., and LANDSBERG, GERALD, Editors. *Emerging Developments in Mental Health Program Evaluation.* New York: Argold Press, 1977.

NEWMAN, EDWARD, and TUREM, JERRY. "The Crisis of Accountability," *Social Work,* 19 (January 1974): 5-16.

NYMAN, GARY W., WATSON, DON, and JAMES, SHIRLEY E. "The Role of the Secretary in Community Mental Health: A Training Model for Integrating Secretaries into the Therapeutic Team in Community Mental Health," *Community Mental Health Journal,* 9 (Winter 1973): 368-377.

ORNE, MARTIN T., and WENDER, PAUL H. "Anticipatory Socialization for Psychotherapy: Method and Rationale," *American Journal of Psychiatry,* 124 (March 1968): 1202-1212.

OVERALL, BETTY, and ARONSON, H. "Expectations of Psychotherapy in Patients of Lower Socio-Economic Class," *American Journal of Orthopsychiatry,* 32 (April 1963): 421-430.

OVERBECK, ANN. "Life-Stress Antecedents to Application for Help at a Mental Health Center: A Clinical Study of Adaptation." Unpublished Doctoral Dissertation, Smith College School of Social Work, 1972.

OVERTON, ALICE. "Taking Help from our Clients," *Social Work,* 5 (April 1960).

OXLEY, GENEVIEVE B. "The Caseworker's Expectations and Client Motivation," *Social Casework,* 47 (July 1966): 432-437.

PAPP, PEGGY, SILVERSTEIN, OLGA, and CARTER, ELIZABETH. "Family Sculpting in Preventive Work with 'Well Families,' " *Family Process,* 12 (June 1973): 197-212.

PARK, JANICE. "The Counseling Program—Report of a Client Follow-up Study" Bridgeport, Conn.: Family Services—Woodfield, 1975, mimeo.

PARSONS, TALCOTT, BALES, ROBERT F., and SHILS, EDWARD A. *Working Papers in the Theory of Action.* New York: Free Press, 1953.

PEARLMAN, JOYCE C. CASTRO. "The Psychoanalytic Approach to Termination: A Review of the Literature" unpublished M.S.W. Thesis, Smith College School for Social Work, 1976.

PERLMAN, HELEN H. *Social Casework—A Problem-Solving Process.* Chicago: University of Chicago Press, 1957.

PERLMAN, HELEN H. "Intake and Some Role Consideration," *Social Casework,* 41 (December 1960): 171-177.

PERLMAN, ROBERT. *Consumers and Social Services.* New York: Wiley, 1975.

PFOUTS, JANE H., and RADER, GORDON E. "The Influence of Interviewer Characteristics on the Initial Interview," *Social Casework,* 43 (December 1962): 548-552.

PINCUS, ALLEN, and MINAHAN, ANNE. *Social Work Practice: Model and Method* (Itasca, Ill.: Peacock, 1973).

POLANSKY, NORMAN, and KOUNIN, JACOB. "Clients' Reactions to Initial Interviews: A Field Study," *Human Relations,* 9 (August 1956): 237-263.

POLSKY, NED. *Hustlers, Beats, and Others.* Chicago: Aldine, 1967.

PROSHANSKY, HAROLD M., ITTELSON, WILLIAM H., and RIVLIN, LEANNE G., Editors. *Environmental Psychology: Man and His Physical Setting.* New York: Holt, Rinehart and Winston, 1970.

REES, STUART. "No More Than Contact: An Outcome of Social Work," *British Journal of Social Work,* 4 (1974): 255-279.

REID, KENNETH E. "Non-rational Dynamics of the Client-Worker Relationship," *Social Casework,* 58 (December 1977): 600-606.

REID, WILLIAM J. "Book Review" of *The Client Speaks* in *Social Casework,* 52 (October 1971): 532-534.

REID, WILLIAM J., and EPSTEIN, LAURA. *Task-Centered Casework.* New York: Columbia University Press, 1972.

REID, WILLIAM J., and EPSTEIN, LAURA. *Task-Centered Practice.* New York: Columbia University Press, 1977.

REID, WILLIAM J., and SHAPIRO, BARBARA L. "Client Reactions to Advice," *Social Service Review,* 43 (June 1969): 165-173.

REIK, THEODOR. *Listening with the Third Ear.* New York: Farrar, Straus, 1948.

REYNOLDS, BERTHA C. "Between Client and Community: A Study of Responsibility in Social Case Work," *Smith College Studies in Social Work,* 5 (September 1934): 1-128.

RHODES, SONYA L. "Contract Negotiation in the Initial Stage of Casework Service." Unpublished Doctoral Dissertation, Columbia University, 1975.

RICHAN, WILLARD C., and MENDELSOHN, ALLAN R. *Social Work—The Unloved Profession.* New York: Watts, 1973.

RICHARDSON, STEPHEN A., DOHRENWEND, BARBARA S., and KLEIN, DAVID. *Interviewing—Its Forms and Functions.* New York: Basic Books, 1965.

RICHMOND, MARY E. *Social Diagnosis.* New York: Russell Sage Foundation, 1917.

RILEY, PATRICK V. "Practice Changes Based on Research Findings," *Social Casework,* 56 (April 1975): 242 250.

RIPPLE, LILLIAN, ALEXANDER, ERNESTINA, and POLEMIS, BERNICE W. *Motivation, Capacity, and Opportunity.* Chicago: School of Social Service Administration, University of Chicago, 1964.

ROBERTS, ROBERT W., and NEE, ROBERT H., Editors. *Theories of Social Casework.* Chicago: University of Chicago Press, 1970.

ROSEN, ALBERT. "Client Preferences: An Overview of the Literature," *Personnel and Guidance Journal,* 45 (April 1967): 785-789.

ROSENBERG, CHAIM M., and RAYNES, ANTHONY E. *Keeping Patients in Psychiatric Treatment.* Cambridge, Mass.: Ballinger, 1976.

ROSENBERG, JANET. "Veterans' Perceptions of Their Hospital Care," *Social Work Research and Abstracts,* 13 (Fall 1977): 30-34.

ROSENBLATT, AARON. "The Application of Role Concepts to the Intake Process," *Social Casework,* 43 (January 1962): 8-14.

RUBENSTEIN, HIASAURA, and BLOCH, MARY H. "Helping Clients Who Are Poor: Worker and Client Perceptions of Problems, Activities, and Outcomes," *Social Service Review,* 52 (March 1978): 69-84.

RUBIN, AARON. "Letter to the Editor," *Social Work,* 22 (November 1977): 520.

SACKS, JOEL G., BRADLEY, PANKE M., and BECK, DOROTHY FAHS. *Clients' Progress Within Five Interviews.* New York: Family Service Association of America, 1970.

SAINSBURY, ERIC. *Social Work with Families.* London and Boston: Routledge and Kegan Paul, 1975.

SCHMIDT, JULIANNA T. "The Use of Purpose in Casework Practice," *Social Work,* 14 (January 1969): 77-84.

SCHOEFIELD, W. *Psychotherapy: The Purchase of Friendship.* Englewood Cliffs, N.J.: Prentice-Hall, 1964.

SCHUERMAN, JOHN R. "The Reviewer's Reply," *Social Service Review,* 50 (June 1976): 325-331.

SCHWARTZ, WILLIAM. "The Social Worker in the Group," in *The Social Welfare Forum—1961.* New York: Columbia University Press, 1961.

SCHWARTZ, WILLIAM. "On the Use of Groups in Social Work Practice," in William Schwartz and Serapio R. Zalba, Editors, *The Practice of Group Work.* New York: Columbia University Press, 1971, pp. 3-24.

SEABURY, BRETT A. "Arrangements of Physical Space in Social Work Settings," *Social Work,* 16 (October 1971): 43-49.

SEABURY, BRETT A. "The Contract: Uses, Abuses, and Limitations," *Social Work,* 21 (January 1976): 16-23.

SHACHTER, BURT. "The Client as Collaborator in Social Work Teaching," in *Teaching for Competence in the Delivery of Direct Services.* New York: Council on Social Work Education, 1976, pp. 107-117.

SHIREMAN, JOAN. "Client and Worker Opinions About Fee-Charging in a Child Welfare Agency," *Child Welfare*, 54 (May 1975): 331-340.

SIEGEL, STEPHEN B. "Research on the Outcome of Social Work Interventions: A Review of the Literature," *Journal of Health and Social Behavior*, 13 (March 1972): 3-17.

SILVERMAN, PHYLLIS R. "The Client Who Drops Out: A Study of Spoiled Helping Relationships." Unpublished Doctoral Dissertation, Brandeis University, 1969.

SILVERMAN, PHYLLIS R. "A Re-examination of the Intake Procedure," *Social Casework*, 51 (December 1970): 625-634.

SIPORIN, MAX. "Situational Assessment and Intervention," *Social Casework*, 53 (February 1972): 91-109.

SIPORIN, MAX. *Introduction to Social Work Practice.* New York: Macmillan, 1975.

SJOBERG, GIDEON, and NETT, ROGER. *A Methodology for Social Research.* New York: Harper and Row, 1968.

SLOANE, R. BRUCE, et al. *Psychotherapy Versus Behavior Therapy.* Cambridge, Mass.: Harvard University Press, 1975.

SMALE, GERALD G. *Prophecy, Behavior and Change.* London and Boston: Routledge and Kegan Paul, 1977.

SMALLEY, RUTH. *Theory for Social Work Practice.* New York: Columbia University Press, 1967.

SMITH, M. BREWSTER. "Competence and Socialization," in John A Clausen, Editor, *Socialization and Society.* Boston: Little, Brown, 1968, pp. 270-320.

SMOLAR, H. TERRY. "Stress and Demographic Variables as Related to Mothers' Referral of Children in Need of Treatment." Unpublished Doctoral Dissertation, Columbia University, 1976.

SPECK, ROSS V., and ATTNEAVE, CAROLYN L. *Family Networks.* New York: Pantheon Books, 1973.

SPIEGEL, JOHN P. "The Resolution of Role Conflict Within the Family," in Norman W. Bell and Ezra F. Vogal, Editors, *A Modern Introduction to the Family*, Revised Edition. New York: Free Press, 1968, pp. 393-411.

STARK, FRANCES B. "Barriers to Client-Worker Communication at Intake," *Social Casework*, 40 (April, 1959): 177-183.

STEIN, HERMAN D. "The Concept of the Social Environment in Social Work Practice," *Smith College Studies in Social Work*, 30 (June 1960): 187-210.

STEIN, IRMA. *Systems Theory, Science, and Social Work.* Metuchen, N.J.: Scarecrow Press, 1974.

STOTLAND, EZRA. *The Psychology of Hope.* San Francisco: Jossey-Bass, 1969.

STREAN, HERBERT S., Editor. *Social Casework: Theories in Action.* Metuchen, N.J.: Scarecrow Press, 1971.

STRUPP, HANS S., FOX, RONALD F., and LESSLER, KEN. *Patients View Their Psychotherapy.* Baltimore: Johns Hopkins Press, 1969.

STUDT, ELLIOT. "Social Work Theory and Implications for the Practice of Methods," *Social Work Education Reporter*, 16 (June 1969): 22-24, 42-46.

SWENSON, CAROL. "Social Networks, Mutual Aid and the Life Model of Practice," in Carel B. Germain, Editor, *The Ecological Perspective in Social Work Practice: People and Environments*. New York: Columbia University Press, in press.

TAYNOR, JANET, PERRY, JAMES, and FREDERICK, PAUL. "A Brief Program to Upgrade the Skills of Community Caregivers," *Community Mental Health Journal*, 12 (January 1976): 13-19.

THOMAS, EDWIN, POLANSKY, NORMAN, and KOUNIN, JACOB. "The Expected Behaviors of a Potentially Helpful Person," *Human Relations*, 8 (May 1955): 165-174.

TOFFLER, ALVIN. *Future Shock*. New York: Random House, 1970.

TOLSDORF, CHRISTOPHER C. "Social Networks, Support, and Coping," *Family Process*, 15 (December 1976): 407-417.

TRIPODI, TONY, FELLIN, PHILLIP, and MEYER, HENRY J. *The Assessment of Social Research*. Itasca, Ill.: Peacock, 1969.

TROPP, EMANUEL. "Expectations, Performance, and Accountability," *Social Work*, 19 (March 1974): 139-148.

TRUAX, CHARLES, and CARKHUFF, ROBERT. *Toward Effective Counseling and Psychotherapy: Training and Practice*. Chicago: Aldine, 1967.

TRUAX, CHARLES B., and MITCHELL, KEVIN M. "Research on Certain Therapist Interpersonal Skills in Relation to Process and Outcome," in Allen E. Bergin and Sol L. Garfield, Editors, *Handbook of Psychotherapy and Behavior Change: An Empirical Analysis*. New York: Wiley, 1971, pp. 299-344.

TURNER, FRANCIS J. *Psychosocial Therapy*. New York: Free Press, 1978.

VAN DYKE, NORMA. "Discomfort and Hope: Their Relationship to Outcome of Referral," *Smith College Studies in Social Work*, 32 (June 1962): 205-219.

WHITE, ROBERT W. *Ego and Reality in Psychoanalytic Theory*. New York: International Universities Press, 1963.

WHITTAKER, JAMES K. *Social Treatment—An Approach to Interpersonal Helping*. Chicago: Aldine, 1974.

WHITTAKER, JAMES K. *The Ecology of Child Treatment: Helping Environments for Troubled Children*. Chicago: Aldine, in press.

WIKLER, MARVIN E. "Using Photographs in the Termination Phase," *Social Work*, 22 (July 1977): 318-319.

WILSON, G. T., HANNON, A. E., and EVANS, W. I. "Behavior Therapy and the Therapist-Patient Relationship," *Journal of Consulting and Clinical Psychology*, 32 (April 1968): 103-109.

WISEMAN, J. P. *Stations of the Lost: The Treatment of Skid Row Alcoholics*. Englewood Cliffs, N.J.: Prentice-Hall, 1970.

WITTMAN, FRIEDNER D., and WITTMAN, MILTON. "Architecture and Social Work: Some Impressions About Educational Issues Facing Both Professions," *Journal of Education for Social Work*, 12 (Spring 1976): 51-58.

WOLBERG, LEWIS. *The Technique of Psychotherapy*. New York: Grune and Stratton, 1954.

WORBY, MARSHA. "The Adolescent's Expectations of How the Potentially Helpful Person Will Act," *Smith College Studes in Social Work*, 26 (October 1955): 19-59.

Wursmer, Jeanne H. "Use of a Client Representative to Monitor Consumer Feedback," in William Neigher, Roni J. Hammer, and Gerald Landsberg, Editors, *Emerging Developments in Mental Health Program Evaluation.* New York: Argold Press, 1977, pp. 378–390.

Index

Acceptance, as workers' quality, 123–29
Advice-giving, expectations about, 74–77
Agency environment (or setting), 156–73
  evaluating quality of, 172–73
  operational environment, 168–72
  physical environment, 162–68, 195
  sectarian affiliation, 160–62
  social environment or climate, 157–62, 195
Agency staff, 158–60; see also Receptionist
Aldrich, C. Knight, 169
Alexander, Ernestina, 64n
Alexander, Franz, 152
Anthony, E. James, 117n
Appointments, scheduling, 6, 169–70
Argelander, Hermann, 59
Aronson, H., 56, 75, 91
Attention, total, 124–25
Attneave, Caroyln L., 149n
Attraction, interpersonal, 12
Authenticity (genuineness), workers', 123–29

Baker, Frank, 147n
Bales, Robert F., 9
Barber, Elinor, 185
Barish, Samoan, 74
Barker, Roger G., 8, 168
Beck, Dorothy Fahs, 17, 19, 22, 25n, 33, 43, 85, 86, 98–100, 108n, 110, 116, 150, 187, 204, 205
Becker, Howard, 205n
Beginning phase, see Getting engaged
Benedeck, Therese, 117n
Bent, Russell J., 125
Bernstein, Arnold, 6, 7, 10, 11, 55, 61, 64, 77, 78, 82, 110, 125, 169, 173, 185–87, 191

Biller, Henry B., 149n
Blenkner, Margaret, 59
Bloch, Mary H., 154
Blumenthal, David L., 17
Blumer, Herbert, 9, 25n, 30, 191, 205
Boatman, Francis L., 64
Bodgan, Robert, 25n
Bolman, W. M., 84
Borgatta, Edgar F., 21
Bott, Elizabeth, 149n
Bounous,, Ronald C., 64
Bradley, Panke M., 22, 110, 187
Briar, Scott, 84
Bush, Malcolm, 204

Cannell, Charles F., 28
Caplan, Gerald, 147, 149n
Carkhuff, Robert, 11, 123, 127, 134, 192n
Carter, Elizabeth, 15
Chance, Erika, 11, 125n, 126
Change, triggering, 152–55, 188–89
Church, agency affiliation with, 160–62
Client:
  as active partcipant in helping process, 12–15, 195
  socialization into role of, 10–11
Clients (participants in the study):
  characteristics of (as a group), 39–42
  characteristics of (as individuals), 43–46
  compared to agency's total clientele, 42
  compared to clients in related studies, 42–43
  expectations of, 55–58
  initial encounter with social worker, see Initial client-social worker encounter
  obtaining participation of, 39
  presenting problems of, 49–50

316